Estuarine Ecology of the Southeastern United States
and Gulf of Mexico

Estuarine Ecology of the Southeastern United States and Gulf of Mexico

By ROBERT R. STICKNEY

TEXAS A&M UNIVERSITY PRESS
College Station

Library of Congress Cataloging in Publication Data

Stickney, Robert R.
    Estuarine ecology of the southeastern United States and
Gulf of Mexico.

    Includes bibliographies and index.
    1. Estuarine ecology—Southern States.   2. Estuarine
ecology—Mexico, Gulf of.   I. Title.
QH104.5.S59S75   1984   574.5'26365'0975   84-40136
ISBN 0-89096-203-0

Manufactured in the United States of America
FIRST EDITION

To Carolan, for your love and patience.
Also, to those colleagues and students
who helped me maintain my enthusiasm
for the subject matter.

Contents

Illustrations

Preface

ECOLOGY, the relationship between an organism and its environment, became one of the catchwords of the 1960s and 1970s. The news media assailed the public with stories about the need to "save our environment" and "protect the ecology," although it was not really clear what was meant by either expression. Before the discovery of ecology and environment by the general public, the subject was just another among many to which biology students were exposed as a part of their academic training. Once ecology was popularized, the formerly limited discipline began to expand, and various subdisciplines were developed. When popular interest led to increased levels of funding for research and to an expansion of jobs in government, industry, and consulting, ecologists began to appear in rapidly increasing numbers.

Dissatisfied with the traditional time-consuming methods of scientific procedure, and sometimes convinced that an ecological disaster was imminent, both well-trained and self-styled ecologists took to the field to decry the problems they perceived. Problems did exist, and continue to exist, though the immediate threat to the well-being of the planet was somewhat overemphasized. In any event, the crusading spirit of the last two decades helped promulgate various laws and regulations that have noticeably improved our air and water.

The United States was able to repair some of its environmental damage largely because we as a nation could afford to become interested in our environment. Most nations are not as fortunate. Because of limited resources they are forced to ignore or at least overlook environmental concerns and place their emphasis on direct support of their people. Even in the United States, the costs of environmental protection have begun to concern the average consumer. Most citizens still consider environmental protection to be important, as long as it does not lead to significant increases in taxes and in the costs of goods and services. It is economics that will finally determine how far our country or any other can go toward fully protecting the environment. Currently, we are facing some difficult decisions with respect to how much further we are willing to go in that direction. In some areas the costs are already perceived as being too high; standards have actually been lowered, again largely on the basis of economics.

The intent in this work is to present the reader with an objective account of the estuarine ecosystem of a major portion of the United States. Some of man's effects on the estuarine environment are discussed in the final chapter, and a few are mentioned in other chapters. Bringing man into the picture is important, I think, since estuaries represent areas where man has had an enormous impact over the past several decades.

In the end, man must learn to live within the world in which he finds himself; that is, he must not only be a resident but must also remain aware that his activities can produce profound change. Learning to live in harmony with the environment involves, to some extent, learning how that environment functions. Estuaries are among the most demanding ecosystems on earth because of their harshness, which is traceable to constant physical and chemical change. Yet estuaries support some of the densest populations of organisms found in any aquatic ecosystem. Because estuaries are often located adjacent to cities, they have received large quantities of pollutants. Even so, estuaries continue to survive and thrive in most areas. Estuaries serve man as sources of food, as locations for highways, and as places of recreation. Mankind must ensure that estuaries are preserved if the present quality of life is to be maintained.

The great diversity that exists not only in the varieties of estuaries throughout the world but also in their abundant flora and fauna precludes a global treatment of the subject. Because my experience has been largely limited to estuaries within the southeastern United States and the Gulf of Mexico, and because the estuaries in those regions are quite similar physically, chemically, geologically, and biologically, this book focuses on those regions. Information from other estuaries, both in the United States and in other parts of the world, is provided as necessary to help illustrate points and furnish additional information where little is available from the region of primary interest.

Acknowledgment

CHAPTER 2, a discussion of freshwater inflow to estuaries, was drafted by Johnie Crance. It has been reduced considerably in order to avoid repetition, and some editorial style changes have been made. Mr. Crance's contribution is gratefully acknowledged: his work represents a major contribution to the area of freshwater inflow, which has recently generated a great deal of interest. Mr. Crance, who was formerly with the National Coastal Ecosystems Team, Fish and Wildlife Service, in Slidell, Louisiana, is currently with the Western Energy and Land Use Team, Fish and Wildlife Service, in Fort Collins, Colorado.

Estuarine Ecology of the Southeastern United States
and Gulf of Mexico

CHAPTER 1

Marine and Estuarine Science

The World Ocean

IN order to place estuaries into their proper environmental framework, an introduction to marine science is warranted. Though estuaries are extremely important, they represent only a small fraction of the world ocean. They act as a buffer zone between the truly fresh inland waters of continents and the high salinity waters of the open seas.

Menard and Smith (1966) determined the areas, volumes, mean depths, and other information about the world ocean (table 1). Approximately 71% of the earth's surface, or over 362,000,000 km^2, is covered by salt water. The greatest depth, over 11,000 m, occurs in the Marianas trench, though the average depth is only about 3,700 m. About 8% of the world ocean is less than 200 m deep, lying over what is called the conti-

TABLE 1. World Ocean and Its Constituent Water Bodies

Water Body	Area (10^6 km^2)	Volume (10^6 km^3)	Mean Depth (m)	Percentage of World Ocean
Pacific Ocean and adjacent seas[a]	181.3	714.4	3,940	50.1
Atlantic Ocean and adjacent seas	94.3	337.2	3,575	26.0
Indian Ocean and adjacent seas[b]	74.1	284.6	3,840	20.5
Arctic Ocean and adjacent seas	12.3	13.7	1,117	3.4

Source: Sverdrup, Johnson, and Fleming, 1942.
[a] Includes the Bering Sea, Sea of Okhotsk, Yellow Sea, East China Sea, and Gulf of California.
[b] Includes the Red Sea.

nental shelf. That 8% is responsible for roughly 80% of the commercial fish landings in the world (Tait and DeSanto, 1972).

Classification of Marine Environments

Subdivision of the world ocean into units that can be readily identified and understood is necessary because of the extent of the marine ecosystem. The most basic division separates the water column into two provinces. The first, the neritic, lies over the continental shelf; the second, the oceanic, includes all water over 200 m.

Hedgpeth (1957) developed a benthic classification scheme widely accepted among oceanographers (figure 1). The uppermost portion of that classification is the supralittoral zone, which involves regions above the highest normal high-tide level, but which may occasionally be wetted by seawater during storms or periods of unusually high tides. Below the supralittoral is the littoral zone, which can also be defined as the intertidal zone. The littoral is submerged at high tide and exposed at low tide. Everything below the littoral zone is called the sublittoral. In estuaries, the sublittoral is small enough to be easily identified, but in the deep sea, further subdivision of the sublittoral is required.

All sublittoral areas of 200 m or less are located over continental

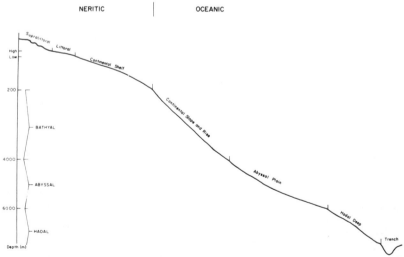

Fig. 1. One scheme by which marine environments can be classified (from Hedgpeth, 1957).

shelves. Beginning at approximately 200 m in most regions of the world, the slope of the bottom increases noticeably as one proceeds offshore. This region, known as the continental slope, extends to some indefinite depth, until the slope becomes more gradual again at the continental rise. Both the continental slope and the continental rise lie at depths between 200 and 4,000 m.

The abyssal plain is found where water depth ranges from 4,000 to 6,000 m. Water deeper than 6,000 m lies over what are known as hadal deeps.

Divisions of Oceanography

Oceanography is commonly divided into four disciplines: physical, chemical, geological, and biological. Although no individual can be an expert in all four, it is important that each oceanographer have a working knowledge in all areas so that communication is possible among scientists from different disciplines. A brief introduction to some of the subjects covered by each discipline is provided below, along with a limited discussion of those subjects of critical importance to estuarine systems. Some of the same topics are then considered in more detail in other chapters.

PHYSICAL OCEANOGRAPHY

Physical oceanographers are interested in such phenomena as tides, waves, currents, temperature, and salinity. Among the most dramatic, though not the newest, theories of modern physical oceanography is that of plate tectonics (also known as seafloor spreading and continental drift). That theory, though based upon physical laws, has been supported by data obtained in other disciplines within oceanography. Briefly, the theory states that the earth's crust is made up of a series of plates that essentially float upon the molten magma beneath. Currents in the magma cause the plates to drift relative to one another. Regions where plates are pushing against one another are characterized by actively building mountain ranges, trenches, large fault lines, and high levels of tectonic activity (earthquakes and volcanism). Some of those activities occur in estuarine areas.

Tides. The rhythmic rise and fall of the surface of the sea relative to some stationary reference point on land is a phenomenon known as tide. Tides are actually manifestations of the presence of a standing wave, which moves around the earth as the planet rotates.

Sir Isaac Newton was the first to provide a satisfactory explanation for the tidal phenomenon when he related tides to his Law of Universal Gravitation. The law states that the attraction between two celestial bodies is directly proportional to the product of their masses and inversely proportional to the square of the distance between them. Although in theory all objects in the universe exhibit some gravitational influence upon each other, proximity and mass are the critical factors. Tides result from the attraction for the earth by the sun and the moon.

As explained by Gross (1967), the gravitational pull of such bodies as the sun and moon on the earth is balanced by the centrifugal forces exhibited by those bodies. That balance is not constant everywhere on the surface of the earth, however. The side of the earth nearest the moon receives a gravitational pull somewhat greater than that of the offsetting centrifugal force. On the opposite side of the planet, centrifugal force exceeds the offsetting gravitational pull. Those differences are small, but they are observable in the behavior of the world ocean, showing up as the phenomenon called tides.

If the world were completely covered with water, the ideal case with respect to tides would exist. For illustration, a hypothetical water-covered planet is convenient. As any point on the surface of a water-covered earth moves directly under the moon, the water is pulled perceptibly toward that satellite. This creates a bulge in the water on the side facing the moon as well as on the opposite side (because of reduced gravitational pull and increased centrifugal force on the latter). Those bulges represent the crests of a wave of tide on the surface of the planet. The troughs in that wave would occur at right angles to the crests. The crests and troughs correspond to the high and low tides, respectively.

When the sun and moon are positioned along the same plane as the earth, they reinforce each other, causing spring tides. This relationship occurs at two-week intervals during periods of new and full moon. When the sun and moon are at right angles relative to the earth, the net effect is to reduce the tidal bulges through cancellation by each other of the effects of sun and moon, and neap tides result. During spring tides the highest high and lowest low tides of the cycle will be produced. During neap tides, the lowest highs and highest lows will occur. More simply, tidal amplitude is highest during spring tides and lowest during neap tides.

Intermediate phases of the moon lead to tidal amplitudes between the ranges of spring and neap tides. It is important to remember that spring tides occur at fourteen-day intervals throughout the year and are not related to the season of the year for which they were named. The fourteen-day interval stems from the fact that a lunar day is twenty-five hours and forty minutes. Thus, it takes fourteen days for the moon to complete one-half an orbit around the earth, or twenty-eight days for a complete lunar cycle.

Because the earth is not covered with water, the tidal phenomenon is not as simple as that presented above. The presence of land masses causes the tidal wave moving around the globe to become deflected and distorted in some areas. In addition, friction causes some drag on the tidal wave, slowing it down, while the rotation of the earth tends to accelerate the motion of tidal waves. Therefore, amplification or depression of the tide range, alteration in the normal pattern of highs and lows, or the production of spring and neap tides somewhat out of phase with the lunar cycle can result.

Where the expected tidal cycle is followed, two high and two low tides occur every twenty-four hours and fifty minutes. Such a pattern is called semidiurnal. In cases where there is only one high and one low tide daily, the tides are called diurnal. In regions such as the Gulf of Mexico, some days may be characterized by semidiurnal tides, some by diurnal tides, and some by a combination. Such a region is said to have mixed tides.

Predictions of the times of high and low tides at given locations along the coasts of the United States and in other regions of the world are available in tide tables. Such tables not only provide information on the time of day at which high and low tides will be experienced but also show the elevation of each tide relative to mean sea level.

Waves. As wind blows over the surface of the sea, waves are generated. Other sources of waves include the tidal wave discussed above, the falling of bodies into the water, and tectonic activity. Man-made explosions can also generate waves.

In its simplest form, wave theory deals with standing waves that move past a given point in what are known as wave trains. The top portion of each wave is known as the crest, while the bottom is called the trough. The vertical distance between the crest and trough is referred to as the wave height, while the horizontal distance between the two is the wavelength. The amount of time that elapses between the passage of two successive crests or troughs is called the wave period. Wave velocity is defined by

$$V = L/T, \tag{1}$$

where V is velocity, L is wavelength, and T is wave period.

Standing waves have constant wavelength, period, and height. As a wave train moves across the surface of the water, there is little actual movement of the water itself, except in the case of breaking waves. This lack of movement is easily demonstrated by a floating object on the water. As a wave crest moves past the floating object, the object will move in the direction of the wave. When the crest passes, however, the object will move in the opposite direction through the wave trough. Thus, the object will go in a circle with little net motion unless it has a surface that catches the wind, in which case movement will be with the wind.

Since the influence of waves on a column of water diminishes with depth, the orbital motion of an object carried by wave action will also diminish with depth. At a depth of $L/4$, the diameter of the orbit exhibited by a particle is only one-fifth of its diameter at the water surface (Ross, 1970). At one-half the wavelength ($L/2$), there is virtually no motion of a particle attributable to surface waves (Gross, 1967).

Since orbital motion is negligible at depths greater than $L/2$, the ocean bottom does not influence the configuration of waves until the waves enter shallow water. At $L/2$ the wave begins to respond to friction from the seafloor, and the crest will start to move faster than the trough. At a depth of $L/20$, the wave will break. Whitecaps, which resemble breaking waves, are caused by the wind blowing the tops off of standing waves.

Factors affecting wave height include the distance over which the wind blows (fetch), wind velocity, and the amount of time the wind has been blowing. Wavelength is also related to wind fetch (Ross, 1970).

Simple wave trains can be generated in the laboratory. They are not readily apparent in nature, however, because the surface of the sea is usually covered with wave trains having a variety of heights, wavelengths, and velocities—but occurring simultaneously. Sometimes wave trains generated at different times and in different areas will combine to reinforce each other, or they may cancel each other out if they are out of phase.

When the sea is nearly calm with respect to wind, long-period waves of uniform wavelength can often be observed. Those waves, which make up the swell, often have shorter-period waves superimposed over them. The smaller waves are referred to as chop. Waves vary from the extremely small capillary variety caused by small puffs of wind during calm weather to the seismically generated tsunamis. The latter are long-period waves of insignificant height at sea but which may rise to heights of 10 m or more when they reach land.

Currents. Large ocean currents, such as the Gulf Stream, exert some control over continental climates and may also affect biological productivity. Ocean currents tend to move clockwise in the northern hemisphere and counterclockwise in the southern hemisphere because of the Coriolis effect.

The Coriolis effect is most readily explained by the example of a cannon placed at the equator in the northern hemisphere and pointed toward the north pole. When the cannon is fired, the trajectory of the projectile will appear to an observer standing at the equator to veer right. This is true because although the projectile is following a straight path through the air, the earth continues to rotate under it. In the southern hemisphere, a projectile shot toward the south pole will appear to move to the left for the same reason. The amount of deflection is dependent upon the velocity of the projectile and the latitude at which it is shot. An observer who stood directly on the equator and shot a projectile along the equator would notice no deviation.

Currents are created in coastal regions by tidal flows, by the input of river water into estuarine areas, and through such phenomena as longshore drift and rip currents. Longshore drift develops when waves strike a beach at an angle (figure 2). Rip currents result where longshore currents from opposite directions meet, and the water is carried offshore in a relatively strong but narrow band. Such currents are dangerous to swimmers who try to move against them. Because rip currents move offshore only a short distance, swimmers are best advised to drift with the current until it dissipates or to swim laterally to exit the rip current area.

Temperature. The temperature of the ocean varies with latitude and depth. At the bottom, in deep water, the temperature in the Arctic and Antarctic is not much different from that near the equator, though surface temperatures in the higher and lower latitudes are significantly different throughout the year. Ross (1970) recognized three layers in the world ocean based upon their temperatures. On the surface is a well-mixed layer, varying from 10 to as much as 500 m deep, which is relatively warm compared with the rest of the water column. Below the mixed layer is a transition zone or thermocline in which temperature decreases rapidly with depth. The thermocline is usually between 500 and 1,000 m thick. Below that is a region of cold water of relatively homogeneous temperature descending to the bottom.

Salinity. The total quantity of dissolved solids in a water sample is a measure of the salinity of that sample. Because of dissolved and particulate

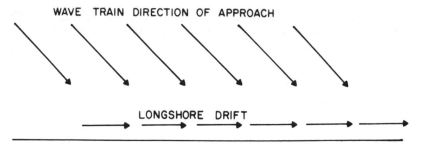

Fig. 2. Propagation of longshore drift occurs when waves approach a beach at an acute angle.

organic matter and other complications, salinity cannot be accurately measured by merely evaporating a water sample to dryness. This is apparent from the general definition of salinity that was established by an international commission in 1902 as described by Sverdrup et al. (1942, pp. 50, 51): "Salinity is the amount of solid material in grams contained in one kilogram of sea water when all the carbonate has been converted to oxide, the bromine and iodine are replaced by chlorine and all organic matter is completely oxidized"; or

$$\text{Salinity} = 0.03 \times 1.805 \times \text{Chlorinity.} \qquad (2)$$

Chlorinity was defined as "the total amount of chlorine, bromine and iodine in grams contained in one kilogram of sea water, assuming that the bromine and iodine have been replaced by chlorine."

The relationship presented in equation 2 was developed by Knudsen near the beginning of the present century and is still widely accepted. As indicated by Perkins (1974), however, Knudsen developed the relationship in the Baltic Sea, and the 0.03 constant was required because of the relatively high rate of freshwater inflow into that body of water. Thus, the International Association of Physical Oceanography in 1963 and the International Council for the Exploration of the Sea in 1964 adopted a slightly modified definition of salinity:

$$\text{Salinity} = 1.80655 \times \text{Chlorinity,} \qquad (3)$$

which is supposed to more accurately reflect the relationship between salinity and chlorinity.

TABLE 2. Water Bodies Classified by Salinity

Salinity (o/oo)	Classification
0.0–0.5	Fresh water
0.6–3.0	Oligohaline
3.1–16.5	Mesohaline
16.6–30.0	Polyhaline
30.1–40.0	Marine
>40.0	Hypersaline

Source: Hedgpeth, 1957.

The primary standard for determining salinity has been called normal water, or Copenhagen seawater. Samples of normal water were first prepared by the Hydrographical Laboratories in Copenhagen, Denmark, in 1902 and became the standard to which most other seawater samples were compared by means of a titration procedure.

Salinity is still measured by titration in some laboratories, but other techniques have been developed. Since salinity is directly related to density, it can be measured with a hydrometer and the appropriate conversion tables. The refractive index is also related to density, so a measure of the refractive index of a water sample can be related back to salinity. In addition, salinity can be measured from conductivity.

Salinity is measured in units of parts per thousand. A part per thousand is equivalent to 0.1% and is often abbreviated o/oo or "per mille."

Aquatic environments can be classified relative to their salinity range. One such classification is presented in table 2.

CHEMICAL OCEANOGRAPHY

The chemical oceanographer is interested in all of the elements and compounds in seawater. Chemical oceanographers are also interested in how those materials cycle through the marine environment and how they influence geological processes and biological productivity.

Early oceanographers concluded that the major chemical constituents in seawater remain present in constant proportions throughout the world ocean, regardless of salinity. That fact, found to be universal, led to formulation of the Law of Constant Proportions: "Regardless of the absolute concentration of total dissolved solids in sea water, the ratios between the more abundant substances are virtually constant in the world ocean" (Baker et al., 1966, s.v. "Law of Constant Proportions").

The Law of Constant Proportions applies only to the conservative constituents of seawater; that is, those not affected by biological activity. Constituents such as dissolved oxygen, the various forms of nitrogen and phosphorus, and other biologically active components vary considerably, both spatially and temporally.

Synergisms—the relationships among chemicals—are poorly understood in any body of water. As increasing numbers of man-made compounds find their way to the ocean, their impacts on organisms can be expected to increase; thus, it is important that their synergistic effects be documented and quantified. To date, that has not been accomplished with most chemicals.

Salinity is a variable of great importance to chemical oceanographers. The constituents that make up the salinity of the world ocean have been widely studied by chemists, and the impact of salinity on chemical equilibria is an important subject within chemical oceanography. For example, the solubility of oxygen in water is controlled to some extent by salinity (temperature and altitude are also important). As salinity increases, the solubility of oxygen in water decreases.

Dissolved oxygen is crucial for the survival of most organisms in the sea. In general, a level of 5 mg/l of oxygen will sustain life in animals that do not depend upon atmospheric oxygen. Oxygen is added to water through dissolution from the atmosphere and by photosynthesis. Many marine scientists report dissolved oxygen in terms of ml/l, while estuarine and freshwater scientists frequently report it in mg/l. The relationship between the two is

$$1 \text{ mg/l } O_2 = 0.7 \text{ ml/l } O_2. \tag{4}$$

Although salinity and dissolved oxygen are among the most important chemical variables affecting marine organisms, many other chemical considerations are also crucial. Life in the sea as we know it could not exist if the medium were not well buffered and maintained at a pH above 7.0. Under acidic conditions, calcium carbonate becomes soluble in water. If the ocean were an acidic medium, corals, molluscs, many protozoans and other organisms containing calcium carbonate exoskeletons could not survive.

Suspended organic and inorganic compounds in seawater can affect biological productivity as well as chemical reactions. Suspended particles have been defined as those larger than 0.45 microns in diameter. Sediment particles, organic detritus, fecal material, and other substances contribute to the total load of suspended solids within a column of water. In most instances that total is only a few mg/l, though in coastal waters it may reach into the hundreds or even thousands of mg/l.

Suspended sediment particles are important sites for chemical reactions. Clay particles are heavily charged and can attract oppositely charged ions to them. Important nutrients may be scrubbed from the water by suspended particulates. Also, particles of various types can provide nuclei for the formation of manganese nodules and other kinds of concretions found on the ocean floor.

Among the chemicals dissolved in seawater are such biologically important substances as amino acids, fatty acids, and carbohydrates. Various petroleum fractions, also of biological origin, are sometimes present. When present at high enough levels, such organic substances lead to the production of foam on the surface of the sea. Organic foams can support a variety of microscopic organisms.

Chemical interactions between air and sea, as well as between sediment and water, are of interest to chemical oceanographers. Many chemicals enter the marine system from either the atmosphere or the sediments, so it is important to determine the nature of the chemical reactions that occur at those interfaces.

GEOLOGICAL OCEANOGRAPHY

Geological oceanographers are interested in beach erosion, geomorphology, sedimentation, geochemistry, petroleum production, marine mining, and numerous other topics relating to the structure and dynamics of the ocean floor and the margins of the sea. Marine geologists and engineers are constantly battling against the forces of nature in their attempts to protect shorelines from erosion. They have provided information critical to the support of the theory of plate tectonics; learned to identify oil and mineral deposits under and on the seafloor; and mapped the major features associated with the ocean bottom. Geologists have contributed important information to all of the other oceanographic disciplines.

Minerals and Oil. Interest in mining the floor of the ocean for various minerals has developed recently. Large deposits of such substances as phosphates have been found in some areas, though other minerals have also received attention. Manganese nodules, formed by the precipitation from seawater of manganese oxides and other minerals around a nucleus (often a particle of bone or sediment), are present in high concentrations in some areas. In addition to quantities of manganese, which alone make mining at least potentially profitable, concentrations of other elements are also high enough to warrant extraction. Wenk (1969) indicated that the average manganese nodule contains 24% manganese, 14% iron, 1% nickel, 0.5% copper, and slightly less than 0.5% cobalt. Other resources to be mined include oyster shell, gas, oil, coal, diamonds, and salt.

Salt domes, large evaporite deposits buried beneath more recent sediments, also occur in the ocean. Interest in them has centered on their use as storage vessels. Salt domes in the Gulf of Mexico, off the coasts of Louisiana and Texas, are currently being developed as storage depots for petroleum. The concept involves pumping water into the salt domes, dissolving the salt to form a brine solution, pumping the brine from the salt dome, and introducing crude oil to replace the removed material.

Sediments. Marine sediments have been widely studied by geologists. Sediments fall into two basic classifications: those found in coastal and nearshore waters and derived from land (terrigenous); and those of the deep sea (pelagic). The latter contain particles of both oceanic and land origin.

Terrigenous sediments range from boulders that fall off a cliff and into the sea to clay particles carried into the ocean in suspension by rivers, storm runoff, or the wind. Pelagic sediments are either biogenous, inorganic, authigenic, or volcanic (Ross, 1970). Biogenous deposits have also been called oozes. Such deposits are composed of the calcareous or siliceous skeletal remains of diatoms, foraminiferans, pteropods, or radiolarians. Inorganic deposits consist of particles that originated on land, while authigenic deposits arise *in situ*. The latter include manganese nodules, salt domes, and phosphorus. Volcanic sediments provide a layer convenient for dating sediments if the time of eruption leading to the sedimentation can be fixed. Problems with dating sediments arise from bioturbation, the reworking and redistribution of sediments by animals. Bioturbation is a particular problem in areas such as estuaries that have high standing crops of benthic organisms.

BIOLOGICAL OCEANOGRAPHY

Members of every living phylum of organism inhabit the world ocean. Many have been intensively studied at the species level, while others have been more widely examined with respect to their community dynamics. In addition, representative marine organisms have been subjected to every sort of gross and minute examination, using not only visual but also chemical techniques. Because of the diversity of marine life, no attempt can be made here to completely cover all organisms. Instead, an outline of the kind of communities found in the ocean is provided. Particulars regarding estuarine members of each community are provided in later chapters.

Decomposers. Largely made up of bacteria and fungi, decomposers are responsible for much of the nutrient recycling on earth. In the deep ocean, large concentrations of decomposers cannot typically be found because of low overall productivity. Their levels in near-shore waters, however, are often quite high. Bacteria and fungi grow best when attached to some kind of substrate. Suspended particulate matter supports their growth as, of course, do sediments.

Interest in decomposer organisms by biological oceanographers has largely centered on determination of their abundance, taxonomy, and distribution. Relatively little work has been undertaken with the decomposer community compared with that expended on higher organisms.

Plants. Because of limitations in the depth to which light can penetrate water, plants of all kinds are restricted to what is called the photic zone—the region where light is present at or above 1% of its incident level at the surface. Many higher plants and seaweeds are found only in shallow areas, though some that float on the surface of the water can be found at sea. Among the latter is the gulfweed, *Sargassum* spp., for which the Sargasso Sea was named. Two species, *S. fluitans* and *S. natans*, are responsible for nearly all of the macroscopic plant life in the Sargasso Sea. Other plants generally restricted to near-shore waters are the kelps, which attach to the substrate by holdfast organs.

Microscopic plants are the dominant primary producers in the open ocean. Thousands of species of single-celled algae exist in the sea as members of the phytoplankton community. The phytoplankters often have limited vertical mobility provided by cilia or flagella, which allows them to remain in the photic zone. They may also contain oil droplets, which give them positive buoyancy.

Benthic algae, which grow attached to substrates, can be found in the ocean within the photic zone. In deep water, floating objects may be colonized by benthic algal species. In fact, many species considered to be primarily phytoplanktonic can attach to substrates and exist as attached algae.

Some primary producer species may grow either as autotrophs or heterotrophs. That is, they can make their own food through photosynthesis if light is available or consume fixed energy in the absence of light. Classification of such organisms as either plants or animals is difficult.

Zooplankton. Animals that drift at the mercy of currents have been called zooplankton. A wide variety of zooplanktonic forms is found in the ocean—some as adults, others as transients. Copepods (figure 3) are perhaps the most widely studied of the organisms that spend their entire lives in the plankton community (holoplankters). Species that are planktonic through their larval or juvenile stages and then become members of other communities are termed meroplanktonic.

Among the more common zooplanktonic organisms (in addition to copepods) are such animals as ostracods, euphausiids, mysid shrimp, arrow worms, ctenophores, coelenterates, fish larvae, and the larvae of such benthic organisms as penaeid shrimp and crabs (figures 3 and 4).

Various species of protozoans can also be found in the zooplankton community, though they are often overlooked by planktologists. Protozoans may be important with respect to overall productivity, and the exoskeletons of certain forms are the dominant sources of various biogenous sediments.

Benthic organisms. Animals that live on or within the sediments are members of the benthos community. Those forms may be attached (oysters, barnacles, mussels, tunicates), or they may be free-living. Common examples of the latter are crabs, shrimp, polychaetes, amphipods, harpacticoid copepods, and isopods (figure 5). Such molluscs as clams and scallops as well as echinoderms are also members of the benthic community.

Benthic organisms provide food for various higher organisms, are important in stabilizing sediments, and furnish an indication as to the environment of any given area. Because benthic organisms are not (with certain exceptions) particularly motile, they can be used to characterize changes within a given environment as a result of natural or man-made processes.

The nekton. Animals that can swim strongly enough to overcome currents are members of the nekton community. Included are squids, fishes, and marine mammals. Historically, much of the impetus for the study of nekton has been to advance our understanding of that community so that effective harvest techniques can be developed. Although nektonic animals do not provide all of the food man obtains from the sea, fishes in particular contribute a significant percentage. Certain nektonic species are also very valuable to sportsmen.

Fig. 3. Members of the zooplanktonic community include such organisms as (*left to right*) copepods, mysids, and ctenophores.

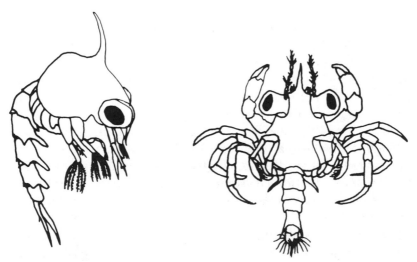

Fig. 4. Swimming crabs go through various larval stages, as characterized by the zoea (*left*) and megalops larvae depicted here.

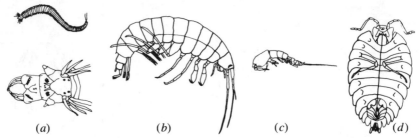

(a)   (b)   (c)   (d)

Fig. 5. Examples of benthic organisms: (a) a polychaete annelid (with close-up of the head region), (b) an amphipod, (c) a harpacticoid copepod, and (d) an isopod.

Defining an Estuary

Estuaries are commonly defined as regions where rivers enter the sea, or they may be defined as the lower, tidal reaches of rivers. Neither definition adequately describes the ecosystem, but each represents the many attempts to devise a good working definition for estuaries (e.g., Ketchum, 1951; Emery and Stevenson, 1957; Hedgpeth, 1966). Perhaps the most widely accepted definition was the one presented by Pritchard (1967a, p. 3), who described an estuary as "a semi-enclosed coastal body of water which has free connection with the open sea, and within which sea water is measurably diluted with freshwater from land drainage." That concept may be conveniently reduced to the form:

$$P + R > E, \tag{5}$$

where P is precipitation, R is runoff, and E is evaporation.

Although the Pritchard definition adequately fits most estuaries, exceptions do exist. The definition and equation above are appropriate to what are more precisely called positive estuaries. Two other possibilities exist: negative estuaries and neutral estuaries. In a negative estuary precipitation and runoff are less than evaporation:

$$P + R < E, \tag{6}$$

while in a neutral estuary, precipitation and runoff equal evaporation:

$$P + R = E. \tag{7}$$

Positive estuaries have salinities below that of the open ocean. Negative estuaries are more saline than the adjacent sea, and neutral estuaries tend

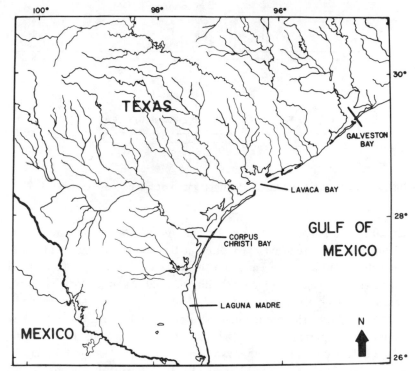

Fig. 6. Some of the major rivers and estuaries of Texas.

to retain the same salinity over long periods (their salinity may or may not be the same as that of the adjacent ocean). Most estuaries along the coasts of the United States are positive (Cronin and Mansueti, 1971).

The Laguna Madre of Texas (figure 6) is the best United States example of a negative estuary. That estuary is characterized by high evaporation coupled with low annual rainfall and runoff, leading to hypersaline conditions during all or part of most years.

The Mediterranean Sea is perhaps the classic example of a negative estuary (figure 7). Though a true sea, the Mediterranean behaves like an estuary in terms of its circulation patterns. As in the Laguna Madre, the rate of evaporation exceeds the volume of freshwater inflow. Evaporation of surface water leads to increased salinity and, consequently, to an increase in surface water density. The dense water sinks and eventually forms a bottom current of high salinity, which flows over a sill at the Strait of

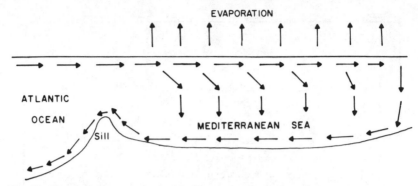

Fig. 7. Circulation pattern in the Mediterranean Sea, a negative estuary.

Gibraltar and enters the Atlantic Ocean. As the volume of water in the Mediterranean is reduced by outflow at the bottom, replacement water from the Atlantic Ocean enters on the surface. Therefore, although the Mediterranean Sea has a higher salinity than the Atlantic Ocean, it is not continually increasing in salinity.

Neutral estuaries are not common, but they do exist. Galveston Bay (figure 6) is reported to act as a neutral estuary during some periods. One of the best documented neutral estuaries is Alligator Harbor, Florida. As reported by Glooschenko and Harriss (1974), Alligator Harbor has a salinity range of from 28 to 36 o/oo with temperature variations controlled by air temperature. According to the authors, neutral estuaries are characterized by low turbidity and sedimentation and a complex pattern of seasonal variations in biota. Circulation in a neutral estuary such as Alligator Harbor largely depends on the amount of wind stress on the surface, tidal regime, temperature, and configuration of the bottom. Sediments appear to arise mostly from the ocean and not from river inflow.

Estuarine Classification Schemes

Besides the relative amounts of precipitation, runoff, and evaporation that dominate a particular estuary, classification can be based on many other factors (e.g., Pritchard, 1967a, 1967b; Bowden, 1967; Dyer, 1973; Schweitzer, 1977). Classification is often based on the developmental stage of the estuary.

Estuarine development can be thought of as similar to succession in lakes, in that estuaries, like lakes, are formed, age, and eventually become unrecognizable as they are incorporated into the land or become part of the sea. Their ephemeral nature has been discussed by Morgan (1967) and Russell (1967).

Various physical forces act upon coastal regions to create and destroy estuaries. According to Reid and Wood (1976), coastlines can be classified as either initial or sequential. Initial coastlines develop as a result of the sea and land moving relative to one another—in response to a tectonic event, glaciation, climatic change, or some related phenomenon. Sequential coastlines are created where marine forces, mainly waves, have altered the configuration of the edge of the land mass.

Barnes (1974) indicated that most modern estuaries date only from the rise in sea level that occurred during the last ice age, about eight thousand years before present (B.P.). The loss of estuaries may be traceable to either sedimentation or erosion. This notion can be extended to coastlines in general, where it appears that major changes in shorelines are often associated with the emergence and submergence of land masses. Gorsline (1967, p. 219), in discussing geologically recent changes in sea level, noted: "The prevailing opinion now seems to be in favor of a relatively rapid rise from about 100 meters below the present level commencing around 17,000 B.P. and reaching a level three to five meters below present datum about 6,000 B.P. after which the sea rose slowly to its present level about 2,000 years ago and may still be rising."

Gorsline (1967) went on to describe present estuaries as the products of processes only recently active, probably during the past three thousand years. He characterized modern estuaries as the result of coastal submergence (initial development) modified by secondary (sequential) processes such as waves and climatic effects.

Based upon the amount of wave energy present in a given area and the width of the continental shelf, some fairly common kinds of estuaries have developed. Narrow coastlines along the continental shelf with high energy and bluffs or cliffs at the shoreline contain estuaries separated from the open sea by spits or beach deposits. This sort of estuary is common along the Pacific coast of the United States. Low- to medium-energy coasts commonly have estuaries fronted by barrier islands. Coastal lagoons (elongate bodies of water lying parallel to the beach and separated from it by dunes or islands with few or no channels to connect with the sea) are also common along coastlines with low to moderate energy. Such estuaries are common along U.S. coasts of the southeastern Atlantic and the Gulf of Mexico. Exceptions are such areas as Beaufort, North Carolina, and Port Aransas, Texas, which are characterized by high energy (Riedl and McMahan, 1974).

Pritchard (1967a), Reid and Wood (1976), Schweitzer (1977), and others have described four classifications of estuaries based on geomorphology: (1) drowned river valleys, (2) bar-built estuaries, (3) fjords, and (4) tectonic estuaries. Each is distinct in origin, though in some cases a combination of forces may have worked in concert to shape a given estuary, making classification somewhat less straightforward.

DROWNED RIVER VALLEY ESTUARIES

Drowned river valley estuaries are often referred to as coastal plains estuaries. Examples along the coast of the United States include such estuaries as Chesapeake Bay and the Mississippi River delta. The latter is an example of a bird's-foot delta formed by the deposition of enormous quantities of sediment over relatively short periods.

The Mississippi River watershed covers 1,330,400 km^2 and carries an estimated 728,000,000,000 m^3 of water annually. Sediments are discharged at the rate of 662,000,000 metric tons a year (Gunter, 1957). The modern bird's-foot delta has been in its present form some five hundred to six hundred years (Morgan, 1967).

Mobile Bay, another drowned river valley estuary of the Gulf of Mexico coast, does not receive a heavy sediment load and is quite different from the Mississippi River delta. Reid (1961) subclassified drowned river valley estuaries as either simple or irregular. Simple estuaries have a single channel (the Delaware and Hudson rivers), while irregular estuaries have a main flood channel and a number of tributaries (Chesapeake Bay and the Mississippi River delta).

In a newly forming drowned river valley, headlands, or promontories, are often present on either side of the river mouth. The headlands contribute sediments to the system as a result of erosion. A delta then forms at the river mouth, and the upper portion of the delta becomes a tidal flat. Similar tidal flats form at the edges of the river, with sediments contributed by the main stream, tributaries, and continued erosion of adjacent land. Spits and sand beaches associated with the developing estuary may be formed by waves reworking marginal sediments.

In time, deposition of sediments at the head of the system and at its mouth may lead to shortening of the estuary. Also, a baymouth bar (sand bar extending partly or completely across the mouth of the embayment) may form. At the end of the life of a drowned river valley estuary, the system becomes filled with sediments and ceases to exist as a recognizable entity. This successional pattern was first described in detail by Johnson (1919).

BAR-BUILT ESTUARIES

Bar-built estuaries are similar in some respects to drowned river valley estuaries. Both have often originated through incision during a period of glaciation and subsequent inundation. Bar-built estuaries, however, are typified by the presence of barrier islands and spits composed of sand, which rise above sea level and extend in a chain between headlands. Inlets occur in one or more places in the barrier island chain. Such estuaries are typically found along the Gulf of Mexico. They may be positive, negative, or neutral in character and tend to be fairly shallow. Excellent examples of bar-built estuaries are found along the panhandle of Florida and include Apalachicola Bay and Alligator Harbor. The Laguna Madre of Texas is also a bar-built estuary.

FJORDS

Fjords are estuaries gouged out by glaciers. They are generally U-shaped in cross-section and have a sill at the mouth. The sill was formed by sediments deposited at the terminus of the glacier that created each fjord. Fjords usually occur in areas of high relief and at high latitudes and may have basins as deep as 300–400 m. When cut off from the sea they may form lakes or lochs. Shorelines of the North Atlantic, the North Pacific, and southeast Alaska have been affected by glaciers, and fjords occur in those regions. Puget Sound is a good example of a fjord estuary.

Because of the shallow sill depth as compared to the rest of the basin and the relatively high rates of freshwater inflow, fjord salinities tend to be lower than those in the adjacent ocean. Lochs are generally characterized by fresh or nearly fresh water.

TECTONIC ESTUARIES

Tectonic estuaries are created as a result of land movement relative to sea level. Those movements are caused by slips in faults, by subsidence, or through volcanic activity. San Francisco Bay is an example (Cronin and Mansueti, 1971). Tectonic unrest may lead to the rapid formation of an estuary. San Francisco Bay, for example, was formed when a fault block subsided: the resulting basin was quickly filled with seawater. In time, fresh water began to flow into the bay from the adjacent watershed.

Volcanism can lead to slower estuary formation, or, in the case of devastating eruptions, to rapid changes. Had Mount St. Helens been adjacent to a coastline, the huge masses of material that poured down the side of the mountain during its initial eruptions could have greatly affected shoreline geomorphology. The estuaries of Hawaii are characteristically small and were formed largely by volcanoes.

OTHER ESTUARIES

A final method for classifying estuaries is based on the dominant physical factors present. In wind-dominated estuaries, the force mostly responsible for water movement is wind generated. Bar-built estuaries, for example, tend to be wind dominated, while coastal plains estuaries are usually tide dominated. In the latter, flow direction changes with the tide, and turbulence may cause mixing of the fresh and salt waters to form a downstream gradient in salinity. In river-dominated estuaries mixing is less apparent, and salinity tends to increase with depth as well as with a downstream direction. Surface waters may remain fairly fresh for some distance down-estuary, occasionally even offshore. Such estuaries may have a salt wedge formed in them that is detectable for many kilometers upstream. Salt wedges (figure 8) form when there is a salinity gradient from the surface to the bottom. While less-dense fresh water flows out of the estuary near the surface, the higher-density salt water actually moves upstream along the bottom. Isohaline lines (regions of the same salinity) become distorted as indicated in figure 8.

Linton (1968) avoided a general classification scheme for estuaries in the United States along the coasts of the southeastern Atlantic and Gulf of Mexico. Instead, he elected to describe them with respect to regional char-

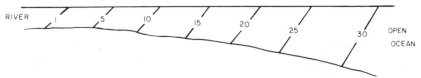

Fig. 8. Cross-section through the lower reaches of a river. The isohaline lines indicate the shape of a typical salt wedge.

acteristics. That method tends to avoid a certain amount of ambiguity and seems realistic, since most estuaries within a given region are similar. Demarkations between regions are usually manifested by some major difference in continental geomorphology.

Use of Estuaries

Man's use of the estuarine environment has been rather extensive. In the United States, there is evidence that American Indians widely used oysters, fish, and other estuarine species for at least several thousand years. This is attested to by the numerous and often extensive middens that have been unearthed (Rounsefell, 1975).

Estuaries have provided safe harbors for ships and many of the world's largest ports lie within estuaries. Also the Intracoastal Waterway system of the United States depends heavily on transit through estuaries. This system was developed to support coastal shipping without exposing the vessels to the open ocean.

With increasing immigration into North America from Europe, estuarine regions were rapidly settled and developed. Most of the people in the United States have always lived in close proximity to the ocean, and that trend continues. Some of the major cities established in estuarine areas include New York City, Los Angeles, Baltimore, San Francisco, Miami, Seattle, New Orleans, Washington, D.C., and Honolulu.

Estuaries are extremely valuable as sources of food for man. Species of commercial importance in United States estuaries include penaeid shrimp, crabs, oysters, various species of fishes, waterfowl, and mammals. According to the National Estuary Study (U.S. Department of the Interior, 1970), the value of commercial fisheries containing species native to estuaries was $300 million to the fishermen and $1.5 billion in the retail market.

The estuaries of the United States harbor several species currently on the endangered or threatened lists. Helping to protect them are over one hundred wildlife refuges, forty areas controlled by the National Park Service, and numerous state parks and historical sites that prohibit hunting. Between 80 and 90% of U.S. coasts along the southeastern Atlantic and Gulf of Mexico are estuarine in nature, compared with only 10 to 20% on the Pacific coast. Most of the estuaries in the former group are of the drowned river valley or bar-built variety. Their geology, physical features, chemistry, biology, and relationships with man are the subjects of the bulk of this book.

LITERATURE CITED

Baker, B. B., Jr., W. R. Deebel, and R. D. Geisenderfer. 1966. *Glossary of oceanographic terms*. Washington, D.C.: U.S. Naval Oceanographic Office.

Barnes, R. S. K. 1974. *Estuarine biology*. London: Edward Arnold.

Bowden, K. F. 1967. Circulation and diffusion, pp. 15–36. In: G. H. Lauff, ed. *Estuaries*. American Association for the Advancement of Science Publication no. 83. Washington, D.C.: AAAS.

Cronin, L. E., and A. J. Mansueti. 1971. The biology of the estuary, pp. 14–39. In: P. A. Douglas and R. H. Stroud, eds. *A symposium on the biological significance of estuaries*. Washington, D.C.: Sport Fishing Institute.

Dyer, K. R. 1973. *Estuaries: A physical introduction*. New York: John Wiley and Sons.

Emery, K. O., and R. E. Stevenson. 1957. Estuaries and lagoons. I. Physical and chemical characteristics, pp. 673–93. In: J. W. Hedgpeth, ed. *Treatise on marine ecology and paleoecology*. Vol. I. Memoir 67. New York: Geological Society of America.

Glooschenko, W. A., and R. C. Harriss. 1974. Neutral embayments, pp. 488–98. In: H. T. Odum, B. J. Copeland, and E. A. McMahan, eds. *Coastal ecological systems of the United States*. Vol. II. Washington, D.C.: Conservation Foundation.

Gorsline, D. S. 1967. Contrasts in coastal bay sediments on the Gulf and Pacific coasts, pp. 219–25. In: G. H. Lauff, ed. *Estuaries*. American Association for the Advancement of Science Publication no. 83. Washington, D.C.: AAAS.

Gross, M. G. 1967. *Oceanography*. Columbus, Ohio: Chas. E. Merrill Publ. Co.

Gunter, G. 1957. Wildlife and flood control in the Mississippi Valley. *Trans. N. Amer. Wildl. Conf.* 22: 189–95.

Hedgpeth, J. W. 1957. Classification of marine environments, pp. 17–27. In: J. W. Hedgpeth, ed. *Treatise on marine ecology and paleoecology*. Vol. I. Memoir 67. New York: Geological Society of America.

———. 1966. Aspects of the estuarine environment, pp. 3–11. In: *A symposium on estuarine fisheries*. American Fisheries Society Special Publication no. 3. Bethesda, Md.: American Fisheries Society.

Johnson, D. W. 1919. *Shore processes and shoreline development*. New York: John Wiley and Sons.

Ketchum, B. H. 1951. Flushing of tidal estuaries. *Sew. Indust. Wastes* 23: 198–209.

Linton, T. L. 1968. A description of the south Atlantic and Gulf coast marshes and estuaries, pp. 15–25. In: J. D. Newsom, ed. *Proceedings of the marsh and estuary management symposium*. Baton Rouge: Louisiana State University Division of Continuing Education.

Menard, H. W., and S. M. Smith. 1966. Hypsometry of ocean basin provinces. *J. Geophysical Res*. 71: 4305–25.

Morgan, J. P. 1967. Ephemeral estuaries of the deltaic environment, pp. 115–20. In: G. H. Lauff, ed. *Estuaries*. American Association for the Advancement of Science Publication no. 83. Washington, D.C.: AAAS.

Perkins, E. J. 1974. *The biology of estuaries and coastal waters*. New York: Academic Press.

Pritchard, D. W. 1967a. What is an estuary: Physical viewpoint, pp. 3–5. In: G. H. Lauff, ed. *Estuaries*. American Association for the Advancement of Science Publication no. 83. Washington, D.C.: AAAS.

———. 1967b. Observations of circulation in coastal plain estuaries, pp. 37–44. In: G. H. Lauff, ed. *Estuaries*. American Association for the Advancement of Science Publication no. 83. Washington, D.C.: AAAS.

Reid, G. K. 1961. *Ecology of inland waters and estuaries*. New York: D. Van Nostrand Co.

Reid, G. K., and R. D. Wood. 1976. *Ecology of inland waters and estuaries*. Princeton, N.J.: D. Van Nostrand Co.

Riedl, R., and E. A. McMahan. 1974. High energy beaches, pp. 180–251. In: H. T. Odum, B. J. Copeland, and E. A. McMahan, eds. *Coastal ecological systems of the United States*. Vol. I. Washington, D.C.: Conservation Foundation.

Ross, D. A. 1970. *Introduction to oceanography*. New York: Appleton-Century-Crofts.

Rounsefell, G. A. 1975. *Ecology, utilization, and management of marine fishes*. Saint Louis: C. V. Mosley Co.

Russell, R. J. 1967. Origins of estuaries, pp. 93–99. In: G. H. Lauff, ed. *Estuaries*. American Association for the Advancement of Science Publication no. 83. Washington, D.C.: AAAS.

Schweitzer, J. P. 1977. Estuarine circulation, pp. 614–23. In: J. R. Clark, ed. *Coastal ecosystem management*. New York: John Wiley and Sons.

Sverdrup, H. U., M. W. Johnson, and R. H. Fleming. 1942. *The oceans*. Englewood Cliffs, N.J.: Prentice-Hall.

Tait, R. V., and R. S. DeSanto. 1972. *Elements of marine ecology*. New York: Springer-Verlag.

U.S. Department of the Interior. 1970. *National estuary study*. Vol. V. Washington, D.C.: Bureau of Sport Fisheries and Wildlife and Bureau of Commercial Fisheries.

Wenk, E., Jr. 1969. The physical resources of the ocean, pp. 83–91. In: *The ocean*. Scientific American Book. San Francisco: W. H. Freeman and Co.

CHAPTER 2

Freshwater Inflow

Introduction

FRESHWATER inflow is defined as water that enters an estuary from contributory streams. Chapman (1977, p. 634) described freshwater inflow alterations as "the modification by man of freshwater tributary flows destined for and received by estuaries." That definition does not take into account natural events such as earthquakes, volcanism, landslides, siltation, and erosion, all of which can alter freshwater inflow.

Historically, there has been a tendency to view coastal ecosystems too narrowly. Attention has been focused primarily on the inner portions of estuaries, ignoring the influences of outside forces and the functional relationships between processes and components of the entire ecosystem. As a result inadequate data have reached decision makers charged with assessing the causes and ecological impacts of altered freshwater inflow and other perturbations of the coastal zone.

The need for fresh water flowing into estuaries is a recognized part of most definitions of the term *estuary*. Many riverine land-use and water management programs and policies, however, do not recognize the need for freshwater inflow as a legitimate use of water. Officials sometimes consider it wasteful to release fresh water into the ocean or into an estuary when water shortages impede urban, industrial, and agricultural development upstream of the estuary. This approach is being modified, however: water allocations for all rivers in the United States will be required in the future. Those allocations will be used to guide water-resource development programs (reservoirs, navigation, irrigation) that are federally funded. In addition, the need for minimum stream flow standards to protect fish and wildlife resources has been recognized, and programs are underway to establish them—thus ensuring that at least some water will reach the estuaries located in areas that have always had continuous input.

Historical Perspective

Concerns over degradation of the coastal environment and research efforts to learn more about estuaries have lagged far behind human settlement and industrial development in the coastal zone. Cronin (1967) wrote that the effects of humans on estuaries were probably unimportant before about 1850. Since then, however, expanding cities and industrial development have transformed coastal areas. All continental U.S. estuaries have therefore suffered from reduced environmental quality; many of them have also experienced a reduction of freshwater inflow.

Initial efforts to increase our knowledge of the physical and biological aspects of estuaries began about 1900 but gained little momentum until 1940. Widespread interest in estuarine pollution and in the degradation of fish and wildlife habitats did not gain momentum until about 1950, but the number of estuarine pollution and habitat studies has significantly increased. Only since the 1960s, however, have scientists made substantial efforts to protect, improve, and better understand coastal ecosystems. Yet, to date, very little has been done to determine the causes and effects of altered freshwater inflow to specific estuaries.

Hopkins (1973) compiled a comprehensive bibliography dealing with the effects of salinity and its changes on life in coastal waters. The most important effect of altered freshwater inflow appears to be the change in salinity and resulting damage to fish, wildlife, and their habitats. Gunter et al. (1973) reviewed the influence of salinity on specific estuarine invertebrates and vertebrates. Snedaker (1977) and Snedaker et al. (1977) compiled bibliographies and summarized the available literature discussing the role of fresh water in estuarine ecosystems. Hackney (1978) summarized information on the relationship of freshwater inflow to estuarine productivity along the Texas coast—an area currently suffering from reduced freshwater inflow.

Snedaker et al. (1977) reported that no one has yet done a quantitative evaluation of direct or indirect influence of fresh water on biological activity, nor do any recent investigations prove or unambiguously demonstrate the quality of fresh water needed to maintain normal conditions within Florida's west coastal estuaries. These conclusions can be extended to most other U.S. estuaries. It is abundantly clear that this aspect of estuarine research needs to be included in water and development projects and estuarine studies in the future.

By 1980, researchers had begun to identify the freshwater inflow requirements of estuaries as a national environmental problem and to develop recommendations that included these requirements in land and coastal planning. The first national symposium on freshwater inflow to estuaries, sponsored by the U.S. Fish and Wildlife Service, was held in 1980. The symposium focused attention on the importance of estuarine ecosystems to our nation and the dependency of estuaries on fresh water (Cross and Williams, 1981).

Ecosystem Boundaries

The ecosystem is a basic unit of nature. It comprises living and non-living parts, which function together as a whole. The essential attributes of any ecosystem are (1) system boundaries, (2) interacting internal parts, and (3) external driving forces. Full appreciation of an ecosystem requires knowledge of the important components and processes that make up the system and an understanding of their functional relationships. In some cases the interrelationships are obvious; for example, an abrupt and severe decrease in freshwater inflow should affect stenohaline organisms. A sudden increase in salinity associated with the decrease in fresh water might lead to the death of some plants and animals. In other cases, such as a slight reduction in the amount of freshwater inflow, ecological effects may be so subtle as to pass unnoticed.

The watershed is a key portion of a coastal ecosystem and must be considered in its entirety in coastal zone planning and management. Many activities within a watershed, especially those affecting the quality and quantity of freshwater inflow, could damage coastal ecosystems. Landward boundaries must therefore be drawn on an ecological rather than an arbitrary basis. The seaward boundary of a coastal ecosystem is often nebulous and difficult to set. The defined ecosystem must, however, embrace a complete and integrated unit. The unit includes a coastal water basin and the adjacent shorelands and watershed to the extent that the area and its combined activities significantly influence the estuary. Offshore, the boundary of the coastal ecosystem might be defined as the extent to which estuary-dependent species move seaward in the course of their lives.

Terrell (1979) has discussed the positive and negative aspects of various schemes to delineate or regionally classify coastal ecosystems. He concluded that no existing schemes could suitably predict how specific kinds of perturbations in identified geological areas would affect coastal ecosystems. Therefore, he developed and recommended adoption of a hierarchical regional classification scheme for coastal ecosystems of the United States based upon physical characteristics.

Terrell (1979) also suggested that the most appropriate landward boundaries of coastal ecosystems are either the marine and estuarine boundaries, as defined by the National Wetlands Inventory Classification Scheme (Cowardin et al., 1977); or the landward limit of the major coastal processes. These suggested landward boundaries do not necessarily include the entire watershed and its network of streams that contribute fresh water to estuaries. The entire watershed must, however, be considered as a part of the coastal ecosystem, since freshwater inflow is a part of the hydrologic process. It is also one of the external driving forces necessary for the existence of positive estuaries.

The Conservation Foundation (1977) considered that a coastal ecosystem included all the landscape and waters of a distinct water basin but did not include the entire watershed. Boundaries of coastal watersheds were limited to land surfaces that drained directly into coastal waters, arbitrarily excluding watershed basins that drained completely into freshwater tributaries.

The Coastal Zone Management Act of 1971 defined shorelands as those lands having a potential direct and significant impact on the coastal waters. That definition recognizes that certain events anywhere within a watershed may affect the included estuary.

The Hydrologic Cycle

An overview of the hydrologic cycle is necessary to understand the sources of freshwater inflow and to gain insight into some of the problems that can be expected if the cycle is disrupted. Details of the hydrologic cycle have been presented by Ackerman et al. (1955), Todd (1970), Leopold (1974), Foin (1976), and Reid and Wood (1976).

The driving forces for the constant recycling of water are evaporation, transpiration, and gravity, which together act as water redistribution agents. Water moves from the surface of the earth into the atmosphere as vapor. In the atmosphere, water vapor collects as clouds, which are blown about by prevailing winds. When the clouds cool through rising or by meeting cooler air masses, the water vapor condenses and returns to the earth as precipitation. This cycle is continuous, though it may be interrupted by man's activities.

Some of the precipitation released by clouds evaporates and is recycled back into the atmosphere before it reaches the surface of the earth. Of the precipitation that does reach the surface and soaks into the ground, some is used by plants and is returned to the atmosphere through transpiration. A portion goes into groundwater recharge, and some runs off or percolates through the soil and accumulates in streams. Streams, in turn, eventually deliver water to the sea, though only between 2 and 27% of the precipitation reaching land is carried to the sea by streams (Ackerman et al., 1955; Reid and Wood, 1976).

Fundamentally, the development of water resources entails modifying the natural hydrologic cycle to meet the needs of man. Regardless of how certain parts of the system are altered, the equilibrium will be changed, and other components of the system will be affected. Consequently, one of the main questions concerning any water development project is, how will the proposed modification affect existing stream, riverine, and estuarine systems?

The Role of Freshwater Inflow

The amount of freshwater inflow and the rate of its exchange with seawater determine the salinity regime in a positive estuary. The abundance and distribution of species are related to salinity. Three key functional roles of freshwater inflow are (1) reduction of salinity, (2) induction of mixing, and (3) delivery to the estuary of nutrients and sediments derived from the watershed.

Reduced salinity is a prerequisite for all positive estuaries. The average salinity of estuarine waters is less than seawater and above 0.1 o/oo. No two estuaries have precisely the same salinity patterns, and those patterns tend to fluctuate both daily and seasonally. The tidal cycle, for example, might cause wide variations in salinity in the lower reaches of an estuary. Large volumes of freshwater inflow stemming from heavy precipitation or strong tidal surges caused by a storm at sea may temporarily alter salinities over an entire estuary. Subtle but permanent changes may be caused by altered freshwater inflow as a result of poor land-use practices, diversion or retention of stream flows, or increased consumption of water in the watershed. Permanent or long-term salinity changes may cause the shifting of species or populations of organisms to different parts of an estuary or could eliminate them altogether.

The role of freshwater inflow as a regulator of salinity is probably its most important function. Salinity is crucial to the survival, optimum growth, spawning, larval rearing, movement, and general well-being of various important estuarine species. Good sources of information on that subject include reviews by Gunter et al. (1973) and Hopkins (1973).

Animal Responses to Freshwater Inflow

When confronted with a marked change in the environment, such as a significant alteration in salinity, estuarine animals will generally respond predictably (Vernberg, 1967). Some animals will become inactive; others might enter a resistant stage or withdraw their soft parts. Oysters, for example, do the latter and can remain isolated from their environment for considerable periods. Gunter (1967) observed that the effects of salinity on any given species may vary at different life stages. For example, penaeid shrimp are typically found in higher salinities as adults than as juveniles.

Gunter (1967) proposed that populations of estuarine animals can be broadly separated into two groups. First are those that complete their life cycles entirely within estuaries; second, those that use the estuaries only as rearing grounds. A third group that passes through estuaries at some stage in their life also seems appropriate. Anadromous species pass through estuaries en route upstream to freshwater spawning areas and on their return to the sea, while catadromous species pass through estuaries on their way to offshore spawning grounds and on their return as larvae or juveniles to fresh water.

Factors Influencing Freshwater Inflow

Clark (1974) proposed as standard management practice that the natural volume, pattern, and seasonal rates of freshwater inflow be maintained intact. The flow of fresh water to most United States estuaries has already been changed by man. Increasing demand for water and for water development projects will make it difficult to prevent additional changes or to maintain the present volume, quality, and patterns of freshwater flow into estuaries.

To achieve inland water and land-use management goals for the benefit of estuarine fish and wildlife, planning and management authorities must be keenly aware of the variables that can influence freshwater inflow. They must also be able to predict, measure, and document changes in freshwater inflow resulting from human activities in the watershed. In addition, they should be able to predict, measure, and document losses that result if the quantity, quality, or seasonal patterns of freshwater inflow are altered.

Man has little or no control over climatic or geologic factors that affect freshwater inflow. Resource planning and management agencies have known for decades, however, that large dams and water diversion projects can alter freshwater inflow and cause widespread losses of fish and wildlife through a changed habitat. Natural resource agencies and the public are increasingly aware of and concerned by the subtle and insidious losses inflicted on coastal ecosystems by man.

Streambed Alterations

Cronin et al. (1971) reviewed the effects of thirteen different kinds of engineering projects on coastal geology. Several of those reviewed (dams, levees, spillways, diversions, and hurricane barriers) alter freshwater inflow. Dams are usually built to store a given volume of water and to regulate its release. Dams, levees, spillways, and stream diversion projects involve purposeful changes in a stream's pattern of flow by changing one or more characteristics of that flow. Changes might include volume, rate, timing, direction, and quality of water flow. Any change may cause alterations in freshwater inflow and affect estuarine organisms and processes.

Dams are one of the more common causes of reduced flow of fresh water into U.S. estuaries. Dams are designed and built to store water for a number of reasons, including hydroelectric power generation, flood control, domestic and industrial water supplies, recreation, irrigation, and fish production. Dams can reduce the volume of stream flow, change peak and seasonal flow patterns, trap sediments, and reduce the silt and nutrient content of freshwater inflow. An impoundment that holds only 1% of the yearly flow of a river is capable of trapping nearly one-half of that river's yearly sediment load (Clark, 1977). The nutrient-rich sediment loads carried to estuaries by some of the large rivers of Georgia and the Carolinas have been reduced to only one-third of their 1910 levels, mainly because of the construction of dams for hydroelectric power and flood control.

According to Blackwater (1977), few human actions can have such far-reaching ecological effects as the construction of a large dam. He used the Aswan High Dam in Egypt as an example and pointed out that the dam blocked the flow of nutrients to the lower Nile River and altered conditions in the Nile Delta, causing Egypt's sardine fishery to decline by about eighteen thousand metric tons annually. Sharaf el Din (1977) summarized how the Aswan High Dam has modified the nutrient budget, biological characteristics, water circulation, and hydrographic conditions in the Nile River.

Dams also prevent fish such as certain species of salmon, shad, herring, and striped bass from migrating upstream to spawn. Over 60% of the riverine grounds for salmon and steelhead trout in the Pacific Northwest have been cut off by the construction of dams with no provision for fish passage (Blackwater, 1977).

The Wallisville Barrier Dam in Texas is an example of how dams in coastal areas might change the character of coastal marshes. The Wallisville dam, although designed at a height of less than 3 m, is supposed to inundate 4,000 ha of marshland in Trinity Bay. According to Blackwater (1977), the brackish water and marshlands eliminated by the dam could result in an annual loss of over seven million metric tons of commercial fish and shellfish.

Levees and spillways may also divert or alter the volume and time of arrival of freshwater inflow and change the patterns of sedimentary deposits and nutrient levels in the coastal zone. Leveeing along the Mississippi River began as early as 1717 (Gunter, 1952). The levees have resulted in channeling and increased rates of river flow to the Gulf of Mexico, leading to greater instability of the estuarine system around the river mouth and probably to a decrease in the fertility of the region (Gunter, 1967).

The Bonnet Carre spillway, located a few kilometers above New Orleans, Louisiana, is a classic example of a man-made structure with a great capacity for altering freshwater inflow. The spillway is essentially a diversion structure, designed to shunt flood waters from the Mississippi River away from the city of New Orleans and into Lake Pontchartrain, thence through Lake Borgne and the Mississippi Sound into the Gulf of Mexico.

Other areas of the United States where levees and water diversion have altered freshwater inflow and caused concern over fish and wildlife losses include the Everglades of Florida (Idyll, 1965; Smith, 1966; Higman, 1967; Dragovich et al., 1968; Kolipinski and Higer, 1969; Heald, 1970; Clark, 1971); the Sacramento–San Joaquin delta of California (Orlob, 1976); and south Texas (U.S. Army Corps of Engineers, 1977). Cronin (1967) discussed the planned diversion of water from the Delaware River for use by New York City. The controversial Tennessee-Tombigbee Water Project, now under construction by the U.S. Army Corps of Engineers, will divert water from the Mississippi River basin to the Mobile River basin.

Hurricane barriers constructed across bays and passes to protect cities and other populated areas in the coastal zone may retain fresh water in the upper estuary for longer periods than normal and change mixing and circulation patterns in certain estuaries. Such a structure has been constructed to protect Galveston and Texas City, Texas. Huge bay-straddling hurricane barriers have also been proposed for such places as Biscayne Bay and Tampa Bay, Florida (Cronin et al., 1971).

Watershed Disturbances

Disturbances in the watershed that may influence the quality or quantity of runoff, stream flow, and thus freshwater inflow are many and varied. Human activities that disturb the watershed and alter the runoff include the development and maintenance of transportation systems (highways, railroads, airports); food production systems (animal and plant crops, feedlots, slaughterhouses); mineral extraction (strip mining, quarries, oil and gas wells); forest industries (timber production and harvesting, sawmills, lumber treatment plants, log rafts); and urban and industrial development.

URBAN DEVELOPMENT

Urban development includes the building and maintenance of roads, parking lots, shopping centers, homes, service stations, sewer lines, sewage treatment plants, and storm-water drainage systems. Most of those activities can affect freshwater inflow.

The removal of vegetation and the resulting disturbance of topsoil associated with urban development can increase erosion. The surfacing of land with impervious material can also increase the runoff rate, the temperature of runoff water, and the rate of evaporation. Also associated with urban development are increases in human population density along with that of their pets, automobiles, and other motor vehicles. All of that leads to greater demands for water and to increased pollutant loads in runoff. The latter can arise from street litter, motor vehicle emissions, biocides, and other sources.

Clark (1977) discussed potential problems associated with urban run-off. The runoff is usually removed as quickly as possible to avoid flooding (resulting from large areas covered with impervious surfaces where water tends to pool). In cities near the coast, runoff is often collected and delivered by pipelines to the estuary with little or no artificial treatment or natural purification.

In the natural system, runoff seeps through the soil or passes over vegetated land. En route to the estuary from the watershed and through unaltered meandering streams, pollutants are biodegraded; removed by filtration, adsorption, or deposition; or reduced and broken down chemically. Whereas pipelines or channeled waterways are usually built in a straight line to save costs, natural watercourses tend to meander through the coastal area, resulting in reduced flow rates and allowing more time for natural purification. Burke (1977) discussed the basic character of contaminants of storm-water runoff and pointed out that natural runoff and stream systems provide examples of efficiency in the management of storm-water removal.

AGRICULTURE

Certain agricultural practices may result in altered freshwater inflows, even if those activities occur many kilometers inland. If the practices are carried out near the coast, they are likely to be more damaging to estuaries than those of a similar nature and magnitude inland. According to Hart (1977), sediment is the most important agricultural nonpoint source pollutant. Agricultural biocides may, however, contaminate runoff and result in serious losses of estuarine life.

Eutrophication, the natural or artificial addition of nutrients to water bodies and the effects of such additions (National Academy of Sciences, 1969), may be accelerated as a result of runoff from farmlands. Nitrogen and phosphorus containing fertilizers are commonly used to increase crop production. High levels of organic wastes containing the same nutrients are found on feedlots and in slaughterhouses. Nutrients may be transported from farmland either in a water-soluble form or adsorbed to sediment or detritus particles.

Circulation

Freshwater inflow is one of the driving forces that powers circulation, mixing, and flushing in estuaries. Circulation and flushing are important in diluting and removing pollutants from the system. Circulation and currents play key roles in the mixing, distribution, and recycling of nutrients essential to primary producers in the estuarine food web. The contribution of estuarine circulation to the nutrient trapping ability of estuaries has been discussed by Odum (1970). Mineral cycling in estuaries has been described by Duke and Rice (1967). Other aspects of estuarine circulation have been examined by Pritchard (1955, 1967), Bowden (1967), Hansen (1967), Rathray (1967), Wiley (1976), and Schweitzer (1977).

Regional Concerns

Some of the largest and most productive estuaries in the United States are located along the coast of the Gulf of Mexico in Florida, Alabama, Mississippi, Louisiana, and Texas. The dominant estuary and source of freshwater inflow in that region is the Mississippi delta–Mississippi River ecosystem. With its massive annual runoff, this estuarine system contributes more fresh water to the Gulf of Mexico than do all of the rivers of the southeastern Atlantic and remainder of the Gulf of Mexico combined (Linton, 1968). The freshwater inflow from the Mississippi River has contributed greatly to the formation of the vast deltaic system developed around the mouth of the Mississippi River. That portion of the Gulf of Mexico from Pascagoula, Mississippi, to Port Arthur, Texas (a distance of 700 km) has been referred to as the "fertile crescent," because of its high fish productivity. This area may be the most productive in the world for fishes, with the possible exception of the coast of Peru (Gunter, 1967).

Many of the estuaries along the Gulf of Mexico have been radically changed by man (Chapman, 1968). These estuaries have coexisted with industrial development and human settlement; the watersheds of most have been altered by urban water development programs and by agriculture, forestry, and other land-use practices. The flow of fresh water into most estuaries of the Gulf of Mexico has been curtailed, and fish and wildlife resources have been reduced or even lost in some estuaries. Nationally, coastal ecosystems are being degraded and diminished at the rate of about 12,000 ha annually (Council on Environmental Quality, 1977). In the Gulf of Mexico alone, nearly 200,000 ha of estuarine habitat were lost by the early 1970s (Chapman, 1971).

Presently, the coast of Texas has inspired more interest, concern, and effort relative to altered freshwater inflow than has any other area within the Gulf of Mexico, and probably within the entire United States. The

Texas coast was identified by Warinner and Lynch (1976) as one of the three areas in the United States where problems in water supply and demand are critical and where they are expected to become increasingly severe over the next several years. Concern over the importance and scarcity of freshwater inflow to the Texas coast grew to the point that the Texas Legislature enacted a law in 1972 requiring the Texas Department of Water Resources (formerly the Texas Water Development Board) to develop information on the flow of fresh water required to maintain the productivity of Texas estuaries.

A positive relationship appears to exist on the Texas coast between freshwater inflow and the production of fishes dependent on estuaries. Chapman (1966) reported that estuaries in eastern Texas contribute more to the commercial fisheries of the state than do the waters lying to the west. The eastern estuaries receive much more fresh water than do their western counterparts and are therefore able to produce many more marketable fishes.

Several studies on freshwater inflow have been conducted in Texas. Childress et al. (1975) studied the effects of freshwater inflow on hydrological and biological conditions in the San Antonio Bay system, and the Texas Department of Water Resources (1978) conducted a similar study of the Colorado River delta. Other studies that have contributed to our knowledge of the role of freshwater inflow on the Texas coast include those of Gunter (1950, 1967), Gunter and Hildebrand (1954), Parker (1955), Chapman (1966, 1972), Bouma and Bryant (1967), Gunter and Edwards (1969), Parker (1970), Shanker and Masch (1970), Copeland et al. (1972), Melton (1973), McGowen and Brewton (1975), Armstrong and Brown (1976), and Henley and Rauschuber (1978). Hackney (1978) summarized the relationship of freshwater inflow to estuaries along the Texas coast.

Plans to build flow-control structures such as dams and diversion canals on the Guadalupe and San Antonio rivers in Texas (which terminate in the San Antonio Bay system) prompted a response from the Texas Parks and Wildlife Department. The department undertook a study of the composition and extent of freshwater inflow and the corresponding effects on San Antonio Bay. Childress et al. (1975) conducted the study and inferred from their data that any major deviation in the annual amount or timing of freshwater inflow from the historic average range of 1,900,000,000 to 3,000,000,000 m^3 will greatly change the ecology of the bay system. Altered freshwater inflows to estuaries elsewhere in the Gulf of Mexico have been discussed by Viosca (1927), Gunter (1952, 1953, 1956, 1967), Smith (1966), and Cronin (1967).

Changes in freshwater inflow to the Everglades of Florida have been of concern for many years. Historically, the drainage of the Florida penin-sula was south to Lake Okeechobee and thence through the Everglades into Florida Bay and the Gulf of Mexico. Leveeing and impoundment of water in Lake Okeechobee; release of flood waters to the west through the Caloo-sahatchee Canal and east through the Saint Lucie Canal; and impoundment of water in conservation pools for industrial and municipal users along the southeast coast of Florida have altered the natural overflow to and through the Everglades (Smith, 1966). Of great concern has been how those altera-tions in freshwater inflow will affect the Tortugas shrimp fishery and the general ecology of Everglades National Park (Idyll, 1965; Higman, 1967; Dragovich et al., 1968; Kolipinski and Higer, 1969; Heald, 1970; Clark, 1971; Lindall, 1973; Michel et al., 1975).

Conclusions

As a general statement, it is recognized that the flow of fresh water into estuaries plays an important role in controlling production, circula-tion, nutrient inputs, and the distribution of organisms. Other important roles can also be related to the rate of entry and volume of freshwater in-flow received by estuaries. It also seems abundantly clear that although freshwater inflow is recognized as important, man has taken little care to preserve historical patterns and rates of inflow. Also, the responses of the environment to alterations in freshwater inflow have been poorly documented.

Most studies conducted on estuaries and their processes and orga-nisms have ignored or only cursorily examined freshwater inflow. This may soon change, since the acknowledged role of fresh water in the life and death of estuaries is becoming more widely recognized. However, the precise role of freshwater inflow in many perturbations afflicting estuaries can only be inferred.

LITERATURE CITED

Ackerman, W. C., E. A. Coleman, and H. O. Ogorsky. 1955. Pp. 44–51. In: *Water, the yearbook of agriculture*. Washington, D.C.: U.S. Department of Agriculture.

Armstrong, N. E., and B. A. Brown. 1976. Exchange of carbon, nitrogen, and phosphorus in Lavaca Bay, Texas, marshes. Vol. I. The role of sediments in nutrient exchange in the Lavaca Bay brackish marsh system. Final Report to Texas Water Development Board, University of Texas at Austin, CRWR-147.

Blackwater, B. 1977. Dams, impoundments, reservoirs, pp. 600–604. In: J. R. Clark, ed. *Coastal ecosystem management*. New York: John Wiley and Sons.

Bouma, A. H., and W. R. Bryant. 1967. Rapid delta growth in Matagorda Bay, Texas, pp. 171–83. In: *Lagunas costeras: Un simposio*. Mem. Simp. Inter. Lagunas Costeras. México, D.F.: UNAM-UNESCO.

Bowden, K. F. 1967. Circulation and diffusion, pp. 15–36. In: G. H. Lauff, ed. *Estuaries*. American Association for the Advancement of Science Publication no. 83. Washington, D.C.: AAAS.

Burke, R., III. 1977. Storm-water runoff, pp. 727–33. In: J. R. Clark, ed. *Coastal ecosystem management*. New York: John Wiley and Sons.

Chapman, C. R. 1966. The Texas basins project, pp. 83–92. In: *A symposium on estuarine fisheries*. American Fisheries Society Special Publication no. 3. Bethesda, Md.: American Fisheries Society.

———. 1968. Channelization and spoiling in Gulf coast and south Atlantic estuaries, pp. 93–106. In: J. D. Newsom, ed. *Proceedings of the marsh and estuary management symposium*. Baton Rouge: Louisiana State University Division of Continuing Education.

———. 1971. The Texas water plan and its effect on estuaries, pp. 40–42. In: P. A. Douglas and R. H. Stroud, eds. *A symposium on the biological significance of estuaries*. Washington, D.C.: Sport Fishing Institute.

———. 1972. The impact on estuaries and marshes of modifying tributary runoff, pp. 235–38. In: R. H. Chabreck, ed. *Proceedings of the coastal marsh and estuary management symposium*. Baton Rouge: Louisiana State University.

———. 1977. Freshwater discharge, pp. 634–39. In: J. R. Clark, ed. *Coastal ecosystem management*. New York: John Wiley and Sons.

Childress, R., B. Eddie, E. Hagen, and S. Williamson. 1975. The effects of freshwater inflows on hydrologic and biological parameters in the San Antonio Bay system, Texas. Texas Parks and Wildlife Department, Coastal Fisheries Branch, Austin. Mimeo.

Clark, J. R. 1974. *Coastal ecosystems: Ecological considerations for management of the coastal zone*. Washington, D.C.: Conservation Foundation.

———. 1977. *Coastal ecosystem management*. New York: John Wiley and Sons.

Clark, S. H. 1971. *Factors affecting the distribution of fisheries in Whitewater Bay, Everglades National Park, Florida*. University of Miami Sea Grant Program Technical Bulletin no. 8. Miami: University of Miami Sea Grant Program.

Conservation Foundation. 1977. *Physical management of coastal floodplains: Guidelines for hazards and ecosystems management*. Washington, D.C.: Conservation Foundation.

Copeland, B. J., H. T. Odum, and D. C. Cooper. 1972. Water quantity for preservation of estuarine ecology, pp. 107–26. In: E. F. Gloyna and W. S. Butcher, eds. *Symposium: Conflicts in water resources planning*. Austin: Center for Research in Water Resources, University of Texas.

Council on Environmental Quality. 1977. *The president's environmental program*. Washington, D.C.: U.S. Government Printing Office.

Cowardin, L. M., V. Carter, F. C. Golet, and E. T. LaRoe. 1977. Classification of wetlands and deep-water habitats of the United States (an operational draft). U.S. Fish and Wildlife Service, Office of Biological Services, Washington, D.C.

Cronin, L. E. 1967. The role of man in estuarine processes, pp. 667–89. In: G. H. Lauff ed. *Estuaries*. American Association for the Advancement of Science Publication no. 83. Washington, D.C.: AAAS.

Cronin, L. E., G. Gunter, and S. Hopkins. 1971. Effects of engineering activities on coastal geology. Report to the Office of the Chief of Engineers, U.S. Army Corps of Engineers.

Cross, R., and Williams, D. L. eds. 1981. Proceedings of the National Symposium on Freshwater Inflow to Estuaries. 2 vols. U.S. Fish and Wildlife Service, Office of Biological Services, FWS/OBS-81/04.

Dragovich, A., J. A. Kelly, Jr., and H. G. Goodell. 1968. Hydrological and biological characteristics of Florida's west coast tributaries. *Fish. Bull*. 66: 463–77.

Duke, T. W., and T. R. Rice. 1967. Cycling of nutrients in estuaries. *Proc. Gulf and Caribb. Fish. Inst*. 19: 59–67.

Foin, T. C., Jr. 1976. *Ecological systems and the environment*. Boston: Houghton Mifflin Co.

Gunter, G. 1950. Seasonal population changes and distributions, as related to salinity, of certain invertebrates of the Texas coast, including the commercial shrimp. *Publ. Inst. Mar. Sci., Univ. Tex*. 1: 7–51.

———. 1952. Historical changes in the Mississippi River and the adjacent marine environment. *Publ. Inst. Mar. Sci., Univ. Tex*. 2: 119–39.

———. 1953. The relationship of the Bonnet Carre spillway to oyster beds in Mississippi Sound and the "Louisiana marsh," with a report on the 1950 opening. *Publ. Inst. Mar. Sci., Univ. Tex*. 3: 17–71.

———. 1956. A revised list of euryhaline fishes of North and Middle America. *Am. Midl. Natur*. 56: 345–54.

———. 1967. Some relationships of estuaries to the fisheries of the Gulf of Mexico, pp. 621–38. In: G. H. Lauff, ed. *Estuaries*. American Association for the Advancement of Science Publication no. 83. Washington, D.C.: AAAS.

Gunter, G., and H. H. Hildebrand. 1954. The relation of total rainfall of the state and catch of the marine shrimp (*Penaeus setiferus*) in Texas waters. *Bull. Mar. Sci. Gulf Caribb*. 4: 95–103.

Gunter, G., and J. C. Edwards. 1969. The relation of rainfall and freshwater drainage to the production of the penaeid shrimps (*Penaeus fluviatilis* Say and *Penaeus aztecus* Ives) in Texas and Louisiana waters. *FAO Fish. Rep.* 3: 873–92.

Gunter, G., B. S. Ballard, and A. Venkataramaiah. 1973. *Salinity problems of organisms in coastal areas subject to the effect of engineering works.* Vicksburg, Miss.: U.S. Army Corps of Engineers.

Hackney, C. T. 1978. *Summary of information: Relationships of freshwater inflow to estuarine productivity along the Texas coast.* U.S. Fish and Wildlife Service Biological Services Program FWS/OBS-78-73. Albuquerque, N. Mex.: U.S. Fish and Wildlife Service Regional Office.

Hansen, D. V. 1967. Salt balance and circulation in partially mixed estuaries, pp. 45–51. In: G. H. Lauff, ed. *Estuaries.* American Association for the Advancement of Science Publication no. 83. Washington, D.C.: AAAS.

Hart, R. D. 1977. Cropland pollution control, pp. 595–600. In: J. R. Clark, ed. *Coastal ecosystem management.* New York: John Wiley and Sons.

Heald, E. J. 1970. The production of organic detritus in a south Florida estuary. *Univ. Miami Sea Grant Tech. Bull.* no. 6.

Henley, D. E., and D. G. Rauschuber. 1978. *Studies of freshwater needs of fish and wildlife resources in Nueces–Corpus Christi Bay area, Texas.* Phase 1 Final Report. 2 vols. Austin: U.S. Fish and Wildlife Service.

Higman, J. B. 1967. Relationships between catch of sport fish and environmental conditions in Everglades National Park. *Proc. Gulf and Caribb. Fish. Inst.* 19: 129–40.

Hopkins, S. H. 1973. Annotated bibliography on effects of salinity and salinity changes on life in coastal waters. Department of Biology, Texas A&M University, College Station.

Idyll, C. P. 1965. Freshwater requirements of Everglades National Park. *Fla. Nat.* 38: 97.

Kolipinski, M. C., and A. L. Higer. 1969. Some aspects of the effects of the quality and quantity of water on biological communities in Everglades National Park. U.S. Geological Survey, Open-Field Report. Mimeo.

Leopold, L. B. 1974. *Water: A primer.* San Francisco: W. H. Freeman and Co.

Lindall, W. N. 1973. Alterations of estuaries of South Florida: A threat to its fish resources. *Mar. Fish. Rev.* 35: 26–33.

Linton, T. L. 1968. A description of the south Atlantic and Gulf coast marshes and estuaries, pp. 15–25. In: J. D. Newsom, ed. *Proceedings of the marsh and estuary management symposium.* Baton Rouge: Louisiana State University Division of Continuing Education.

McGowen, J. H., and J. L. Brewton. 1975. *Historical changes and related coastal processes, Gulf and mainland shorelines, Matagorda Bay area, Texas.* Austin: Bureau of Economic Geology, University of Texas.

Melton, H. E. 1973. A history of Texas' water problems. M.A. thesis, University of Texas, Arlington.

Michel, J. F., R. C. Work, F. W. Rose, and R. G. Rehrer. 1975. A study of the effects of freshwater withdrawal on the lower Peace River (Florida). Rosensteil School of Marine and Atmospheric Sciences, University of Miami Report no. 75002.

National Academy of Sciences. 1969. *Eutrophication: Causes, consequences, correctives*. Washington, D.C.: NAS.

Odum, W. E. 1970. Pathways of energy flow in a south Florida estuary. Ph.D. diss. University of Miami.

Orlob, G. T. 1976. Impact of upstream storage and diversions on salinity balance in estuaries, pp. 3–17. In. M. Wiley, ed. *Estuarine processes*. Vol. II. Circulation, sediments, and transfer of material in the estuary. New York: Academic Press.

Parker, J. C. 1970. Distribution of juvenile brown shrimp (*Penaeus aztecus* Ives) in Galveston Bay, Texas, as related to certain hydrographic features and salinity. *Cont. Mar. Sci*. 15: 1–12.

Parker, R. H. 1955. Changes in the invertebrate fauna, apparently attributable to salinity changes, in the bays of central Texas. *J. Paleon*. 29: 193–211.

Pritchard, D. W. 1955. Estuarine circulation patterns. *Proc. Am. Soc. Civil Eng*. 81: 117–19.

———. 1967. Observations of circulation in coastal plain estuaries, pp. 37–44. In: G. H. Lauff, ed. *Estuaries*. American Association for the Advancement of Science Publication no. 83. Washington, D.C.: AAAS.

Rathray, M., Jr. 1967. Some aspects of the dynamics of circulation in fjords, pp. 52–62. In: G. H. Lauff, ed. *Estuaries*. American Association for the Advancement of Science Publication no. 83. Washington, D.C.: AAAS.

Reid, G. K., and R. D. Wood. 1976. *Ecology of inland waters and estuaries*. New York: D. Van Nostrand Co.

Schweitzer, J. P. 1977. Estuarine circulation, pp. 614–23. In: J. R. Clark, ed. *Coastal ecosystem management*. New York: John Wiley and Sons.

Shanker, N. J., and D. F. Masch. 1970. Influence of tidal inlets on salinity and related phenomena in estuaries. Hydrological Engineering Laboratory, University of Texas at Austin, Technical Report HYD 16-7001.

Sharaf el Din, S. H. 1977. Effect of Aswan High Dam on the Nile flood and on the estuarine and coastal circulation patterns along the Mediterranean Egyptian coast. *Limnol. Oceanogr*. 22: 194–207.

Smith, S. H. 1966. Effects of water use activities in Gulf of Mexico and South Atlantic estuarine areas, pp. 93–101. In: *A symposium on estuarine fisheries*. American Fisheries Society Special Publication no. 3. Bethesda, Md.: American Fisheries Society.

Snedaker, S. 1977. Bibliography: Role of fresh water in estuarine ecosystems. University of Miami. Mimeo.

Snedaker, S., D. deSylva, and D. Cottrell. 1977. Rosensteil School of Marine and Atmospheric Sciences, University of Miami Final Report to Southwest Florida Management District.

Terrell, T. T. 1979. Physical regionalization of coastal ecosystems of the United States and its territories. U.S. Fish and Wildlife Service Biological Services Program FWS/OBS-78-80.

Texas Department of Water Resources. 1978. *Hydrological and biological studies of the Colorado River delta, Texas*. Austin: Engineering and Environmental Systems Section, Texas Department of Water Resources, LP-79.

Todd, D. K., ed. 1970. *The water encyclopedia*. Port Washington, N.Y.: Water Information Center.

U.S. Army Corps of Engineers. 1977. *Mouth of Colorado River, Texas*. Phase 1. General design memorandum, navigation feature. Galveston: USCE, Galveston District.

Vernberg, J. F. 1967. Some future problems in the physiological ecology of estuarine animals, pp. 554–57. In: G. H. Lauff ed. *Estuaries*. American Association for the Advancement of Science Publication no. 83. Washington, D.C.: AAAS.

Viosca, P., Jr. 1927. Flood control in the Mississippi Valley and its relation to Louisiana fisheries. *Trans. Am. Fish. Soc.* 57: 49–61.

Warinner, J. E., and M. P. Lynch. 1976. Impacts of predicted water resource utilization, pp. 109–22. In: *An assessment of estuarine and near-shore marine environments*. Gloucester Point: Virginia Institute of Marine Sciences.

Wiley, M., ed. 1976. *Estuarine processes*. Vol. II. Circulation, sediments, and transfer of material in the estuary. New York: Academic Press.

CHAPTER 3

Sedimentary Processes

Sources of Estuarine Sediments

SEDIMENTS have been defined as "solid granular matter heavier than sea-water, the separate pieces or 'grains' of which, irrespective of their size, are or were at one time loose upon the sea bed or are in the process of falling through the sea" (Bagnold, 1963, p. 507). The standard breakdown of sediment particles by size classes is presented in table 3. Since estuarine ecologists generally examine sediments only on the basis of a few size classes, a somewhat simplified scheme seems to be more appropriate. For many ecological purposes the classification of particles into clay (smaller than 4 microns), silt (4 to 63 microns), and sand (larger than 63 microns) is often sufficient. Sediments containing particles of 2.0 mm and larger may be classified as gravel. In many estuaries of the southeastern United States and Gulf of Mexico, particles of gravel size are composed not of pieces of rock but, in most cases, of shell fragments and other animal hard parts.

Most important to estuarine ecologists are sediments that enter the system with river inflow; those brought into the estuaries from the near-shore coastal area; those carried in by the wind; and those that arise from within the system. Estuaries can only become filled in by sedimentary material arising from outside the estuarine system. As indicated by Rusnak (1967), those sediments may be carried in by rivers, tides, winds, or biological activity, but the so-called self-digestion (equivalent to internal changes in sedimentary patterns) of estuaries can only be a redistribution of sediments already present. Thus, that process cannot result in a decrease in the total volume of an estuary. Self-digestion does not, of course, generally occur in the absence of sedimentation from outside sources.

RIVER-BORNE SEDIMENTATION

The Nile, the Amazon, and the Mississippi are examples of large, well-known rivers with high levels of sedimentation. Thousands of other

TABLE 3. Sediment Particle Sizes

Classification	Millimeter Equivalent	Phi Equivalent[a]
Boulder	4096.0	− 12
	2048.0	− 11
	1024.0	− 10
	512.0	− 9
Cobble	256.0	− 8
	128.0	− 7
Pebble	64.0	− 6
	32.0	− 5
	16.0	− 4
	8.0	− 3
	4.0	− 2
Granules	2.0	− 1
Sand	1.0	0
	0.50	+ 1
	0.25	+ 2
	0.125	+ 3
	0.0625	+ 4
Silt	0.0313	+ 5
	0.0156	+ 6
	0.0078	+ 7
	0.0039	+ 8
Clay	0.00195	+ 9
	0.00098	+10
	0.00049	+11
	0.00024	+12

Source: Encyclopaedia Britannica Macropaedia 16:467.
[a]Determined on the basis of the negative logarithm to the base 2 of the diameter of the particle.

rivers and lesser streams around the world also enter estuaries. Each carries sediments with it.

Rivers may flow serenely into estuaries and carry small amounts of sediment. The rate of sedimentation may, in some cases, be equal to or less than that of eustatic changes in sea level. If the eustatic change is in the direction of an apparent rise in sea level, the estuary may actually increase in volume over time, despite sedimentation.

Rivers may also carry enormous quantities of sediment into estuaries, either as a normal consequence of high rate of flow or intermittently, during floods. In an extended period of high sedimentation a delta may form, such as the bird's-foot delta on the mouth of the Mississippi River. Sedimentation rates in the Mississippi River delta have been shown to reach 30 cm/yr or more (Nelson, 1974).

With regard to sediment loads, rivers of the southern United States carry much more than do their northern counterparts relative to the size of the river valleys in each area. Consequently, the estuaries of the South tend to be mostly filled with sediments, while those of the North are not (Meade, 1969). Southeastern estuaries generally contain high levels of silts and clays (collectively referred to as mud). Many of the Florida estuaries are exceptions, particularly those of the Atlantic coast, the Florida Keys, and the Gulf coast up to at least Tampa Bay. Little or no silt from coastal Georgia moves along the Atlantic seaboard farther south than the Saint Johns River in northern Florida (Tanner, 1960). The quartz sand sediments typical of the upper Florida Atlantic coast give way to carbonate sediments at about Biscayne Bay. The latter variety of sediment is dominant throughout the Florida Keys, having its source primarily from coral reefs.

Georgia, South Carolina, and the Gulf coast all contain areas crossed by rivers, which drain large expanses of the interior and carry significant volumes of fine sediment (produced from weathering of the geological formations in the river valleys and erosion of soils from agricultural and other land). In Georgia and South Carolina, as a result, extensive salt marshes have formed. Vast salt and freshwater marshes are also found in Louisiana, but the coastal marshes of the other Gulf states are rather poorly developed. For example, although about 160,000 ha of marshland lie along the Georgia coast, only about 14,000 ha of tidal marsh can be found in Alabama (Crance, 1971).

River flow must be considered one of the major controllers of the rate of estuarine sedimentation. The Mississippi River can be used as an example. During periods of low river flow, there is generally no significant shoaling around the entrance to Southwest Pass, a region maintained for shipping by a great deal of dredging. As river flow increases, so does the rate of shoaling. As reported by Ippen (1966), continuous dredging is periodically required to maintain the channel. During one two-week stretch when dredges were not operating, nearly 10 m of sediment were deposited in some areas.

The sediments in certain estuaries are nearly uniform with respect to particle size and composition, while in others a great deal of variability can be found. For example, the sediments of Tampa Bay, Florida, are surprisingly uniform throughout the estuary. They are composed primarily of reworked quartz sand and biogenic carbonate detritus. Organic and clay fractions are high only in the upper parts of the bay and in a few other isolated areas (Goodell and Gorsline, 1961), and it can be assumed that their sources are largely from surface water inflow.

Sands are often composed of quartz or silicate particles, and gravels are commonly pieces of larger rocks. Most silt particles are agglomerates of clay; to understand both, clays must be defined. Clay particles are composed of clay minerals, the three most common of which are illite, kaolinite, and montmorillonite. All are charged particles but behave differently. Illites are smaller than kaolinites, but both are larger than montmorillonites (Whitehouse et al., 1960). Turekian and Scott (1967) determined that the Mississippi River and other rivers of the central United States have higher suspended sediment loads than eastern rivers; they also noted that river sediments within the central United States tend to be rich in montmorillonite, while those in the East have larger proportions of kaolinite and illite. The charges associated with clay minerals influence the behavior of those particles while they are in suspension.

When colloidal or semicolloidal clay mineral particles are suspended in a freshwater stream, the water may appear clear to the naked eye; yet when the stream enters an estuary and the fresh and salt waters begin to mix, a phenomenon called flocculation occurs. The rate and extent of flocculation depend upon the preferential absorption of ions by the different kinds of clay particles; substitution of cations within the crystal lattice of the clay mineral; and broken bonds, which may be present at particular edges on the particle (Postma, 1967). The negative charge on the surface of the clay mineral particle becomes balanced by a layer of hydrated cations, which tends to move away from the surface of the particle. At some critical thickness of this double layer, the particle may become attached to other particles, and flocculation occurs (Postma, 1967). As more and more particles stick together, the mass may become great enough that the particle can no longer be carried in suspension by existing current velocity: settling, with resultant sedimentation, then occurs.

Structural differences in clay minerals tend to cause them to flocculate differently. Illites and kaolinites begin to flocculate at lower salinities than do montmorillonites (Whitehouse et al., 1960). In fact, while illites and kaolinites may be flocculated out of suspension at a few parts per thousand salinity, montmorillonites may continue to flocculate throughout the range of estuarine salinities.

Popular theory indicates that flocculation of river-borne sediments is the major cause of both high concentrations of suspended sediment and high sedimentation rates in estuaries. This theory has been widely documented in the literature (Luneburg, 1939; Postma and Kalle, 1955; Freitag, 1960; Ippen, 1966). Deflocculation is also thought to result from flocculated particles being carried into plumes of fresh water flowing out of estuaries (Barnes, 1974).

Coarse sediments, clearly, do not flocculate but can only be carried in suspension when current flow rate is sufficient to scour them from the bottom. They may be carried into suspension, or they may be bounced and rolled along the streambed until they enter the estuary (McDowell and O'Connor, 1977). Thereafter, it is a simple matter of the particles resettling to the bottom once current velocity fails to maintain them in suspension or cause them to move further as bed load. Resuspension or additional movement along the bottom can result from significant increases in the flow of fresh water into the estuary or from strong tidal or storm-generated currents.

It is widely recognized that silts and clays do not always remain where they first settled. Settling to the bottom generally results from reduced current velocity, perhaps because as a river enters the estuary the current tends to spread laterally and begins to slow. Tide stage will also have an effect, particularly in regions with relatively strong tidal currents. If the tide is flooding when a given particle enters the estuary and begins to join with other particles, the speed of the current may be rapidly reduced, and the floc will settle in the upper estuary. If, on the other hand, the tide is ebbing, the floc could be carried well down the estuary before current velocity is reduced sufficiently for settling. The particle could, in fact, be carried out to sea. Studies have revealed that very little sediment reaches the continental shelf from the estuaries along the East Coast of the United States (Dyer, 1979), but the Apalachicola and Mobile rivers have been shown to supply clay to the continental shelf of the Gulf of Mexico (Griffin, 1962).

Once a clay or silt particle settles to the bottom, it usually sticks to the bed. If it is not soon resuspended, it may remain where it settled. The longer a particle remains in one position, the more consolidated the mud becomes because of the water loss (Dyer, 1979). With time an individual particle will become buried by other particles, making it less available for resuspension by currents, though storms can disrupt the pattern. The consolidation process is much swifter within sandy sediments than it is in silts and clays.

INCOMING COASTAL SEDIMENTS

At times a significant contribution to the sedimentation within an estuary can be made from the sea instead of the river. Because of longshore drift, it is not difficult to visualize the movement of sedimentary material into estuarine systems. Waves continually disturb the sedimentary particles within the surf zone, which results in the constant displacement of sediments. Sand dunes may also be a source of sedimentary material for the surf zone.

Submerged sediments in the near-shore waters of the continental shelf can also provide sediments for estuaries. Currents are just as capable of moving sediments from subtidal regions into the estuary as they are of moving intertidal beach sediments, so long as the shear strength holding the particles in place is overcome.

The extent to which sediments within estuaries originate from the river or the sea varies considerably. The Seine estuary appears to be considerably influenced by sediments of marine origin (Rajcevic, 1957; Vigarie, 1965). Other European estuaries have also been shown to receive sediments primarily from the sea (Guilcher, 1967).

The origin of estuarine sediments is often determined by comparing the sediments of interest with those close to the estuary, offshore and upstream. Analyses of clay minerology and grain sizes can then generally indicate the point of origin. For example, Windom et al. (1971) examined the minerology of suspended and bottom sediments from the Ogeechee, Altamaha, and Satilla rivers in Georgia and showed that the fine material was derived from the continental shelf, while the clastics (fragmented, irregularly shaped particles) were formed from coastal plain and inland detritus.

In many cases, the material entering an estuary from the seaward side is composed of the larger grain sizes. This is particularly true the farther away from shore that the material originates. Deep offshore sediments tend to be large grained because fine materials are normally not carried far from shore (Postma, 1967). (An exception would be volcanic ash that settled offshore, downwind from an eruption.) Deep offshore sediments do not, in general, return to the coastal zone, because the forces responsible for sediment movement cannot transport those sediments. Thus, near-shore sub-tidal regions and beaches are the most likely sources of marine sediments to enter an estuary (Meade, 1969).

When marine sediments dominate those of an estuary, it is generally because they are carried upstream along the bottom by the salt wedge (Guilcher, 1967). When marine sediments are dominant the influence of river-borne sediments must obviously be limited, as are the influences of other sediment sources. Net transport of sediments up the estuary have been reported. Wright and Sonu (1975) examined Choctawhatchee Bay in Florida and found that density stratification within the estuary as a result of tidal movement led to vertical segregation of the velocities of flood and ebb currents. During flood tide, flows were concentrated near the bottom, where they carried sediments into the bay from the seaward side. During ebb flow, however, currents were concentrated near the surface, reducing the outward movement of sediments.

Sources and net movements of sediments in estuaries are difficult to predict and take considerable time and effort to document in the field. One way around extensive field work has been by modeling. This procedure can be done through simulation models on computers but can also be accomplished through mechanical modeling. The most extensive application of the latter has been at the U.S. Army Corps of Engineers Waterways Experiment Station in Vicksburg, Mississippi, where researchers have constructed and tested scale models of many of the estuaries of the United States.

WIND-DRIVEN SEDIMENTATION

Wind effectively transports sediment particles of fine and very fine sand. Excellent sources of such materials are beaches and dunes that front the ocean adjacent to estuaries. While the general configuration of a beach is not significantly altered over the short term by normal winds blowing over the sand, enough material may eventually be moved to influence the sedimentary patterns within an estuary. The most dramatic effects of wind, however, result from storms. Storms have been identified as a major factor in the emplacement and modification of coarse-grained sediments along the Texas coast (McGowen and Scott, 1975).

The most dramatic kind of storm is, of course, the hurricane. The effects of hurricanes on sedimentation include storm surges, which create strong currents that carry suspended and bedload sediments into the estuary; high waves; and intense flooding resulting from heavy rainfall (Hayes,

1978). River-borne sediments are often increased by the greatly increased runoff. In addition, extremely turbulent coastal waters may move marine sediments, which normally are not easily dislodged, into the estuarine zone, and flooding within an estuarine basin can redistribute large amounts of supratidal, intertidal, and subtidal material. Hayes (1978) noted that one storm may cause more changes in a few hours than might otherwise occur over several decades. If a storm is sufficiently large, the changes may be greater than would otherwise occur for centuries.

Gross et al. (1978) examined the amount of sediment entering the upper Chesapeake Bay in suspension from the Susquehanna River from 1966 to 1976. They determined that approximately 50 million metric tons of material were involved. But the sediments did not enter the estuary at the rate of 5 million tons per year; instead, it appeared that about 40 million tons resulted directly from Hurricanes Agnes in 1972 and Eloise in 1975. Thus, about 80% of the total suspended load entering the bay from the Susquehanna over that decade was storm related. Since that study evaluated only the Susquehanna River, it may have accounted for a mere fraction of the total sediment load entering Chesapeake Bay during those ten years. Other major rivers feeding into the bay include the Patuxent, Rappahannock, York, and James.

INTERNAL REDISTRIBUTION

In most estuaries currents and waves are continually in motion, occasionally augmented by storms. All of these forces are important in redistributing sediments within estuaries and in eroding supratidal lands bordering any given estuary. As indicated by Hayes (1975), the morphology of sand deposits in estuaries is a function of tidal range, tidal currents, wave conditions, and storm action.

Sand, although quite motile, is commonly found in high-energy parts of an estuary, while silts and clays are not. Within the sand are shell fragments and other larger sedimentary particles (Sanders, 1958). Low-energy environments are dominated by silts and clays.

The most rapid currents found in estuaries are normally around inlets where sediments of all sizes are mobilized and redistributed. Sand flats adjacent to inlets are often dynamic and transient because of their continuous redistribution of material. Many of these areas are nearly devoid of benthic organisms because of the instability of the substrate (Peterson and Peterson, 1979).

Intertidal flats tend to have fine sediments within them, and the mean grain size of the particles becomes finer as one moves up the estuary from the inlet (Peterson and Peterson, 1979). This general picture can be quickly changed by the passage of a storm, however. Large deposits of oyster shell in the midst of sediments dominated by silts and clays often represent shoals formed during storms.

The erosion of primary or secondary dunes by wind or rain and the resulting deposits into the estuary through surface runoff represent one way in which sediments near the borders of an estuary become deposited as intertidal or subtidal sediments. Some of the estuaries of Brittany contain sediments that reflect their origin in the lower slopes of the land bordering them (Guilcher, 1967). Other examples of this nature have been reported by Guilcher and King (1961) and Stevenson and Emery (1958). Similarly, sloughing of the banks of tidal creeks and erosion of upland areas contribute to shoaling within an estuary.

BIOGENIC DEPOSITS

Many species of both plants and animals contain body parts, usually skeletal, that may contribute to estuarine sediments when the organisms die and decay. Some of these bits of material are very small (e.g., the frustules of diatoms and the tests of foraminifera), while others may be quite large (e.g., the bones of a marine mammal that died inside the estuary or was washed in from the sea). Perhaps the most commonly observed and most abundant variety of biogenic deposit is the remains of molluscs. Shells and shell hash (pieces of shell formed by waves and frictional forces acting upon whole shells) are often plentiful, particularly in high-energy areas, such as the inlets of many estuaries.

The sands in parts of south Florida and in many regions of the tropics are composed almost entirely of the remains of corals. Degradation of coral skeletons to fragments the size of sand results from physical and biological activity. Certain fish feed upon coral and may grind off pieces of the coral skeleton (calcium carbonate) as a part of their feeding. Other fish pick up bites of sediment in search of living animals within and may crush not only corals but also molluscs in the process, again contributing to the reduction of large particles into what eventually become sand grains.

Estuarine sediments have been found in some cases to contain high levels of organic matter, often composed of algal particles, small pieces of roots, remnants of planktonic animals, and other organic residues

(Guilcher, 1963). These organic particles are transient in nature because of their ultimate decomposition into carbon dioxide, water, and small amounts of trace elements; nevertheless, the continuous supply of these particles to the system is often responsible for the maintenance of a fairly constant level of organic matter in the sediments.

Marshland Sediments

Marshlands associated with estuaries of the southeastern United States and the Gulf of Mexico vary in extent, but they usually include a system of tidal creeks that meander through them. As water spills over the top of a channel and across a tidal flat (a tidal flat differs from marshland in that the former is devoid of vegetation) and as the creek widens, current speed is reduced. Fine particles unable to settle within the creek because of the rate of flow are deposited on tidal flats. The same process occurs when tidal water spreads across marshlands, though in that case sedimentation is assisted by the plants, which tend to further slow the flow of water and may physically trap suspended particles in their leaves, stems, or exposed portions of their root systems.

Along the sides of the larger channels passing through estuaries, natural levees are commonly present that may, in some cases, rise as much as 30 cm above the prevailing level of the adjacent marshland. As the water overflows the creek banks during flood tide, particulate matter drops out of solution and is deposited. If that happens immediately after the water overflows the banks of the creek, a levee is formed. When such a natural levee is found near a stream enclosing a marshland, a small pond may be formed in the center of the enclosure (Emery and Stevenson, 1957).

Factors that control sedimentation in marshes include (1) vegetation density, (2) the elevation of the marsh above sea level, and (3) the distance between a particular point in a marsh and the margin of a river or creek (Chapman, 1960). Thus, it is obvious that sedimentation will not occur at the same rate in all parts of a marsh; it is even likely that the composition of the sediments within a marsh will vary somewhat from one area to another. According to Kolumbe (1931), tidal currents and the physico-chemical flocculation of colloidal particles as a result of the mixing of fresh with saline water are also important in marsh development.

Sediment Accretion Rates

Studies to date reveal that the general accretion rate in marshes ranges from about 2 to 18 mm/yr (Redfield, 1972; Harrison and Bloom, 1974; Richard, 1978), with several investigators coming up with intermediate values (reviewed by Nixon, 1980). The upper end of the cited range is almost insignificant when compared with the marshes of the Bay of Fundy, which have been shown to accumulate sediments at rates as high as 76 cm in 122 days (Chapman, 1960).

McCaffrey (1977) examined the sediments of Long Island Sound using radioactive lead and determined that the rate of accretion in the high marsh of that region had increased since 1900. Through the use of long-term readings to gauge the tide, he also determined that the rate at which sea level rose had also increased; the marsh was therefore remaining relatively stable with respect to its elevation above sea level. Because of the generally rising sea level, marshes must accumulate much of the sedimentary material that enters estuaries in order to maintain their vertical position (Settlemyre and Gardner, 1975).

Salt marshes along the Gulf coast in the Mississippi delta region are in a rapidly subsiding zone, where accretion is important if the marshes are to maintain themselves. Accretion rates of 13.5 mm annually have been shown to be sufficient to maintain those marshes (DeLaune and Patrick, 1980). Deteriorating marshes were found by the same authors in regions that received only 7.5 mm/yr of accretion.

Various estimates of the filling rates common to most estuaries have been developed, and scientists generally feel that the life of an estuary will be on the order of thousands of years, providing some catastrophe does not reduce that life span. Chesapeake Bay is thought to have formed ten thousand years ago and is far from being filled with sediments (Massmann, 1971).

The estuaries associated with the Mississippi River delta are not only somewhat unusual with respect to the amount of sediments passing through them but are also filling much more rapidly than are other estuaries. Estimates of the rates of accretion of sediments near the Mississippi delta are about 300 m/1,000 years (Scrutton, 1960; Shephard, 1960), while most estuaries and bays appear to be filling at the rate of from 2 to 4 m/1,000 years (Shephard, 1953; Shephard and Moore, 1960). The lagoons of semiarid regions are only accreting at the rate of about 1 m/1,000 years (Rusnak, 1960).

Barnes (1974) noted that on the average, estuaries accumulate mud sediments at the rate of about 2 mm/yr. A study by Richard (1978), on the other hand, indicated that over a period of 173 years, the average accretion rate in the estuary under study was 3.4 mm/yr. Accretion rates depend to some extent upon the position in the estuary where samples are taken.

Influence of the Biota on Sedimentary Processes

Considerable research has been conducted on the relationships between benthic animals and the sediments in which they are found. Recent reviews on animal-sediment relationships have been contributed by Gray (1974) and Rhodes (1974). The study of benthic organisms does not require consideration of their sedimentary environment, but no ecological evaluation of benthic communities would be complete if the sediments were ignored.

The relationship between animals (or plants) and the surrounding sediments is two-directional. On the one hand, organisms are influenced by the sediments in which they exist; on the other, the organisms may be important in restructuring the sedimentary environment, even to the extent of changing the kinds and rates of certain chemical reactions. Sedimentary materials not only affect benthic creatures but may also influence both plants and animals in the water column.

In estuaries, the turbidity often present in the water column is more often associated with high levels of suspended sediments than with other substances. While this material frequently settles to the bottom, as previously discussed it also often undergoes constant replacement. In the short term, therefore, the level of turbidity remains relatively constant except during storms.

Suspended sediments and detritus can clog gills, impair respiration, and hinder feeding in animals (Cairns, 1967). They can also reduce primary productivity by limiting the light required for photosynthesis. Turbidity can influence other aspects of water quality and, hence, can affect organisms (reviewed by Saila, 1980). The literature on the effects of suspended and deposited sediments on estuarine organisms has been reviewed by Sherk (1971).

Loosanoff and Tommers (1948) reported that as little as 1.0 g/l of silt can reduce the pumping rate in adult American oysters (*Crassostrea virginica*) by 57%. At levels of 3 to 4 g/l, pumping rates may be reduced by 94%. On the other hand, small quantities of suspended material may stimulate pumping and growth (Loosanoff, 1961).

Direct burial of benthic epifaunal organisms can result when sedimentation rates are high. Motile forms can often survive by moving to the surface at the same rate at which the sediments accumulate, but sedentary and attached forms may be unable to move. Corals, sponges, oysters, tunicates, and barnacles are examples of animals that will rapidly succumb if subjected to direct sedimentation.

The effects of organisms upon sediments may be substantial, not only on distributing the sediments but also on controlling the kinds of organisms that can inhabit those sediments. A considerable amount of sediment processing may occur, including burrowing, ingestion and defecation of sedimentary particles, construction of tubes and related activities, and biodeposition of exoskeletons and other parts of organisms (Myers, 1977a).

The burrowing and ingestion and defecation of sedimentary material by benthic animals can have a considerable impact on sediment structure. Sorting and the disruption of any layering or bedding that may otherwise have been present in the sediments often result from animal activity. Many studies have been undertaken on the effects of sediment reworking, but few have provided information on the actual amount of sediment handled by organisms involved in reworking. Mangum (1964) reported that individuals of the polychaete *Clymenella torquata* have been shown to process about 1 ml/day of sediment in Puerto Rico. In New Brunswick, Canada, where mean temperatures are much lower, the annual rate of sediment processing by each individual of the same species is about 96 ml/yr, while in North Carolina (intermediate temperature regime) the rate is 274 ml/yr. The pelycepod mollusc *Yoldia limulata* has been found to process up to 257 ml/yr in Buzzards Bay, Massachusetts (Rhodes, 1963). In regions where high concentrations of these benthic animals are found, the total amount of reworking possible within a year is extremely great. Rhodes (1963) reported that the sediments can be reworked by *Y. limulata* more rapidly than they are deposited, even though the clam makes up only about 10% of the total benthos present.

The intensive reworking of sandy sediments by some animals may limit other organisms by creating an interface layer between sediment and water that is easily suspended, unstable, and tends to clog gills. This has been documented by Rhodes and Young (1970, 1971) and Young and Rhodes (1971). The exclusion of one kind of organism by another is called ammensalism and has been discussed in more detail by Myers (1977b).

The activities of benthic invertebrates can cause the agglomeration of particles, again changing the character of the originally sedimented particles. Lund (1957) calculated that a continuous single layer of *Crassostrea virginica* would be capable of depositing 12 tons/ha of dry mass sediment weekly! Haven and Morales-Alamo (1966) further calculated that a typical oyster bed in the York River estuary of Virginia could deposit 1 to 2 tons/ha/week of dry weight sediment.

In addition to bioturbation, particles can be cemented together and stabilized by microbial activity. Changes affecting the erodibility of the sediments through such processes have been discussed by Rhodes et al. (1978a, 1978b). The construction of tubes in the sediment and the irrigation of those tubes by the animals inhabiting them have been shown to lead to complex changes in the patterns of chemical reactions and in the diffusion gradients within the sediments.

Miscellaneous Characteristics of Sediments

In addition to characteristic grain sizes within a given area of an estuary, other features of sediments should be acknowledged. For example, sediments act as sources and sinks for various chemicals, including pollutants and nutrients.

The amount of organic matter in sediments is highly variable. The rich, black, pungent-smelling muds of the Southeast, for example, often contain several percent organic matter and are high in hydrogen sulfide as a result of the decomposition of organic material. By contrast, some sandy estuarine regions may be nearly devoid of organic matter.

As a general rule, positive estuaries have water of low dissolved oxygen and high salinity moving into them along the bottom. This pattern leads to sediments with characteristically black muds and high organic content. Negative estuaries, on the other hand, usually contain gray mud of low organic content resulting from well-oxygenated water moving out of the estuary on the bottom (Emery and Stevenson, 1957).

The association between high organic content and the black color found in many estuarine sediments is generally recognized. In Chesapeake

Bay, the "natural" color of the sediments is apparently gray-green. The black found in some sediments in the region is caused by the chemical hydrotroilite (Biggs, 1967). The chemistry of hydrotroilite has been discussed by Berner (1967). The substance appears to result from conversion of FeS to pyrite.

The immediate surface of most sediments is oxidized and will usually appear as brown, except in a region with anaerobic water over the sediments. The brown oxidized layer may be very thin, perhaps with an olive-gray, equally thin layer immediately below it. Next comes a black, anoxic layer of variable depth, followed by a gray layer.

Black sediments are generally characteristic of reducing environments. The reworking of those sediments can affect certain chemical reactions and the speed with which they take place. Sulfate reduction, for example, is accelerated by benthic organisms in such environments (Aller, 1978).

Another feature of sediments, including those found in estuaries, is bedding structures. The kind of bedform in estuaries is governed by the maximum velocities of flood and ebb tides, the time span during which a given velocity exists, and the difference in maximum velocities of flood and ebb tides (Boothroyd and Hubbard, 1975). Bedding structures are also partly dependent on the sort of sediment surrounding them. For example, ripples can be found in sand but not in mud (Reineck, 1967).

Some of the various bedding structures include:

1. Lamella bedding. Individually recognizable sand layers may form from the action of single waves, causing between six and sixteen lamellae to be set down during a given tidal cycle.
2. Ripple bedding. Ripples are made up of spoon-shaped lamellae developed from currents. Large ripples (megaripples) occur if currents usually exceed 80 cm/sec. Megaripples are frequently found in coarse sand.
3. Flaser bedding. Sand may be deposited in ripples during current flow, while mud is held in suspension. At slack tide the mud settles and covers the surface of the ripples, or it may collect only in the troughs.
4. Lenticular bedding. This results from the presence of sand lenses in a muddy matrix.
5. Mud deposits. These are mostly muds, but with sand grains included in a nonhomogeneous formation.

6. Salt marsh or flood deposits. Shell deposits inserted into the salt marsh strata are an example. Root canals with iron hydroxide on their surfaces are characteristic.
7. Bioturbate structures. Normal bedding planes may be disturbed by the activity of benthic animals, including demersal fishes.

Thus, we have seen that sediments differ widely from one estuary to another and even within a given estuary. Dyer (1973, p. 3) pinpointed the profile in an observation that will become increasingly relevant as other subjects cogent to estuarine ecology are discussed.

The main drawback in studying estuaries is that flow, tidal range and sediment distribution are continually changing and consequently some estuaries may never really be steady-state systems. . . . Because of the interaction of so many variables no two estuaries are alike and one never knows whether one is observing general principles or unique details.

LITERATURE CITED

Aller, R. C. 1978. The effects of animal-sediment interactions on geochemical processes near the sediment-water interface, pp. 157–72. In: M. L. Wiley, ed. *Estuarine interactions*. New York: Academic Press.

Bagnold, R. A. 1963. Mechanics of marine sedimentation, pp. 507–28. In: M. N. Hill, ed. *The sea*. Vol. III. New York: Wiley-Interscience.

Barnes, R. S. K. 1974. *Estuarine biology*. London: Edward Arnold.

Berner, R. A. 1967. Diagenesis of iron sulfide in recent marine sediments, pp. 268–72. In: G. H. Lauff, ed. *Estuaries*. American Association for the Advancement of Science Publication no. 83. Washington, D.C.: AAAS.

Biggs, R. B. 1967. The sediments of Chesapeake Bay, pp. 239–60. In: G. H. Lauff, ed. *Estuaries*. American Association for the Advancement of Science Publication no. 83. Washington, D.C.: AAAS.

Boothroyd, J. C. and D. K. Hubbard. 1975. Genesis of bedforms in mesotidal estuaries, pp. 217–34. In: L. E. Cronin, ed. *Estuarine research*. Vol. II. New York: Academic Press.

Cairns, J., Jr. 1967. Suspended solids standards for the protection of aquatic organisms. *Purdue University Engin. Bull.* 129: 16–27.

Chapman, V. J. 1960. *Salt marshes and salt deserts of the world*. New York: Wiley-Interscience.

Crance, J. H. 1971. Description of Alabama estuarine areas—cooperative Gulf of Mexico estuarine inventory. *Alabama Marine Resources Bull.* 6: 1–85.

DeLaune, R. D., and W. H. Patrick. 1980. Rate of sedimentation and its role in nutrient cycling in a Louisiana salt marsh, pp. 401–12. In: P. Hamilton and

K. B. Macdonald, eds. *Estuarine and wetland processes—with emphasis on modeling*. New York: Plenum Press.

Dyer, K. R. 1973. *Estuaries: A physical introduction*. New York: John Wiley and Sons.

———. 1979. Estuaries and estuarine sedimentation, pp. 1–18. In: K. R. Dyer, ed. *Estuarine hydrography and sedimentation*. Cambridge, England: Cambridge University Press.

Emery, K. O., and R. E. Stevenson. 1957. Estuaries and lagoons. I. Physical and chemical characteristics, pp. 673–93. In: J. W. Hedgpeth, ed. *Treatise on marine ecology and paleoecology*. Vol. I. Memoir 67. New York: Geological Society of America.

Freitag, D. R. 1960. Soil as a factor in shoaling processes: A literature review. *Tech. Bull.* 4: 1–47. Comm. on Tidal Hydraulics, U.S. Army Corps of Engineers, Washington, D.C.

Goodell, H. G., and D. S. Gorsline. 1961. A sedimentological study of Tampa Bay, Florida. *Inter. Geol. Congress, XXI Session*. 23: 75–78.

Gray, J. S. 1974. Animal-sediment relationships. *Oceanogr. Mar. Biol. Ann. Rev.* 12: 223–61.

Griffin, G. M. 1962. Regional clay-mineral facies: Products of weathering intensity and current distribution in the northeastern Gulf of Mexico. *Geol. Society of America Bull.* 73: 737–68.

Gross, M. G., K. Karweit, W. B. Cronin, and J. R. Schubel. 1978. Suspended sediment discharge of the Susquehanna River to northern Chesapeake Bay, 1966 to 1976. *Estuaries* 1: 106–10.

Guilcher, A. 1963. Estuaries, deltas, shelf, slope, pp. 620–54. In: M. N. Hill, ed. *The sea*. Vol. III. New York: Wiley-Interscience.

———. 1967. Origin of sediments in estuaries, pp. 149–57. In: G. H. Lauff, ed. *Estuaries*. American Association for the Advancement of Science Publication no. 83. Washington, D.C.: AAAS.

Guilcher, A., and C. A. M. King. 1961. Spits, tombolos, and tidal marshes in Connemara and West Kerry, Ireland. *Proc. Roy. Irish Acad.* 61: 283–338.

Harrison, E. Z., and A. L. Bloom. 1974. The response of Connecticut salt marshes to the recent rise in sea level. *Geological Society of America*, Abstr. 6: 35–36.

Haven, D. S., and R. Morales-Alamo. 1966. Aspects of biodeposition by oysters and other invertebrate filter feeders. *Limnol. Oceanogr.* 11: 487–98.

Hayes, M. O. 1975. Morphology of sand accumulation in estuaries: An introduction to the symposium, pp. 3–22. In: L. E. Cronin, ed. *Estuarine research*. Vol. II. New York: Academic Press.

———. 1978. Impact of hurricanes on sedimentation in estuaries, pp. 323–46. In: M. L. Wiley, ed. *Estuarine interactions*. New York: Academic Press.

Ippen, A. T. 1966. Sedimentation in estuaries, pp. 648–72. In: A. T. Ippen, ed. *Estuary and coastline hydrodynamics*. New York: McGraw-Hill.

Kolumbe, E. 1931. *Spartina townsendii*: Anpflanzungen in Schleswig-Holstein-ischen Wattenmeer. *Wiss. Meer. Kiel*. 21–22: 67.

Loosanoff, V. L. 1961. Effects of turbidity on some larval and adult bivalves. *Proc. Gulf and Carrib. Fish. Inst.* 14: 80–95.

Loosanoff, V. L., and F. D. Tommers. 1948. Effect of suspended silt and other substances on rate of feeding of oysters. *Science* 107: 69–70.

Lund, E. J. 1957. A quantitative study of clearance of a turbid medium and feeding by the oyster. *Publ. Inst. Mar. Sci., Univ. Tex.* 4: 296–312.

Luneburg, H. 1939. Hydrochemische untersuchungen in der Elbmundung mittels elektrokolorimeter. *Arch. Deutsch. Seewarte* 59: 1–27.

McCaffrey, R. J. 1977. A record of the accumulation of sediment and trace metals in a Connecticut, U.S.A., salt marsh. Ph.D. diss. Yale University, New Haven, Conn.

McDowell, D. M., and B. A. O'Connor. 1977. *Hydraulic behaviour of estuaries*. New York: John Wiley and Sons.

McGowen, J. H., and A. J. Scott. 1975. Hurricanes as geologic agents on the Texas coast, pp. 23–46. In: L. E. Cronin, ed. *Estuarine research*. Vol. II. New York: Academic Press.

Mangum, C. P. 1964. Activity patterns in metabolism and ecology of polychaetes. *Comp. Biochem. Physiol.* 11: 239–56.

Massmann, W. H. 1971. The significance of an estuary on the biology of aquatic organisms of the Middle Atlantic region, pp. 96–109. In: P. R. Douglas and R. H. Stroud, eds. *A symposium on the biological significance of estuaries*. Washington, D.C.: Sport Fishing Institute.

Meade, R. H. 1969. Landward transport of bottom sediment in estuaries of the Atlantic coastal plain. *J. Sed. Pet.* 39: 222–34.

Myers, A. C. 1977a. Sediment processing in a marine subtidal sandy bottom community. I. Physical aspects, *J. Mar. Res.* 35: 609–32.

———. 1977b. Sediment processing in a marine subtidal sandy bottom community. II. Biological consequences. *J. Mar. Res.* 35: 633–47.

Nelson, B. W. 1974. Sedimentary deltas, pp. 278–311. In: H. T. Odum, B. J. Copeland, and E. A. McMahan, eds. *Coastal ecological systems of the United States*. Vol. I. Washington, D.C.: Conservation Foundation.

Nixon, S. W. 1980. Between coastal marshes and coastal waters. A review of twenty years of speculation on the role of salt marshes in estuarine productivity and water chemistry, pp. 437–525. In: P. Hamilton and K. B. Macdonald, eds. *Estuarine and wetland processes—with emphasis on modeling*. New York: Plenum Press.

Peterson, C. H., and N. M. Peterson. 1979. The ecology of intertidal flats in North Carolina: A community profile. U.S. Fish and Wildlife Service Biological Services Program. FWS/OBS 79-39.

Postma, H. 1967. Sediment transport and sedimentation in the estuarine environment, pp. 158–79. In: G. H. Lauff, ed. *Estuaries*. American Association for the Advancement of Science Publication no. 83. Washington, D.C.: AAAS.

Postma, H., and K. Kalle. 1955. Die Entstehung von Truebungszonen in Unterlauf der Fluesse. *Deutsch. Hydrograph. Zeit.* 8: 137–44.

Rajcevic, B. M. 1957. Etude des conditions de sedimentation dans l'estuaire de la Seine. *Ann. Inst. Tech Batiment et Trav. Publ.* 10: 743–75.

Redfield, A. C. 1972. Development of the New England salt marsh. *Ecol. Monogr.* 42: 201–37.

Reineck, H. E. 1967. Layered sediments of tidal flats, beaches, and shelf bottoms of the North Sea, pp. 191–206. In: G. H. Lauff, ed. *Estuaries*. American Association for the Advancement of Science Publication no. 83. Washington, D.C.: AAAS.

Rhodes, D. C. 1963. Rates of sediment reworking by *Yoldia limulata* in Buzzards Bay, Massachusetts, and Long Island Sound. *J. Sed. Pet.* 33: 723–27.

———. 1974. Organism-sediment relations on the muddy sea floor. *Oceanogr. Mar. Biol. Ann. Rev.* 12: 263–300.

Rhodes, D. C., and D. K. Young. 1970. The influence of deposit-feeding organisms on sediment stability and community trophic structures. *J. Mar. Res.* 28: 150–78.

———. 1971. Animal-sediment relations in Cape Cod Bay, Massachusetts. II. Reworking by *Molpadia oolitica* (Holothuroidea). *Mar. Biol.* 11: 255–61.

Rhodes, D. C., J. Y. Yingst, and W. J. Ullman. 1978a. Seafloor stability in central Long Island Sound. Part I. Temporal changes in erodibility of fine-grained sediments, pp. 221–44. In: M. L. Wiley, ed. *Estuarine interactions*. New York: Academic Press.

———. 1978b. Seafloor stability in central Long Island Sound. Part II. Biological interactions and their potential importance for seafloor erodibility, pp. 245–60. In: M. L. Wiley, ed. *Estuarine interactions*. New York: Academic Press.

Richard, G. A. 1978. Seasonal and environmental variations in sediment accretion in a Long Island salt marsh. *Estuaries* 1: 29–35.

Rusnak, G. A. 1960. Sediments of Laguna Madre, Texas, pp. 153–96. In: F. P. Shephard, F. B. Phleger, and Tj. H. Van Andel, eds. *Sediments, northwest Gulf of Mexico*. Tulsa, Okla.: American Association of Petroleum Geologists.

———. 1967. Rates of sediment accumulation in modern estuaries, pp. 180–84. In: G. H. Lauff ed. *Estuaries*. American Association for the Advancement of Science Publication no. 83. Washington, D.C.: AAAS.

Saila, S. B. 1980. Estuarine fishery resources and physical estuarine modifications: Some suggestions for impact assessment, pp. 603–29. In: P. Hamilton and

K. B. Macdonald, eds. *Estuarine and wetland processes—with emphasis on modeling*. New York: Plenum Press.

Sanders, H. L. 1958. Benthic studies in Buzzards Bay. I. Animal-sediment relationships. *Limnol. Oceanogr.* 3: 245–58.

Scrutton, P. C. 1960. Delta building and deltaic sequence, pp. 82–102. In: F. P. Shephard, F. B. Phleger, and Tj. H. Van Andel, eds. *Sediments, northwest Gulf of Mexico*. Tulsa, Okla.: American Association of Petroleum Geologists.

Settlemyre, J. L., and L. R. Gardner. 1975. *Chemical and sediment budgets for a small tidal creek, Charleston Harbor, S.C.* Water Resources Research Institute Clemson University Report no. 57. Clemson, S.C.: Clemson University.

Shephard, F. P. 1953. Sedimentation rates in Texas estuaries and lagoons. *Amer. Assoc. Petrol. Geol.* 37: 1919–34.

———. 1960. Gulf coast barriers, pp. 197–220. In: F. P. Shephard, F. B. Phleger, and Tj. H. Van Andel, eds. *Sediments, northwest Gulf of Mexico*. Tulsa, Okla.: American Association of Petroleum Geologists.

Shephard, F. P., and D. G. Moore. 1960. Bays of central Texas coast, pp. 117–52. In: F. P. Shephard, F. B. Phleger, and Tj. H. Van Andel, eds. *Sediments, northwest Gulf of Mexico*. Tulsa, Okla.: American Association of Petroleum Geologists.

Sherk, J. A., Jr. 1971. The effects of suspended and deposited sediments on estuarine organisms. Cont. no. 443, Chesapeake Biol. Lab., Solomons, Maryland. Mimeo.

Stevenson, R. E., and K. O. Emery. 1958. *Marshlands at Newport Bay, California*. Allan Hancock Publication no. 20, p. 110. Los Angeles: University of Southern California Press.

Tanner, W. F. 1960. Florida coastal classification. *Trans. Gulf Coast Assoc. Geol. Soc.* 10: 259–66.

Turekian, K. K., and M. R. Scott. 1967. Concentrations of Cr, Ag, Mo, Ni, Co, and Mn in suspended material in streams. *Envir. Sci. & Tech.* 1: 940–42.

Vigarie, A. 1965. Les modalities du remblaiement alluvial dans l'estuarie de la Seine. *Cah. Oceanog.* 17: 301–30.

Whitehouse, U. G., L. M. Jeffrey, and J. D. Debbrecht. 1960. Differential settling tendencies of clay minerals in saline waters. *Proc. Natl. Conf. Clays, Clay Minerals* 7: 1–79.

Windom, H. L., W. J. Neal, and K. C. Beck. 1971. Mineralogy of sediments in three Georgia estuaries. *J. Sed. Pet.* 41: 497–504.

Wright, L. D., and C. J. Sonu. 1975. Processes of sediment transport and tidal delta development in a stratified tidal inlet, pp. 63–76. In: L. E. Cronin, ed. *Estuarine research*. Vol. II. New York: Academic Press.

Young, D. K., and D. C. Rhodes. 1971. Animal-sediment relations in Cape Cod Bay, Massachusetts. I. A transect study. *Mar. Biol.* 11: 242–54.

CHAPTER 4

Physical Relationships

Extent of Estuaries

ESTUARIES occupy about 0.25% of the earth's surface, so in that respect they constitute a relatively insignificant percentage of the world ocean. Approximately 20% of the total estuarine area is marshland, and the remainder is open water, according to Woodwell et al. (1973). Those authors estimated that 3.1 billion metric tons of organic matter are produced annually in estuaries, or about 2% of worldwide production. Some of the most important estuaries of the United States can be found in our area of interest, which extends from Chesapeake Bay to the extreme southern coast of Texas.

Chesapeake Bay is about 300 km long and between 6 and 56 km wide, a total area of roughly 1,100,000 ha (Massmann, 1971). Formed about ten thousand years ago by rising sea level and the drowning of the Susquehanna River Valley, Chesapeake Bay has become an important source for fishery products and is heavily used by commercial and military ships as well as by sportsmen. Salinity in Chesapeake Bay ranges from about 30 o/oo in the bottom waters at the mouth to fresh water at the head (Massmann, 1971).

The estuaries near Beaufort, North Carolina, have received a great deal of attention by estuarine ecologists. That region, about 400,000 ha, has been widely studied, since several university and federal government laboratories are in the immediate vicinity. Maximum depth in those estuaries is about 13 m with a mean of about 1.2 m (Williams, 1966).

The estuaries of Georgia, particularly those around Sapelo Island, have been extensively studied. Georgia has about 160,000 ha of salt marsh. Most of the marshland is composed of smooth cordgrass, *Spartina alterniflora*, though various other aquatic plants are present and may dominate at certain elevations within the marsh.

Florida has about 1,200,000 ha of estuaries: open water fills some 800,000 ha, mangrove swamps about 160,000 ha, and tidal marshes the remainder (McNulty et al., 1972). About half of the estuaries of Florida are unvegetated; the other half is divided among mangroves, marshgrasses, and submerged vegetation.

Alabama's coastline is dominated by Mobile Bay. That body of water, which can be classified as an estuary, is some 1,036,000 ha in area. The bay is about 50 km long, 13 to 16 km wide at the upper end, and 39 km wide at the lower end (April and Raney, 1980).

The effects of limited tidal range on the extent of coastal salt marshes are apparent along much of the coast of the Gulf of Mexico except for Louisiana, where the Mississippi River and extensive areas of freshwater marshes change conditions considerably. Mississippi has only about 27,000 ha of tidal marshland. The total area of the Mississippi estuaries is some 200,000 ha at mean high water. Submerged vegetation covers roughly 7,000 ha within the state (Christmas, 1973).

According to Day et al. (1973), Louisiana has an estuarine area of some 2,800,000 ha, of which about 1,600,000 ha are salt and freshwater marshes. That is in sharp contrast to the Texas coast, which, although nearly 1,000 km long (Diener, 1975), has only about 500,000 ha of open water and lagoons and 240,000 ha of marshlands. Louisiana and Texas contain 68% of the estuaries of the Gulf of Mexico and 80% of the marshes. They also account for 24% of the total estuarine area of the United States and 55% of the marshes in the contiguous forty-eight states.

Marshlands

Salt marshes can be defined as beds of intertidal rooted vegetation alternately inundated and drained by the rise and fall of the tide (Cooper, 1974). The harshness of the environment may have greatly influenced these areas, in that both the plants and the animals found in marshes throughout the United States are similar. *Spartina alterniflora* tends to dominate the coastal marshes of the southeastern United States and the Gulf of Mexico. Other species of *Spartina*, along with various species of *Juncus* and *Salicornia* (discussed in chapter 6), are almost universally present (Cooper, 1974).

The coastal zone from Cape Lookout, North Carolina, to Jacksonville, Florida, is the area of optimum development for salt marshes (Linton, 1968). As mentioned earlier, much of Louisiana's marshland comprises freshwater marshes dominated by genera of plants different from those of salt marshes. In coastal areas of the southeastern United States with optimal conditions for the development of marshes, the tides range from slightly less than 2 m in North Carolina and northern Florida to as much as 3 m in portions of Georgia and South Carolina. The marshes in the region from North Carolina to northern Florida have formed behind narrow barrier islands and are heavily influenced by silt deposition from rivers (Linton, 1968). The barrier islands of that region emerged during a decline in sea level with the last ice age; the islands are slowly drowning as sea level rises (Hoyt et al., 1964; Land and Hoyt, 1966; Hoyt and Hails, 1967; Hoyt and Henry, 1967). Inundation may be offset somewhat by the concurrent deposition of river-borne sedimentary material.

According to Chapman (1960), a typical salt marsh develops in three major steps. First, a mud or sand flat is formed, upon which the only plants present are various species of algae, and in certain areas eelgrass or other species of submerged grasses. Second, as elevation increases (from eustatic changes in sea level or deposition of more sediments), the submerged grasses are replaced by intertidal species, predominantly cordgrasses of the genus *Spartina*. Third, a bare phase is often sandwiched between the disappearance of eelgrass and the appearance of cordgrasses.

Salt marshes may occupy narrow fringes along the ocean, or they may be several kilometers wide. Their boundaries often depend upon tidal range as well as upon natural relief. Marshes are found most frequently in high latitudes, because in the tropics and subtropics their ecological niche is usually filled by mangrove swamps (Chapman, 1960).

Typical marshes of the temperate area tend to have two main parts: a lower portion, exposed at low tide and entirely underwater at high tide; and a higher one, covered by water only during spring high tides or storm surges. The lower part can be further divided into an unvegetated portion and a higher vegetated zone. The highest part of the marsh is commonly vegetated by macrophytes (Guilcher, 1963).

Physiographic features of marshlands include rivers and creeks, whose characteristics have been described by Chapman (1960). Riverbanks in estuaries usually have steep mud sides. Lateral channels develop on the mud banks and make up the marsh creek system. Plant colonization leads to increased accretion of sediments and a building of creek banks. Creek development falls into three phases:

1. Active youth, where erosion at the head of the creek parallels rapid accretion of the marsh sediments and deepening of the creek

2. Maturity, where further accretion and erosion result from under-cutting of the creek banks
3. Senility, where vegetation in its final stage dominates, and por-tions of the marsh are cut off from the head of the creek to form what are known as pans

An alternative senility phase involves covering the creek with plants and maintaining the flow of the creek below the sediment surface. This condi-tion may occur in the ultimate branches of a creek, while main channels generally remain open.

A recent development in the study of marshes is the use of remote sensing. The employment of aircraft and satellite imagery has been stan-dard practice by some researchers for several years. As these techniques have become increasingly sophisticated, their use has expanded from gen-eral mapping to the identification of various plants (often to species) and even to providing estimates of primary production. The application of re-mote sensing to marshlands was reviewed by Bartlett and Klemas (1980), who conducted a study of the marshes of Delaware, in which the spectral reflectance properties of the vegetation canopy were used to measure the biomass of emergent *Spartina alterniflora*.

Lagoons and Negative Estuaries

Not all lagoons are hypersaline, though those along the coasts of the United States often fall into the hypersaline category. Following the last ice age, when sea level had risen about 100 m and invaded formerly terrestrial habitats, irregular shorelines were formed, which were later smoothed by currents, waves, and transported sediments (Remane and Schlieper, 1971). Lagoon formation generally followed a patterned sequence. First, a bay was cut off from the sea through the accumulation of sedimentary deposits at the mouth. The embayment then became a lagoon, and perhaps even-tually a freshwater body. Lagoons with some connection to the ocean (such as the Laguna Madre of Texas) continued to be saline. Lagoons are often oriented with their long axes parallel to the beach, and they are nearly al-ways quite shallow (Remane and Schlieper, 1971).

Although the Laguna Madre is the best-known lagoon in the United States, there are others. For example, Bogue Sound, Back Sound, and to some extent Core Sound (all in North Carolina) can be considered lagoons, since they receive little freshwater runoff (Peterson and Peterson, 1979).

Most hypersaline lagoons have expansive pans or flats on their landward sides. Those shallow, flat areas are important in nutrient circulation and net transport of water (Copeland and Nixon, 1974). These regions also experience rapid evaporation with later replacement of water because of tidal flooding. The Laguna Madre and Baffin Bay system of Texas is the most extensive hypersaline lagoon in the United States. Behrens (1966) found a 15 to 40 o/oo salinity difference between the north end of the Laguna Madre and the west end of Baffin Bay (a distance of over 60 km), except during periods of rainfall.

Characteristically, if the water in a hypersaline lagoon is shallow (ca. 10 cm or less) and circulation is poor, algal mats become the dominant primary producer. Under those conditions the water may be saturated or even supersaturated with oxygen during the day and anaerobic at night (Sollins, 1969). In waters deeper than 10 cm but not so deep that light cannot penetrate to the bottom, grass flats may be present. If turbidity becomes too high and light limits the survival of rooted vegetation, or in cases where light is limited because of depth, phytoplankton becomes the dominant form of primary producer (Copeland and Nixon, 1974).

Tides

Tides tend to affect estuarine and near-shore organisms far more than species living offshore. Along much of the southeastern Atlantic and Gulf of Mexico coastline, tidal ranges are sufficient to produce diurnal, semidiurnal, or somewhat irregular flooding of relatively large lateral expanses of intertidal coastal lands. Many of these coastal lands are estuarine in character. Intermittent exposure to the atmosphere and inundation by water in the intertidal zone translate into an unusually hostile environment for most species of organisms, since the majority of them are either strictly terrestrial or exclusively aquatic and do not tolerate changes from one environment to the other. Numerous species, of course, have adapted to, and may even be dependent upon, the conditions existing in intertidal environments.

Among the most obvious effects of living in the intertidal zone are the intermittent threats of desiccation on the one hand and loss of electrolyte balance or drowning on the other, depending upon whether the organism in question is terrestrial or aquatic. Another effect, and one that is often a problem even for species well adapted to the intertidal zone, is extreme and sometimes rapid change in temperature. Many intertidal areas are sandy and absorb and lose heat rapidly depending upon time of day, season of the year, and meterological conditions at any given instant. When an intertidal area is inundated by at least a few centimeters of water, there is some moderation of heat gain or loss at the level of the sediments. Exposure during low tide, however, offers no such protection, and rapid heating or cooling are common. Since the organisms that inhabit the intertidal environment are poikilothermic, metabolic rates and other physiological processes may be significantly affected by rapid changes in temperature. Animals frequenting the intertidal environment to feed or for other purposes may also be poikilothermic, but since they are not permanent residents and are generally highly motile, they may be able to avoid the temperature extremes experienced by the nontransient species.

In general, tidal range decreases toward the head of an estuary. Because of undulations in terrain, patterns of tributary streams and creeks, the presence or absence of levees, and for other reasons, tidal amplitude lateral to any point upstream of the mouth of an estuary may vary somewhat. The effects of tide can, however, sometimes be observed well upstream of a river mouth. Rivers where tidal effects may reach 100 to 1,000 km upstream of the mouth include the Yangtze, Euphrates, Nile, Amazon, and Mississippi.

Tidal amplitudes vary widely from place to place around the world because of latitude, shape of land masses, distance between land masses, and circulation patterns within ocean basins. Table 4 presents tidal amplitudes for some places along the Atlantic seaboard and the Gulf of Mexico as well as for Puerto Rico.

Although the Gulf of Mexico and Puerto Rico tend to have relatively low tidal amplitudes, in other places there are extremely high tides; in still others, virtually no tide. The latter are known as amphidromic points. One such place is the island of Tahiti, in the south Pacific.

Some of the highest tides in the world are reported in the Bay of Fundy on the east coast of Canada, where maximum tidal range is 16.3 m (Dalrymple et al., 1975). This extreme range is caused, in part, by the presence of a sill near the mouth of the bay, which leads to friction between the bottom and the incoming water. The narrow river channel also contributes to the phenomenon, as does the outflowing river water, which helps to hold back the tide. After a period, the flooding tide overcomes the resistant forces operating against it and begins to move rapidly upstream. When the

TABLE 4. Approximate Spring Tides at Selected Locations

Location	Amplitude (m)
Puerto Rico	0.10
Galveston, Texas	0.30
Miami Beach, Florida	0.75
Savannah, Georgia	3.0
Bar Harbor, Maine	3.2
Bay of Fundy, Canada	16.3

Source: U.S. Coast and Geodetic Survey. 1983. Tide tables, high and low water predictions, east coast of North and South America including Greenland. Rockville, Md: National Ocean Service.

flood tide meets the narrow river channel, it continues to move upstream and forms a wave several centimeters in height. This wave, called a tidal bore, causes the river to flow upstream until it loses momentum, after which normal flow continues.

While tidal bores and other unusual tidal phenomena are of interest, in most cases tides are much less dramatic. Tidal range rarely exceeds 3 m along the coasts of the southeastern Atlantic and the Gulf of Mexico in the United States. As tidal range increases, the extent of tidal marshes also increases. Tidal flats are found in regions that support intertidal vegetation but are often exposed to enough wave action to prevent plants from becoming established.

The amount of water that enters an estuary on the incoming tide and leaves the river and creek channels to emerge onto the marshes or tidal flats will, of course, vary significantly depending upon the shape of the basin and on tidal amplitude. Few studies appear to have examined this relationship, but Ragotzkie and Bryson (1955) calculated that between one-third and one-half of the tidal flood water that enters the Duplin River in Georgia later exits the river to cover adjacent marshlands.

The movement of water through marshes as a function of tide stage is presented in figure 9. At low tide, when the creek channel is completely or nearly empty of water, subsurface water flows toward the creek channel. As the tide begins to rise, the situation is somewhat complicated by the pressure of water within the channel moving through the adjacent sediments away from the channel; at the same time, trapped interstitial water some distance from the creek continues to move toward the channel. As the tide continues to rise, perfusion of water into the sediments from the creek

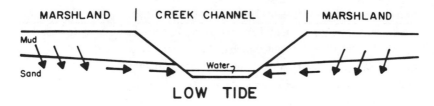

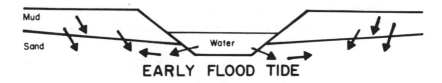

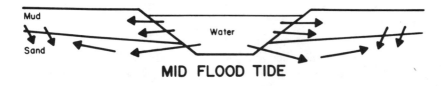

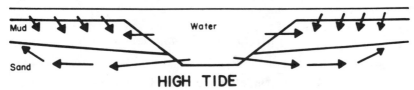

Fig. 9. Water flowing through a salt marsh at various stages in the tidal cycle (adapted from Chapman, 1960).

continues, and the lateral extent of movement increases. If the tide is so high that the water overflows from the creek channel onto the adjacent marshland or tidal flat, water will also begin to perfuse into the sediments from above. The process is reversed during the ebb portion of the cycle.

Turbidity often increases as the tides rise and fall. Flowing water, particularly over fine sediments, leads to increased turbidity in many cases. As described by Peterson and Peterson (1979), turbidity is at its lowest during slack tide, in part because many of the intertidal areas are left exposed to the atmosphere and do not continue to be available for erosion. The exception, of course, would be during a period of precipitation, when freshwater runoff could mobilize the sediments and increase turbidity.

Waves

Although waves are commonly observed in estuaries, they usually have a relatively short wavelength and low amplitude because of the limited fetch within the system. Incoming wave trains that enter a fairly deep estuary perpendicular to the entrance may significantly influence sediment movement and biota within the estuary; usually, however, protective bars, barrier islands, or beachfronts with restricted openings to the inner estuary disperse wave energy along the coastline. Localized weather disturbances may give rise to waves over 1 m in height even within a fairly small estuary. Such waves are only present during high winds, and they quickly dissipate once the storm has passed.

Since waves in estuaries usually range from 30 to 60 cm or less (virtually calm water is not uncommon in many estuarine systems), the amount of erosion attributable to them is often quite small. Waves, working in conjunction with longshore drift, cause migrations in barrier islands, lead to the development and destruction of channels between these islands, and create problems for persons wishing to maintain open channels for shipping.

Currents and Circulation

Most currents within estuaries result directly from tides. The flooding and ebbing tides are responsible for currents that change direction every few hours and virtually disappear at slack tide. In systems dominated by a large amount of river inflow, incoming fresh water has a definite impact. The flow may change directions as the tide turns, but because of the greater volume of water moving downstream with the ebbing tide, currents during that stage may be somewhat greater than during flood tides.

The maximum flow rates of currents tend to occur near mid-tide, with steady increases from slack high or low water to mid-tide and gradual decreases from mid-tide to high or low water. In regions with low tidal amplitude, tidal currents may be insignificant; in areas where the tidal range is high, however, strong currents may exist. Differences in current velocities from one estuary to another are related to the volume of water moved during a typical tidal cycle, the total area and volume of the estuary, and the shape of the estuarine basin, including the existing relief.

The wind may augment surface currents if it blows in the same direction as the current is flowing, or it may retard a current if it blows from the opposite direction. In Galveston Bay, Texas, winds not only affect current velocity, they tend to control the amount of water in the bay, overcoming even the predicted amplitudes and times of high and low tides. Drift bottles placed along the Texas coast near Mustang Island and Padre Island (Watson and Behrens, 1970) demonstrated a drift to the north in the summer along the shoreline and either north or south in the winter, depending upon wind direction.

Four major kinds of estuaries can be identified based upon their patterns of circulation: highly stratified, partly stratified, vertically homogeneous, or sectionally homogeneous. The different sorts of stratification are based upon salinity patterns but also relate to the currents and circulation patterns within the basin. Other things being equal, it appears that an estuary will shift from highly stratified through moderately stratified to vertically homogeneous as it develops. This pattern of change coincides with (1) decreasing river flow, (2) decreased depth, (3) increasing tidal velocity, and (4) increased width (Pritchard, 1955).

The details of estuarine circulation and mixing are quite complex and can only be completely understood through an in-depth mathematical treatment. Readers interested in the calculations involved in these and other physical phenomena in estuaries should consult such sources as Bowden (1967), O'Kane (1980), and Sundermann and Holz (1980). The latter provide a great deal of information on the development of models to predict the physical dynamics of estuaries.

More simplistically, the general conclusion can be drawn that currents provide much of the energy that causes the mixing of fresh and salt water in estuaries. In a gross fashion, the degree of mixing is predictable based on the ratio of water volume at flood tide to the volume of river flow. If the ratio is between one hundred and one thousand, partial mixing may result. If the ratio is less than unity, a salt wedge is likely to be present (Drake et al., 1979).

The rate of flushing in estuaries is important with respect to mass movements of water and is thus of general interest to physical oceanographers. This subject has become of increasing general importance, however, as scientists seek to examine the rate at which pollutants move through estuaries. The effects of pollution on estuaries and their organisms are related to how long the pollutant remains within the system and, thus, to the flushing time (Stowe, 1979). Various treatments of flushing times can be found in the literature. Some are highly complex, such as that of O'Kane (1980), while others are as simple as the following from Stowe (1979):

$$\text{Flushing time} = \text{freshwater content/freshwater input.} \qquad (8)$$

In unstratified estuaries flushing is usually slow because of little net downstream flow. In highly stratified estuaries, a particle in the low-salinity surface water may be rapidly carried through the estuary; but if that particle enters the underlying salt water, it may be trapped indefinitely and may even move upstream with the salt wedge.

A final current phenomenon sometimes found within estuaries is called a seiche. A seiche is a periodic current system in the form of a standing wave, where the water within a basin oscillates about one or two nodal points. A rocking motion of the water results (Reid, 1961). Seiches are observed in ocean basins and have been reported from large lakes. They can also occur in estuaries with suitably large expanses of open water. Perhaps the best example of the seiche phenomenon is a bathtub or basin of water. A small seiche is formed when an object is placed into or removed from a bathtub or when a basin of water is tilted and then returned to the horizontal. Seiches can normally be perceived only with specialized instrumentation. The Bay of Fundy experiences an extremely high tidal range when seiches are synchronized with the tide. San Francisco Bay and other estuaries have also been reported to have seiches within them (Reid, 1961).

Light

Although the deep water of the open ocean can be divided into distinct photic, dysphotic, and aphotic zones, in the shallow waters that dominate estuaries the entire water column often exists within the photic and dysphotic zones. Light intensity in many estuaries, however, is considerably reduced by the time it reaches the bottom, particularly in deep water and where turbidity is high.

Even in turbid estuaries significant levels of primary productivity are often present in the form of phytoplankters. In well-mixed estuaries, a given algae cell can be carried up into the photic zone often enough to ensure a net photosynthetic advantage over respiration.

Benthic algae may receive sufficient light for photosynthesis only during low tide or when the tide is approaching or just leaving its mean low level. By contrast, intertidal plants may be able to obtain enough light for considerable photosynthetic activity even during high tide. The decrease in light intensity that occurs in the photic zone as turbidity increases has been investigated by numerous authors, including Ellis (1936), Nash (1947), Wilson (1956, 1960), Emery and Stevenson (1957), Odum and Hoskin (1958), Ragotzkie (1959), Riley and Schurr (1959), Bartsch (1960), Odum and Wilson (1962), Brehmer (1965), Stross and Stottlemyer (1965), Biggs (1967), Brown and Clark (1968), and Flemer et al. (1967). As a general rule, estuaries receive sufficient light to produce a high level of primary production. Without the support of the primary producers, there would not be enough food to support the animals in the estuaries of the world.

Salinity

As we have seen, salinity gradients are a common feature of estuaries, with the usual pattern being increasing salinity from the head toward the mouth of the system. The salt wedge in a typical estuary will change spatially as the tide ebbs and flows. For example, the bottom salinity at a given point in a stratified estuary will, in general, increase during flood tide and decrease as the tide ebbs. The salt wedge of the Mississippi River has been known to migrate as far as 216 km upstream from the entrance to Southwest Pass; thus, the phenomenon can be of impressive magnitude (Ippen, 1966). In most cases, however, less dramatic salt wedges exist.

The estuaries of much of the southeastern United States and the Gulf of Mexico are not noted for well-developed salt wedges. Wedges are found in channels such as those constructed to allow the passage of ships. The channels may be several meters deep around the entrances to major ports, or they may be relatively shallow in the intracoastal waterways.

In most cases, biologists report salinity only to the nearest part per thousand. Although it would be possible to measure salinity to fractions of a part per thousand, as pointed out by Mangelsdorf (1967), the local and transient nature of a given salinity in an estuary leaves little to be gained from more precise measurement. In the case of estuaries, salinity range may be far more important than a high level of precision on an instantaneous basis.

Although estuarine organisms are usually euryhaline, they can be damaged and even killed during salinity extremes. Also, if the normal range of salinity in an estuary is altered by an increase or decrease either diurnally or over extended periods, the effects on organisms within the estuary can be substantial, although not always detrimental. For example, when the Gulf Intracoastal Waterway (GIWW) was completed in 1948, mortality due to hypersalinity in the upper Laguna Madre of Texas was virtually eliminated (Simmons, 1957). Before construction of the GIWW, salinities as high as 114 o/oo were reported; after construction the maximum reported was 79 o/oo. On the other hand, a drought along the Texas coast from 1948 to 1953 led to an invasion of marine species, both vertebrate and invertebrate, into the bays of the state. The establishment and growth of oyster reefs suffered and oyster production dropped (Parker, 1955).

Simmons (1957) reported that the copepod *Acartia tonsa* was abundant in the Laguna Madre at salinities ranging from 47 to 75 o/oo; the only penaeid shrimp species found above 45 o/oo was the brown shrimp, *Penaeus aztecus*, which did not tolerate salinities above 60 o/oo. The ranges in which various common fish species were collected from Texas waters were presented by Simpson and Gunter (1956). The ability of some species to tolerate extreme ranges (table 5) is well demonstrated by such fishes as *Fundulus grandis*, *F. similis*, and *Cyprinodon variegatus*.

Increased annual rainfall has been shown to improve shrimp production, thus providing additional evidence of the importance of freshwater inflow as discussed in chapter 2. Hildebrand and Gunter (1952) found that the production of white shrimp (*Penaeus setiferus*) was high following years with generous rainfall and low following dry years. A later study (Gunter and Hildebrand, 1954) concluded that the fast growth of *P. setiferus* during wet years was related to low salinity instead of higher nutrient levels associated with increased freshwater inflow. The authors also determined that the catch was correlated with rainfall patterns of the previous year, indicating a lag between the increased input of fresh water and the rise in shrimp production.

The euryhalinity, or lack of it, expressed by a particular species of marine organism relates to the ability of that organism to osmoregulate or osmoconform. Many invertebrates have only limited, if any, ability to con-

TABLE 5. Salinity Tolerance of Selected Estuarine Fishes

Species	Salinity Range (o/oo)	Mean Salinity (o/oo)
Gambusia affinis	1.0–20.6	8.5
Fundulus jenkinsi	3.4–20.6	14.0
Poecilia latipinna	1.0–53.9	24.1
Lucania parva	1.0–48.2	24.9
Fundulus pulvereus	11.6–47.6	28.9
Fundulus grandis	1.8–76.1	30.1
Adinia xenica	13.1–53.9	30.4
Fundulus similis	13.1–76.1	33.5
Cyprinodon variegatus	1.8–142.4	34.5

Source: Simpson and Gunter, 1956.

trol the osmotic concentration within their bodies; most of them experience intracellular osmotic pressures that nearly duplicate those of the surrounding medium. Higher animals, on the other hand, are generally able to maintain a fairly constant internal osmotic pressure over at least a small range of salinity. The ability to osmoregulate is as highly developed in many animals living at constant salinity as it is in those experiencing wide ranges of salinity in their natural environments. Take for example a stenohaline marine fish that maintains its internal cell concentration at about 1% salt (equivalent to about 10 o/oo salinity) in a surrounding medium of about 35 o/oo salinity. A great deal of energy must be expended to maintain the internal environment constant with respect to salt balance.

Estuarine organisms may be hypotonic, isotonic, or hypertonic to the external medium at any given moment. Vernberg and Vernberg (1970) reported four kinds of osmoregulators: (1) perfect osmoregulators, (2) perfect osmoconformers, (3) hyperosmoregulators, and (4) hyper- and hypo-osmoregulators. The relative internal and external salt concentrations of each kind are depicted in figure 10.

Animals that can osmoregulate efficiently include those with well-developed kidneys. The kidneys of freshwater and marine teleost fishes can function either in salt retention or salt excretion, depending upon the environment. In species unable to adapt from one salinity extreme to the other, kidney function is set; that is, the kidney is not adapted to secrete salt in one instance and conserve it in another. Yet many species spend portions

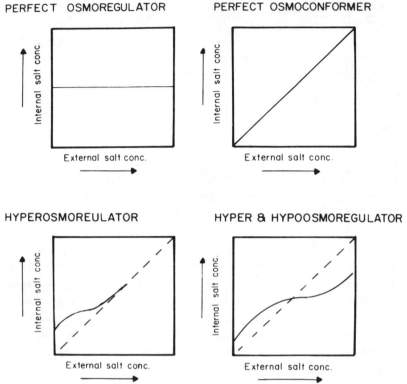

Fig. 10. The four different types of osmoregulators found in estuarine environments (adapted from Vernberg and Vernberg, 1970).

of their lives in fresh water and the remainder at sea. The American eel, *Anguilla rostrata*, and the various species of salmon are examples.

Striped mullet, *Mugil cephalus*, and certain flounders, *Paralichthys* spp., are also commonly found in fresh water. In fact, large mullet can often be observed in the freshwater springs of Florida. *Paralichthys lethostigma*, the southern flounder, appears to be physiologically adapted to different salinities at different ages (Stickney and White, 1973).

The elasmobranchs (sharks, skates, and rays), for example, maintain their blood isotonic or nearly isotonic with the surrounding medium, though the internal salt levels in those fishes are not significantly elevated in comparison with the bony fishes. Instead, osmotic pressure is increased in the cartilaginous fishes by the presence of high levels of blood urea (Hickman and Trump, 1969).

The fact that invertebrate blood is essentially isotonic with the external medium does not mean that those animals cannot osmoregulate. Actually, the ionic composition of the internal fluids of invertebrates does differ somewhat from that of the external medium, indicating that some selective replacement of ions, and thus osmoregulation, occurs (Lockwood, 1967). Vernberg and Vernberg (1970) noted that such organisms as fiddler crabs (*Uca* sp.) are good hyper- and hyporegulators and that grass shrimps (*Palaemonetes* sp.) are good hyperregulators. The brine shrimp (*Artemia salina*) is a good hyporegulator.

Freshwater fish, being in a hypoosmotic medium, are constantly absorbing water through their tissues as the surrounding medium passes through semipermeable membranes in an attempt to dilute the concentrated salts in the body fluids. Therefore, freshwater fish do not drink but, instead, produce copious amounts of dilute urine. Their kidneys are efficient at retaining salts. In addition, salt is pumped into the fish through the gills.

Marine fish, on the other hand, are constantly forced to consume water in order to replace the losses through their integument. This water consumption, however, leads to the intake of large quantities of excess salt that must be eliminated. The kidneys of marine fishes thus secrete concentrated or isosmotic urine, so that water loss via the kidneys is minimized. Marine fishes also eliminate salts through the gills. Euryhaline fishes may be isotonic with the surrounding medium at times but are under osmostic stress at other times. Their internal fluids in some cases change from hypertonic to hypotonic and back every several hours.

Benthic organisms may be subjected to frequent changes in salinity, or they may live in a relatively constant environment. Epifaunal benthic organisms are exposed to salinity changes as a result of the flooding and ebbing tides, while the interstitial waters surrounding benthic infauna tend to remain constant with respect to salinity. Sanders et al. (1965) determined that although epifauna exposed to rapid fluctuations in salinity were sparse, the infauna dominated, since their environment was much stabler. The salinity of interstitial waters has been found to be persistently stable, even when the overlying water is of higher or lower salinity than that of the interstitial water (Smith, 1955). Although surface-living benthic organisms must adapt to changing salinity (Pantin, 1931), the infaunal community is often not severely stressed by alterations in the water column. A stream of fresh water passing over intertidal sand has little effect on the salinity of interstitial water to a depth of 25 to 30 cm (Reid, 1930, 1932). At those depths salinity is often similar to that of seawater, and burrowing animals can find an environment of suitable and fairly constant salinity.

Low-salinity water passes over sediments when rainfall runoff crosses the exposed sediments during low tide. As determined by Reid (1932), rapidly flowing water of low salinity leaches salt from the sediments more rapidly than does slowly flowing water of the same salinity.

Benthic infaunal organisms may be concentrated in interstitial waters of a particular salinity range. For example, *Nereis diversicolor* (a polychaete) has been found in areas having a water column salinity of 0.5 o/oo, though the interstitial salinities were somewhat higher (Smith, 1956). An earlier study (Smith, 1955) indicated that *N. diversicolor* was concentrated within a belt of water of relatively low salinity. Thus, if the interstitial water is of the proper salinity, the animal may live above or below the elevations that might indicate its optimum salinity as determined from overlying water.

Temperature

Temperature is one of the most important physical characteristics of every aquatic environment because of its control over metabolic rates of poikilotherms. Temperature is thus extremely important in controlling productivity. With the exception of homoiothermic whales, porpoises, seals, walruses, and manatees, the activity of aquatic organisms largely depends upon the environmental temperatures surrounding the marine animals. Unlike salinity, temperature within the shallow sediments is usually similar to that of the overlying water column. Because of the physical nature of water, atmospheric temperature may be somewhat warmer or colder than that of the water itself. Water tends to cool and warm slowly, so even with fairly drastic changes in atmospheric temperature as for example during cold fronts, the water temperature may be little affected. Extended periods of cold or warm weather will, of course, eventually modify water temperature. In any case, the extremes faced by terrestrial animals are generally broader than those experienced by aquatic organisms.

The estuaries of the southeastern Atlantic and the Gulf of Mexico can be considered to lie in temperate and, in some cases, subtropical areas. Thus, extreme cold is not common, though the upper temperature extremes within the water column may surpass those found in tropical climates. The estuaries near Beaufort, North Carolina, have mean temperatures of 27.6 C in June and 7.9 C in January (Williams, 1966) and represent about the northern extreme of many species that are common year round in southern U.S. estuaries. Higher maximum and minimum temperatures generally occur south of Beaufort.

Although deep waters usually minimize abrupt changes in water temperature, rapid changes have been known to harm estuarine organisms. For example, winter cold fronts have been known to kill large numbers of fish in the shallow coastal waters of Texas. In two cases (1940 and 1951), the effects were extreme (Gunter and Hildebrand, 1951). The ability of fishes in Florida waters to tolerate periods of freezing weather has been found to be directly related to the normal ranges of the species involved (Storey, 1937). Tropical species are nearly always harmed, while subtropical ones usually are much less affected. Temperate species survive without difficulty in most instances. Studies in Florida waters have demonstrated that variations in water temperature influence fish populations more profoundly than do salinity changes (Zilberberg, 1966).

Devastation of estuarine fish by cold waves is not restricted to estuaries in the Gulf of Mexico. In January, 1970, a cold front in Georgia killed many star drum (*Stellifer lanceolatus*) and white shrimp (*Penaeus setiferus*). According to Dahlberg and Smith (1970), mortality among other species was limited, even though air temperature dropped to − 10 C during this period.

The amount of diurnal temperature range experienced by estuarine organisms depends, in part, upon whether they exist subtidally or intertidally. Johnson (1965) determined that animals in the upper 1.0 cm of intertidal sands may encounter diurnal temperature ranges three times greater than those experienced by the same species living subtidally. Depth in the sediments, however, is a mitigating feature. In the California study of Johnson (1965), intertidal animals living at depths of 10 cm or greater experienced the same diurnal temperature range as those living subtidally.

In neutral estuaries, temperature is largely dependent on location, water depth, exchange rate with the open ocean, and the existence of any artificial heat sources in the embayment (Glooschenko and Harriss, 1974). Although this is generally true of all estuaries, the effects of river inflow can be expected to have some impact on positive estuaries. Thermal effects associated with high evaporative losses and high salinity, on the other hand, may be more important in negative estuaries. Skogsberg (1936) found a distinct annual thermal pattern in Monterey Harbor, California, in response to the seasonal upwelling of deep bottom water that entered the bay. In Alligator Harbor, Florida, the annual temperature pattern was based upon fluctuations in air temperature (Glooschenko and Harriss, 1974), as is probably common in most estuaries.

LITERATURE CITED

April, G. C., and D. C. Raney. 1980. Predicting the effects of storm surges and abnormal river flow on flooding and water movement in Mobile Bay, Alabama, pp. 217–45. In: P. Hamilton and K. B. Macdonald, eds. *Estuarine and wetland processes—with emphasis on modeling*. New York: Plenum Press.

Bartlett, D. S., and V. Klemas. 1980. Quantitative assessment of emergent *Spartina alterniflora* biomass in tidal wetlands using remote sensing, pp. 425–36. In: P. Hamilton and K. B. Macdonald, eds. *Estuarine and wetland processes—with emphasis on modeling*. New York: Plenum Press.

Bartsch, A. F. 1960. Settleable solids, turbidity, and light penetration as factors in water quality, pp. 118–27. In: C. Tarzwell, ed. *Biological problems in water pollution*. Cincinnati: U.S. Public Health Service Publication no. W60-3.

Behrens, E. W. 1966. Surface salinities for Baffin Bay and Laguna Madre, Texas, April 1964–March 1966. *Publ. Inst. Mar. Sci., Univ. Tex.* 11: 168–73.

Biggs, R. B. 1967. Overboard spoil disposal. I. Interim report on environmental effects, pp. 134–51. In: P. L. McCarty and R. Kennedy, chairmen. *Proceedings of the National Symposium on Estuarine Pollution*. Stanford, Calif.: Stanford University Press.

Bowden, K. F. 1967. Circulation and diffusion, pp. 15–36. In: G. H. Lauff, ed. *Estuaries*. American Association for the Advancement of Science Publication no. 83. Washington, D.C.: AAAS.

Brehmer, M. L. 1965. Turbidity and siltation as forms of pollution. *J. Soil Water Conserv.* 20: 132–33.

Brown, C. L., and R. Clark. 1968. Observations on dredging and dissolved oxygen in a tidal waterway. *Water Resour. Res.* 4: 1381–84.

Chapman, V. J. 1960. *Salt marshes and salt deserts of the world*. New York: Wiley-Interscience.

Christmas, J. Y., ed. 1973. *Cooperative Gulf of Mexico estuarine inventory and study, Mississippi*. Ocean Springs, Miss.: Gulf Coast Research Laboratory.

Cooper, A. W. 1974. Salt marshes, pp. 55–98. In: H. T. Odum, B. J. Copeland, and E. A. McMahan, eds. *Coastal ecological systems of the United States*. Vol. II. Washington, D.C.: Conservation Foundation.

Copeland, B. J., and S. W. Nixon. 1974. Hypersaline lagoons, pp. 312–30. In: H. T. Odum, B. J. Copeland, and E. A. McMahan, eds. *Coastal ecological systems of the United States*. Vol. I. Washington, D.C.: The Conservation Foundation.

Dahlberg, M. D., and F. G. Smith. 1970. Mortality of estuarine animals due to cold on the Georgia coast. *Ecology* 51: 931–33.

Dalrymple, R. W., R. J. Knight, and G. V. Middleton. 1975. Intertidal sand in Cobequid Bay (Bay of Fundy), pp. 293–307. In: L. E. Cronin, ed. *Estuarine research*. Vol. II. New York: Academic Press.

Day, J. W., W. G. Smith, P. R. Wagner, and W. C. Stowe. 1973. Community structure and carbon budget of a salt marsh and shallow bay estuarine system in Louisiana. Louisiana State University Center for Wetland Resources Publication no. LSU-SG-72-04.

Diener, R. A. 1975. Cooperative Gulf of Mexico estuarine inventory and study— Texas: Area description. NOAA Technical Report, NMFS Circular 393.

Drake, C. L., J. Imbrie, J. A. Knauss, and K. K. Turekian. 1979. *Oceanography*. New York: Holt, Rinehart and Winston.

Ellis, M. M. 1936. Erosion silt as a factor in aquatic environments. *Ecology* 17: 29–42.

Emery, K. O., and R. E. Stevenson. 1957. Estuaries and lagoons. I. Physical and chemical characteristics, pp. 673–93. In: J. W. Hedgpeth, ed. *Treatise on marine ecology and paleoecology*. Vol. I. Memoir 67. New York: Geological Society of America.

Flemer, D. A., C. Dovel, H. J. Pfitzenmeyer, and D. E. Ritchie, Jr. 1967. Spoil disposal in upper Chesapeake Bay. II. Preliminary analysis of biological effects, pp. 152–87. In: P. L. McCarty and R. Kennedy, chairmen. *Proceedings of the National Symposium on Estuarine Pollution*. Stanford, Calif.: Stanford University Press.

Glooschenko, W. A., and R. C. Harriss. 1974. Neutral embayments, pp. 488–98. In: H. T. Odum, B. J. Copeland, and E. A. McMahan, eds. *Coastal ecological systems of the United States*. Vol. II. Washington, D.C.: Conservation Foundation.

Guilcher, A. 1963. Estuaries, deltas, shelf, slope, pp. 620–54. In: M. N. Hill, ed. *The sea*. Vol. III. New York: Wiley-Interscience.

Gunter, G., and H. H. Hildebrand. 1951. Destruction of fishes and other organisms on the south Texas coast by the cold wave of January 2–February 3, 1951. *Ecology* 32: 731–36.

———. 1954. The relation of total rainfall of the state and catch of the marine shrimp (*Penaeus setiferus*) in Texas waters. *Bull. Mar. Sci. Gulf Caribb.* 4: 95–103.

Hickman, C. P., Jr., and B. F. Trump. 1969. The kidney, pp. 91–239. In: W. S. Hoar and D. J. Randall, eds. *Fish physiology*. Vol. I. New York: Academic Press.

Hildebrand, H. H., and G. Gunter. 1952. Correlations of rainfall with the Texas catch of white shrimp. *Trans. Am. Fish. Soc.* 82: 151–55.

Hoyt, J. H., and J. R. Hails. 1967. Pleistocene shoreline sediments in coastal Georgia: Deposition and modification. *Science* 155: 1541–43.

Hoyt, J. H., and V. J. Henry, Jr. 1967. Influence of island migration on barrier island sedimentation. *Geol. Society of America Bull.* 78: 77–86.

Hoyt, J. H., R. J. Weimer, and V. J. Henry, Jr. 1964. Late Pleistocene and recent sedimentation, central Georgia coast., U.S.A., pp. 171–76. In: L. J. U. Van Straaten, ed. *Developments in sedimentology.* Vol. I. New York: Elsevier.

Ippen, A. T. 1966. Sedimentation in estuaries, pp. 648–72. In: A. T. Ippen, ed. *Estuary and coastline hydrodynamics.* New York: McGraw-Hill.

Johnson, R. G. 1965. Temperature variation in the infaunal environment of a sand flat. *Limnol. Oceanogr.* 10: 114–20.

Land, L. S., and J. H. Hoyt. 1966. Sedimentation in a meandering estuary. *Sedimentology* 6: 191–207.

Linton, T. L. 1968. A description of the south Atlantic and Gulf coast marshes and estuaries, pp. 15–25. In: J. D. Newsom, ed. *Proceedings of the marsh and estuary management symposium.* Baton Rouge: Louisiana State University Division of Continuing Education.

Lockwood, A. P. M. 1967. *Aspects of the physiology of crustacea.* San Francisco: Freeman.

McNulty, J. K., W. N. Lindall, Jr., and J. E. Sykes. 1972. Cooperative Gulf of Mexico estuarine inventory and study—Florida: Phase 1, area description. NOAA Technical Report, NMFS Circular 368.

Mangelsdorf, P. C., Jr. 1967. Salinity measurements in estuaries, pp. 71–79. In: G. H. Lauff, ed. *Estuaries.* American Association for the Advancement of Science Publication no. 83. Washington, D.C.: AAAS.

Massmann, W. H. 1971. The significance of an estuary on the biology of aquatic organisms of the middle Atlantic region, pp. 96–109. In: P. R. Douglas and R. H. Stroud, eds. *A symposium on the biological significance of estuaries.* Washington, D.C.: Sport Fishing Institute.

Nash, C. B. 1947. Environmental characteristics of a river estuary. *J. Mar. Res.* 6: 147–74.

Odum, H. T., and C. M. Hoskin. 1958. Comparative studies on the metabolism of marine waters. *Publ. Inst. Mar. Sci. Univ. Tex.* 5: 16–46.

Odum, H. T., and R. F. Wilson, 1962. Further studies on reaeration and metabolism of Texas bays, 1958–1960. *Publ. Inst. Mar. Sci., Univ. Tex.* 8: 23–55.

O'Kane, J. P. 1980. *Estuarine water-quality management.* London: Pitman Publishing.

Pantin, C. F. A. 1931. The adaptation of *Gunda ulvae* to salinity. I. The environment. *J. Exp. Biol.* 8: 63.

Parker, R. H. 1955. Changes in the invertebrate fauna, apparently attributable to salinity changes, in the bays of central Texas. *J. Paleon.* 29: 193–211.

Peterson, C. H., and N. M. Peterson. 1979. The ecology of intertidal flats in North Carolina: A community profile. U.S. Fish and Wildlife Service Biological Services Program FWS/OBS 79-39.

Pritchard, D. W. 1955. Estuarine circulation patterns. *Proc. Am. Soc. Civil Eng.* 81: 117–19.

Ragotzkie, R. A. 1959. Plankton productivity in estuarine waters of Georgia. *Publ. Inst. Mar. Sci., Univ. Tex.* 6: 146–58.

Ragotzkie, R. A., and R. A. Bryson. 1955. Hydrography of the Duplin River, Sapelo Island, Georgia. *Bull. Mar. Sci. Gulf Caribb.* 5: 297–314.

Reid, D. M. 1930. Salinity interchange between seawater in sand and overflowing freshwater at low tide. *J. Mar. Biol. Assoc. U.K.* 16: 609–14.

———. 1932. Salinity interchange between seawater in sand and overflowing freshwater at low tide. II. *J. Mar. Biol. Assoc. U.K.* 18: 299–306.

Reid, G. K. 1961. *Ecology of inland waters and estuaries.* New York: D. Van Nostrand Co.

Remane, A., and C. Schlieper. 1971. *Biology of brackish water.* Die Binnengewasser. Bund XXV. New York: Wiley-Interscience.

Riley, G. A., and H. M. Schurr. 1959. Transparency of Long Island Sound waters. *Bull. Bingham Oceanogr. Coll.* 17: 66–82.

Sanders, H. L., P. C. Manglesdorf, Jr., and G. R. Hampson. 1965. Salinity and faunal distribution in the Pocasset River, Massachusetts. *Limnol. Oceanogr.* 10 (suppl.): R216–29.

Simmons, E. G. 1957. An ecological survey of the upper Laguna Madre of Texas. *Publ. Inst. Mar. Sci., Univ. Tex.* 4: 156–200.

Simpson, D. G. and G. Gunter. 1956. Notes on habitats, systematic characters, and life histories of Texas saltwater Cyprinodontes. *Tulane Stud. Zool.* 4: 115–34.

Skogsberg, T. 1936. Hydrography of Monterey Bay, California: Thermal conditions, 1929–1936. *Trans. Am. Philos. Soc.* 29: 1–152.

Smith, R. I. 1955. Salinity variation in interstitial water of sand at Kames Bay, Millport, with reference to the distribution of *Nereis diversicolor*. *J. Mar. Biol. Assoc. U.K.* 34: 33–46.

———. 1956. The ecology of the Tamar estuary. VII. Observations on the interstitial salinity of intertidal muds in the estuarine habitat of *Nereis diversicolor*. *J. Mar. Biol. Assoc. U.K.* 35: 81–104.

Sollins, P. 1969. Measurement and similation of oxygen flows and storages in a laboratory blue-green algal mat ecosystem. M.A. thesis, University of North Carolina, Chapel Hill.

Stickney, R. R., and D. B. White. 1973. Effects of salinity on growth of *Paralich-*

thys lethostigma postlarvae reared under aquaculture conditions. *Proc. S.E. Assoc. Game and Fish Comm.* 27: 532–40.

Storey, M. 1937. The relation between normal range and mortality fish due to cold at Sanibel Island, Florida. *Ecology* 18: 10–26.

Stowe, K. S. 1979. *Ocean science.* New York: John Wiley and Sons.

Stross, R. G., and J. R. Stottlemyer. 1965. Primary production in the Patuxent River. *Ches. Sci.* 6: 125–40.

Sundermann, J., and K. -P. Holz. 1980. *Mathematical modeling of estuarine physics.* New York: Springer-Verlag.

Vernberg, F. J., and W. B. Vernberg. 1970. *The animal and the environment.* New York: Holt, Rinehart and Winston.

Watson, R. L., and E. W. Behrens. 1970. Near-shore surface currents, southeastern Texas Gulf coast. *Cont. Mar. Sci.* 15: 131–43.

Williams, R. B. 1966. Annual phytoplanktonic production in a system of shallow temperate estuaries, pp. 699–716. In: H. Barnes, ed. *Some contemporary studies in marine science.* London: George, Allen, and Unwin.

Wilson, J. N. 1956. Effects of turbidity and silt on aquatic life, pp. 235–39. In: C. Tarzwell, ed. *Biological problems in water pollution, first seminar.* Cincinnati: U.S. Public Health Service.

———. 1960. The effects of erosion, silt, and other inert materials on aquatic life, pp. 269–71. In: C. Tarzwell, ed. *Biological problems in water pollution.* Cincinnati: U.S. Public Health Service Publication no. W60-3.

Woodwell, G. M., P. H. Rich, and C. A. Hall. 1973. Carbon in estuaries, pp. 221–40. In: G. M. Woodwell and E. V. Pecan, eds. *Carbon and the biosphere.* Washington, D.C.: Technical Information Center, Office of Information Services, U.S. Atomic Energy Commission.

Zilberberg, M. H. 1966. Seasonal occurrence of fishes in a coastal marsh of northwest Florida. *Publ. Inst. Mar. Sci., Univ. Tex.* 11: 126–34.

CHAPTER 5

Estuarine Chemistry

Introduction

NATURAL waters are a repository for virtually all of the elements and compounds known to exist on earth. Because of salinity gradients, current patterns, and land runoff, the chemistry of estuaries is extremely complex. In this chapter we examine some of the more important chemical phenomena and characteristics of estuaries, but by no means all of them. Although man's role in the additions of high levels of both naturally occurring and man-made compounds is acknowledged throughout this chapter, the emphasis is on natural chemical reactions. Pollution and other effects directly attributable to man are considered in chapter 11. The primary focus is on aspects of chemistry that have direct bearing on, or that are under the complete or partial control of, biological processes.

Perhaps the least understood aspect of water chemistry involves synergisms—the effects various water quality variables have upon one another. In most cases, synergisms are not well understood; in fact, so little is known about them that a documented presentation of synergistic behavior is not possible beyond the interactions of two or three variables. As each new variable is added, the complexity of interactions increases greatly, and documentation of the various responses becomes increasingly difficult.

The addition of chemicals to estuaries from freshwater inflow, the atmosphere, and the sediments is particularly important because the volume of water within an estuary is small relative to that of the open ocean. Thus, estuaries are more easily influenced by external substances. Diffusion often controls the transfer of chemicals from sediments to water and vice versa for non-reactive chemical species, while reactive species are under the control of both diffusion and the reactions they undergo (Bricker and Troup, 1975). The atmosphere frequently contributes chemicals through settling of aerosols or dissolution of gases. Freshwater inflow carries in both dissolved and particulate materials, which may become reactive once they enter estuarine waters.

The Carbonate-Bicarbonate Buffer System

Buffering of the water in estuaries, as in the open ocean and fresh water, is mainly controlled by the carbonate-bicarbonate buffer system. This system is directly related to the addition and removal of carbon dioxide (CO_2) from the water. Carbon dioxide is added by diffusion from the atmosphere and is also present, in relatively high concentrations, in precipitation. The primary manner in which CO_2 becomes dissolved in water, however, is through respiration. Photosynthesis is the most important mechanism for remvoal of CO_2 from water. Thus CO_2 levels are largely controlled by biological activities. The addition of CO_2 to water leads to the formation of carbonic acid:

$$CO_2 + H_2O \rightleftharpoons H_2CO_3. \tag{9}$$

The dissociation of carbonic acid then proceeds as follows:

$$H_2CO_3 \rightleftharpoons H^+ + HCO_3^-, \tag{10}$$

$$HCO_3^- \rightleftharpoons H^+ + CO_3^=. \tag{11}$$

Thus addition of carbon dioxide by respiration will yield free hydrogen ions (H^+) which, if not neutralized, will reduce the pH of the water.

So long as carbonate ions ($CO_3^=$) and bicarbonate ions (HCO_3^-) are available in the system, they will combine with H^+ ions to maintain the pH relatively constant, and the system is considered to be buffered. Similarly, if H^+ ions are removed from the system, HCO_3^- will give up H^+ ions, again keeping the pH constant.

The quantity of carbonate and bicarbonate ions present in an aquatic system is known as alkalinity. Total alkalinity tends to remain constant in a well-buffered system, though the relative contributions of HCO_3^- and $CO_3^=$ may change temporally. Total alkalinity can be altered by additions of bicarbonate from marshland runoff (Gardner, 1975).

If carbonate ions become depleted, pH can change dramatically. If a pool of calcium carbonate is present, however (as is generally the case in estuaries where organisms with $CaCO_3$ exoskeletons are common), dissolution will provide additional carbonate ions for the pool:

$$CaCO_3 \rightleftharpoons Ca^{++} + CO_3^=. \tag{12}$$

In freshwater environments, calcium carbonate may be present only in limited quantities. That, coupled with the fact that once dissolved, the ions must diffuse throughout the water column, means that pH may fluctuate considerably each day. Marine and estuarine environments are usually better buffered because of their generally higher alkalinities and greater availability of carbonates. Their pH levels usually exceed 8.0.

Each of the reactions presented in equations 9–12 is reversible. As a result of photosynthesis, H^+ are removed from the system and carbonic acid or bicarbonate dissociate. The reverse occurs when respiration adds CO_2 to the system and leads to the formation of bicarbonate or carbonic acid as H^+ are absorbed.

The process described above is an oversimplification but is basically how the carbonate-bicarbonate system functions. Other chemical processes in estuaries will alter the system; a mitigating factor, however, is the concentration of organic matter present. As discussed by Chave (1970), the precipitation of calcium carbonate from seawater that is highly saturated with carbonate can be impeded by the presence of dissolved organic matter. Similarly, alkalinity may affect chemical reactions beyond those within the buffer system. For example, Carpenter et al. (1975) found a relationship between alkalinity and the concentrations of several trace metals in the Susquehanna River and northern Chesapeake Bay. They concluded that variations in the composition of river water mixed with seawater are a major cause of temporal changes in the chemical composition of estuarine waters.

Interstitial water may be of somewhat different salinity than that of the overlying water column. The same is true with respect to other water-quality variables. As discussed by Riedl and McMahan (1974), free carbon dioxide levels in interstitial waters vary with depth. Hardness, a measure of the amount of calcium and magnesium ions in water, increases in interstitial water with distance from the coast.

Estuaries, which have variable and wide-ranging salinities, may also fluctuate both spatially and temporally with respect to buffering capacity. The levels of primary and secondary productivity will influence diurnal changes in pH, particularly where buffering capacity is low.

Man and his activities have long affected the ability of estuarine organisms to add and remove CO_2. The buffer system is based upon a weak acid-base equilibrium. If strong acids or bases are imposed upon the system, as through release from an industrial plant, its natural buffering capacity may be overcome, with consequent dramatic changes in pH.

Phosphates and borates undergo a series of reactions similar to those of the carbonate-bicarbonate buffer system. Thus, they also provide some buffering of natural waters, although their importance is generally over-shadowed by the reactions presented above.

Dissolved Oxygen

Oxygen enters water by diffusion from the atmosphere and as a result of photosynthesis. Diffusion is a simple process of oxygen gas moving from a concentration of 20% in the atmosphere into the water, where its concentration rarely exceeds a few parts per million. Winds and waves increase the rate of diffusion by physically mixing air bubbles into the liquid, thus exposing more gas surface area to the water. Although diffusion will eventually saturate a body of water with oxygen, and mechanical mixing of air and water will increase the rate at which saturation is reached, a high rate of photosynthesis will have a much more rapid effect on oxygen concentrations in water. Respiration, on the other hand, leads to the removal of oxygen from water.

The amount of oxygen present in water at saturation will vary with temperature, salinity, and altitude. As any of those variables increases, the level of dissolved oxygen (DO) at saturation will decrease.

Under normal conditions, some diurnal cycling of DO can be expected in estuarine waters. Respiration continues day and night and is common to both plants and animals. Photosynthesis, however, is limited to the daylight. Because of respiratory demands on oxygen during darkness without concomitant additions from photosynthesis, there is usually a decline in DO between dusk and dawn. Some time shortly after dawn, photosynthesis begins to add oxygen to the water once again. The rate of photosynthesis can be expected to increase until the sun reaches its zenith, because depth of light penetration increases as the angle of incidence changes. As the afternoon proceeds, the production of photosynthetic oxygen will gradually decrease until photosynthesis ceases at about dusk.

The level of DO in water generally rises throughout the day as a result of photosynthesis. This oversimplified picture can be modified by weather fronts, declines in primary productivity, and man's activity. Normal fluctuations in primary and secondary productivity can significantly affect DO levels. Algal blooms and crashes may greatly increase or decrease diurnal variations in DO. Such fluctuations in primary productivity may result from changes in nutrient availability, grazing rates, shading by suspended sediments, self-shading, and extended periods of either clear or cloudy weather.

In shallow, calm water, diurnal changes in DO may be dramatic because photosynthesis will add a great deal of oxygen during the day, while respiration will cause a similarly large reduction at night. In turbulent, shallow water, loss of oxygen during the day as supersaturation is reached and continued input of oxygen by turbulent mixing at night may lead to a relatively constant daily DO level.

With the exception of highly turbid estuaries, the photic zone normally extends to or near the bottom of the water column. Although there is usually little variation in DO from surface to bottom within estuaries, the bottom waters of highly stratified estuaries where the photic zone is also limited may actually become anaerobic, making them uninhabitable for most organisms. Oxygen depletions of this sort are most common in the summer, when high rates of secondary productivity place a great demand on available oxygen reserves. The problem is compounded when pollutants, particularly those with high biochemical oxygen demands (BOD), are added to the system.

The concept of BOD was developed and is used most commonly by sanitary engineers to evaluate the efficiency of sewage treatment plants, but it is also a meaningful determination in many natural water bodies. Determination of BOD provides a measurement of how much oxygen will be used as a result of bacteriological decomposition of organic materials within a water sample during a specified period (usually five days).

The presence of suspended sediments in the water tends to increase BOD (Zobell, 1942; Zobell and Feltham, 1942). Suspended particles provide excellent substrates for bacterial growth (Cairns, 1967). Decomposition of organic matter not only places a demand on oxygen, it also leads to the release of ammonia, nitrate, and phosphate, all of which are nutrients (Zobell and Feltham, 1942; Hayes, 1964).

Aquatic organisms can usually survive, grow, and carry out their normal life functions when DO concentration meets or exceeds 5.0 mg/l. Problems generally arise when DO falls below about 3.0 mg/l, though most organisms can survive the latter level for at least limited periods.

While the water column in estuaries generally contains sufficient DO to support plants and animals living within the system, the sediments commonly contain anaerobic layers. Benthic species can survive in anaerobic sediments by either extending their gills into the oxygen-containing overlying water or by pumping oxygen-rich water down to the level at which their bodies are resting. In many cases the sediments are characterized by a narrow anaerobic band at or near the surface, under which the interstitial water may be aerobic. In those conditions, benthic infauna can obtain oxygen from either the interstitial or overlying waters.

Oxygen depletions may occur in estuarine waters. Mobile Bay, Alabama, is well known for a phenomenon called "jubilee"—periods when large numbers of marine organisms die along the beaches of the bay. Summer salinity stratification creates pockets of oxygen-depleted water in the bay. Some years those pockets may be pushed shoreward, moving marine organisms, which will not enter the depleted water, along in front of them. When they reach shore in edible condition, the moribund fishes, crabs, and other animals provide a bonanza for beachcombers (May, 1973).

Nutrients

Major limiting nutrients in aquatic environments are phosphorus, nitrogen, and silicon. The first two are required by all plants and animals, while the third is required by such organisms as diatoms, which have silicious tests. The focus of this discussion is on nitrogen and phosphorus.

Estuaries have been called nutrient traps by many investigators. According to Peterson and Peterson (1979), there are three main reasons for that viewpoint. First, clay particles, so prevalent in estuaries, adsorb nutrients. Second, tidal flow often leads to minimal net movement of particles and water, so residence time is long in estuaries. Finally, rapid biodeposition of nutrients occurs after they have been removed from the water by filter feeders and lost to the sediments in feces and pseudofeces.

Although many of the nutrients present in estuarine waters enter with freshwater inflow, atmospheric additions, influxes from offshore, diffusion from the sediments, and various sources of pollution should not be overlooked. As discussed by Ketchum (1967), rivers bring in nutrients that were leached from the soil in the drainage basin, while pollutants may enter from a variety of locations.

Nutrients and nutrient cycling have been the focus of numerous scientific papers and books. A simplified treatment of nutrient cycling in estuaries is presented in figure 11.

NITROGEN

The nitrogen cycle common to aquatic environments is presented in figure 12. Of particular importance is that although freshwater inflow is a significant source of nitrogen, the element also occurs in high concentrations within the atmosphere and can be fixed by certain kinds of aquatic

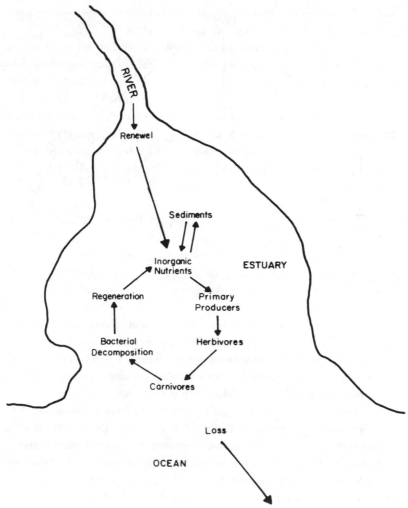

Fig. 11. The general pattern of nutrient cycling in estuaries (adapted from Duke and Rice, 1967).

organisms—notably blue-green algae and certain bacteria. Gaseous nitrogen is of little value as a nutrient until it is nitrified from N_2 to ammonia (NH_3 or NH_4^+), after which it can be denitrified through nitrite (NO_2^-) to nitrate (NO_3^-) by bacteria. The bacterial genus *Nitrosomonas* is responsible for the step from ammonia to nitrite, while a complementary genus, *Nitrobacter*, converts nitrite to nitrate.

Nitrogen is present in the ocean in four chemical states. In decreasing

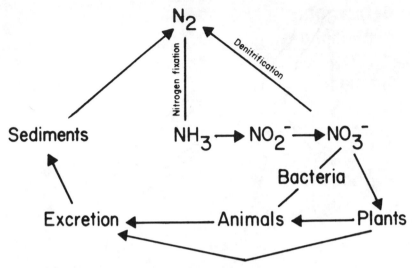

Fig. 12. The nitrogen cycle (redrawn from Stickney, 1979).

order of importance they are: organic matter, nitrate, nitrite, and ammonia. Ammonia, like nitrite, is toxic to aquatic organisms, though it is a natural waste product of metabolism. In most natural environments, excreted ammonia is rapidly converted to nitrate by the appropriate bacteria. Nitrate is then rapidly removed from solution by plants.

The major source of nitrogen to estuaries is from freshwater inflow, according to the general view. DeLaune and Patrick (1980) found that incoming sediments provide the main source of nitrogen and other nutrients for *Spartina alterniflora*. According to those authors, the delta of the Mississippi River receives annual inputs of 231, 23.1, and 991 kg/ha of nitrogen, phosphorus, and potassium, respectively.

PHOSPHORUS

The cycling of phosphorus in aquatic ecosystems is somewhat more complex than that of nitrogen. Phosphorus is not a constituent of the atmosphere and thus does not have a pathway corresponding to that of nitrogen fixation. A simplified version of the phosphorus cycle in estuaries is presented in figure 13. For purposes of simplicity, losses to sedimentation and adsorption are not shown in the figure, though they are important to the overall cycle. Phosphorus inputs, similar to those of nitrogen, are from

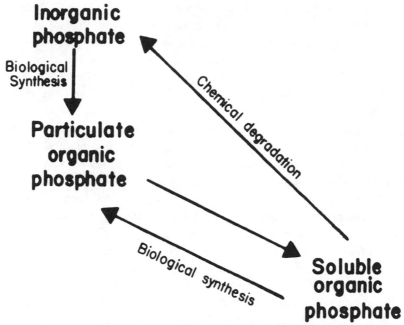

Fig. 13. The phosphorus cycle.

freshwater inflow, runoff of interstitial waters from marshlands, intrusion of enriched offshore waters, and pollution. Phosphorus is found on the surface of the earth almost exclusively in the form of orthophosphate, and it is in that form that phosphorus exists in solution in rivers (Aston, 1978).

The residence time of phosphorus in water is short because of the high reactivity of the element. Phytoplankton and bacteria equilibrate with phosphorus additions within a few minutes. Hayes and Phillips (1958) found that the removal of bacteria from a laboratory system greatly reduced the rate at which phosphorus was taken up by higher organisms. Dead plankton were found to readily absorb phosphorus, but that action could be blocked by the addition of antibiotics, indicating that bacteria were responsible. In a review of phosphorus in natural waters, Pomeroy (1960) indicated that the residence time of dissolved phosphate varies from 0.05 to 200 hours. Since plants are able to absorb phosphorus at levels far exceeding their immediate needs, they serve as a sink for the element.

The turnover rate of phosphate is between 0.1 and 1.0 mg P/m³/hr, regardless of phosphorus concentration, except when biological activity is very high, in which case the rate of turnover is between 1.0 and 2.0 mg P/ m^3/hr (Pomeroy, 1960). Thus, the high productivity found in many aquatic environments may be more dependent on the rate at which phosphorus is cycled than on the absolute concentration of the element in the water. The exchanges between water and sediments with respect to phosphorus have been studied in Georgia estuaries. Pomeroy et al. (1965) concluded that a two-step exchange occurs: the first between clay minerals and the water, and the second between interstitial microorganisms and the water.

Nutrients such as phosphate can be trapped and absorbed from water by the roots of submerged vegetation. Once absorbed, the nutrient can be translocated throughout the plant (McRoy and Barsdate, 1970; Bristow and Whitcombe, 1971; McRoy et al., 1972; DeMarte and Hartman, 1974). The fluxes of phosphorus through a tidal marsh, periphyton, and plankton in estuaries have been investigated by Correll et al. (1975).

An adsorption reaction between dissolved phosphate and suspended matter could not be demonstrated from field data by Carritt and Goodgal (1954). Those authors did, however, find some support for adsorption in laboratory studies and suggested a mechanism by which it might occur. They hypothesized that under conditions of low salinity and pH along with high turbidity, adsorption of phosphate is favored. On the other hand, when salinity and pH are higher, competing ions may release or regenerate phosphate, which would then become available for photosynthetic removal from the water. Jitts (1959) found that phosphate adsorption by silt was directly related to the ratio of iron to organic matter in the water. He also discovered that organic matter in the absence of iron depressed phosphate adsorption.

Organic Matter in Estuaries

Organic matter in water is generally referred to as dissolved and particulate carbon and excludes living organisms. Dissolved organic carbon (DOC) is, by convention, organic material that passes through a 0.45 micron filter, while particulate organic carbon (POC) is retained by the same size filter. POC may be thought of as equivalent to organic detritus. The pathways by which carbon cycles within estuaries are illustrated in figure 14.

Estuarine DOC is derived from three sources: (1) the sea, in which background levels are about 1 mg C/l (McAllister et al., 1964) but can be

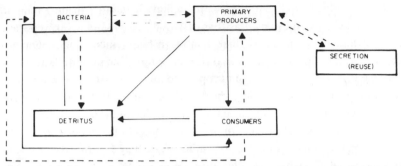

Fig. 14. Primary pathways of organic carbon flow in estuaries (particulate carbon movement is indicated by solid lines, dissolved carbon by dashed lines).

found at levels as high as 20 mg C/l (Strickland, 1965); (2) river water, which contains variable levels of DOC with a mean suggested by Beck et al. (1974) of 10 mg C/l; and (3) estuarine water, which tends to range between that of the open sea and rivers, with a mean of 5 mg C/l suggested by Riley and Chester (1971).

Examples of riverine DOC levels include 25 mg C/l in the Satilla River, Georgia (Beck et al., 1974), and 2.8 to 7.0 mg C/l in the Brazos River, Texas (Brooks, 1970). In a Louisiana study, Happ et al. (1977) found a clear gradient in both DOC and total organic carbon (TOC) from marshlands into the Gulf of Mexico. In the marshes, DOC averaged 6.7 mg C/l, while it decreased to 4.7 mg C/l in the lower bays and was further reduced to 2.4 mg C/l in the Gulf of Mexico. TOC followed the same pattern. Both DOC and TOC had late winter–early spring peaks that may have reflected the washing in of organic matter during periods of increased runoff. In Texas, levels of dissolved organic matter (DOM) in estuaries were found to range from 2.0 to 5.3 mg/l, while concentrations of 1.0 to 3.7 mg/l were found in continental-shelf waters (Maurer and Parker, 1972). In places where oceanic DOC levels are only a few milligrams per liter, the ratio of organic carbon (in the sediments) to DOC (in seawater) to POC (in seawater) to carbon (in living organisms) is approximately 1000:100: 10:1 (Kalle, 1972).

The literature is ambiguous about the extent to which river-borne organic matter passes through estuaries into the open ocean or is precipitated (or otherwise removed) when it contacts salt water (Handa, 1977). Although most authors agree that organics precipitate in estuaries, Sholkovitz

(1976) concluded that the level of precipitation is only on the order of 3–20%. Other studies, such as that of Woodwell et al. (1973), reported that, at least in some areas, there is no significant outwelling of organic carbon from estuarine marshes into coastal waters. The same authors noted that the flow may, in fact, be in the opposite direction. Additional information on the subject of organic carbon levels in natural waters can be found in the proceedings of a symposium edited by Hood (1970).

The most logical mechanism for development of DOC is by degradation of POC, but the direction of carbon flow may be reversed in some instances. DOC may be secreted into the water by living organisms and thus does not necessarily pass through a nonliving POC stage. Conversion of DOC to particulate matter and subsequent removal of POC from water have been discussed by Aston (1978).

DOM in seawater is found in two fractions: (1) stable, inert material that represents the bulk of the total and is only slowly degraded, either chemically or biologically; and (2) trace organic compounds derived directly from living organisms. The latter are rapidly degraded (Bada and Lee, 1977). Organic molecules in seawater can be rapidly adsorbed on detrital particles after they are hydrolized by microorganisms. This process may be an important mechanism by which organic macromolecules return to the food chain (Khaylov and Finendo, 1968). Organic matter of colloidal size was examined in Tokyo Bay by Ogura (1977), who found the material to be refractory to bacterial attack. The colloidal material did tend to aggregate on small particles in the water, after which it sank to the sediments.

Many of the rivers of the southeastern United States and at least part of the coast along the Gulf of Mexico are highly colored (generally appearing tea colored) because of the high levels of DOM. Beck et al. (1974) characterized the rivers of the southeastern Georgia coastal plain as having low levels of suspended solids, low ionic strength, low pH, and a predominance of organic over inorganic constituents. The organics were found to be similar to soil fulvic acids in their chemical properties. Those rivers were determined to be significantly different from much of the rest of the world. Many Florida panhandle rivers are highly colored with organic acids and may share the characteristics outlined by Beck et al. (1974) for Georgia coastal rivers.

DOM present in natural waters is generally considered to be in the form of humic compounds (defined as organic acids of high molecular weight) or nonhumic compounds. The latter are compounds of low molecular weight, which are rapidly removed from solution. Nonhumic compounds usually consist of carbohydrates, lipids, amino acids, and polypeptides. Among the dissolved free amino acids released by zooplankton, for example, are alanine, glycine, and taurine (Webb and Johannes, 1967). Allen (1978) reported that dissolved organic substances with molecular weights of less than 500 may indicate productivity or trophic state (oligotrophy, hypereutrophy, or dystrophy), at least in fresh waters.

Organisms occurring in natural waters can release DOC into the water. For example, Gallagher et al. (1976) calculated that DOC was released from *Spartina alterniflora* leaves into the water at the rate of at least 61 kg/ha/yr in Georgia marshes. Phytoplankton can also release organic carbon. In a study of the phenomenon in a Georgia estuary, Thomas (1971) estimated that between 0.2 and 6.8% of the carbon fixed through phytoplanktonic photosynthesis was subsequently released back into the water.

In laboratory experiments, phytoplankton have been shown to excrete as much as 35–40% of their photoassimilated carbon (Hellebust, 1967). Field studies in South Carolina demonstrated that the DOC released from phytoplankton ranged from 3–55% of total daily primary production (Sellner et al., 1976). Glycolic acid, an algal excretory product readily metabolized by marine bacteria, was found to turn over twelve times annually in Ipswich Bay, Massachusetts (Wright and Shah, 1977). The authors concluded that glycolic acid contributed significantly to bacterial metabolism and was as important as many other substrates for bacterial growth.

In addition to DOC release by *S. alterniflora* and phytoplankton, other primary producers have also been shown to excrete dissolved organic substances. The DOC released by eelgrass (*Zostera marina*) and associated epiphytes was studied in North Carolina by Penhale and Smith (1976). The percentage of total photosynthate excreted was only 1.5% for the eelgrass and 2% for the epiphytic community. Excretion was found to be less in the dark than in the light.

Kalle (1937) hypothesized a relationship between yellow substances (*Gelbstoffe*) in water and the presence of organic matter. Many investigators have attempted to quantify that relationship, but according to Pocklington (1977), those attempts have largely been abandoned.

Organic compounds are considered to be important in controlling the abundance, distribution, and metabolism of bacteria and fungi (Gunkel, 1972). Organic material, whether dissolved or particulate, can serve as a substrate for the growth of microorganisms. Heterotrophic marine bacteria can use such compounds as simple sugars, polysaccharides, organic acids, alcohols, aldehydes, lipids, and hydrocarbons (Gunderson, 1976). In addition, it has long been held that at least some higher organisms can obtain direct nutrient benefit from DOM. This concept, known as the Pütter hypothesis (Pütter, 1909), was debated for many years until Collier et al. (1953) reported that carbohydrate dissolved in seawater was removed and retained by oysters.

Since the work of Collier et al. (1953), various investigators have found that other species can remove DOM from water. Included in the list are both plants and animals. Organic substances have, in fact, been found significant to plant growth in many instances, though their contribution to animal nutrition remains doubtful. Trace organics may be important to phytoplankton growth and may even control the development and reproduction of attached algae. Fogg (1972) reviewed the literature on that subject.

As an example of how organics may be used by algae, Hellebust (1970) determined that the diatom *Melosira nummuloides* takes up amino acids through active transport from the water. The same study indicated that amino acids alone would not support the growth of the diatom in the absence of light and that some amino acids actually inhibited diatom growth if they were the only acids present in the medium. Hellebust (1970) also found that another diatom, *Cyclotella cryptica*, had a low capacity for glucose transport and that such species as *Coccolithus huxleyi, Isochrysis galbana, Dunaliella tertiolecta, Pyramimonas* sp., and *Skeletonema costata* did not take up the substrates offered at measurable rates. Another study, which involved the green alga *Chlorella vulgaris*, demonstrated that when that species was grown in the light it could use citrulline, arginine, or urea as substitutes for inorganic nitrogen (Arnow et al., 1953). The same study revealed that other amino acids, purines, pyrimidines, and nucleic acids stimulated growth but did not induce chlorophyll synthesis in *C. vulgaris*.

The uptake of dissolved organic substances by animals has been reviewed by Stephens (1967) and Wilber (1972). In addition, Jorgensen (1966) reviewed laboratory and field experiments in which the effects of DOC uptake on growth of suspension-feeding organisms were analyzed. Studies by Stephens and Schinske (1961) and Stephens (1964) are good examples of the kind of information that has been developed. In the first study, thirty-five species of animals from eleven phyla were examined as to their ability to remove glycine from seawater. Stephens and Schinske (1961) found that representatives from the taxa Porifera, Cnidaria, Rhynchocoela, Ectoprocta, Annelida, Sipunculoidea, Mollusca, Echinodermata, Hemichordata, and Chordata (no vertebrates were tested among the Chordata) could absorb glycine, while Crustacea apparently could not. In the second study, Stephens (1964) demonstrated that the polychaetes *Nereis limnicola* and *N. succinea* could remove glycine from seawater of intermediate and high salinity.

Trace Metals

In most cases trace metals occur at levels too low to damage organisms. Those required for proper nutrition may be obtained directly from the water or from the food, in the case of heterotrophic organisms. Necessary trace metals include but are not limited to:

1. Zinc—required for carbohydrate metabolism
2. Copper—used in the blood pigment hemocyanin in invertebrates
3. Iron—used in the blood pigment hemoglobin by vertebrates and certain invertebrates
4. Cobalt—used in the hemoglobin molecule
5. Strontium—used in the exoskeleton in certain species of invertebrates

Any of the trace metals mentioned above (and others) can be toxic when present at high concentrations.

The primary routes of the input of trace metal into coastal waters are from the atmosphere and through freshwater runoff (Nixon, 1980). Marshes are considered to be trace metal sinks (Windom, 1975). The actual forms in which trace metals appear in natural waters have not been well documented. Aston (1978) indicated that they may exist as ions, ion pairs, complexes, or polymers. The same author also noted that speciation is partly dependent on the complexing of metals with organic compounds and that precipitation of such things as hydrated oxides of iron and manganese from seawater is important in trace metal exchanges. Oxides often form in estuaries as pH increases when fresh and salt waters mix.

The form and behavior of mercury in estuaries are largely controlled by organic processes. Mercury in sediments, for example, is usually found within particulate organic matter. Decomposition of estuarine plant material appears to provide detrital organic material that is enriched in mercury compared with living plants (Lindberg et al., 1975).

Various studies have examined the form and concentration of trace metals in estuarine sediments. Because many estuaries contain oxidized and reduced layers within their sediments, the forms in which trace metals appear can vary considerably with depth. Since the demarcation between oxidized and reduced sedimentary material is generally sharp, transition in the oxidation state of trace metals may also be abrupt. In addition, migration of metals within the sediments is common. Exchange from the sediments to the water and vice versa is another regular phenomenon. A study by Brooks et al. (1968) revealed that cadmium and strontium concentrations in estuarine sediments decreased with depth, probably due to precipitation reactions. Increases in the concentrations of cadmium, cobalt, and zinc at the sediment surface were reported and attributed to biological concentration and release.

In a study of a coastal pond in Massachusetts, Horne and Woernle (1972) found that the concentrations of iron and manganese reached marked maxima at a depth corresponding to that of the anoxic layer in the sediments. Thus, those metals were thought to migrate toward the reducing environment. Cross et al. (1970) reported that manganese, iron, and zinc were all present at higher concentrations in muddy sediments than in sand. Moreover, manganese and iron concentrations increased in the water column toward the sea while zinc was fairly constant throughout the estuary. Windom et al. (1971) found that dissolved iron was rapidly removed from river water entering an estuary. There was some loss of dissolved manganese but little or no effect on dissolved copper.

Duchart et al. (1972) determined that the manganese concentration in the interstitial waters of a loch in Scotland decreased with depth; this effect, they theorized, indicated recycling between the solid phase of the metal and the dissolved phase. Cobalt, copper, iron, nickel, lead, and zinc were evaluated in the same study: some increased and some decreased with depth. The authors concluded that the changes depended upon organic content, accumulation rates, the physiochemical environment, and other factors.

Various metals have been found to be enriched in interstitial waters as compared with their concentrations in overlying salt water. Studies by Brooks et al. (1968) and Presley et al. (1972) demonstrated the phenomenon with cobalt, copper, iron, lithium, manganese, molybdenum, nickel, strontium, and zinc. Enrichment was generally two to five times that of seawater except for iron, manganese, and zinc, which were often more greatly enriched.

The flux of trace metals through salt marshes has been studied to some extent in the southeastern United States and has been reviewed by Windom (1975). Control of trace metal flux through marshes seems to depend upon processes occuring at the boundary between the river and estuary proper and at the salt marsh–sediment boundary. Important processes include precipitation, flocculation, adsorption-desorption reactions, and sedimentation. Biological processes are also implicated in trace metal cycling. Metals that might otherwise be lost to the sediments are often taken up by plants and later released.

Windom (1975) reported that the behavior of various metals differs considerably. For example, much of the dissolved iron and manganese entering a salt marsh precipitates and accumulates in the sediments. Most soluble cadmium and copper, on the other hand, is transported through the marsh and may be carried out of the estuary. Particulate forms of the latter two metals, however, appear to be lost to the sediments within the estuary.

Historical changes in the rates at which trace metals have been added to estuaries and other water bodies have been cited as indicators of increased pollution, and various studies examining the phenomenon have been undertaken. Thomson et al. (1975) analyzed the levels of trace metals in sediments on Long Island Sound over the seventy years preceding the study and determined that temporal increases appeared to be related to man's activities. McCaffrey (1977) found that lead within the sediments of a *Spartina patens* marsh increased beginning about the time of the Civil War (1860s); no correlation, however, seems to exist between the introduction of leaded gasoline and increased lead content in the sediments.

Dunstan and Windom (1975) reported no correlation between heavy metal concentrations in *S. alterniflora* and the marsh sediments or nearby river and estuarine waters in association with six major river systems along the coast of the southeastern United States. Ranges of metal concentrations in the marshgrass were low compared with those in the sediments and water. Although most metals were not concentrated within the marshgrass beyond levels appearing in the sediments, mercury was up to four times higher in the *S. alterniflora*. Among the effects of high mercury concentrations on marshgrass were inhibition of germination and death of seedlings.

Other trace metals did not inhibit germination, but copper and lead killed seedlings if present at high enough levels.

One concept of modern ecology is that of biological magnification. Simply stated, pollutants are often found to increase in concentration from one trophic level to another within the food web. Thus, while primary producers may contain a low level of a particular pollutant, herbivores and carnivores will have increasingly higher levels. Ultimately, the concentration may become so high in top carnivores that toxicity occurs. This phenomenon has been well documented for such pesticides as DDT but may not be generally applied to pollutants. For example, little biological magnification in trace metals was observed by Stickney et al. (1975) in their examination of various estuarine animals. Similarly, Cross et al. (1970) examined the levels of manganese, iron, and zinc in sediments, water, and six species of polychaetes. They concluded that either the polychaetes were able to regulate internal levels of the metals, or the metals were in a form that did not lead to uptake by the annelids.

LITERATURE CITED

Allen, H. L. 1978. Low molecular weight dissolved organic matter in five softwater ecosystems: A preliminary study and ecological implications. *Verh. Internat. Verein. Limnol.* 20: 514–24.

Arnow, P., J. J. Oleson, and J. H. Williams. 1953. The effect of arginine on the nutrition of *Chlorella vulgaris*. *Amer. J. Bot.* 40: 100–104.

Aston, S. R. 1978. Estuarine chemistry, pp. 361–440. In: J. P. Riley and R. Chester, eds. *Chemical oceanography*. New York: Academic Press.

Bada, J. L., and C. Lee. 1977. Decomposition and alteration of organic compounds dissolved in seawater. *Mar. Chem.* 5: 523–34.

Beck, K. C., J. H. Reuter, and E. M. Perdue. 1974. Organic and inorganic geochemistry of some coastal plain rivers of the southeastern United States. *Geochim. et Cosmochim. Acta*, 38: 341–64.

Bricker, O. P., III., and B. N. Troup. 1975. Sediment-water exchange in Chesapeake Bay, pp. 3–27. In: L. E. Cronin, ed. *Estuarine research*. Vol. I. New York: Academic Press.

Bristow, J. M., and W. Whitcombe. 1971. The role of roots in the nutrients of aquatic vascular plants. *Amer. J. Bot.* 58: 8–13.

Brooks, J. M. 1970. The distribution of organic carbon in the Brazos River basin. M.S. thesis, Texas A&M University, College Station.

Brooks, R. R., B. J. Presley, and I. R. Kaplan. 1968. Trace elements in the interstitial waters of marine sediments. *Geochim. et Cosmochim. Acta* 32: 397–414.

Cairns, J., Jr. 1967. Suspended solids standards for the protection of aquatic organisms. *Purdue University Eng. Bull.* 129: 16–27.

Carpenter, J. H., W. L. Bradford, and V. Grant. 1975. Processes affecting the composition of estuarine waters (HCO3, Fe, Mn, Zn, Cu, Ni, Cr, Co, and Cd), pp. 188–214. In: L. E. Cronin, ed. *Estuarine research.* Vol. I. New York: Academic Press.

Carritt, D. E., and S. Goodgal. 1954. Sorption reactions and some ecological implications. *Deep Sea Res.* 1: 224–43.

Chave, K. E. 1970. Carbonate-organic interactions in sea water, pp. 373–85. In: D. W. Hood, ed. *Symposium on organic matter in natural waters.* College: University of Alaska Institute of Marine Science.

Collier, A., S. M. Ray, A. W. Magnitsky, and J. O. Bell. 1953. Effect of dissolved organic substances on oysters. *Fish. Bull.* 54: 167–85.

Correll, D. L., M. A. Faust, and D. J. Severn. 1975. Phosphorus flux and cycling in estuaries, pp. 108–36. In: L. E. Cronin, ed. *Estuarine research.* Vol. I. New York: Academic Press.

Cross, F. A., T. W. Duke, and J. N. Willis. 1970. Biogeochemistry of trace elements in a coastal plain estuary. Distribution of manganese, iron, and zinc in sediments, water, and polychaetous worms. *Ches. Sci.* 11: 221–34.

DeLaune, R. D., and W. H. Patrick. 1980. Rate of sedimentation and its role in nutrient cycling in a Louisiana salt marsh, pp. 401–12. In: P. Hamilton and K. B. Macdonald, eds. *Estuarine and wetland processes—with emphasis on modeling.* New York: Plenum Press.

DeMarte, J. A. and R. I. Hartman. 1974. Studies on the absorption of P32, Fe59, and Ca45 by water milfoil *Myriophyllum exalbescens* (Fernalt). *Ecology* 55: 188–94.

Duchart, P., S. E. Calvert, and N. B. Price. 1973. Distribution of trace metals in the pore waters of shallow water marine sediments. *Limnol. Oceanogr.* 18: 605–10.

Duke, T. W., and T. R. Rice. 1967. Cycling of nutrients in estuaries. *Proc. Gulf and Caribb. Fish. Inst.* 19: 59–67.

Dunstan, W. M., and H. L. Windom. 1975. The influence of environmental changes in heavy metal concentrations on *Spartina alterniflora*, pp. 393–404. In: L. E. Cronin, ed. *Estuarine research.* Vol. II. New York: Academic Press.

Fogg, G. E. 1972. Organic substances. Plants, pp. 1552–63. In: O. Kinne, ed. *Marine ecology.* Vol. I. New York: John Wiley and Sons.

Gallagher, J. L., W. J. Pfeiffer, and L. R. Pomeroy. 1976. Leaching and microbial utilization of dissolved carbon from leaves of *Spartina alterniflora*. *Est. and Coast. Mar. Sci.* 4: 467–71.

Gardner, L. R. 1975. Runoff from an intertidal marsh during tidal exposure—recession curves and chemical characteristics. *Limnol. Oceanogr.* 20: 81–89.

Gunderson, G. 1976. Cultivation of micro-organisms. Bacteria, pp. 301–35. In:

O. Kinne, ed. *Marine ecology*. Vol. III. New York: John Wiley and Sons.

Gunkel, W. 1972. Organic substances: Bacteria, fungi, and blue-green algae, pp. 1533–49. In: O. Kinne, ed. *Marine ecology*. Vol. I. New York: John Wiley and Sons.

Handa, N. 1977. Land sources of marine organic matter. *Mar. Chem.* 5: 341–59.

Happ, G., J. G. Gosselink, and J. W. Day, Jr. 1977. The seasonal distribution of organic carbon in a Louisiana estuary. *Est. and Coast. Mar. Sci.* 5: 695–705.

Hayes, F. R. 1964. The mud-water interface. *Oceanogr. Mar. Biol. Ann. Rev.* 2: 121–45.

Hayes, F. R., and J. E. Phillips. 1958. Lake and water sediment. IV. Radio-phosphorus equilibrium with mud, plants, and bacteria under oxidized conditions. *Limnol. Oceanogr.* 3: 459–75.

Hellebust, J. A. 1967. Excretion of organic compounds by cultured and natural populations of marine phytoplankton, pp. 361–66. In: G. H. Lauff, ed. *Estuaries*. American Association for the Advancement of Science Publication no. 83. Washington, D.C.: AAAS.

———. 1970. The uptake and utilization of organic substances by marine phyto-plankters, pp. 225–56. In: D. W. Hood, ed. *Symposium on organic matter in natural waters*. College: University of Alaska Institute of Marine Science.

Hood, D. W. ed. 1970. *Symposium on organic matter in natural waters*. College: University of Alaska Institute of Marine Science.

Horne, R. A., and C. H. Woernle. 1972. Iron and manganese profiles in a coastal pond with an anoxic zone. *Chem. Geol.* 9: 299–304.

Jitts, H. R. 1959. The adsorption of phosphate by estuarine bottom deposits. *Aust. J. Mar. Freshw. Res.* 10: 7–21.

Jorgensen, C. B. 1966. *Biology of suspension feeding*. New York: Pergamon Press.

Kalle, K. 1937. Meereskundliche chemische Untersuchen mit Hilfe des Zeisschen Pulfrich Photometers. *Ann. Hydrogr. Berl.* 65: 276–82.

———. 1972. Organic substances. General introduction, pp. 1527–31. In: O. Kinne, ed. *Marine ecology*. Vol. II. New York: John Wiley and Sons.

Ketchum, B. H. 1967. Phytoplankton nutrients in estuaries, pp. 329–35. In: G. H. Lauff, ed. *Estuaries*. American Association for the Advancement of Science Publication no. 83. Washington, D.C.: AAAS.

Khaylov, K. M., and Z. Z. Finendo. 1968. The interaction of detritus with high molecular weight components of dissolved organic matter in sea water. *Oceanology* 8: 776–85.

Lindberg, S. E., A. W. Andren, and R. C. Harriss. 1975. Geochemistry of mercury in the estuarine environment, pp. 64–107. In: L. E. Cronin, ed. *Estuarine research*. Vol. I. New York: Academic Press.

McAllister, C. D., N. Shah, and J. D. H. Strickland. 1964. Marine phytoplankton photosynthesis as a function of light intensity: A comparison of methods. *J. Fish. Res. Bd. Can.* 21: 159–81.

McCaffrey, R. J. 1977. A record of the accumulation of sediment and trace metals in a Connecticut, U.S.A., salt marsh. Ph.D diss. Yale University, New Haven, Conn.

McRoy, C. P., and R. J. Barsdate. 1970. Phosphate absorption in eelgrass. *Limnol. Oceanogr.* 15: 6–13.

McRoy, C. P., R. J. Barsdate, and M. Nebart. 1972. Phosphorus cycling in an eelgrass (*Zostera marina* L.) ecosystem. *Limnol. Oceanogr.* 17: 58–67.

Mauer, L. G., and P. L. Parker. 1972. The distribution of dissolved organic matter in the near-shore waters of the Texas coast. *Cont. Mar. Sci.* 16: 109–24.

May, E. B. 1973. Extensive oxygen depletion in Mobile Bay, Alabama. *Limnol. Oceanogr.* 18: 353–66.

Nixon, S. W. 1980. Between coastal marshes and coastal waters: A review of twenty years of speculation on the role of salt marshes in estuarine productivity and water chemistry, pp. 437–525. In: P. Hamilton and K. B. Macdonald, eds. *Estuarine and wetland processes—with emphasis on modeling.* New York: Plenum Press.

Ogura, N. 1977. High molecular weight organic matter in seawater. *Mar. Chem.* 5: 535–49.

Penhale, P. A., and W. O. Smith, Jr. 1976. Excretion of dissolved organic carbon by eelgrass (*Zostera marina*) and its epiphytes. *Limnol. Oceanogr.* 22: 400–407.

Peterson, C. H., and N. M. Peterson. 1979. The ecology of intertidal flats in North Carolina: A community profile. U.S. Fish and Wildlife Service Biological Services Program FWS/OBS 79-39.

Pocklington, R. 1977. Chemical processes and interactions involving marine organic matter. *Mar. Chem.* 5: 479–96.

Pomeroy, L. R. 1960. Residence time of dissolved phosphate in natural waters. *Science* 131: 1731.

Pomeroy, L. R., E. E. Smith, and C. M. Grant. 1965. The exchange of phosphate between estuarine water and sediments. *Limnol. Oceanogr.* 10: 167–72.

Presley, B. J., Y. Kolodny, A. Nissenbaum, and I. R. Kaplan. 1972. Early diagenesis in a reducing fjord, Saanich Inlet, British Columbia. II. Trace element distribution in interstitial water and sediment. *Geochim. et Cosmochim. Acta* 36: 1073–90.

Pütter, A. 1909. *Die Ernährung der Wassertiere und der Stoffhaushalt der Gewässer.* Jena: Fischer.

Reidl, R., and E. A. McMahan. 1974. High energy beaches, pp. 180–251. In: H. T. Odum, B. J. Copeland, and E. A. McMahan, eds. *Coastal ecological systems of the United States.* Vol. I. Washington, D.C.: Conservation Foundation.

Riley, J. P., and R. Chester. 1971. *Introduction to marine chemistry.* New York: Academic Press.

Sellner, K. G., R. G. Zingmark, and T. G. Miller. 1976. Interpretations of the 14C method of measuring the total annual production of phytoplankton in a South Carolina estuary. *Bot. Mar.* 19: 119–25.

Sholkovitz, E. R. 1976. Flocculation of dissolved organic and inorganic matter during the mixing of river water and seawater. *Geochim. et Cosmochim. Acta* 40: 831–45.

Stephens, G. C. 1964. Uptake of organic material by aquatic invertebrates. III. Uptake of glycine by brackish water annelids. *Biol. Bull.* 126: 150–62.

———. 1967. Dissolved organic material as a nutritional source for marine and estuarine invertebrates, pp. 367–73. In: G. H. Lauff, ed. *Estuaries*. American Association for the Advancement of Science Publication no. 83. Washington, D.C.: AAAS.

Stehens, G. C., and R. A. Schinske. 1961. Uptake of amino acids by marine invertebrates. *Limnol. Oceanogr.* 6: 175–81.

Stickney, R. R. 1979. *Principles of warmwater aquaculture*. New York: Wiley-Interscience.

Stickney, R. R., H. L. Windom, D. B. White, and F. E. Taylor. 1975. Heavy metal concentrations in selected Georgia estuarine organisms with comparative food habit data, pp. 257–67. In: F. G. Howell, J. B. Gentry, and M. H. Smith, eds. Chemical cycling in southeastern ecosystems. ERDA Symposium Series (CONF-740513).

Strickland, J. D. H. 1965. Production of organic matter in the primary stages of the marine food chain, pp. 477–610. In: J. P. Riley and G. Skirrow, eds. *Chemical oceanography*. Vol. I. New York: Academic Press.

Thomas, J. P. 1971. Release of dissolved organic matter from natural populations of marine phytoplankton. *Mar. Biol.* 11: 311–23.

Thomson, J., K. K. Turekian, and R. J. McCaffrey. 1975. The accumulation of metals in and release from sediments of Long Island Sound, pp. 28–44. In: L. E. Cronin, ed. *Estuarine research*. Vol. I. New York: Academic Press.

Webb, K. L., and R. E. Johannes. 1967. Studies of the release of dissolved free amino acids by marine zooplankton. *Limnol. Oceanogr.* 12: 376–82.

Wilber, C. G. 1972. Organic substances. Animals, pp. 1566–77. In: O. Kinne, ed. *Marine ecology*. Vol. I. New York: John Wiley and Sons.

Windom, H. L. 1975. Heavy metal fluxes through salt-marsh estuaries, pp. 137–52. In: L. E. Cronin, ed. *Estuarine research*. Vol. I. New York: Academic Press.

Windom, H. L., W. J. Neal, and K. C. Beck. 1971. Mineralogy of sediments in three Georgia estuaries. *J. Sed. Pet.* 41: 497–504.

Woodwell, G. M., P. H. Rich, and C. A. Hall. 1973. Carbon in estuaries, pp. 221–40. In: G. M. Woodwell and E. V. Pecan, eds. *Carbon and the biosphere*. Washington, D.C.: Technical Information Center, Office of information Services, U.S. Atomic Energy Commission.

Wright, R. T., and N. M. Shah. 1977. The trophic role of glycolic acid in coastal seawater. II. Seasonal changes in concentration and heterotrophic use in Ipswich Bay, Massachusetts, USA. *Mar. Biol.* 43: 257–63.

Zobell, C. E. 1942. Changes produced by microorganisms in sediments after deposition. *J. Sed. Pet.* 12: 127–36.

Zobell, C. E., and C. B. Feltham. 1942. The bacterial flora of a marine flat as an ecological factor. *Ecology* 23: 69–78.

CHAPTER 6

Primary Producers, Decomposers, and Detritus

Introduction

ACCORDING to Wetzel (1975), production is defined as the weight of new organic material formed over a period of time. If that organic material is composed of plants, then the appropriate term is primary production. For example, the amount of production in a *Spartina alterniflora* marsh may be several thousand kg/ha. Productivity is defined as the rate of production (Wetzel, 1975). Phytoplankton productivity, for example, might be on the order of several mg/l/day. In some cases production and productivity are expressed as wet weight of tissue elaborated, but it is often desirable to use dry weights for the expression of production or productivity. That eliminates the variability in percentage of water. Other ways of expressing production and productivity are related to the amount of carbon fixed per unit time, the amount of chlorophyll present, and the amount of oxygen generated.

Another term commonly used with respect to both plant and animal communities is standing crop. Standing crop (or standing stock) is the weight of material or number of individuals existing at the time of sampling, expressed as either area or volume. For example, submerged and intertidal macrophytes may be measured on the basis of g/m^2 standing crop. Differences in standing crops over time can provide an estimate of productivity.

Primary producers grow within estuaries but may also be carried into estuaries from offshore or with incoming fresh water. As indicated by Walker (1973), generalizing from the value of one source of primary productivity is often inappropriate, since the situation will change from one estuary to another. One group of primary producers may dominate a given estuary, but all producers contribute to the food web (Marshall, 1970). A relatively small number of primary producers may support a highly diverse consumer community (Peterson and Peterson, 1979). Breuer (1957) revealed some of the dominant organisms in a typical estuarine community and outlined the food web in Baffin Bay, Texas. Since then, various authors have examined the tropic relationships in coastal ecosystems. Much of that work was reviewed in Odum et al. (1974).

Since much of the primary productivity in estuaries enters the consumer trophic levels as detritus, bacteria and the role of detritus are discussed in this chapter. The primary producer groups considered are phytoplankton, benthic algae, submerged plants, intertidal and supratidal marsh plants, and mangroves.

The primary producers in estuaries of the southeastern Atlantic and Gulf of Mexico are composed of both cosmopolitan and locally endemic species. Those tolerating wide ranges in environment can be expected to inhabit larger ranges than those narrowly limited by such factors as temperature, salinity, turbidity, and tidal range.

Beaches, dunes, and their flora are technically not parts of the estuarine environment unless the watershed is included in the definition of the ecosystem. Since dunes often contribute sediments to estuaries, however, a few words about the plants that inhabit sand dunes are pertinent. Two dunegrasses effective in stabilizing sand dunes are American beachgrass (*Ammophilia breviligulata*) and sea oats (*Uniola paniculata*). Woodhouse et al. (1977) studied experimentally planted dunes for ten years and concluded that American beachgrass was good for early stabilization and dune development, easy to propagate, and quick to become established. Sea oats, on the other hand, was difficult to propagate and became established slowly; it was, however, an excellent long-term stabilizing agent. The authors concluded that a mixture of the two species should be used for dune stabilization.

The two grasses discussed above, along with other plant species commonly found on dunes and their distributions, are presented in table 6. Various species of plants—subtidal, marshland, and mangrove swamp— appear in the table.

Phytoplankton and Benthic Algae

The phytoplankton community is composed of plants, generally unicellular algae, that are suspended in the water column. The benthic com-

TABLE 6. Representative Plants of the Southeastern Atlantic and the Gulf of Mexico

Common Name	Scientific Name	Distribution
Beach and Dune Vegetation		
Sea rocket	*Cakile edentula*	Virginia to South Carolina
Saltwort	*Salsola kaki*	Virginia to Florida
Dusty miller; silver king	*Artemisia stelleriana*	Virginia
Seabeach knotweed	*Polygonum glaucum*	Virginia to Georgia
Gray orach	*Atriplex patula*	Virginia to South Carolina
Seabeach orach	*Atriplex arenaria*	Southeastern Atlantic and Gulf of Mexico
Seaside goldenrod	*Solidago sempervirens*	Southeastern Atlantic and Gulf of Mexico
Cocklebur; sea burdock	*Xanthium echinatum*	Virginia
Horn; sea poppy	*Glaucium flavium*	Virginia
Pigweed; lamb's quarter	*Chenopodium album*	Southeastern Atlantic and Gulf of Mexico
Primrose	*Oenothera humifusa*	Virginia to Florida
Wild morning glory	*Convolvulus sepium*	Southeastern Atlantic and Gulf of Mexico
Yarrow	*Achillea millefolium*	Southeastern Atlantic and Gulf of Mexico
Virginia creeper; woodbine	*Parthenocissus quinquefolia*	Southeastern Atlantic and Gulf of Mexico
Jointweed	*Polygonella articulata*	Virginia to North Carolina
Ragweed	*Ambrosia artemisiifolia*	Southeastern Atlantic and Gulf of Mexico
Bayberry	*Myrica pensylvanica*	North Carolina
Knawel	*Scleranthus annuus*	Virginia to Florida
Carpet weed	*Molluga verticillata*	Southeastern Atlantic and Gulf of Mexico
Old field toadflax	*Linaria canadensis*	Southeastern Atlantic and Gulf of Mexico
Sheep sorrel	*Rumex acetosella*	Virginia
Beachgrass; marramgrass	*Ammophilia breviligulata*	Virginia to North Carolina
Common sow thistle	*Sonchus oleraceus*	Virginia to Florida
Salt marsh hay; salt meadow cordgrass	*Spartina patens*	Southeastern Atlantic and Gulf of Mexico

TABLE 6. (*continued*)

Common Name	Scientific Name	Distribution
Cheat	*Bromus tectorum*	Virginia
Terrellgrass	*Elymus virginicus*	Virginia
Sea blite	*Suaeda maritima*	Virginia
Sea blite	*Suaeda linearis*	Southeastern Atlantic and Gulf of Mexico
Black nightshade	*Suaeda nigrum*	Virginia to Florida
Sea purselane	*Sesuvium maritinum*	Southeastern Atlantic and Gulf of Mexico
Sea oats	*Uniola paniculata*	Southeastern Atlantic and Gulf of Mexico
Beach heather; povertygrass	*Hudsonia tomentosa*	Virginia to North Carolina
Seaside pinweed	*Lechea maritima*	Virginia
Poison ivy	*Rhus radicans*	Southeastern Atlantic and Gulf of Mexico
Scrub oak; holly oak	*Quercus ilicifolia*	Virginia to North Carolina
Red cedar; juniper	*Juniperus virginiana*	Southeastern Atlantic and Gulf of Mexico
Sea myrtle; groundsel tree	*Baccharis halmifolia*	Southeastern Atlantic and Gulf of Mexico
Red fescuegrass	*Festuca rubra*	Virginia to North Carolina
Wormwood	*Artemisia caudata*	Southeastern Atlantic and Gulf of Mexico
Seaside spurge	*Euphorbia poygonifolia*	Virginia to Georgia
Canadian rush	*Juncus canadensis*	Virginia to Georgia
Gray's sedge	*Cyperus grayii*	Virginia to Florida
Common hairgrass	*Deschampsia flexuosa*	Virginia to North Carolina
Seaside heliotrope	*Heliotropium curassavicum*	Southeastern Atlantic and Gulf of Mexico
Gray nickerbean	*Caesalpinia crista*	Florida
Coin vine; fish poison vine	*Dalbergia ecastophyllum*	Florida
Necklace pod	*Sophora tomentosa*	Florida
Vidrillos	*Batis maritima*	Texas
Keygrass	*Monanthochloë littoralis*	Florida and Texas
Sea oxeye	*Borrichia frutescens*	Southeastern Atlantic and Gulf of Mexico

TABLE 6. (*continued*)

Common Name	Scientific Name	Distribution
White gulf dune paspalum	*Paspalum monostachyum*	Texas
Salt jointgrass	*Paspalum vaginatum*	Southeastern Atlantic and Gulf of Mexico
Lantana	*Lantana involucrata*	Florida and Texas
Dwarf saltwort	*Salicornia bigelovii*	Southeastern Atlantic and Gulf of Mexico
Subtidal Vegetation		
Eelgrass	*Zostera marina*	Virginia to North Carolina
Widgeongrass	*Ruppia maritima*	Southeastern Atlantic and Gulf of Mexico
Turtlegrass	*Thalassia testudinum*	Florida to Texas
Manateegrass	*Cymodocea manatorum*	Florida and Texas
Pond weed	*Potamogeton* spp.	Southeastern Atlantic and Gulf of Mexico
Tidal Marsh Vegetation		
Smooth cordgrass; salt marsh cordgrass	*Spartina alterniflora*	Southeastern Atlantic and Gulf of Mexico
Salt marsh hay; salt meadow cordgrass	*Spartina patens*	Southeastern Atlantic and Gulf of Mexico
Spikegrass; saltgrass; alkaligrass; seashore saltgrass	*Distichlis spicata*	Southeastern Atlantic and Gulf of Mexico
Black rush; needle rush	*Juncus roemerianus*	Southeastern Atlantic and Gulf of Mexico
Switchgrass	*Panicum virgatum*	Virginia to Mississippi
Reedgrass	*Phragmites australis*	Southeastern Atlantic and Gulf of Mexico
Red fescuegrass	*Festuca rubra*	Virginia to North Carolina
Redtopgrass	*Agrostis alba*	Nearly cosmopolitan in Southeastern Atlantic and Gulf of Mexico
Sea blite	*Suaeda maritima*	Virginia to Florida
Sea blite	*Suaeda linearis*	Southeastern Atlantic and Gulf of Mexico
Perennial glasswort	*Salicornia virginica*	Southeastern Atlantic and Gulf of Mexico
Samphire	*Salicornia europea*	Virginia to Georgia

TABLE 6. (*continued*)

Common Name	Scientific Name	Distribution
Dwarf saltwort	*Salicornia bigelovii*	Southeastern Atlantic and Gulf of Mexico
Marsh aster	*Aster tenufolius*	Virginia to Louisiana
Salt marsh fleabane	*Pluchea purpurascens*	Virginia to Florida
Salt marsh fleabane	*Pluchea camphorata*	Southeastern Atlantic and Gulf of Mexico
Sea purselane	*Sesuvium portulacastrum*	Nearly cosmopolitan in Southeastern Atlantic and Gulf of Mexico
Marsh samphire	*Philoxerus vermicularis*	Southeastern Atlantic and Gulf of Mexico
Sea myrtle; groundsel tree; cotton tree; saltbush	*Baccharis halimifolia*	Southeastern Atlantic and Gulf of Mexico
Sea oxeye	*Borrichia frutescens*	Southeastern Atlantic and Gulf of Mexico
Sea oxeye	*Borrichia arborescens*	Florida
Marsh elder	*Iva frutescens*	Virginia to Louisiana
None	*Melanthera aspera*	Florida
Seaside goldenrod	*Solidago sempervirens*	Southeastern Atlantic and Gulf of Mexico
Saltwort	*Batis maritima*	North Carolina to Texas
Seaside heliotrope	*Heliotropium curassivicum*	Southeastern Atlantic and Gulf of Mexico
Necklace pod	*Sophora tomentosa*	Florida
Orach	*Atriplex putula*	Virginia to South Carolina
Sand spurry	*Spergularia marina*	Virginia to Florida
Link	*Eleocharis parvula*	Nearly cosmopolitan in Southeastern Atlantic and Gulf of Mexico
Swamp rose; mallow	*Hibiscus palustris*	Virginia and North Carolina
Olney threesquare	*Scirpus olneyi*	Southeastern Atlantic and Gulf of Mexico
Threesquare rush	*Scirpus americanus*	Southeastern Atlantic and Gulf of Mexico
Bullrush	*Scirpus maritimus*	Texas
Terrellgrass	*Elymus virginicus*	Virginia
Cardinal flower	*Lobelia cardinalis*	Southeastern Atlantic and Gulf of Mexico

TABLE 6. (*continued*)

Common Name	Scientific Name	Distribution
Spiked loosestrife	*Lythrum salicaria*	Virginia
Shadbush	*Amelanchier laevis*	Virginia to Georgia
Sea lavender	*Limonium carolinianum*	Southeastern Atlantic and Gulf of Mexico
Keygrass	*Monanthochloë littoralis*	Florida and Texas
Virginia dropseed	*Sporobolus virginicus*	Southeastern Atlantic and Gulf of Mexico
Water pimpernel	*Samolus ebracteatus*	Florida to Texas
Christmas berry	*Lycium carolinianum*	South Carolina to Texas
Horned rush	*Rhynchospora corniculata*	Texas
Mangrove Swamps and Their Borders		
Black mangrove	*Avicennia germinans*	Florida to Texas
Button mangrove; buttonwood	*Conocarpus erectus*	Florida
White mangrove	*Laguncularia racemosa*	Florida
Red mangrove	*Rhizophora mangle*	Florida
Sea oxeye	*Borrichia frutescens*	Southeastern Atlantic and Gulf of Mexico
Sea oxeye	*Borrichia arborescens*	Florida
Seaside goldenrod	*Solidago sempervirens*	Southeastern Atlantic and Gulf of Mexico
Gray nickerbean	*Caesalpinia crista*	Florida
Coin vine; fish poison vine	*Dalbergia ecastophyllum*	Florida
Necklace pod	*Sophora tomentosa*	Florida
None	*Eustoma exaltatum*	Florida
Keygrass	*Monanthochloë littoralis*	Florida and Texas

Sources: Adapted from Moul, 1973, and Carlton, 1975.

munity comprises species associated with substrates. Although the term *benthic algae* implies that the plants are attached to bottom sediments, the definition may be extended to include association with or attachment to any substrate. Much of the biomass produced by phytoplankton and benthic algae enters the benthic invertebrate food web of intertidal and shallow subtidal flats. Benthic algae may be the most important food source for benthic organisms (Peterson and Peterson, 1979).

Species found in the phytoplankton and benthic algal communities are not necessarily restricted to these communities. Both have many species in common. Some of the most frequently occurring members are species of green algae, blue-green algae, and diatoms. Brown and red algae may also be present. Rather large algal species, such as the kelps (e.g., *Macrocystis pyrifera* and *Laminaria* spp.) and sea lettuce (*Ulva* spp.) are macroscopic and would more appropriately be considered macrophytic plants.

PHYTOPLANKTON

Many phytoplanktonic species occur in estuaries. In a typical study, Phillips (1960) found 195 taxa of marine algae in Tampa Bay, Boca Ciega Bay, and Tarpon Springs, Florida, over a salinity range of 24.7 to 31.3 o/oo. In a North Carolina study, Carpenter (1971) found 203 taxa, including 134 species of diatoms, twenty-five chlorophytes, fifteen dinoflagellates, nine cryptomonads, nine cyanophytes, three xanthophytes, two loricate flagellates, and one euglenoid flagellate.

Seasonal trends in phytoplanktonic activity are frequently observed in estuaries. The usual pattern in aquatic environments includes spring and fall blooms, with reduced numbers and low production in the summer and winter. Thayer (1971) measured phytoplankton productivity in North Carolina estuaries and determined it to be maximum in June and minimum in December. The spring and fall peaks appear linked to the various environmental changes of those seasons. Temperature often changes rapidly and may become optimum for phytoplankton productivity at some intermediate between the summer and winter means. In addition, rainfall and associated runoff are often higher during spring and fall, resulting in greater nutrient inputs. Reductions in standing crops of phytoplankton after the seasonal peaks may be caused, in part, by zooplankton grazing.

If phytoplankton cells are not maintained above the compensation depth, respiration will equal or exceed photosynthetic production. Turbidity often controls the depth of the photic zone in estuaries, and reductions in light penetration resulting from turbidity can reduce primary productivity and stimulate respiration (Odum and Wilson, 1962). Odum and Hoskin (1958) demonstrated that primary production was highest in shallow, clear bays and lowest in turbid, deep bays.

Where respiration exceeds photosynthesis because of light limitation or other environmental stresses, inorganic nutrients will be released from the declining phytoplankton community and may accumulate within the estuary. That accumulation may stimulate renewed photosynthesis (Odum and Wilson, 1962). Self-shading of phytoplankton during a bloom can also be a cause of increased turbidity and may lead to retardation of photosynthesis if turbulent mixing does not frequently bring the cells into the photic zone.

Primary productivity can be expressed as the total amount of carbon fixed per day (gross productivity) or the total amount fixed less that lost to respiration (net productivity). Although in most cases there is a daily net gain in primary productivity, that is not always true. Ragotzkie (1959) found gross phytoplanktonic productivity in Georgia to be 0.68 g $C/m^2/$ day, while net productivity was -0.038 g $C/m^2/$day. Clearly, if net productivity is negative, the phytoplankton present cannot support a consumer population. It is also apparent that a negative net photosynthetic rate cannot last for long without decimating the phytoplankton community.

Chlorophyll a is commonly measured as an indication of primary production. Flemer (1970) found that the level of chlorophyll a in Chesapeake Bay was highest during warm months. Stross and Stottlemyer (1965) reached the same conclusion with the Patuxent River, indicating that the most productive period was from June through October, disregarding variability from year to year. In Louisiana estuaries, primary productivity, also determined by measuring chlorophyll a, peaked in January and July (Happ et al., 1977).

The radioisotope carbon-14 was used by Sellner et al. (1976) to measure phytoplanktonic productivity in a South Carolina estuary. They found that the lowest rate of fixation occurred in November (6.4 mg $C/m^2/$hr) and the highest in August (234 mg $C/m^2/$hr). Thayer (1971) reported a range of from 16 to 153 g $C/m^2/$yr fixed in North Carolina estuaries, with a mean of 66 g $C/m^2/$yr.

Phytoplankton productivity in estuaries reaches a maximum of 22.6 g $C/m^2/$day gross and 16.4 g $C/m^2/$day net. Annual rates of production range from about 100 to 550 g C/m^2 gross and from -11 to 220 g C/m^2 net (Williams, 1972).

Phytoplankton productivity has been shown to vary considerably with respect to location within estuaries, both in depth and in distance from the estuary mouth. Williams (1966) determined that levels of both gross production and respiration were highest at the 50% light level in North Carolina estuaries. In the same study he found that the rate of photosynthesis of phytoplankton was highest at the head of the estuary in shallow, turbid water. Averaged over the water column, the photosynthetic rate was 99.6 g $C/m^2/day$ fixed. Similar results were reported by Stross and Stottlemyer (1965) for the Patuxent River. In the latter study and in one of Chesapeake Bay (Flemer, 1970), primary production was highest in the upper estuary when examined volumetrically. Aerially, however, productivity in both studies was higher downstream, probably because the upper stations were deeper than those near the estuary mouth. In the Patuxent River area, mean productivity was 1.2 g $C/m^2/day$ fixed upstream and 1.8 $g/m^2/day$ downstream. In Chesapeake Bay productivity was 0.2 g $C/m^2/day$ fixed in the upper bay and 1.0 $g/m^2/day$ in the lower bay.

When comparing one study with another or analyzing samples taken from different locations or at different times within the same estuary, presenting the information volumetrically may make the most sense. In most cases, whether the data are reported in area or volume, determinations are generally made at a single depth and extrapolated over the water column. To document that sort of extrapolation, information should be obtained from discrete samples taken at various depths throughout the photic zone.

Because of constraints on time and money, samples from several depths are not often obtained. Instead, the 50% light level is frequently selected as the sampling depth of choice, since that depth is generally thought to be representative of the depth of maximum photosynthesis. Studies using a standard light level instead of an arbitrary depth avoid some errors of interpretation caused by different turbidities at a given sampling depth.

One area of marine science intimately related to phytoplankton is the phenomenon of red tides. Red tides are actually intense blooms of dinoflagellates that produce toxins affecting other marine organisms. Red tides are perhaps most common in Florida, but significant problems have arisen in many other areas. Estuarine dinoflagellate blooms of *Gymnodinium* sp. and *Cochlodinium* sp. have been documented in La Jolla Bay, California (Holmes et al., 1967). Blooms of *Gymnodinium* sp. in Georgia occurred in 1955 and 1956 (Ragotzkie and Pomeroy, 1957).

The dinoflagellate *Prorocentrum mariae-lebouriae* has been responsible for outbreaks of red tide in Chesapeake Bay. That alga is present year round in the southern part of the bay in high salinity water. During the summer it has been found to migrate up-estuary to the northern part of the

bay along the bottom, aided by subsurface currents. The organism becomes tolerant to low salinity during the summer, and blooms may lead to
red tide outbreaks in the nothern part of the bay (Tyler and Seliger, 1981).

BENTHIC ALGAE

There are two kinds of benthic diatoms: those that are motile and
those that attach to sedimentary particles (Pomeroy, 1959). Certain diatoms that live within the sediments can migrate vertically to seek the desired light intensity. Sediments rich in diatoms are often brown, while
green sediments may be attributable to chlorophytes. Such blue-green algal genera as *Lyngbya, Microcoleus,* and *Phormidium* may dry intertidally
into hard black or bluish-green crusts at low tide (Peterson and Peterson,
1979). Naturally occurring blue-green algal mats are typically found in
warm water. Shallow coastal areas around the Gulf of Mexico and north-
ward on the Atlantic seaboard to New Jersey support such communities, at
least seasonally (Pomeroy, 1959; Sorenson and Conover, 1962). The formation of blue-green algal mats may also be a response to pollution (Birke,
1974).

Blue-green algal mats have been found in tidal basins, small depres-
sions near shore, and in broad lagoons containing from 1 to 50 cm of water
(Sorenson and Conover, 1962). Most algal mats appear in water less than
10 cm (Odum, 1967). Once a dehydrated blue-green algal mat is rehy-
drated, vigorous photosynthesis can be expected (Sollins, 1969). Such
mats are rich in fatty acids (Parker and Leo, 1965).

Besides the dominant blue-green algae, such organisms as unicellular
green algae, flagellates, diatoms, and pink and purple bacteria may be
present in algal mats (Sorenson and Conover, 1962; Odum et al., 1963).
High concentrations of such bacteria as *Desulfovibrio* and *Beggiatoa* have
been observed (Armstrong and Odum, 1964).

In Texas, blue-green algal mats have been found on sandy shallows
around Baffin and Alazan bays and in the Laguna Madre. Thin water layers
trapped on sand flats support algal mats of *Lyngbya confervoides* (Birke,
1974). Other species present in such mats include *Oscillatoria, Microcoleus, Schizothrix, Phormidium,* and *Anacystis,* though none of them is
generally dominant (Armstrong and Odum, 1964; Odum, 1967).

Turbidity, cloudy weather, and shading out by other species of plants
can limit light penetration and thus benthic algal productivity. Limitations

on benthic algae under stands of *Spartina patens* and *Distichlis spicata* have been reported (Blum, 1968).

Differences in primary productivity of intertidal benthic algae are determined by whether a given site is exposed or is inundated by water (Pomeroy, 1959). At high tide, production of submerged benthic algae in Georgia was 200 mg $C/m^2/hr$ in August and 50 mg $C/m^2/hr$ in winter. At low tide, gross productivity was 150 mg $C/m^2/hr$ in winter and from 20 to 30 mg $C/m^2/hr$ in summer. Pomeroy (1959) concluded that daily production was nearly constant when averaged across the year, with annual gross production being about 200 g C/m^2. The lack of seasonal variation in total benthic algal productivity was supported by Gallagher and Daiber (1974). Those authors, working in Delaware, found that gross algal production was about one-third of that attributable to marshgrasses.

Pomeroy (1959) indicated that net productivity of the benthic algal community was 90% of gross productivity. Coles (1979) found that benthic algal populations were high in salt marshes and in the upper portions of mud flats in Britain but low on sand flats. The small number of algae on sand flats appeared to result from grazing by macroinvertebrates. The most abundant species were motile diatoms, which produce mucus that traps and binds fine sediments. Coles (1979) determined that the accretion of mud on salt marshes can be stopped by eliminating the algae and that such accretion on sand flats can be initiated by removing macroinvertebrates that are feeding upon the algae.

Leach (1970) found that epibenthic algal production in an estuary in Scotland was 31 $g/m^2/yr$. That accounted for about one-third of the mean level of organic carbon present in the sediments. In Boca Ciega, Florida, the relative importance of macrophytes, phytoplankton, and benthic algae appeared to be about equal in water of 2 m or less (Pomeroy, 1960). In deeper water, phytoplankton appeared to be the most important primary producer.

Macrophytic Vegetation

Macrophytes are perhaps most simply defined as macroscopic plants. Most estuarine species are rooted, though some floating species also occur. From upstream, such freshwater species as water hyacinths may move into estuaries, while sargassum weed may drift in from offshore.

Upper estuarine marshlands commonly grade into freshwater marshes. One study of that transition zone was conducted by Philipp and Brown (1965). General references on marsh vegetation include those of Shreve et al. (1910), Johnson and York (1915), Fassett (1929), Taylor (1939), Kurz and Wagner (1957), Chapman (1960), and Reimold and Queen (1974). Studies on macrophytic vegetation around the Gulf of Mexico, including early literature on marshgrasses, mangroves, and shoreline plants, have been reviewed by Thorne (1954). The literature on submerged marsh-grasses, with emphasis on Chesapeake Bay, was analyzed by Stevenson and Confer (1978).

Extensive freshwater marshes above estuaries are most common in areas with large rivers flowing through them (e.g., Chesapeake Bay and the Louisiana marshes). The salt- and freshwater marshes around the mouth of the Mississippi River in Louisiana constitute the largest marsh area of the Gulf of Mexico (Penfound and Hathaway, 1938; Shiflet, 1963; Hoese, 1967). In areas periodically flooded by salt water, *Spartina alterniflora* dominates. In brackish areas the dominant marshgrasses are *Spartina patens, Distichlis spicata*, and *Juncus roemerianus*. At the transition to higher elevations and consequent lower salinity, the marshes become dominated by *S. cynosuroides* and *Phragmites australis*.

FRESHWATER MARSH PLANTS

Elodea canadensis, or elodea, is a typical freshwater marsh species. It is widely used in home aquaria, grows most successfully over a temperature range of 15 to 18 C, and seems to prefer soft sediments over sand (Yeo, 1965). Elodea, which can tolerate only low salinity (Stevenson and Confer, 1978), is found in fairly shallow water, with maximum density at about 3 m (Hutchinson, 1975).

Ceratophyllum demersum, or hornwort, is a freshwater macrophyte found only in warm, nearly tropical climates (Martin and Uhler, 1939). Optimal growth occurs at 30 C, and only minimal growth has been reported at 20 C (Wilkinson, 1963). Bourn (1932) determined that *C. demersum* develops normally at salinities up to 6.5 o/oo. Since it lacks a root system (Stevenson and Confer, 1978), it is not depth limited. Sculthorpe (1967) indicated that the plant is of some use as food for waterfowl.

Najas (*Najas quadalupensis*), or bushy pondweed, is also essentially a freshwater plant. Growth has been reported at 0.17 o/oo salinity (Haller et al., 1974). Najas prefers sandy substrates but can sometimes be found on mud bottoms and is an excellent source of food for waterfowl (Martin and Uhler, 1939).

Another freshwater marsh plant with wide distribution is water celery, and tapegrass (*Vallisneria americana*). The plant grows best between 33 and 36 C, and growth is arrested below 19 C (Wilkinson, 1963). Studies by Bourn (1934) suggest that the species cannot be maintained in the laboratory at salinities below 4.2 o/oo. Ball (1965) indicated that water celery has been used by wildlife managers as food for waterfowl.

Potamogeton (or pondweed), one common species of which is *Potamogeton pectinatus*, germinates and grows when planted at 15 to 18 C (Yeo, 1965). Maximum seed production, germination, and growth of vegetation occur in fresh water. Growth and germination decrease by 50% at 8 to 9 o/oo salinity, though 3 o/oo may stimulate tuber production (Teeter, 1965). Sculthorpe (1967) reported that potamogeton grows best in silt, but it has also been found growing in sand (Rickett, 1923). Pondweed is widely used as food by waterfowl (Martin and Uhler, 1939; Fassett, 1960; Bergman, 1973).

Another species, *P. perfoliatus*, has a broad temperature tolerance and does not die until the temperature reaches 45 C (Anderson, 1969). This pondweed tolerates salinities of 2 to 25 o/oo (Anderson, 1969; Stevenson and Confer, 1978) and appears to prefer still or standing water of 0.6 to 1.5 m depth (Martin and Uhler, 1939), where it is freely consumed by waterfowl.

Myriophyllum spicatum grows over a temperature range of 0.1 to 30 C and has been found growing under 25 cm of ice (Anderson, 1964; Anderson et al., 1965). *Myriophyllum* tolerates salinities of 0 to 20 o/oo (Rawls, 1964) and seems to grow best in soft sediments with high levels of organic matter (Anderson, 1972). Patten (1956) noted that the plant is commonly eaten by waterfowl. *M. spicatum* can absorb iron and calcium from the sediments and can also release those elements (DeMarte and Hartman, 1974).

SUBTIDAL PLANTS

More information exists on the productivity and ecology of eelgrass, *Zostera marina*, than on most other subtidal plants, though eelgrass is not common throughout much of the southeastern Atlantic coastal region. Because the concepts developed from studies on eelgrass beds appear to be generally applicable to other kinds of submerged plants, much of this discussion is focused on *Z. marina*.

The most abundant submerged macrophytes in Mississippi include *Halodule (Diplanthera) wrightii, Cymodocea manatorum, Thalassia testudinum,* and *Ruppia maritima* (Christmas, 1973). Turtlegrass (*T. testudinum*) is also common in Florida, while widgeongrass (*R. maritima*) is found in many estuaries and was reported along with *Halodule beaudettei* and *Halophilia engelmanni* (shoalgrass and halophilia, respectively) in the upper Laguna Madre (Rickner, 1979).

Turtlegrass in Apalachee Bay, Florida, was found to be quantitatively the most important of the thirty-six benthic macrophytes identified (Zimmerman and Livingston, 1976). Measurements of leaf production in south Florida by Wood et al. (1967) and Zieman (1968) averaged 1,500 g/m^2/yr of organic matter production. In south Florida, the leaves of turtlegrass account for only about 10 to 20% of total plant biomass. Between six and eight crops of leaves are produced annually.

T. testudinum appears to have an optimum temperature of about 30 C and an optimum salinity near 30 o/oo (Zieman, 1975). The leaves of the plant do not appear to be heavily grazed upon by most marine organisms but are consumed by certain species of waterfowl and at least a few fishes. The cownose ray (*Rhinoptera bonasus*), common carp (*Cyprinus carpio*), and mute swan (*Cygnus olor*) have been known to uproot or overgraze turtlegrass beds, although not often enough to have a significant impact (Stevenson and Confer, 1978).

Ruppia martima grows in water of 18 to 30 C (Joanen and Glasgow, 1965) and dies when the temperature reaches 45 C (Anderson, 1969). Widgeongrass exhibits a broad tolerance for salinity, from 5 to 40 o/oo (Anderson, 1972). The plant appears to prefer soft, muddy substrates (Anderson, 1972) and has shown optimum productivity in the laboratory in water 60 cm deep (Joanen and Glasgow, 1965). *R. maritima* is eaten by ducks, coots, geese, swans, marsh birds, and shore birds (Martin and Uhler, 1939; Sculthorpe, 1967).

Eelgrass thrives along the Atlantic coast of the United States as far south as North Carolina. The species can tolerate salinities from 8 to 35 o/oo (Phillips, 1974) but grows best in the range of 10 to 30 o/oo. Eelgrass can withstand temperatures as low as −6 C (Biebel and McRoy, 1971) and as high as 40 C for short periods but grows best from 10 to 20 C (Thayer et al., 1975b). In North Carolina, eelgrass and the attached epiphytic algae showed similar trends in seasonal production (Penhale, 1977). Both had their highest standing crops in March, with a general decline during the remainder of the year. Mean biomass was 105.0 g/m^2 dry weight, with 80.3 g/m^2 attributable to eelgrass and the rest to the epiphytes. Thayer et al. (1975b) indicated that the roots of eelgrass are important in binding sedimentary particles and that the leaves retard currents and stimulate sedimentation.

McRoy and Barsdate (1970) and McRoy et al. (1978), have analyzed the rate at which phosphorus is absorbed and the cycling of phosphorus in eelgrass communities. Phosphorus absorption was found to be greatest in the light. The element was first taken into the plant through both the leaves and the roots; once absorbed, it was rapidly transported to all parts of the plant. McRoy and Barsdate (1970) reported that eelgrass could remove phosphorus from both the water and the sediments. They also determined that some phosphorus was returned to the water by the grass, indicating that eelgrass may be both a sink and a source of that nutrient in estuaries. McRoy et al. (1972) found that eelgrass could absorb as much as 166 mg $P/m^2/day$ from sediments, of which 104 $mg/m^2/day$ were assimilated and 62 $mg/m^2/day$ were excreted into the water.

Ammonia, nitrate, and nitrite are translocated from the roots of *Z. marina* after absorption (McRoy and Goering, 1974). The same authors demonstrated that those forms of nitrogen are also excreted by eelgrass.

Studies on the macrofauna in eelgrass beds have established that the amount of energy consumed by heterotrophic organisms within a bed may amount to 55% of the net production of the eelgrass, benthic algae, and phytoplankton produced in the bed (Thayer et al., 1975a). Eelgrass does not enter the food web directly but becomes important only as detritus (Thayer et al., 1975b).

MANGROVES

Mangroves generally are found only between the latitudes 25° N and 25° S. On the east coast of Africa, in Australia, and in New Zealand, they often extend another 10 to 15° farther south and may have an even greater southward range in Japan (Kuenzler, 1974). In the United States, the most extensive mangrove swamps are in Florida, where they cover over 200,000 ha (Craighead, 1964). Extensive mangrove communities also occur in Puerto Rico.

Mangrove communities in Florida consist of the red mangrove (*Rhizophora mangle*), white mangrove (*Laguncularia racemosa*), and black mangrove (*Avicennia germinans*). In some mangrove communities, the buttonwood, or button mangrove (*Conocarpus erectus*), also grows. Habitat preference by mangroves is based upon temperature and tolerance for wave energy. Mangroves can be found on nearly any kind of substrate, including rocks (if there are cracks where the roots can penetrate). Most Florida mangroves grow in either calcereous or siliceous sands (Kuenzler, 1974).

Cold appears to be the major impediment to the growth and survival of mangroves. They may be found in tidal ranges of from less than 0.33 m in Puerto Rico (Biebl, 1962) to over 3 m in Australia (Macnae, 1967). Mangroves tolerate wide ranges in salinity and may thrive where salinity limits the development of competing plant species (Kuenzler, 1974). The transpiration rate in mangroves is low compared with other plants (Scholander et al., 1962). That may be partly due to the mangrove leaves, which have a heavily cutinized epidermis and lack stomata on the upper surface (Bowman, 1917).

Mangroves provide a habitat for a variety of organisms, including waterfowl. They are also beneficial to man, since the plants may diminish hurricane damage (Davis, 1940). Although the mangroves may be defoliated, broken, or even swept away during a major storm, damage to structures and other living organisms is often reduced when mangroves are present (Craighead and Gilbert, 1962). Red mangrove seedlings sprout in marl soil below the tide line and generally form the seaward band of the mangrove community. They have arching prop roots and long, slender seeds that germinate before dropping from the tree.

Black mangroves grow farther inland on flats that are flooded only during high tide. They have characteristic aerial roots called pneumatophores. Nearby are buttonwood communities, which are transitional between other species of mangroves and either tropical forests or sawgrass (*Mariscus jamaicensis*). Buttonwoods are often found with needle rush (*Juncus roemerianus*). White mangroves appear in all zones but are usually not dominant (Davis, 1940).

The mangrove communities of Florida are visited by various animal species of economic importance, including menhaden, mullet, spotted seatrout, snook, tarpon, red drum, mangrove snapper, pompano, and pink shrimp (Tabb and Yokel, 1968). Idyll (1965) indicated that pink shrimp use mangrove-dominated estuaries as nursery grounds.

According to Odum (1970a), the food web in Florida mangrove communities is based upon vascular plant detritus derived mainly from the leaves of red mangroves. Turtlegrass is also present and contributes to the detritus-based food web (Heald and Odum, 1969). Degradation of leaves and the enrichment of the resulting detritus with fungi, bacteria, and protozoans provide food for higher organisms. Of 120 species examined by Odum and Heald (1975), about one-third were detritus consumers (having at least 20% detritus in their digestive tracts).

The production of mangrove leaves in the North River estuary system of the Florida Everglades was found to exceed 800 g/m^2/yr of dry matter (Heald and Odum, 1969). The same study also determined that within 6 mo of leaf fall, over 30% of the leaves were removed by scavengers, among which the snail (*Melampus* sp.) and crab (*Rhithropanopeus harrissi*) were shown to ingest newly deposited plant detritus (Odum et al., 1972). Algae growing near mangroves may also be important to community metabolism and productivity, but the extent of their importance and that of phytoplankton to total primary productivity have not been well documented.

Although plant diversity is usually low around mangroves, many animal species can be found. The most important benthic species appear to be crustaceans and molluscs, most of which are either deposit or filter feeders (Kuenzler, 1974). Crabs on the intertidal flats of mangrove islands in Florida Bay include *Uca pugilator, U. speciosa, U. thayeri,* and *Eurytium liosum*. Above high water such crabs as *Aratus pisonii, Sesarma curacacense,* and *S. reticulatum* are abundant (Tabb et al., 1962). The barnacle, *Balanus eburneus,* and coon oyster, *Ostrea frons,* are also commonly found near mangrove roots (Kuenzler, 1974). The American oyster, *Crassostrea virginica,* is important in Florida Bay (Tabb et al., 1962). Snails that browse on the roots and surface of mangroves include the genera *Cerithium, Melogena, Cypraea,* and *Littorina* (Davis, 1940; Tabb et al., 1962). Davis (1940) reported such vertebrates as turtles, crocodiles, alligators, bears, wildcats, pumas, and rats. A variety of amphipods, isopods, and fishes also live in mangrove communities.

INTERTIDAL MARSHGRASSES

The dominant species of marshgrasses along the coasts of the forty-eight contiguous states are members of the genus *Spartina*. Along the Atlantic and the Gulf of Mexico, smooth cordgrass and salt meadow cordgrass (*S. alterniflora* and *S. patens*, respectively) are the most common. The former is an intertidal species, and the latter grows at elevations only infrequently wetted by salt water. On the Pacific coast, the dominant plant in the lower intertidal zone is *S. foliosa* (Munz and Keck, 1959). Along the coasts of the southeastern United States and the Gulf of Mexico alone, there are approximately 2.25×10^6 ha of marshland (Thorne, 1954).

Even the casual observer of marshes along the coasts of South Carolina and Georgia gets the impression that a tremendous amount of primary production is present. Odum (1959) compared the productivity of Georgia marshes with other kinds of vegetation. The net production of *Spartina*, 3,300 g/m^2/yr, was exceeded only by such phenomena as mass algae culture and forest plantations. The production of wheat, oats, corn, rice, hay, and sugar beets was below that of *Spartina*, while marshgrass production was similar to that of Hawaii sugarcane. When compared with the world average for the production of sugarcane, marshgrass was over twice as productive.

Despite a great deal of information on the productivity of *S. alterniflora*, only limited data have been collected on such species as *S. patens*, *S. cynosuroides* (big cordgrass), *Phragmites australis* (reedgrass), *Zizaniopsis miliacea* (giant cutgrass), *Distichlis spicata* (saltgrass), *Eleocharis* spp. (spikerushes), *Panicum regens* (dogtoothgrass), and *Fimbristylis spadicea* (fimbristylis). Examples of irregularly flooded marshes dominated by *S. patens* and *D. spicata* can be found in such places as Pamlico Sound, North Carolina; Cedar Key to Apalachee Bay, Florida; and near the mouth of the Mississippi River (Marshall, 1974). In North Carolina, irregularly flooded marshes cover an area of about 82,000 ha, while the regularly flooded ones cover only about 23,000 ha (Wilson, 1962).

As one moves upstream, *S. alterniflora* becomes less and less abundant and is replaced by *J. roemerianus* and *D. spicata*. Finally, marsh species give way to freshwater macrophytes (Cooper, 1974). In some instances, *S. alterniflora* is first replaced by *S. patens*, or the latter grass may appear above the *Juncus* marsh (Waits, 1967).

Although the upper elevation of *S. alterniflora* appears to be a good marker of mean high water, that is not necessarily the case. In a study by Lagna (1975) the two items were not correlated, and the author concluded that other factors influenced the elevation at which *Spartina* would colonize. Regardless, the general pattern of macrophytic growth in estuaries is relatively well defined by the tides, as indicated in figure 15.

Stalter and Batson (1969) recognized two forms of *S. alterniflora*: a dwarf or short form, which occupies the upper intertidal part of the marsh, and a tall form, which grows in the lower intertidal zone along the creek and riverbanks. A medium form is also recognized by some authors. The short and tall forms of smooth cordgrass appear distinct enough to be considered races, if not subspecies.

Teal (1962) reported that 20% of the marsh associated with Sapelo Island, Georgia, was composed of tall form *S. alterniflora*. He also noted that 45% of the area was colonized by the short form of the grass together with *Salicornia* sp. Medium *S. alterniflora*, Teal concluded, covered 35% of the marshland. In a similar study, Cooper (1974) reported that the marshes in Brunswick County, North Carolina, consisted of 6% tall, 11% medium, and 47% short form *S. alterniflora*. *J. roemerianus* occupied 9% of the area, with creeks making up 27%.

J. roemerianus grows from Maryland to Texas (Gleason and Cronquist, 1963). It has been reported from 1.2 to 43.3 o/oo salinity but is best developed in a range from 5 to 20 o/oo (Penfound and Hathaway, 1938). Stalter (1968) found that the interstitial water in a *Juncus* marsh ranged from 1 to 26 o/oo.

Succulents of the genus *Salicornia* generally grow above high tide. Yet growth of such species as *S. bigelovii* and *S. herbacea* is optimum when interstitial salt concentration is at or above 1% as NaCl (van Eijk, 1939; Baumeister and Schmidt, 1962). At salt levels above optimum, root and shoot growth are impaired (Webb, 1966).

Two groups of insects feed on marshgrass, according to Kraeuter and Wolf (1974). One group feeds on the living plant tissues, while the other takes over once the grass dies back and begins to enter the detritus food web. Most estimates indicate that direct feeding on living plant tissues involves no more than 10% of total production.

The area occupied by estuarine macrophytes has been found to correlate directly with the production of commercially important species of

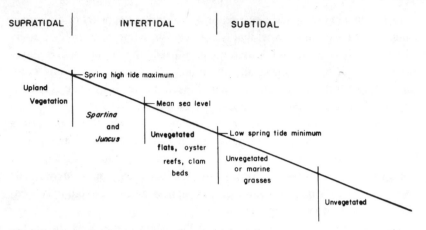

Fig. 15. Macrophyte vegetation zones in a typical estuary. (Adapted from Miller, W. R., and F. E. Egler. 1950. Vegetation of the Wequetequok-Pawcatuck tidal marshes, Connecticut. *Ecol. Monogr.* 20: 141–72.)

shrimp (Turner, 1977). Inshore yields of shrimp were directly related to the area occupied by estuarine intertidal macrophytes but were not correlated with total area, average depth, or volume of the estuary.

Annual net production of *S. alterniflora* apparently decreases with latitude (Cooper, 1974). Turner and Gosselink (1975) demonstrated that late summer live biomass of *S. alterniflora* in eight Texas and Florida marshes was equivalent to or slightly greater than that of the north Atlantic coast. They also found that the dead plant biomass in the southern region was considerably higher. The longer growing season in the South may lead to a disparity in annual production between the two regions.

While reviewing studies of marsh production, Keefe (1972) determined that *S. alterniflora* averaged 445 to 3,300 g/m^2/yr dry weight, while *S. patens* and *J. roemerianus* averaged 1,296 and between 849 and 1,360 g/m^2/yr, respectively. That study considered only net production of the aboveground biomass. In the same review, the author determined that the production of aerial *S. cynosuroides* averaged 1,456 g/m^2/yr, with a range of 1,000 to 2,000 g/m^2/yr. Keefe (1972) reported that the production of *S. townsendii* ranges from 700 to 1,060 g/m^2/yr. Turner (1976) reviewed the literature on marshgrass production and included estimates for *D. spicata* ranging from 603 to 985 g/m^2/yr.

Differences between production in tall and short form *S. alterniflora* have been noted. The short form ranges from 500 to 1,000 g/m^2/yr dry weight; the tall form, from 1,100 to over 3,000 g/m²/yr. Mann and Chapman (1975) reported that marshgrasses may produce from 200 to 1,000 g C/m² annually in tropical waters, while turtlegrass produces from 500 to 1,500 g C/m²/yr. Thus, under some circumstances submerged vegetation may contribute more to production than do intertidal grasses, on a unit area basis. The relative areas colonized by each group, along with productivity per unit area, will determine the absolute contribution of each to overall primary production.

Latitude also affects the annual production of marshgrasses. In Nova Scotia, near the northern extreme of its range, the production of aboveground *S. alterniflora* was reported to be 710 g/m²/yr dry weight (Hatcher and Mann, 1975). For New England marshes, the tall form of *S. alterniflora* averages 840 g/m²/yr; the short form, only 432 g/m²/yr. Those values are similar to ones reported from New York marshes but are somewhat less than many in the southern United States (Nixon and Oviatt, 1973).

Williams and Murdoch (1969) reported the production of *S. alterniflora* near Beaufort, North Carolina, as 650 g/m²/yr dry weight or 248 g/m²/yr of carbon fixed. Those values were calculated to be about one-third of phytoplankton production. The marshes of Georgia have been shown to produce as much as 3,300 g/m²/yr dry weight (Odum, 1959). Schelske and Odum (1962) outlined several reasons for the high productivity of these marshes: (1) ebb and flow of tidal water; (2) abundant supply of nutrients; (3) rapid regeneration and conservation of the available nutrients; (4) availability of three kinds of primary producers (marshgrasses, phytoplankton, and benthic algae), resulting in efficient use of available light; and (5) year-round production because of the successive crops.

Gabriel and de la Cruz (1974) found that maximum production of the Bay Saint Louis, Mississippi, was 1,051 g/m²/yr dry weight. The marshes examined contained thirty-four species of plants, dominated by *J. roemerianus, S. cynosuroides, Scirpus americanus* and *D. spicata*. Louisiana marshes, dominated by *S. alterniflora*, produce up to 2,960 g/m²/yr of dry weight biomass in areas immediately adjacent to the creeks and 1,484 g/m²/yr inland from the creek banks (Day et al., 1973). In another Louisiana study, net aboveground production of *S. alterniflora* ranged from 750 to 2,600 g/m²/yr (Kirby and Gosselink, 1976).

Some investigators have tried to place a monetary value on salt marshes. Gosselink et al. (1974) claimed that total social values attributable to marshes ranged from $125,000 to $200,000/ha. Inflation since the time of that study would greatly increase those figures. Included in that assessed value were such items as fisheries production, use in tertiary treatment of nutrient-rich wastes, and proposed intensive uses for such activities as oyster culture.

Considerable debate has arisen over the actual value of marshes—not only in dollars, but as a place of beauty and as a contributor to secondary productivity. As indicated by Nixon (1980), the debate has not only been complex but, as in all issues of this nature, it has been emotional. As is commonly true, a resolution to the satisfaction of the majority with minimum damage to the environment lies somewhere between the extremes of strict protectionism and wanton destructionism. It may not be necessary to prove conclusively the monetary or biological value of marshes in order to obtain a consensus to preserve them as far as possible. In that regard, the words of Nixon (1980, p. 508) are compelling:

I do not know if salt marshes are really important for waterfowl or mammals, or as sources of sulfur dioxide, or as storm buffers, or for a host of other possible reasons. They are important to me and to many other people who enjoy looking across the sweep and green openness of them, who like to walk out across them and observe their patterns of life and form. And these are not trivial reasons for maintaining that the marshes are important.

The propagation of *S. alterniflora* in nature has become important recently as man has begun to establish marshlands on bare intertidal areas. Although it is well known that smooth cordgrass produces seedheads in the fall, it is also widely acknowledged that a primary means of propagation is by rhizomes. Rhizomes are essentially roots that extend laterally from the parent plant. As the rhizomes grow, they in turn send up new aboveground vegetation. Rapid colonization of a large area from a fairly small number of planted sprigs can result, and this method has been the most successful among attempts to recolonize marshlands on bare areas of suitable elevation (Webb et al., 1978).

Examination of the seedheads of mature *Spartina* has repeatedly indicated that only a few viable seeds are present (Chapman, 1960; Larimer, 1968). Early attempts at storage and subsequent germination of the seeds met with only limited success, but recently developed techniques have helped achieve relatively high percentages of germination. On the Pacific coast it was found that the seeds of *S. foliosa* can be stored in estuarine water for twenty-one weeks at appropriate temperatures and that they would later germinate when exposed to an alternating 20 to 35 C temperature cycle (Seneca, 1974). Germination of seeds after dry storage or storage in demineralized water was not as successful.

In a similar study, 52% of the seeds of *S. alterniflora* germinated when exposed to an 18 to 35 C diurnal thermal regime after storage for eight months in seawater (Mooring, 1970). Dry seeds stored in the same manner did not remain viable. Cooper (1974) reported that germination of marshgrasses, in general, seems best in fresh water and concluded that germination in nature may occur during periods of high rainfall at low tide.

Increased growth of *S. alterniflora* after the addition of fertilizer has been demonstrated (Broome et al., 1975b; Webb et al., 1978), suggesting nutrient limitations in at least some salt marshes. It has also been established that tissue concentrations of several nutrients and soil properties are correlated with variations in the height and yield of *S. alterniflora* (Broome et al., 1975a).

Teal (1962) proposed the theory that estuaries are a major source of organic matter in coastal waters. That concept was later extended by other researchers to nutrients, trace metals, and a few other substances. Nixon (1980) discussed the commonly held belief that marshes act as nutrient traps. This theory he noted was confounded by E. P. Odum (1968), who indicated that estuaries are outwelling sources of nutrients and organic matter and are thus important to the maintenance of coastal fisheries. Odum (1979) later modified this statement to identify his opinion on outwelling as a hypothesis, not a proven fact. Nixon (1980) suggested that the outwelling hypothesis, which had been accepted by many in the scientific community, was based upon virtually no empirical data. Recent data have been collected supporting the opposite conclusions—that salt marshes, in fact, contribute little organic matter to coastal waters (Haines and Dunstan, 1975; Haines, 1975, 1976a, 1976b, 1979).

Nutrient fluxes in estuaries are also somewhat problematical, though one widely held view is that marshes act as sinks for nutrients. Nixon (1980) reported that fluxes are most easily measured by multiplying the difference in concentration of a nutrient between flood and ebb tides by the volume of water exchanged between the tidal extremes. Although Nixon's method is superficially simple, such things as tidal asymmetries compound the calculation so that, at best, the numbers derived are only rough approximations.

Some data do indicate that salt marshes contribute certain substances to coastal waters. Settlemyre and Gardner (1975) concluded that SiO_2 and PO_4 are exported from marshes. There is also evidence that marshes act as sinks for trace metals and other elements. According to Nixon (1980), the literature supports the contention that Pb, Cu, Zn, Fe, and Mn accumulate in marshes (Pb and Cu being mainly derived from the atmosphere).

One paradox in the literature is the apparent unconcern among some experts that marshes are simultaneously considered both traps and exporters of nutrients and minerals. According to one theory, phosphorus is rapidly removed from the water in marshes and stored in sediments and plants for a while before being exported from the marsh in detritus and living organisms (Pomeroy et al., 1967). This temporary storage and later release provides one possible explanation of how fluxes might occur, but not all cases are as easily rectified.

After careful review of the literature on nutrient fluxes in estuaries, Nixon (1980) concluded: (1) marshes export dissolved organic nitrogen; (2) marshes export dissolved phosphorus; and (3) marshes appear to be sinks for nitrate and nitrite, but the status of ammonia is unclear.

Bacteria and Fungi

Bacteria and fungi play major roles in the formation of detritus. When plants or parts of plants die, they quickly decompose through a combination of mechanical and microorganism-related activities. Thereafter, the small pieces of detritus that are formed may be eaten by herbivores, thus cycling nutrients into the consumer food web by a somewhat circuitous route.

Both bacteria and fungi are important in the decomposition of all organic matter. This discussion therefore not only relates to the formation of plant detritus but offers a brief overview of estuarine microbiology. The amount of information available on estuarine fungi is limited; thus, beyond recognizing that fungi are important members of the decomposer food web, little mention of them is possible.

It is well known that the standing crops of both bacteria and fungi are higher in sediments containing small grains than in those made up of larger particles. Dale (1974) found that the numbers of bacteria are also related to other sediment properties. Organic carbon and total nitrogen levels in the sediments, for example, were found to be positively correlated with bacterial counts. Some bacteria have been shown to extract nutrients from the water column and appear able to use organic matter.

Microorganisms are vital in breaking down cellulose and lignins, which are largely undigestible by higher organisms. Bacteria and fungi colonize not only detritus particles but also fecal pellets and increase the nutritional content of the pellets for coprophagous species. There is some conflict about whether higher animals feeding on detritus obtain their primary nourishment from the detritus or from the microorganisms that have colonized the particle (Fenchel, 1970; Adams and Angelovic, 1970). It seems reasonable to assume that a detritus particle heavily colonized by decomposers and allied organisms will have more nutritional value than one lacking such a community.

Zobell and Feltham (1942) showed that natural levels of bacteria in water from Mission Bay, California, ranged from several thousand to a few million bacteria per milliliter, while levels in the sediments reached several million bacteria per gram. In contrast, water flowing into the bay contained only a few hundred bacteria per milliliter. The same study reported that sediment bacteria decreased exponentially with depth to about 5 m, below which no living organisms were found. Unpolluted marine waters normally exhibit their highest bacterial levels at the sediment surface. Rublee and Dornseif (1978) found that cell numbers in a North Carolina salt marsh decreased from a range of 8.36 to 10.90×10^9 cells/cm^3 at the sediment surface to a range of 2.19 to 2.58×10^9 cells/cm^3 at a depth of 20 cm. Those authors found no differences between subtidal and intertidal patterns.

With respect to bacterial levels in the water, Fehon and Oliver (1979) found that bacterial density of the surface microlayer was 130 to 5,000 times higher than that in the underlying water. Studies leading to similar results were conducted by Sieburth (1971) and Crow et al. (1975). Levels of bacteria in the water column appear to be highest within the photic zone. Measurements of adenosine triphosphate (ATP) production over a range of salinity from 11.5 to 32.7 o/oo by Weiland et al. (1979) showed little effect of salinity on bacterial concentration.

Pathogenic bacteria are a real or potential problem in many estuaries. *Vibrio parahaemolyticus*, a major cause of gastroenteritis in man, has been isolated from white shrimp (*Penaeus setiferus*) in Galveston Bay, Texas, and has been found toxic to brown shrimp (*P. aztecus*) from the same area (Vanderzant et al., 1970). The same bacterium was isolated from thirty-nine of sixty-six oysters sampled in Galveston Bay (Vanderzant et al., 1973). Other studies on pathogenic bacteria in estuaries indicate that such organisms as *Clostridium botulinum*, *V. parahaemolyticus*, fecal streptococci, and fecal coliforms survive much longer than was once thought. In addition, certain bacteria are resistant to heavy metals and antibiotics (Colwell and Kaper, 1978). The resistance to seawater reported by some scientists relates, at least in the case of coliform bacteria, to BOD. When BOD ranges from 1 to 10 mg/l, seawater is at least temporarily less toxic to coliforms (Savage and Hanes, 1971). Where sufficient nutrients were present, the same authors found that both total and fecal coliform levels actually increased in seawater.

Oyster beds in various areas have been closed to fishing because of contamination by pathogenic bacteria. In a study of bacteria associated with the clam, *Rangia cuneata*, a species with human food potential, Comar et al. (1979) found that plate counts were generally higher than for other species of shellfish. Potentially pathogenic bacteria of the genera *Salmonella, Shigella, Vibrio,* and *Staphylococcus* were recovered at low levels. The small numbers of pathogenic bacteria and near compliance with current coliform standards were cited by the authors as evidence that no unique health problem was present in *R. cuneata*. Monitoring would be warranted, however, if the clam became more widely used as human food. Such monitoring is currently being conducted on other seafoods.

The Role of Detritus

The view proposed and elaborated upon by Odum (1962, 1963), Teal (1962), and Odum and de la Cruz (1963, 1967) that detritus forms the base of the food chain in estuaries was not challenged until recently. The extensive salt marshes of Georgia led to the development of the theory, and the expansiveness of those marshes strengthens the concept that grass is important in the food web. The death of aboveground cordgrass biomass each fall, forming large windrows of dead and decaying leaves and stems (wrack), also proves that large amounts of nutrients are being recycled. Reidenbaugh and Banta (1980) tracked the movements of tidal *S. alterniflora* wrack in a Virginia salt marsh and found that the material may become stranded in the high marsh, where it will decompose; it may, on the other hand, become temporarily fixed at lower elevations. The dead material eventually decays through mechanical and microbiological means and becomes detritus of small particle sizes.

The importance of detritus in estuarine food webs has been extended by various authors from the expansive marshes of the southeastern Atlantic coast to mangrove communities, to submerged estuaries dominated by grass beds, and to estuaries with little macrophytic vegetation. The detritus theory has been so dominant over the past several years that the relative roles of phytoplankton and benthic algae have been largely ignored.

A review of recent literature on the subject reveals that the classic view of detritus in estuarine food webs is simplistic. As discussed by Christian and Wetzel (1978), the number of microorganisms that are attached to detritus particles is small relative to the number that are not. The maximum conversion efficiency of microbes is about 60% but drops to about 20% as the complexity of the microbial community increases. Although this line of reasoning is not overwhelmingly convincing, it does bring into question the importance of detritus. Even while the theory was gaining widespread acceptance, Darnell (1967) was pointing out that information on the role of detritus in estuarine food webs was inferred, with few data to support the theory.

According to Odum et al. (1972), the degradation of plant material is as follows: (1) there is a loss of soluble components to the water, (2) microorganisms colonize the dead material, and (3) the particles become fragmented through mechanical processes. The rate of decomposition of marsh plants into detritus is often measured with the litter bag technique. That is, plant material is placed in a mesh bag, and the rate of loss of material from the bag is measured. A summary of studies on losses from litter bags (Gulf South Research Institute, 1977) indicated that the decrease was 50 to 96% annually for *S. alterniflora*, 35 to 47% for *J. roemerianus*, and 38 to 53% for *D. spicata*. Mangrove leaves fell within the range of 38 to 53%. The mesh size of the bag will affect the loss rate, as do the texture and fiber strength of the plants, the time intervals between measurements, the species of plant, the latitude from which the plants were collected, and various environmental conditions.

Many studies have focused on the rate of decomposition of smooth cordgrass and other marsh plants, with or without use of the litter bag technique. May (1974) determined that the microbial decomposition of dead *Spartina* in Georgia is the result of attack by fungi, although macroinvertebrates were also implicated in the degradation process. In another Georgia study, Reimold et al. (1975) measured changes in the amount of detritus at four-week intervals. Detritus production (areal rate of disappearance) was calculated. The average standing crop of dead material was highest in *J. roemerianus* and lowest in the short form of *S. alterniflora*. The areal rate of disappearance of detritus averaged 7 mg/g/day for tall form *S. alterniflora* and 18 mg/g/day for the short form. The rate of disappearance of *J. roemerianus* detritus was the same as that of the tall form of smooth cordgrass. The average monthly production of detritus by tall form *S. alterniflora* (197.9 g/m^2) was significantly greater than for the short form (113.6 g/m^2). The average monthly production of detritus by *J. roemerianus* (188.4 g/m^2) was also significantly greater than that of short form *S. alterniflora* but not significantly different from that of the tall form of the cordgrass. Mean annual detritus production was found to be 1,845.8 g/m^2.

In another study to determine the rate at which *S. alterniflora* decomposes, stems and leaves were ground, dried, and separated into four size fractions (Gosselink and Kirby, 1974). The samples were then incubated in the dark at 30 C in artificial seawater, and decomposition was followed for thirty days. The efficiency with which microorganisms converted the substrate into microbial biomass was found to range from 28 to over 60%, with efficiency decreasing as particle size increased.

Studies of the fatty acid composition of *S. alterniflora* at monthly intervals in Narragansett Bay, Rhode Island, led Schultz and Quinn (1973) to conclude that both aerobic and anaerobic processes are important in the formation of detritus. Proximate nutritive values of other marshgrasses have been computed to evaluate how the plants change during decomposition (de la Cruz, 1975). Evaluations of *S. cynosuroides, D. spicata,* and *Scirpus americanus* in Mississippi showed that the plants retained 60 to 70% of their organic content during decomposition. The caloric level within the plants either remained constant or rose slightly. Crude fiber, carbohydrate, and lipid levels declined, but protein increased from 96 to 300% during the transition to detritus.

Decomposition of *J. roemerianus* leaves in a litter bag was found by de la Cruz and Gabriel (1974) to be 40% annually. Caloric, elemental, and proximate nutritive analyses at various stages during the life and decay of the plants revealed the following temporal changes: (1) an increase in caloric content; (2) a decrease in carbon, nitrogen, and phosphorus, and (3) a decrease in crude fiber, carbohydrate, protein, and lipid.

Other macrophytic ecosystems have also been examined. Odum and Heald (1975) constructed a model of the detritus food web in Florida mangrove communities, and Fenchel (1970) showed that samples of detritus coming primarily from turtlegrass harbored large numbers of microorganisms. The *T. testidinum* samples were found to contain 3×10^9 bacteria, 5×10^7 flagellates, 5×10^4 ciliates, and 2×10^7 diatoms per gram dry weight.

In a laboratory experiment run on dead eelgrass, Harrison and Mann (1975) discovered that the leaves lost a maximum of 35% of their original dry biomass in 100 days at 20 C. Leaching accounted for 82% of the loss. Bacteria were found to only slowly degrade the leaf material, but the rate of degradation increased when protozoans were present.

Estimates suggest that less than 5% of living estuarine macrophytes are consumed by herbivores (Smalley, 1959; Heald, 1969). Among the organisms that do eat living macrophytes are the insects *Orchelimum* (which eats living *S. alterniflora*) and *Prokelisia* (which consumes the juices of marshgrasses). Those insects in turn support spiders, wrens, and sparrows (Teal, 1962). Cattle will consume *S. patens*, and sheep and goats will graze on various marshgrasses. Once the plants have died and begun the transition to microscopic particles of detritus, consumption increases by organisms more complex than bacteria, fungi, and protozoans.

Some of the most compelling information about the sources of detritus in salt marshes stems from examination of carbon isotope ratios. Haines (1976a, 1976b, 1977) analyzed the ratios between carbon-12 and carbon-13 in marshes, concluding that the main function of the ratios is to indicate the source of the carbon in an estuary. That is, the ratio of the two isotopes can be used to determine if the carbon source was from vascular plants (e.g., *S. alterniflora*) or algae. She estimated that phytoplankton production is about 770 g/m^2/yr and that terrestrial detritus contributes about 600 g/m^2/yr. Those inputs are about the same magnitude as that of *Spartina*.

Energy transfer up the food chain from detritus is accomplished by myriad organisms. Odum et al. (1972) concluded that amphipods, mysids, cumacea, ostracods, chironomidae, harpacticoid and planktonic copepods, snapping shrimp, crabs, filter-feeding bivalves, and several species of shrimp are direct consumers of detritus. Besides being consumed by higher animals, the feces of detritus consumers may be eaten by coprophagous species. In general, the group of organisms that consumes detritus is composed of few species but contains many individuals.

Some fishes have been regularly found with fairly high proportions of detritus in their digestive tracts. Among them, the striped mullet, *Mugil cephalus*, is perhaps the best documented. Odum (1970b) determined that striped mullet feed either by ingesting the surface layer of the sediment or by grazing on submerged hard surfaces. Major stomach contents of mullet include algae, decaying plant detritus, and inorganic sediment particles. Odum (1970b) showed that given the choice between living plants and detritus, the fish would select the living material almost exclusively. This may indicate that detritus was present incidentally as an accident of feeding behavior. Mullet appear to prefer fine to coarse particles, which may result from the relative richness of microorganisms on particles of various sizes (W. E. Odum, 1968).

There is considerable evidence that invertebrates feed on detritus. Darnell (1961, 1964) reported that organic detritus is a conspicuous item in the food habits of a variety of macroinvertebrates in Lake Pontchartrain, Louisiana. Adams and Angelovic (1970) examined the assimilation of carbon-14–labelled detritus by the gastropod *Bittium varium*, the grass shrimp *Palaemonetes pugio*, and the polychaete *Glycera dibranchiata*. All three were found to assimilate the bacteria associated with detritus. The general information available on the nutritive value of detritus for benthic organisms was reviewed by Tenore (1977).

With respect to the feeding of invertebrates on detritus derived from submerged macrophytes, it has been shown that the amphipod *Parhyalella whelpleyi* consumes *T. testudinum* detritus (Fenchel, 1970) as well as the fecal pellets of its own species. Fenchel postulated that the amphipod obtains nutrients from the microorganisms within the detritus but does not use the macrophytic particles themselves. In south Florida, the primary sources of detritus are the leaves of the red mangrove and turtlegrass (Heald and Odum, 1969).

Among the copepods, the calnoid *Eurytemora affinis* appears to be largely supported by detritus (Heinle et al., 1973). In contrast, the harpacticoid copepod *Scottolana canadensis* was less able to use detritus and associated microorganisms as an energy source.

In conclusion, considerable evidence shows not only that estuarine organisms consume detritus but that they also derive at least some nutrition thereby. The contribution of detritus as a direct source of food energy for vertebrates and invertebrates remains somewhat clouded, though several investigators have claimed that detritus is extremely important and that it, in fact, supports much of the secondary productivity within estuaries. Recent evidence suggests that while detritus is important in estuarine food webs, the influences of phytoplankton and benthic algae should not be overlooked—in some cases, they may be more significant than detritus.

LITERATURE CITED

Adams, S. M., and J. W. Angelovic. 1970. Assimilation of detritus and its associated bacteria by 3 species of estuarine animals. *Ches. Sci.* 11: 249–54.

Anderson, R. R. 1964. Ecology and mineral nutrition of *Myriophyllum spicatum* (L.). M.S. thesis, University of Maryland, College Park.

———. 1969. Temperature and rooted aquatic plants. *Ches. Sci.* 10: 157–64.

———. 1972. Submerged vascular plants of the Chesapeake Bay and tributaries. *Ches. Sci.* 13 (suppl.): S87–89.

Anderson, R. R., R. G. Brown, and R. D. Rappleye. 1965. Mineral composition of Eurasian watermilfoil, *Myriophyllum spicatum*. *Ches. Sci.* 6: 68–72.

Armstrong, N. E., and H. T. Odum. 1964. Photoelectric system. *Science* 143: 256–58.

Ball, E. W. 1965. Waterfowl habitat management. *Proc. Southern Weed Conf.* 17: 308–14.

Baumeister, W., and L. Schmidt. 1962. Über die Rolle des Natrium in pflanzlichen Stoffwechsel. *Flora* 152: 24–56.

Bergman, R. D. 1973. Use of boreal lakes by postbreeding canvasbacks and redheads. *J. Wildl. Man.* 37: 160–70.

Biebl, R. 1962. Protoplasmatisch-okologische Untersuchungen an Mangrovealgen von Puerto Rico. *Protoplasma* 55: 572–606.

Biebl, R., and C. P. McRoy. 1971. Plasmitic resistance and rate of respiration and photosynthesis of *Zostera marina* at different salinities and temperatures. *Mar. Biol.* 8: 48–56.

Birke, L. 1974. Marine blue-green algal mats, pp. 331–45. In: H. T. Odum, B. J. Copeland, and E. A. McMahan, eds. *Coastal ecological systems of the United States.* Vol. I. Washington, D.C.: Conservation Foundation.

Blum, J. L. 1968. Salt marsh spartinas and associated algae. *Ecol. Monogr.* 38: 119–221.

Bourn, W. S. 1932. Ecological and physiological studies on certain aquatic angiosperms. *Cont. Boyce Thompson Inst.* 4: 425–96.

———. 1934. Sea-water tolerance of *Vallisneria spiralis* L. and *Potamogeton foliosus. Cont. Boyce Thompson Inst.* 6: 303–308.

Bowman, H. H. M. 1917. Ecology and physiology of the red mangrove. *Amer. Phil. Soc. Proc.* 56: 589–672.

Breuer, J. P. 1957. An ecological survey of Baffin and Alazan Bays, Tex. *Publ. Inst. Mar. Sci., Univ. Tex.* 4: 133–55.

Broome, S. W., W. W. Woodhouse, Jr., and E. D. Seneca. 1975a. The relationship of mineral nutrients to growth of *Spartina alterniflora* in North Carolina. I. Nutrient status of plants and soils in natural stands. *Proc. Soil Sci. Soc. Amer.* 39: 295–301.

———. 1975b. The relationship of mineral nutrients of growth of *Spartina alterniflora* in North Carolina. II. The effects of N, P, and Fe fertilizers. *Proc. Soil Sci. Soc. Amer.* 39: 301–307.

Carpenter, E. J. 1971. Annual phytoplankton cycle of the Cape Fear River estuary, North Carolina. *Ches. Sci.* 12: 95–104.

Chapman, V. J. 1960. *Salt marshes and salt deserts of the world*. New York: Wiley-Interscience.

Christian, R. R., and R. I. Wetzel. 1978. Interaction between substrate, microbes, and consumers of *Spartina* detritus in estuaries, pp. 93–113. In: M. L. Wiley, ed. *Estuarine interactions*. New York: Academic Press.

Christmas, J. Y., ed. 1973. *Cooperative Gulf of Mexico estuarine inventory and study, Mississippi*. Ocean Springs, Miss.: Gulf Coast Research Laboratory.

Coles, S. M. 1979. Benthic microalgal populations on intertidal sediments and their role as precursors to salt marsh development, pp. 25–42. In: R. L. Jefferies and A. J. Day, eds. *Ecological processes in coastal environments*. London: Blackwell Scientific Publications.

Colwell, R. R., and J. Kaper. 1978. Distribution, survival, and significance of pathogenic bacteria and viruses in estuaries, pp. 443–57. In: M. L. Wiley, ed. *Estuarine interactions*. New York: Academic Press.

Comar, P. G., B. E. Kane, Jr., and D. B. Jeffreys. 1979. Sanitary significance of the bacterial flora of the brackish water clam, *Rangia cuneata*, in Albemarle Sound, North Carolina. *Proc. Nat'l. Shellfish Assoc.* 69: 92–100.

Cooper, A. W. 1974. Salt marshes, pp. 55–98. In: H. T. Odum, B. J. Copeland, and E. A. McMahan, eds. *Coastal ecological systems of the United States*. Vol. II. Washington, D.C.: Conservation Foundation.

Craighead, F. C. 1964. Land, mangroves, and hurricanes. *Fairchild Tropical Gardens Bull.* 19: 5–32.

Craighead, F. C., and V. C. Gilbert. 1962. The effects of hurricane Donna on the vegetation of southern Florida. *Quart. J. Fla. Acad. Sci.* 25: 1–28.

Crow, S. A., D. G. Ahearn, W. L. Cook, and A. W. Borquin. 1975. Densities of bacteria and fungi in coastal surface films as determined by a membrane-adsorption procedure. *Limnol. Oceanogr.* 20: 644–46.

Dale, N. G. 1974. Bacteria in intertidal sediments: Factors related to their distribution. *Limnol. Oceanogr.* 19: 509–18.

Darnell, R. M. 1961. Trophic spectrum of an estuarine community, based on studies of Lake Pontchartrain, Louisiana. *Ecology.* 42: 553–68.

———. 1964. Organic detritus in relation to secondary production in aquatic communities. *Verh. Internat. Verein. Limnol.* 15: 462–70.

———. 1967. Organic detritus in relation to the estuarine ecosystem, pp. 376–82. In: G. H. Lauff, ed. *Estuaries*. American Association for the Advancement of Science Publication no. 83. Washington, D.C.: AAAS.

Davis, J. H., Jr. 1940. The ecology and geologic role of mangroves in Florida. Carnegie Institute, Washington, D.C., Publication no. 517. *Tortugas Lab. Pap.* 32: 303–412.

Day, J. W., W. G. Smith, P. R. Wagner, and W. C. Stowe. 1973. Community structure and carbon budget of a salt marsh and shallow bay estuarine system in

Louisiana. Louisiana State University Center for Wetland Resources Publication no. LSU-SG-72-04.

de la Cruz, A. A. 1975. Proximate nutritive value changes during decomposition of salt marsh plants. *Hydrobiologia* 47: 475–80.

de la Cruz, A. A., and B. C. Gabriel. 1974. Caloric, elemental, and nutritive changes in decomposing *Juncus roemerianus* leaves. *Ecology* 55: 882–86.

DeMarte, J. A., and R. I. Hartman. 1974. Studies on the absorption of P32, Fe59, and Ca45 by water milfoil *Myriophyllum exalbescens* (Fernalt). *Ecology* 55: 188–94.

Fassett, N. C. 1929. The vegetation of the estuaries of northeastern North America. *Proc. Boston Soc. Nat. Hist.* 39: 73–130.

———. 1960. *A manual of aquatic plants.* Madison: University of Wisconsin Press.

Fehon, W. C., and J. D. Oliver. 1979. Taxonomy and distribution of surface microlayer bacteria from two estuarine sites. *Estuaries* 2: 194–97.

Fenchel, T. M. 1970. Studies on the decomposition of organic detritus derived from the turtle grass *Thalassia testudinum. Limnol. Oceanogr.* 15: 14–20.

Flemer, D. A. 1970. Primary production in the Chesapeake Bay. *Ches. Sci.* 11: 117–29.

Gabriel, B. C., and A. A. de la Cruz. 1974. Species composition, standing stock, and net primary production of a salt marsh community in Mississippi. *Ches. Sci.* 15: 72–77.

Gallagher, J. L., and F. C. Daiber. 1974. Primary production of edaphic algal communities in a Delaware salt marsh. *Limnol. Oceanogr.* 19: 390–93.

Gleason, H. A., and A. Cronquist. 1963. *Manual of vascular plants of northeastern United States and adjacent Canada.* Princeton, N.J.: D. Van Nostrand Co.

Gosselink, J. G., and C. J. Kirby. 1974. Decomposition of salt marsh grass, *Spartina alterniflora* Loisel. *Limnol. Oceanogr.* 19: 825–32.

Gosselink, J. G., E. P. Odum, and R. M. Pope. 1974. *The value of the tidal marsh.* Baton Rouge: Center for Wetland Resources, Louisiana State University.

Gulf South Research Institute. 1977. Coastal marsh productivity: A bibliography. U.S. Fish and Wildlife Service Biological Services Program FWS/OBS 77–39.

Haines, E. B. 1975. Nutrient inputs to the coastal zone: The Georgia and South Carolina shelf, pp. 303–22. In: L. E. Cronin, ed. *Estuarine research.* Vol. I. New York: Academic Press.

———. 1976a. Relation between the stable carbon isotope composition of fiddler crabs, plants, and soils in a salt marsh. *Limnol. Oceanogr.* 21: 880–83.

———. 1976b. Stable carbon isotope ratios in the biota, soils, and tidal water of a Georgia salt marsh. *Est. and Coast. Mar. Sci.* 4: 609–16.

———. 1977. On the origins of detritus in Georgia salt marsh estuaries. *Oikos.* 29: 254–60.

————. 1979. Interactions between Georgia salt marshes and coastal waters: A changing paradigm, pp. 35–46. In: R. J. Livingston, ed. *Ecological processes in coastal and marine systems*. Proceedings of the Symposium at Florida State, University, April, 1978.

Haines, E. B., and W. M. Dunstan. 1975. The distribution and relation of particulate organic material and primary productivity in the Georgia Bight, 1973–1974. *Est. and Coast. Mar. Sci.* 3: 431–41.

Haller, W. T., D. I. Sutton, and W. C. Barlowe. 1974. Effects of salinity on growth of several aquatic macrophytes. *Ecology* 55: 891–94.

Happ, G., J. G. Gosselink, and J. W. Day, Jr. 1977. The seasonal distribution of organic carbon in a Louisiana estuary. *Est. and Coast. Mar. Sci.* 5: 695–705.

Harrison, P. G., and K. H. Mann. 1975. Detritus formation from eelgrass (*Zostera marina* L.): The relative effects of fragmentation, leaching, and decay. *Limnol. Oceanogr.* 29: 924–34.

Hatcher, B. G., and K. H. Mann. 1975. Above-ground production of marsh cordgrass (*Spartina alterniflora*) near the northern edge of its range. *J. Fish. Res. Bd. Can.* 32: 83–87.

Heald, E. J. 1969. The production of organic detritus in a south Florida estuary. Ph.D. diss. University of Miami.

Heald, E. J., and W. E. Odum. 1969. The contribution of mangrove swamps to Florida fisheries. *Proc. Gulf and Caribb. Fish. Inst.* 22: 130–35.

Heinle, D. R., D. A. Flemer, J. F. Ustach, R. A. Murtagh, and R. P. Harris. 1973. *The role of organic debris and associated microorganisms in pelagic estuarine food chains*. Technical Report no. 22. College Park: Maryland Water Resources Research Center.

Hoese, H. D. 1967. Effect of higher than normal salinities on salt marshes. *Cont. Mar. Sci.* 12: 249–61.

Holmes, R. W., P. M. Williams, and R. W. Eppley. 1967. Red water in La Jolla Bay, 1964–1966. *Limnol. Oceanogr.* 12: 503–12.

Hutchinson, G. E. 1975. *A treatise on limnology*. Vol. III. New York: John Wiley and Sons.

Idyll, C. P. 1965. Shrimp need fresh water too. *National Parks Magazine*, October, pp. 14–15.

Joanen, T., and L. L. Glasgow. 1965. Factors influencing the establishment of widgeongrass stands in Louisiana. *Proc. S.E. Assoc. Game and Fish Comm.* 19: 78–92.

Johnson, D. A., and H. H. York. 1915. *The relation of plants to tide-levels*. Publication no. 206. Washington, D.C.: Carnegie Institute.

Keefe, C. W. 1972. Marsh production: A summary of the literature. *Cont. Mar. Sci.* 16: 163–81.

Kirby, C. J., and J. G. Gosselink. 1976. Primary production in a Louisiana Gulf coast *Spartina alterniflora* marsh. *Ecology* 57: 1052–59.

Kraeuter, J. N., and P. L. Wolf. 1974. The relationship of marine macroinvertebrates to salt marsh plants, pp. 449–62. In: R. J. Reimold and W. H. Queen,
eds. *Ecology of halophytes*. New York: Academic Press.

Kuenzler, E. J. 1974. Mangrove swamp systems, pp. 346–71. In: H. T. Odum,
B. J. Copeland, and E. A. McMahan, eds. *Coastal ecological systems of the
United States*. Vol. I. Washington, D.C.: Conservation Foundation.

Kurz, H., and K. Wagner. 1957. *Tidal marshes of the Gulf and Atlantic coasts of
northern Florida and Charleston, South Carolina*. Florida State University
Studies no. 24. Tallahassee: Florida State University.

Lagna, L. 1975. The relationship of *Spartina alterniflora* to mean high water. New
York Sea Grant Institute, NYSSGP-RS-75-002.

Larimer, E. J. 1968. An investigation of possibilities for creating saltmarsh in the
estuaries of the Atlantic and Gulf coasts. *Proc. S.E. Assoc. Game and Fish
Comm.* 22: 82–88.

Leach, J. H. 1970. Epibenthic algal production in an intertidal mud flat. *Limnol.
Oceanogr.* 15: 514–21.

Macnae, W. 1967. Zonation within mangroves associated with estuaries in North
Queensland, pp. 432–44. In: G. H. Lauff, ed. *Estuaries*. American Associa-
tion for the Advancement of Science Publication no. 83. Washington, D.C.:
AAAS.

McRoy, C. P., and J. J. Goering. 1974. Nutrient transfer between the seagrass
Zostera marina and its epiphytes. *Nature* 248: 173–74.

McRoy, C. P., and R. J. Barsdate. 1970. Phosphate absorption in eelgrass. *Limnol.
Oceanogr.* 15: 6–13.

McRoy, C. P., R. J. Barsdate, and M. Nebart. 1972. Phosphorus cycling in an
eelgrass (*Zostera marina* L.) ecosystem. *Limnol. Oceanogr.* 17: 58–67.

Mann, K. H., and A. R. O. Chapman. 1975. Primary production of marine macrophytes, pp. 207–25. In: J. P. Cooper, ed. *Photosynthesis and productivity
in different environments*. London: Cambridge University Press.

Marshall, H. L. 1974. Irregularly flooded marsh, pp. 150–70. In: H. T. Odum,
B. J. Copeland, and E. A. McMahan, eds. *Coastal ecological systems of the
United States*. Vol. II. Washington, D.C.: Conservation Foundation.

Marshall, N. 1970. Food transfer through the lower trophic levels of the benthic
environment, pp. 52–66. In: J. H. Steele, ed. *Marine food chains*. Berkeley:
University of California Press.

Martin, A. C., and F. M. Uhler. 1939. *Food of game ducks in the United States and
Canada*. Technical Bulletin no. 634. Washington, D.C.: U.S. Department of
Agriculture.

May, M. S. 1974. Probable agents for the formation of detritus from the halophyte,
Spartina alterniflora, pp. 429–40. In: R. J. Reimold and W. H. Queen, eds.
Ecology of halophytes. New York: Academic Press.

Mooring, M. T. 1970. Seed germination response to temperature and salinity and seeding response to salinity of *Spartina alterniflora* from North Carolina. M.S. thesis, North Carolina State University, Raleigh.

Munz, P. A., and D. D. Keck. 1959. *A California flora.* Berkeley: University of California Press.

Nixon, S. W. 1980. Between coastal marshes and coastal waters: A review of twenty years of speculation on the role of salt marshes in estuarine productivity and water chemistry, pp.437–525. In: P. Hamilton and K. B. Macdonald, eds. *Estuarine and wetland processes—with emphasis on modeling.* New York: Plenum Press.

Nixon, S., and C. Oviatt. 1973. Ecology of a New England salt marsh. *Ecol. Monogr.* 43: 463–98.

Odum, E. P. 1959. *Fundamentals of ecology.* Philadelphia: W. B. Saunders Co.

———. 1962. Relationship between structure and function in the ecosystem. *Japan J. Ecology* 12: 108–18.

———. 1963. Primary and secondary energy flow in relation to ecosystem structure. *Proc. XVI Intern. Cong. Zool.* 4: 336–38.

———. 1968. A research challenge: Evaluating the productivity of coastal and estuarine water, pp. 63–64. In: *Proceedings of the second Sea Grant conference.* Kingston: University of Rhode Island.

———. 1979. The status of three ecosystem-level hypotheses regarding salt marsh estuaries: Tidal subsidy, outwelling, and detritus-based food chains. The fifth biennial international estuarine research conference, Jekyll Island, Georgia, October 7–12.

Odum, E. P., and A. A. de la Cruz. 1963. Detritus as a major component of ecosystems. *AIBS Bull.* 13: 39–40.

———. 1967. Particulate organic detritus in a Georgia salt marsh–estuarine ecosystem, pp. 383–88. In: G. H. Lauff, ed. *Estuaries.* American Association for the Advancement of Science Publication no. 83. Washington, D.C.: AAAS.

Odum, H. T. 1967. Biological circuits and the marine systems of Texas, pp. 99–157. In: T. A. Olson and F. J. Burgess, eds. *Pollution and marine ecology.* New York: Wiley-Interscience.

Odum, H. T., and C. M. Hoskin. 1958. Comparative studies on the metabolism of marine waters. *Publ. Inst. Mar. Sci., Univ. Tex.* 5: 16–46.

Odum, H. T., and R. F. Wilson. 1962. Further studies on reaeration and metabolism of Texas bays, 1958–1960. *Publ. Inst. Mar. Sci., Univ. Tex.* 8: 23–55.

Odum, H. T., B. J. Copeland, and E. A. McMahan, eds. 1974. *Coastal ecological systems of the United States.* 4 vols. Washington, D.C.: Conservation Foundation.

Odum, H. T., R. P. Cuzon du Rest, R. J. Beyers, and C. Allbaugh. 1963. Diurnal metabolism, total phosphorus, Ohle anomaly, and zooplankton diversity of abnormal marine ecosystems of Texas. *Publ. Inst. Mar. Sci., Univ. Tex.* 9: 404–53.

Odum, W. E. 1968. The ecological significance of fine particle selection by the striped mullet, *Mugil cephalus*. *Limnol. Oceanogr.* 13: 92–98.

―――. 1970a. Pathways of energy flow in a south Florida estuary. Ph.D. diss., University of Miami.

―――. 1970b. Utilization of the direct grazing and plant detritus food chains by the striped mullet *Mugil cephalus*, pp. 222–40. In: J. H. Steele, ed. *Marine food chains*. Berkeley: University of California Press.

Odum, W. E., and E. J. Heald. 1975. The detritus-based food web of an estuarine mangrove community, pp. 265–86. In: L. E. Cronin, ed. *Estuarine research*. Vol. I. New York: Academic Press.

Odum, W. E., J. C. Zieman, and E. J. Heald. 1972. The importance of vascular plant detritus to estuaries, pp. 91–144. In: R. H. Chabreck, ed. *Proceedings of the coastal marsh and estuary management symposium*. Baton Rouge: Louisiana State University.

Parker, P. L., and R. F. Leo. 1965. Fatty acids in blue-green algal mat communities. *Science* 145: 373–74.

Patten, B. C., Jr. 1956. Notes on the biology of *Myriophyllum spicatum* L. in New Jersey Lake. *Bull. Torrey Bot. Club* 83: 5–18.

Penfound, W. T., and E. S. Hathaway. 1938. Plant communities of the marshlands of southeastern Louisiana. *Ecol. Monogr.* 8: 1–56.

Penhale, P. A. 1977. Macrophyte-epiphyte biomass and productivity in an eelgrass (*Zostera marina* L.) community. *J. Exp. Mar. Biol. Ecol.* 26: 211–24.

Peterson, C. H., and N. M. Peterson. 1979. The ecology of intertidal flats in North Carolina: A community profile. U.S. Fish and Wildlife Service Biological Services Program FWS/OBS 79-39.

Philipp, C. C., and R. G. Brown. 1965. Ecological studies of transition-zone vascular plants in South River, Maryland. *Ches. Sci.* 6: 73–81.

Phillips, R. C. 1960. Ecology and distribution of marine algae found in Tampa Bay, Boca Ciega Bay, and at Tarpon Springs, Florida. *Quart. J. Fla. Acad. Sci.* 23: 222–60.

―――. 1974. Temperate grass flats, pp. 244–99. In: H. T. Odum, B. J. Copeland, and E. A. McMahan, eds. *Coastal ecological systems of the United States*. Vol. II. Washington, D.C.: Conservation Foundation.

Pomeroy, L. R. 1959. Algal productivity in Georgia salt marshes. *Limnol. Oceanogr.* 4: 386–97.

―――. 1960. Primary productivity of Boca Ciega Bay, Florida. *Bull. Mar. Sci. Gulf Caribb.* 10: 1–10.

Pomeroy, L. R., R. E. Johannes, E. P. Odum, and B. Roffman. 1967. The phosphorus and zinc cycles and productivity of a salt marsh, pp. 412–30. In: D. J. Nelson and F. C. Evans, eds. Proceedings of the second symposium on radioecology held at Ann Arbor, Michigan, May 15–17.

Ragotzkie, R. A. 1959. Plankton productivity in estuarine waters of Georgia. *Publ. Inst. Mar. Sci., Univ. Tex.* 6: 146–58.

Ragotzkie, R. A., and L. R. Pomeroy. 1957. Life history of a dinoflagellate bloom. *Limnol. Oceanogr.* 2: 62–69.

Rawls, C. K. 1964. Aquatic plant nuisances. *Proc. Interstate Comm. Potomac River Basin.* 1: 51–56.

Reidenbaugh, T. G., and W. C. Banta. 1980. Origin and effects of *Spartina* wrack in a Virginia salt marsh. *Gulf Research Reports* 6: 393–401.

Reimold, R. J., and W. H. Queen, eds. 1974. *Ecology of halophytes.* New York: Academic Press.

Reimold, R. J., J. L. Gallagher, R. A. Linthurst, and W. J. Pfeiffer. 1975. Detritus production in coastal Georgia salt marshes, pp. 217–28. In: L. E. Cronin, ed. *Estuarine research.* Vol. I. New York: Academic Press.

Rickett, H. W. 1923. A quantitative study of the larger aquatic plants of Green Lake, Wisconsin. *Wisc. Acad. Sci. Arts Lett.* 21: 381–414.

Rickner, J. A. 1979. The influence of dredged material islands in upper Laguna Madre, Texas, on selected seagrass and macrobenthos. Ph.D. diss., Texas A&M University, College Station.

Rublee, P., and B. E. Dornseif. 1978. Direct counts of bacteria in the sediments of a North Carolina salt marsh. *Estuaries* 1: 188–91.

Savage, H. P., and N. B. Hanes. 1971. Toxicity of seawater to coliform bacteria. *J. Water Poll. Cont. Fed.* 43: 854–60.

Schelske, C. L., and E. P. Odum. 1962. Mechanisms maintaining high productivity in Georgia estuaries. *Proc. Gulf and Caribb. Fish. Inst.* 14: 75–80.

Scholander, P. F., H. T. Hammel, E. Hemmingsen, and W. Gary. 1962. Salt balance in mangroves. *Plant Physiol.* 37: 722–29.

Schultz, D. M., and J. G. Quinn. 1973. Fatty acid composition of organic detritus from *Spartina alterniflora*. *Est. and Coast. Mar. Sci.* 1: 177–90.

Schulthorpe, C. D. 1967. *The biology of aquatic vascular plants.* London: Edward Arnold.

Sellner, K. G., R. G. Zingmark, and T. G. Miller. 1976. Interpretations of the 14C method of measuring the total annual production of phytoplankton in a South Carolina estuary. *Bot. Mar.* 19: 119–25.

Seneca, E. D. 1974. A preliminary germination study of *Spartina foliosa*, California cordgrass. *Wasmann J. of Biology* 32: 215–19.

Settlemyre, J. L., and L. R. Gardner. 1975. *Chemical and sediment budgets for a small tidal creek, Charleston Harbor, S.C.* Water Resources Research Institute, Clemson University Report no. 57. Clemson, S.C.: Clemson University.

Shiflet, T. 1963. Major ecological factors controlling plant communities in Louisiana marshes. *J. Range Man.* 16: 231–35.

Shreve, F., M. A. Chrysler, F. H. Blodgett, and F. W. Besley. 1910. *The plant life of Maryland*. Maryland Weather Services Special Publication. Vol. III. Baltimore: Johns Hopkins University Press.

Sieburth, J. McN. 1971. Distribution and activity of oceanic bacteria. *Deep Sea Res*. 18: 1111–21.

Smalley, A. E. 1959. The growth cycle of *Spartina* and its relation to the insect populations in the marsh, pp. 96–100. In: *Proceedings of the salt marsh conference, Marine Institute*. Sapelo Island: University of Georgia.

Sollins, P. 1969. Measurement and simulation of oxygen flows and storages in a laboratory blue-green algal mat ecosystem. M.A. thesis, University of North Carolina, Chapel Hill.

Sorenson, L. O., and J. T. Conover. 1962. Algal mat communities of *Lyngbya confervoides* (C. Agardh) Gomont. *Publ. Inst. Mar. Sci., Univ. Tex*. 8: 61–74.

Stalter, R. 1968. An ecological study of a South Carolina salt marsh. Ph.D. diss., University of South Carolina, Columbia.

Stalter, R., and W. T. Batson. 1969. Transplantation of salt marsh vegetation, Georgetown, South Carolina. *Ecology* 50: 1087–89.

Stevenson, J. C., and N. M. Confer. 1978. Summary of available information on Chesapeake Bay submerged vegetation. U.S. Fish and Wildlife Service Biological Services Program. FWS/BA 78-66.

Stross, R. G., and J. R. Stottlemyer. 1965. Primary production in the Patuxent River. *Ches. Sci*. 6: 125–40.

Tabb, D. C., and B. J. Yokel. 1968. *Report to the Conservation Foundation: Preliminary ecological study of Rookery Bay Sanctuary, Naples, Florida*. Miami: University of Miami Institute of Marine Science.

Tabb, D. C., D. L. Dubrow, and R. B. Manning. 1962. The ecology of northern Florida Bay and adjacent estuaries. *Fla. Bd. Conserv. Tech. Ser. no. 39*.

Taylor, N. 1939. *Salt tolerance of Long Island salt marsh plants*. Circular 23. Albany: New York State Museum.

Teal, J. M. 1962. Energy flow in the salt marsh ecosystem of Georgia. *Ecology* 43: 614–24.

Teeter, J. W. 1965. Effects of sodium chloride on the sago pondweed. *J. Wildl. Man*. 29: 838–45.

Tenore, K. R. 1977. Food chain pathways in detrital feeding benthic invertebrate communities: A review with new observations on sediment resuspension and detrital recycling, pp. 37–53. In: B. C. Coull, ed. *Ecology of marine benthos*. Columbia: University of South Carolina Press.

Thayer, G. W. 1971. Phytoplankton production and the distribution of nutrients in a shallow unstratified estuarine system near Beaufort, N.C. *Ches. Sci*. 12: 240–53.

Thayer, G. W., D. A. Wolfe, and R. B. Williams. 1975. The impact of man on seagrass systems. *Am. Sci*. 63: 288–96.

Thayer, G. W., S. M. Adams, and M. W. LaCroix. 1975. Structural and functional aspects of a recently established *Zostera marina* community, pp. 518–40. In: L. E. Cronin, ed. *Estuarine research*. Vol. I. New York: Academic Press.

Thorne, R. F. 1954. Flowering plants of the waters and shores of the Gulf of Mexico, pp. 193–202. In: P. Galtsoff, ed. The Gulf of Mexico: Its origin, waters, and marine life. *Fish. Bull.* 89.

Turner, R. E. 1976. Geographic variations in salt marsh macrophytic production: A review. *Cont. Mar. Sci.* 20: 47–68.

———. 1977. Intertidal vegetation and commercial yields of penaeid shrimp. *Trans. Am. Fish. Soc.* 106: 411–16.

Turner, R. E., and J. G. Gosselink. 1975. A note on standing crops of *Spartina alterniflora* in Texas and Florida. *Cont. Mar. Sci.* 19: 113–18.

Tyler, M. A., and H. H. Seliger. 1981. Selection for a red tide organism: Physiological responses to the physical environment. *Limnol. Oceanogr.* 26: 310–24.

Vanderzant, C., C. A. Thompson, Jr., and S. M. Ray. 1973. Microbial flora and level of *Vibrio parahaemolyticus* of oysters (*Crassostrea virginica*), water, and sediment from Galveston Bay. *J. Milk Food Technol.* 36: 447–52.

Vanderzant, C., R. Nickelsen, and J. C. Parker. 1970. Isolation of *Vibrio parahaemolyticus* from Gulf coast shrimp. *J. Milk Food Technol.* 33: 161–62.

van Eijk, M. 1939. Analyse der Wirkung des NaCl auf die Entwicklung, Sukkulenz und Transpiration bei *Salicornia herbacea*, sowie Untersuchungen über den Einfluss der Salzaufnahme auf die Wurzelatmung bei Aster tripolium. *Rec. Trav. Bot. Neerl.* 36: 559–67.

Waits, E. D. 1967. Net primary productivity of an irregularly flooded North Carolina salt marsh. Ph.D. diss., North Carolina State University, Raleigh.

Walker, R. A. 1973. Wetlands preservation and management on Chesapeake Bay: The role of science in natural resource policy. *Coast. Zone Man. J.* 1: 75–101.

Webb, J. W., J. D. Dodd, B. W. Cain, W. R. Leavens, L. R. Hossner, C. Lindau, R. R. Stickney, and H. Williamson. 1978. *Habitat development field investigations: Bolivar Peninsula marsh and upland habitat development site, Galveston Bay, Texas.* App. D. Propagation of vascular plants and postpropagation monitoring of botanical soil, aquatic biota, and wildlife resources. Vicksburg, Miss.: U.S. Army Corps of Engineers.

Webb, K. L. 1966. NaCl effects on growth and transpiration in *Salicornia bigelovii*, a salt-marsh halophyte. *Plant and Soil* 24: 261–67.

Weiland, R. T., T. H. Chrzanowski, and L. H. Stevenson. 1979. Influence of freshwater intrusion on microbial biomass in salt-marsh creeks. *Estuaries* 2: 126–29.

Wetzel, R. G. 1975. *Limnology*. Philadelphia: W. B. Saunders Co.

Wilkinson, R. E. 1963. Effects of light intensity and temperature on the growth of waterstargrass, coontail, and duckweed. *Weeds* 11: 287–89.

Williams, R. B. 1966. Annual phytoplankton production in a system of shallow temperate estuaries, pp. 699–716. In: H. Barnes, ed. *Some contemporary studies in marine science*. London: George, Allen, and Unwin.

———. 1972. Nutrient levels and phytoplankton productivity in the estuary, pp. 59–89. In: R. H. Chabreck, ed. *Proceedings: Second symposium on coastal marsh and estuary management*. Baton Rouge: Louisiana State University.

Williams, R. B., and M. B. Murdoch. 1969. The potential importance of *Spartina alterniflora* in conveying zinc, manganese, and iron into estuarine food chains, pp. 431–39. In: D. J. Nelson and F. C. Evans, eds. Proceedings: Second National symposium on radioecology. CONF-670503, USAEC.

Wilson, K. A. 1962. North Carolina wetlands: Their distribution and management. *N.C. Wildl. Res. Comm.*

Wood, E. J., W. E. Odum, and J. C. Zieman. 1967. Influence of sea grasses on the productivity of coastal lagoons, pp. 495–502. In: *Symposium on coastal lagoons*. Mexico City: UNAM-UNESCO.

Woodhouse, W. W., Jr., E. D. Seneca, and S. W. Broome. 1977. Ten years of development of man-initiated coastal barrier dunes in North Carolina. University of North Carolina Sea Grant College Publication UNC-SG-77-01.

Yeo, R. R. 1965. Yields of propagules of certain aquatic plants. I. *Weeds*. 14: 110–13.

Zieman, J. C. 1968. A study of the growth and decomposition of the sea-grass *Thalassia testudinum*. M.S. thesis, University of Miami.

———. 1975. Quantitative and dynamic aspects of the ecology of turtle grass, *Thalassia testudinum*, pp. 541–62. In: L. E. Cronin, ed. *Estuarine research*. Vol. I. New York: Academic Press.

Zimmerman, M. S., and R. J. Livingston. 1976. Seasonality and physico-chemical ranges of benthic macrophytes from a north Florida estuary (Apalachee Bay). *Cont. Mar. Sci.* 20: 33–45.

Zobell, C. E., and C. B. Feltham. 1942. The bacterial flora of a marine flat as an ecological factor. *Ecology* 23: 69–78.

CHAPTER 7

Zooplankton

Introduction

ZOOPLANKTONIC animals are those that drift at the mercy of currents. A commonly accepted classification of zooplankters by size is as follows:

1. Macroplankton—large organisms, easily visible to the naked eye, larger than 1 mm in diameter
2. Microplankton—animals ranging from 0.06 to 1 mm
3. Nannoplankton—animals ranging from 5 to 60 microns (0.005 to 0.06 mm)
4. Ultraplankton—animals smaller than 5 microns in diameter

Another classification scheme used with the zooplankton community distinguishes between meroplankton and holoplankton. Meroplankters are animals that spend part of their lives in the plankton community and the remainder elsewhere. Examples, particularly numerous in estuaries, include the larvae of a variety of taxa, both the fish and their eggs. Holoplankters, which spend their entire lives in the plankton community, comprise copepods, jellyfishes, various protozoans, and other groups.

The taxonomic groups represented in the zooplankton community include:

1. Phylum protozoa (Orders Foraminifera and Radiolaria and Family Tintinnidae)
2. Phylum Ctenophora
3. Phylum Coelenterata (Classes Hydrozoa and Scyphozoa)
4. Phylum Arthropoda, Class Crustacea (Suborder Cladocera, Order Copepoda, Suborders Mysidacea, Amphipoda, Isopoda, and Cumacea), many meroplanktonic forms in the above taxa, Order Decapoda, and Subclasses Cirripedia and Stomatopoda
5. Phylum Annelida (Class Polychaeta with some four holoplanktonic families)

6. Phylum Chaetognatha
7. Phylum Mollusca (Class Gastropoda with the planktonic heteropods and pteropods)
8. Phylum Chordata (Classes Thaliacea and Larvacea)

The above listing is not exhaustive. In two instances (Phyla Arthropoda and Mollusca) notations on holoplanktonic, as opposed to meroplanktonic, forms are included; as indicated above, however, fish eggs and larvae (Phylum Chordata) could also be mentioned. Phylum Echinodermata and others with meroplanktonic, but not holoplanktonic, species in estuaries do not appear on the list. The chordate class Thaliacea (salps and doliolids) lacks members commonly found in estuaries, though the Larvacea (appendicularians) frequently appear in estuarine plankton samples. The following organisms (Christmas, 1973), collected in the estuaries of Mississippi, demonstrate the variability of taxa in a typical estuary: protozoa, coelenterata, ctenophora, ectoprocta, phoronida, mollusca, polychaeta, ostracoda, cirripedia nauplii, copepoda, isopoda, stomatopoda, cumacea, mysidacea, decapod zoeae, caridea zoeae, anomura, brachyura, cladocera, ophiuroidea larvae, chaetognaths, urochordata, and osteichthyes.

Larvae collected in zooplankton samples may be distinct—so different, in fact, that species identification is relatively simple—but more often, larval crustaceans, molluscs, echinoderms, ectoprocts, hemichordates, and others can only be identified to class or order. In most cases the larvae are sufficiently distinct that a classification to species would be possible if the larvae were taken into the laboratory and reared to metamorphosis. This has often not been done.

Characteristics of Estuarine Zooplankton Communities

A cursory examination of the literature on estuaries quickly proves that the zooplankton community has received little attention compared with plants, benthos, and nekton. Various authors have characterized the organisms in selected estuaries; others have demonstrated spatial as well as temporal abundance; and some indications of grazing rates have resulted. This section discusses the general characteristics of zooplankton communities in estuaries, but the treatment is necessarily somewhat superficial. Productivity studies on zooplankton in fresh water are common; in estuaries, they are scarce. This is perhaps because many of the zooplanktonic species in estuaries are transients. Polychaete, crab, shrimp, and fish larvae, among others, contribute much more to overall productivity after they leave the zooplankton community than when they are members of it.

Perhaps the most ambitious study to date of estuarine zooplankton was conducted in North Carolina over a period of ten years. The variety of papers resulting from that study include Williams (1969, 1971), Williams and Deubler (1968), Williams and Porter (1971), and Williams and Bynum (1972). Those authors examined such members of the community as amphipods, penaeid shrimp, and flounders.

Several general patterns have emerged from studies of estuarine zooplankton communities (Perkins, 1974): (1) zooplankton communities tend to be more diverse than their phytoplankton counterparts; (2) copepods tend to outnumber other organisms in estuarine zooplankton communities; (3) zooplankton distribution appears to be linked to salinity; (4) many species practice diurnal migration and often respond positively to low light intensities; and (5) seasonal fluctuations in zooplankton populations are commonly observed.

Diversity

Diversity indices have been developed to determine how the species and individuals within a given community are related. Diversity can also represent the relative health of a community: generally, high diversity is desirable while low diversity is not. Polluted environments often teem with individuals representing only one or a few species; thus, the diversity in such environments is low. This does not mean that all environments demonstrating low diversity are polluted.

Because of the wide variety of organisms that are either meroplanktonic or holoplanktonic, it seems logical that the ocean generally has a high diversity of zooplankton. Since continuous recruitment into and departure from the community are common with meroplanktonic species, diversity frequently changes with time.

Various diversity indices have been proposed; the most widely used appears to be the Shannon-Wiener function. This index also seems to provide the least biased estimate of diversity (Heip and Engels, 1974). The formula for the Shannon-Wiener function is

$$H = - \sum Pi \, ln \, Pi, \qquad (13)$$

where Pi is the proportion of species i in the sample, and ln is the natural logarithm. Some investigators use modifications of the formula. For example, Dahlberg and Odum (1970) used $\log_{10}$ instead of natural logarithms. In any case, the calculation is relatively simple. Values will generally range from about 0.6 to more than 3.

Other functions that can be calculated from the same data used to determine diversity include richness and evenness. These functions can also be obtained in a number of ways. Dahlberg and Odum (1970) selected the following formula for richness:

$$D = (S - 1)/\log N, \tag{14}$$

where S is the number of species in the sample, and N is the number of individuals. The evenness index used by Dahlberg and Odum (1970) was

$$J = H/H \max = H/\log S, \tag{15}$$

where S is the maximum possible value of H. $H = H$ max when all species are equally abundant. Heip and Engels (1974) discussed a preferable evenness function as developed by Heip (1974):

$$E = e^H - 1/S - 1, \tag{16}$$

where e^H is the natural logarithm raised to the power of the Shannon-Wiener index, and S is the number of species in the sample.

Although zooplankton diversity seems to be higher than that of phytoplankton (Perkins, 1974), the former community is often still limited in its number of species, according to Riley (1967). Much more work is needed on the application of diversity indices to estuarine zooplankton communities.

The diversity concept has augmented and to some extent even replaced the indicator species notion that was popular several years ago. According to the latter theory, the dominance or unusually high abundance of a particular species in the environment reveals the condition of that environment. The theory has been applied to estuarine zooplankton communities by Jeffries (1962a) but has recently fallen into disrepute.

Dominance of Copepods

Copepods tend to outnumber other estuarine zooplankton, though by volume ctenophores are commonly dominant. Christmas (1973) found that *Mnemiopsis mccradyi* were always dominant in Mississippi Sound; this may also be generally true, he reasoned, in other estuaries. Christmas also showed that swarms of ctenophores appeared when temperatures ranged between 20.4 and 24.9 C, with salinities from 5.0 to 19.9 o/oo. Christmas et al. (1966) and Phillips et al. (1969) determined that when ctenophores are abundant in Mississippi estuarine waters, other zooplankters are not as plentiful as usual.

In a study that evaluated the zooplankton community at Beaufort, North Carolina, for one year (Williams et al., 1968), copepods were dominant in volume. They also dominated in samples taken during an intensive summer study of Georgia zooplankton (Stickney and Knowles, 1975) and a less intensive long-term study that measured zooplankton patterns in the same locations during one-day periods from summer through winter (Stickney and Knowles, 1976). The latter two studies used closing water bottles for sampling; the samples may thus have been biased against ctenophores.

Acartia tonsa has been found to be the dominant species of, or at least a significant contributor to, the zooplankton communities of many U.S. estuaries (Deevey, 1948, 1960; Grice, 1956, 1960; Woodmansee, 1958; Cronin et al., 1962; Cuzon du Rest, 1963; Hopkins, 1966; Christmas, 1973; Bellis, 1974). That species has been shown to alternate seasonally with *A. clausi* in estuaries of the New England and Middle Atlantic states (Conover, 1956; Jeffries, 1962b). *Pseudodiaptomus coronatus* is also found throughout the southeastern Atlantic coastal region and in the Gulf of Mexico. Christmas (1973) found that *P. coronatus* was most abundant in water from 25 to 35 C, with salinity from 25 to 30 o/oo.

Distribution with Salinity

It is intuitively obvious that the members of the zooplankton community will change as salinity decreases from near oceanic at the estuary mouth to fresh in the upper estuary. Although salinity is crucial to the distribution of zooplankters, species composition and density may also depend upon food supply, water movement, and the rate of water exchange in estuaries (Bakker and De Pauw, 1975). Temperature is also important in the distribution of zooplankton—not so much up and down an estuary, but certainly with respect to latitude.

Both holoplanktonic and meroplanktonic species vary their locations in estuaries according to salinity. In laboratory studies with various meroplanktonic species, decapod crustaceans have received considerable attention. For example, laboratory studies on the exposure of larval crabs, *Panopeus herbstii*, to twelve combinations of salinity and temperature indicated that the time required for development from hatching to the first crab stage decreased with increasing salinity over the range of 12.5 to 31.1 o/oo (Costlow et al., 1962). In a related study on the crab *Rhithropanopeus harrisii*, Costlow et al. (1966) determined that hatching was normal over the range of 5 to 33 o/oo salinity. Normal molt frequency occurred between 5 and 35 o/oo, but development slowed at 2.5 and 40 o/oo. Survival to the first crab stage was possible in the salinity range of 2.5 to 40 o/oo but not at 1 o/oo. Ong and Costlow (1970) experimented with the stone crab *Menippe mercenaria* and found that optimum conditions for growth were between 30 and 35 o/oo. Under favorable conditions, the megalops stage was reached in fourteen days and the first crab stage in twenty-one days. A salinity of 10 o/oo was lethal to the first zoeal stage at temperatures from 20 to 30 C.

The distribution of mysid crustaceans in estuaries was closely tied to salinity according to Price (1976), in a study undertaken around Galveston Bay, Texas. The most abundant species, *Mysidopsis almyra*, occurred in low salinity shallow waters within bayous and bays. *M. bahia*, which represented 10% of the mysid community, appeared in shallow bay waters of higher salinity. In contrast, *M. bigelowi*, which contributed 5% to the total mysid community, was found in deep bay waters and offshore. Another species, *Metamysidopsis swifti*, was collected in the surf along the beaches, while *Brasilomysis castroi* and *Promysis atlantica* were found only in deeper offshore waters.

In an earlier study, Price (1974) outlined the ranges of salinity over which several mysid species can be expected to occur:

1. *Mysidopsis almyra*—1.3 to 40.0 o/oo
2. *Mysidopsis bahia*—18.4 to 37.8 o/oo
3. *Metamysidopsis swifti*—26.1 to 35.1 o/oo
4. *Mysidopsis bigelowi*—19.4 to 29.7 o/oo
5. *Brasilomysis castroi*, *Promysis atlantica*, and *Bowmaniella brasillensis*—above 23 o/oo

The above listing does not give the tolerance range of any of the species but merely indicates the level of salinity at which they can be commonly collected.

DIURNAL MIGRATIONS

Pelagic copepods have been shown to exhibit striking patterns of diurnal horizontal as well as vertical migrations, which are related to such factors as tide stage and time of day. Jacobs (1968) found that *Acartia tonsa* was most abundant throughout the water column during rising and high tides and was least plentiful when the tide was falling or low. He hypothesized that the copepods were moving upstream with the flooding tide and in the opposite direction during ebb flow. Temperature and salinity gradients were not appreciable, and food supply was ruled out as a controlling factor in migration.

In an intensive study of summer zooplankton, Stickney and Knowles (1975) found *Acartia tonsa* at the surface to be most abundant at night and during periods of rising and high tide. The incidence of that species at other depths under the same conditions was relatively lower. *A. tonsa* at the bottom was most plentiful during daylight when the tide was falling or low. In a later study, Stickney and Knowles (1976) concluded that *A. tonsa* was commonly concentrated near the bottom of the water column, while copepod nauplii and polychaete larvae stayed near the surface. The distributions of harpacticoid copepods and *Pseudodiaptomus coronatus* were similar to those of *A. tonsa* during the summer (Stickney and Knowles, 1975).

Zooplanktonic species have at least limited powers of vertical migration and can move laterally across currents. Passive movement with currents can be controlled if the animals move up in the water column when flow is in the proper direction and to the sediment surface when the desired location in the estuary is reached or when the current direction changes. These movements have been well documented for postlarval flounders of the family Bothidae (Williams and Deubler, 1968; White and Stickney, 1973). Flounder postlarvae have been successfully collected in several estuaries along the southeastern Atlantic coast of the United States during January and February, when the young fish are moving inshore from the spawning grounds. The small fish can be caught in plankton nets at the surface during the night on incoming tides.

Migrations may also be in response to light intensity. The increased abundance of *Acartia tonsa* in the surface waters of Georgia at night suggests negative phototaxic response (Stickney and Knowles, 1975). Also indicative of negative phototaxis is the availability of flounder postlarvae at the surface during the night. Mysids (*Neomysis americana*) were collected at night by plankton net well up in the water column in Georgia in conjunction with flounder postlarvae sampling (White and Stickney, 1973). Few mysids, however, were collected during the daytime.

Seasonal Fluctuations in Zooplankton

Seasonal cycling in zooplankton populations has been documented by various studies conducted in U.S. estuaries. The observed cycles are highly variable, but certain patterns tend to persist. According to Riley (1967), high primary productivity in estuaries is responsible for the frequently observed high levels of summer zooplankton. This phenomenon is not common in the open ocean. Contributing to the abundant summer standing crops in estuaries is the very high recruitment into the zooplankton community of meroplanktonic forms during warm months. Low temperature (Fish and Johnson, 1937; Riley, 1941) and predation (Heinle, 1966; Riley, 1967) also control zooplankton populations in certain instances.

Copepods, ctenophores, and mysids are among the zooplanktonic animals shown to display distinct seasonal trends. Stickney and Knowles (1976), in their study that extends from July through March, found that *A. tonsa* populations were highest from August through November. This study supports the observation of others of a fall population peak in that species. No other species of *Acartia* appeared in the Georgia zooplankton to replace *A. tonsa* when that species declined. Harpacticoid copepods along with *Pseudodiaptomus coronatus* and polychaete larvae, were also most numerous in the Georgia study during the summer and fall. *Oikopleura* sp., an appendicularian, though present only in very low concentrations during any month, was absent from samples collected from January through March. It was most abundant in August and September. Thus, the pattern in *Oikopleura* was similar to that of the more dominant members of the community. McIlwain (1968) found that copepod populations peaked in spring, summer, and fall in Mississippi Sound.

With respect to the total zooplankton community, maximum numbers have generally been found in late spring and late summer in samples collected from Long Island Sound (Deevey, 1956). The population increased during spring and decreased in the fall to a midwinter low. Copepods were the dominant taxon. In a one-year study of estuarine zooplankton near Beaufort, North Carolina (Williams et al., 1968), standing crops were significantly greater during winter than summer. The low overall abundance of zooplankton in that study was not attributable to temperature, tidal flushing patterns, or insufficient food. In fact, the authors estimated that daily consumption of phytoplankton by zooplankton amounted to only 2 to 9% of net primary production.

Christmas (1973) examined the seasonal patterns of ctenophores in Mississippi Sound and determined that the population peaked in August and bottomed out in November. The summer maximum was partly attributed to seasonal occurrences of meroplankters, particularly crustacean and molluscan larvae that were eaten by the ctenophores. Stanlaw et al. (1981) found that newly hatched larvae of the ctenophore *Mnemiopsis mccradyi* were delicate and could be killed by copepods larger than nauplii. Larval ctenophores, on the other hand, were shown to require high concentrations of copepod nauplii in order to sustain their growth. The larval ctenophores could survive starvation for up to a week, but the importance of a ready supply of food appears critical if a large population of ctenophores is to be supported.

The voracious predation by ctenophores on other groups of zooplankters has been documented (Nelson, 1925; Barlow, 1955; Grice, 1956; Conover, 1961; Hopkins, 1966). The same is true of the jellyfishes. Phillips et al. (1969) examined the feeding relationships of the latter in Mississippi Sound. The Portuguese man-o-war, *Physalia physalia*, was the only species found to feed largely on pelagic fishes. Other jellyfishes, such as the sea nettle, *Chrysaora quinquecirrha*, and winter jellyfish, *Cyanea capillata versicolor*, feed mainly on ctenophores; while cabbageheads, *Stomolophus meleagris*, eat microzooplankton. Seawasps, *Chiropsalmus quadrumanus*, were found to consume microcrustacea and crustacean larvae. Concerning the relationship between fishes and jellyfish, Phillips et al. (1969) found that harvestfish, *Peprilus alepidotus*, and bumpers, *Chloroscombrus chrysurus*, appeared to feed on plankters that had been stunned or killed by the nematocysts of jellyfish.

In a two-year study of the mysids in the Delaware River estuary, Hulbert (1957) discovered that *Neomysis americana* was common throughout the estuary, with greater numbers in deep water than near the shore or in the surface waters. The same species was found to be abundant throughout the year in the Indian River Inlet of Delaware (Hopkins, 1965). *N. americana* accounted for 80% of the mysids, while *Mysidopsis bigelowi* contributed 17%. The remainder were *Metamysidopsis munda* and *Gas-*

trosaccus dissimilis. Hopkins (1965) reported that *N. americana* appeared to produce three generations: two were short-lived summer ones; the third, a longer-lived winter one. *N. americana* were most numerous from April through September and could be found in greatest abundance at the surface at night. Studies of the various species of mysids around Galveston Bay, Texas, by Price (1976) led to the conclusion that all mysids reproduced rapidly in summer, causing great population growth at that time. Slower reproduction and lower standing crops were common in winter.

Mysids are generally present in large numbers throughout the estuaries of the United States, though their presence is often missed in samples taken during daylight when the opossum shrimp are within the sediments. One of the reasons for the success of mysids may be that they feed low on the food chain. Kost and Knight (1975) found that California opossum shrimp, *N. mercedis*, feed primarily on detritus and diatoms. That feeding pattern presumably extends to other mysids as well.

Microplankton and Fish Eggs

Although the previous discussion has examined the major planktonic species, little or no information has been presented on microplankton and planktonic fish eggs and larvae. Neither has been studied intensively from a community point of view, though a great deal of descriptive and taxonomic work has been done on fish eggs and larvae. For example, Wheatland (1956) conducted an extensive study of the pelagic fish eggs and larvae of Long Island Sound and provided identifications and ecological information on each of the species collected.

The heterotrophic microplankton found within particulate matter in the estuaries and coastal waters of Georgia were studied by Hanson and Wiebe (1977). Those investigators discovered that in the creeks, rivers, and coastal waters (less than 4 km offshore), at least 80% of all community activity was associated with particles of 3 microns diameter or larger. The highest level of estuarine activity was reached near low ebb tide; the lowest, at slack high water. The implications for overall estuarine productivity and nutrient cycling have not been determined, but, as indicated in chapter 6, protozoans and other microplankton are important in detritus formation.

LITERATURE CITED

Bakker, C., and N. De Pauw. 1975. Comparison of plankton assemblages of identical salinity ranges in estuarine tidal and stagnant environments. II. Zooplankton. *Netherlands J. Sea Res.* 9: 145–65.

Barlow, J. P. 1955. Physical and biological processes determining the destruction of zooplankton in a tidal estuary. *Biol. Bull.* 109: 211–25.

Bellis, V. 1974. Medium salinity plankton systems, pp. 358–96. In: H. T. Odum, B. J. Copeland, and E. A. McMahan, eds. *Coastal ecological systems of the United States.* Vol. II. Washington, D.C.: Conservation Foundation.

Christmas, J. Y., ed. 1973. *Cooperative Gulf of Mexico estuarine inventory and study, Mississippi.* Ocean Springs, Miss.: Gulf Coast Research Laboratory.

Christmas, J. Y., G. Gunter, and P. Musgrave. 1966. Studies of the annual abundance of postlarval penaeid shrimp in the estuarine waters of Mississippi, as related to subsequent commercial catches. *Gulf Research Reports* 2: 177–212.

Conover, R. J. 1956. Oceanography of Long Island Sound, 1952–1954. VI. Biology of *Acartia clausi* and *A. tonsa. Bull. Bingham Oceanogr. Coll.* 15: 156–233.

———. 1961. A study of Charleston and Green Hill ponds, Rhode Island. *Ecology* 42: 119–40.

Costlow, J. D., Jr., C. G. Bookhout, and R. Monroe. 1962. Salinity-temperature effects on the larval development of the crab, *Panopeus herbstii* Milne-Edwards, reared in the laboratory. *Phys. Zool.* 35: 79–93.

———. 1966. Studies on the larval development of the crab, *Rhithropanopeus harrisii* (Gould). I. The effect of salinity and temperature on larval development. *Phys. Zool.* 39: 81–100.

Cronin, L. E., J. C. Daiber, and E. M. Hulbert. 1962. Quantitative seasonal aspects of zooplankton in the Delaware River estuary. *Ches. Sci.* 3: 63–93.

Cuzon du Rest, R. P. 1963. Distribution of the zooplankton in the salt marshes of southeastern Louisiana. *Publ. Inst. Mar. Sci., Univ. Tex.* 9: 132–55.

Dahlberg, M. D., and E. P. Odum. 1970. Annual cycles of species occurrence, abundance, and diversity in Georgia estuarine fish populations. *Am. Midl. Natur.* 83: 382–92.

Deevey, G. B. 1948. The zooplankton of Tisbury Great Pond. *Bull. Bingham Oceanogr. Coll.* 12: 1–44.

———. 1956. Oceanography of Long Island Sound, 1952–1954. V. Zooplankton. *Bull. Bingham Oceanogr. Coll.* 15: 113–55.

———. 1960. The zooplankton of the surface waters of the Delaware Bay region. *Bull. Bingham Oceanogr. Coll.* 17: 5–53.

Fish, C. J., and M. W. Johnson. 1937. The biology of the zooplankton population in the Bay of Fundy and Gulf of Maine with special reference to production and distribution. *J. Biol. Bd. Can.* 3: 189–332.

Grice, G. D. 1956. A qualitative and quantitative seasonal study of the copepods of Alligator Harbor. *Fla. State Univ. Stud.* 22: 37–76.

———. 1960. Calanoid and cyclopoid copepods collected from the Florida Gulf coast and Keys in 1954 and 1955. *Bull. Mar. Sci. Gulf Caribb.* 10: 217–26.

Hanson, R. B., and W. J. Wiebe. 1977. Heterotrophic activity associated with particulate size fractions in a *Spartina alterniflora* salt-marsh estuary, Sapelo Island, Georgia, USA, and the continental shelf waters. *Mar. Biol.* 42: 321–30.

Heinle, D. R. 1966. Production of a calanoid copepod, *Acartia tonsa*, in the Patuxent River estuary. *Ches. Sci.* 7: 59–74.

Heip, C. 1974. A new index measuring evenness. *J. Mar. Biol. Assoc. U.K.* 54: 555–57.

Heip, C., and P. Engels. 1974. Comparing species diversity and evenness indices. *J. Mar. Biol. Assoc. U.K.* 54: 559–63.

Hopkins, T. L. 1965. Mysid shrimp abundance in surface waters of Indian River Inlet, Delaware. *Ches. Sci.* 6: 86–91.

———. 1966. Plankton of the St. Andrew Bay system of Florida. *Publ. Inst. Mar. Sci., Univ. Tex.* 11: 12–64.

Hulbert, E. M. 1957. The distribution of *Neomysis americana* in the estuary of the Delaware River. *Limnol. Oceanogr.* 2: 1–11.

Jacobs, J. 1968. Animal behaviour and water movement as co-determinants of plankton distribution in a tidal system. *Sarsia* 34: 355–70.

Jeffries, H. P. 1962a. Copepod indicator species in estuaries. *Ecology* 43: 730–33.

———. 1962b. Succession of two *Acartia* species in estuaries. *Limnol. Oceanogr.* 7: 354–64.

Kost, A. B., and A. W. Knight. 1975. The food of *Neomysis mercedis* Holmes in the Sacramento–San Joaquin estuary. *Cal. Fish and Game* 61: 35–46.

McIlwain, T. D. 1968. Seasonal occurrence of the pelagic copepoda in Mississippi Sound. *Gulf Research Reports* 2: 257–70.

Nelson, T. C. 1925. On the occurrence and food habits of ctenophores in New Jersey inland coastal waters. *Biol. Bull.* 48: 92–111.

Ong, K.-S., and J. D. Costlow, Jr. 1970. The effect of salinity and temperature on the larval development of the stone crab, *Menippe mercenaria* (Say), reared in the laboratory. *Ches. Sci.* 11: 16–29.

Perkins, E. J. 1974. *The biology of estuaries and coastal waters.* New York: Academic Press.

Phillips, P. J., W. D. Burke, and E. J. Keener. 1969. Observations on the trophic significance of jellyfishes in Mississippi Sound with qualitative data on the associative behavior of small fishes with medusae. *Trans. Am. Fish. Soc.* 98: 703–12.

Price, W. 1974. The Mysidacea of Galveston Island. *Tex. J. Sci.* 25: 1–132.

Price, W. W. 1976. The abundance and distribution of Mysidacea in the shallow waters of Galveston Island, Texas. Ph.D. diss., Texas A&M University, College Station.

Riley, G. A. 1941. Plankton studies. III. Long Island Sound. *Bull. Bingham Oceanogr. Coll.* 7: 1–93.

———. 1967. The plankton of estuaries, pp. 316–26. In: G. H. Lauff, ed. *Estuaries*. American Association for the Advancement of Science Publication no. 83. Washington, D.C.: AAAS.

Stanlaw, K. A., M. R. Reeve, and M. A. Walter. 1981. Growth, food, and vulnerability to damage of the ctenophore *Mnemiopsis mccradyi* in its early life history stages. *Limnol. Oceanogr.* 26: 224–34.

Stickney, R. R., and S. C. Knowles. 1975. Summer zooplankton distribution in a Georgia estuary. *Mar. Biol.* 33: 147–54.

———. 1976. Seasonal zooplankton patterns in a Georgia estuary. *Bull. Ga. Acad. Sci.* 34: 121–28.

Wheatland, S. B. 1956. Oceanography of Long Island Sound, 1952–1954. VII. Pelagic fish eggs and larvae. *Bull. Bingham Oceanogr. Coll.* 15: 234–314.

White, D. B., and R. R. Stickney. 1973. A manual of flatfish rearing. Georgia Marine Science Center Technical Report Series 73-7.

Williams A. B. 1969. A ten-year study of meroplankton in North Carolina estuaries: Cycles of occurrence among penaeidean shrimps. *Ches. Sci.* 10: 36–47.

———. 1971. A ten-year study of meroplankton in North Carolina estuaries: Annual occurrence of some brachyuran developmental stages. *Ches. Sci.* 12: 53–61.

Williams, A. B., and E. E. Deubler. 1968. A ten-year study of meroplankton in North Carolina estuaries: Assessment of environmental factors and sampling success among bothid flounders and penaeid shrimp. *Ches. Sci.* 9: 27–41.

Williams, A. B. and H. J. Porter. 1971. A ten-year study of meroplankton in North Carolina estuaries: Occurrence of postmetamorphal bivalves. *Ches. Sci.* 12: 26–32.

Williams, A. B., and K. H. Bynum. 1972. A ten-year study of meroplankton in North Carolina estuaries: Amphipods. *Ches. Sci.* 13: 175–92.

Williams, R. B., M. B. Murdoch, and L. K. Thomas. 1968. Standing crop and importance of zooplankton in a system of shallow estuaries. *Ches. Sci.* 9: 42–51.

Woodmansee, R. A. 1958. The seasonal distribution of the zooplankton of Chicken Key in Biscayne Bay, Florida. *Ecology* 39: 247–62.

CHAPTER 8

Benthos

Introduction

THE benthic community is inhabited by animals that live around the sediments. Epifaunal organisms occur at the surface of the sediments, while infaunal organisms dwell within them. Oyster reefs are a form of benthic community, as are the communities of animals found attached to pilings, breakwaters, ship hulls, and other objects, whether natural or man-made.

In this discussion, macrobenthic organisms will be defined as those retained by a 0.5 mm standard sieve; meiobenthic organisms, those passing through a 0.5 mm standard sieve. Members of the macrobenthic community may be as small as larval polychaetes and certain species of benthic copepods and as large as adult clams, oysters, and scallops. Meiobenthic organisms include not only the larval stages of animals that later become macrobenthic but also protozoans and other small animals that remain meiobenthic as adults. Some classifications use an additional category called the microbenthos. Microbenthic organisms have been defined as those that pass through a 63-micron standard sieve.

Among the most important physical and chemical features of estuarine organisms within the benthos communities are salinity and sediment type. Some of the early studies demonstrating the dependence of such organisms on these features were reviewed by Carriker (1967). Other variables such as temperature, dissolved oxygen, pollutant levels, and turbidity influence the benthos communities of estuaries both quantitatively and qualitatively. Water temperature over much of the world fluctuates seasonally, and the benthic organisms of temperate or higher latitudes must adapt to often significant seasonal and even diurnal temperature changes. Species that have adapted to tropical waters are, on the other hand, generally stenothermal. Estuarine benthic organisms tend to have salinity preferences and relatively restricted salinity ranges.

Substrate requirements for benthic organisms often relate to feeding mechanisms and food habits. Planktonic larvae of benthic organisms, as discussed by Carriker (1967), often have at least limited ability to select the kind of substrate upon which they will ultimately settle to take up their benthic life stages. With motile or highly adaptable species, the substrate type upon which larvae settle may be relatively insignificant; for certain species, however, particularly those with limited or no motility as adults (e.g., clams, oysters, and barnacles), selection of the proper substrate at the time of settling is critical to survival. Species such as oysters can settle and resuspend themselves into the water column if the substrate is unsuitable. At some point, however, further movement from the sediments into the water column becomes impossible, and the animal will succumb if it has failed to find an appropriate substrate.

Certain species of invertebrates with strong swimming ability, as well as certain fishes, can more likely be found on the substrate than in the water column. Thus, the incorporation of these animals into either the benthic or nekton community is somewhat arbitrary. Among the species that can enter the water column or are strong swimmers but appear to prefer living on or in the sediments are shrimp, swimming crabs, and fishes such as flounders, sting rays, eels, sea robins, and lizardfish. Much of the coastal fishery of the southeastern Atlantic and the Gulf of Mexico is based upon groundfish—species found near the bottom. To enhance continuity, the invertebrates that might be classified as either benthic or nektonic are included in this chapter, while fishes are considered to be members of the nekton and are discussed in chapter 9.

The Meiobenthos

Although some studies include details of the taxonomy of species within the meiobenthic community, classification much below the level of class or order is often difficult, particularly with larval forms. Based on quantity per given volume of sediment, the numbers of organisms inhabiting meiobenthic communities are generally quite large relative to those of the macrobenthos in the same location. The biomass of the macrobenthic organisms, however, generally far exceeds that of the meiobenthos. Qualitatively, both groups are often highly diverse.

Sand-flat meiofaunal species are vermiform organisms that move through the interstitial spaces between sediment grains. The meiofauna of muddy sediments, on the other hand, are usually stockier and are burrowing species (McIntyre, 1969). Muddy-bottom meiofauna live near the sediment surface (often in the upper centimeter) and may inhabit anaerobic areas, while sand-flat meiofaunal can often be found in abundance to depths greater than 10 cm.

Some authors have indicated that the meiobenthic community represents a dead end in the food chain; other evidence, however, suggests that meiobenthic species serve as food for organisms in other communities. Discussion of this point can be found in Bell and Coull (1978), Bell (1979), and Peterson and Peterson (1979). Many general studies of meiofaunal communities have been undertaken. Kerby (1977) reported that meiofaunal density in the intertidal zone ranges from 11,000 to more than 16,000,000 individuals/m². Density in the subtidal zone was found by the same author to range from 4,000 to 3,200,000 individuals/m². Pearse et al. (1942) enumerated both microorganisms and meiobenthic animals on intertidal flats and discovered that a gram of sediment might contain 500,000 bacteria, several thousand diatoms and other algae, and various numbers of nematodes, copepods, ostracods, and amphipods.

A 1957 study of the meiobenthos of Buzzards Bay, Massachusetts (Wieser, 1960), revealed that the numbers of organisms present ranged from 1.69×10^5 to $1.86 \times 10^6/m^2$. Nematodes and kinorhynchs were found to constitute 89 to 99% of the total. Wieser (1960) further determined that distribution of the meiobenthic animals was related to sediment type. In South Carolina, Bell (1979) reported that 73% of the meiofauna was made up of nematodes, with copepods the next most abundant taxon. The copepod assemblages differed both in numbers per unit area and numbers of species during the two years in which the community was studied.

In another study of the meiofauna of South Carolina, Coull and Fleeger (1977) found that the organisms within the top centimeter of the mud varied randomly with respect to community abundance and diversity. Diversity was controlled by the seasonal cycling of occurring species groups. In contrast, the meiofauna in a sandy region of the estuary showed decreased diversity with time, while abundance increased. No marked seasonality of the sand-dwelling meiobenthic organisms was observed during the three-year study. The mud and sand communities appeared to have different species compositions, seasonal responses, dominance relationships, and population controls, though the two communities were equally diverse.

Studies in various *Spartina alterniflora* salt marshes in the southeastern United States have identified distinct zonation patterns among the meiobenthic copepods (Coull et al., 1979). One species, *Microarthridon littorale*, occurs along the entire gradient from the bottom of tidal creeks to the high intertidal zone of the marshes. Most other species have rather limited zonation. Reasons for the broad distribution of *M. littorale* are unknown, but the narrow distribution of other species may result from tolerance of only limited ranges of water depth, inability to avoid desiccation during exposure at low tide, the presence or absence of vegetation, and the presence of macrofaunal disturbers or predators.

In Louisiana, most salt marshes contain pools of water among the stands of *Spartina* spp. and *Distichlis spicata*. Elliott and Bamforth (1975) found 200 species of interstitial ciliates living in the marshes. The distribution of the protozoans was stratified, with algivores and omnivores inhabiting the upper layer and bactivores living more deeply within the sediments. The food habits of 260 species of benthic ciliates were reviewed by Fenchel (1968a).

Although the meiobenthos community is often considered as a whole, at times particular species or groups of species are examined with care because they can be used to predict certain things about the environment. One such group, which has helped identify environmental conditions in the salt water (including estuaries), is the foraminifera. Those protozoans can often be found in benthos communities but are also commonly collected from the water column. Nichols (1974) reported that the number of forams per liter in the water column at any given time should correspond to the general level of organic productivity within the estuary being sampled. Although few studies relative to that point have been conducted, Stewart (1958) found low productivity in the San Miguel Lagoon, Baja California, when forams numbered less than 10/ml. Nichols (1974) presented the ecology of forams in considerable detail. Unless otherwise indicated, the following discussion is from that work.

Forams develop tests composed of calcium carbonate, or they may agglutinate sand particles and, in some cases, chitin. Species that build their tests from sand grains, mica flakes, or other sedimentary particles cement those particles together with calcium carbonate or chitinous secretions. Such species are found primarily in fresh and brackish water. The calcareous species construct tests of calcium carbonate, which is either secreted by the protozoan or precipitated from the water. Such species tend to tolerate higher salinity water than those building their tests from sediment particles. When found in low salinity water, the calcareous species generally have thin tests, and some species have tests with chitinous linings.

Besides their potential for predicting productivity, forams can also be used to identify prevailing environmental conditions. For example, Nichols (1974) cited various authors who determined that when forams are present in environments receiving high levels of seasonal stress or pollutant input, the tests of the protozoans have irregular shapes.

The number of species of forams increases near the sea, though large populations can often be found where rivers enter estuaries, particularly when nutrient levels are high. Their numbers may actually diminish both up- and downstream from such locations.

Although forams with large, thick tests may be common near high-energy beaches, they are usually scarce in high-velocity channels. When present in the latter, the forams are often represented only by minute or attached species. In sedimentary deltas, the foram community commonly comprises large standing crops represented by a small number of species. In marshes, protozoans vary in composition and abundance and are typically low in diversity. Mangrove swamps are dominated by calcareous species. Few forams are found in turbid, poorly vegetated waters around hypersaline lagoons.

The life span of forams ranges from a few months to several years. Forams appear to be bloom feeders—that is, they eat sparingly and reproduce slowly when food is limiting, but when sufficient food is present, they exploit it and greatly increase their reproductive rate (Lee et al., 1965).

Another group of meiobenthic organisms for which considerable data are available is the ciliate protozoans. A great deal of information on these protozoans has been published by Fenchel (1967, 1968a, 1968b, 1969). In those studies he determined that the respiration of the meiofaunal community exceeds that of the macrofauna and that the ciliates are the most important meiofaunal group in sediments composed of fine and medium sand. In addition, Fenchel examined the reproductive capacity of nine species of ciliates in the laboratory at various temperatures and concluded that all of the species evaluated grew best at or above 20 C. At that temperature, generation time ranged from 2.4 to 46 hours.

Studies of the meiobenthic community are few compared with those of the macrobenthos. This may result, in part, from the relatively greater difficulty in separating the meiobenthic organisms from the sediments and in identifying the species collected. Also, though even the most casual observer notices macrobenthic life within estuarine sediments, the meiobenthos are too minute to attract attention. Their inconspicuousness may have fostered the lack of attention paid them by scientists.

The Macrobenthos

Like the meiobenthos, estuarine macrobenthic organisms represent a broad cross section of the aquatic invertebrates (along with a few taxa that are terrestrial at some point in their lives). Among the dominant groups of macrobenthos found on tidal flats are the polychaetes, bivalve and gastropod molluscs, amphipods and other crustaceans, sipunculids, nemerteans, and echinoderms (Peterson and Peterson, 1979).

On most estuarine sand and mud flats, epifaunal species are present but are often sparse relative to the infauna (Moore et al., 1968). Oyster reefs and fouling communities are exceptions, since they are dominated by epifauna. Regarding areal coverage, however, oyster reefs and fouling communities often represent a minor fraction of the total estuary. With respect to biomass, motile epibenthic forms such as shrimp and crabs may dominate in many estuarine systems. If counted, benthic infaunal species generally outnumber the motile forms by orders of magnitude.

Taxonomic variety is often relatively high in benthic communities, though a few species frequently dominate. In twenty samples collected from Buzzards Bay, Massachusetts, over two years, Sanders (1960) found seventy-nine macrobenthic species. Eleven of these species constituted over 95% of the number of organisms present, and ten species accounted for 95% of biomass. Sanders (1960) considered number to be a better measure of the benthic community than biomass, since only 0.15% of the species accounted for 55.17% of the weight. Also, biomass can be misleading when animals with heavy exoskeletons are present within a community. For example, an area dominated by polychaetes may have a sparse population of clams. Even a few of the latter could make up the bulk of the biomass present unless only the weight of the living material is considered. As an example of the dominance of molluscs in biomass, a study conducted in south Florida (Moore et al., 1968) concluded that dry weight biomass in the estuary was 30 g/m^2, of which 96% was contributed by molluscs.

Enumeration studies of benthic organisms are more common than those that consider biomass alone. Many investigations have analyzed both factors. A representative study is that of Sanders et al. (1962) in Barnstable Harbor, Massachusetts. During summer sampling, those investigators found that the numbers of intertidal benthic organisms varied from 7,000 to 355,000/m^2 with a dry weight biomass range of 17.6 to 60.2 g/m^2.

The ecology of sand and mudflat benthic organisms in North Carolina has been considered in detail by Peterson and Peterson (1979). Mudflat benthic ecology in northern California was described by Barbour et al. (1973). That study analyzed the water column, freshwater marshes, and upland flora and fauna as well as the estuarine mudflat community. Other general references on marine benthic ecology include Carriker (1967) and Coull (1977).

Not all benthic studies have used the same sieve sizes to separate animals from the sediments. Although we have limited the macrobenthos to organisms larger than 0.5 mm, many studies have made the separation at 1.0 mm or even larger. Williams and Thomas (1967) collected benthos samples in Chesapeake Bay and examined only those organisms retained by a 6.0 mm sieve.

PHYSICAL AND CHEMICAL CONSIDERATIONS

Physical and chemical factors associated with estuaries often control diversity, speciation, and abundance of macrobenthic organisms. In a study of amphipods of the family Haustoriidae, Dexter (1967) found that seven species cohabited an ocean-inlet beach in North Carolina. Adaptability to different niches characterized by intertidal zonation patterns, varying reproductive seasons, and size differences was invoked to explain how the various species could occur in the same general environment. Thus, mere tolerance of local environmental conditions is not sufficient to explain the presence or absence of a particular benthic species. Biological adaptation may also be important and will sometimes lead to the elimination or allow the cohabitation of species that compete for the same niche.

Euryhalinity is a characteristic shared by various estuarine organisms. Because of tidal ebb and flow, many estuarine animals are exposed to almost constantly changing salinity. The benthic infauna may be less harshly affected than other organisms since interstitial waters tend to maintain a more stable salinity profile than that exhibited by the overlying water column, particularly in estuaries with significant amounts of tidal flow and incoming fresh water. Reid (1930) demonstrated that fresh water flowing over sand in an estuary did not affect infauna that could burrow to a depth of 30 cm, because the salinity did not change significantly at that depth. Stenohaline epibenthic organisms, on the other hand, might be severely stressed or killed when exposed to even slight reductions in salinity as a result of inflowing fresh water.

In general, the more rapid the flow of fresh water over sand, the faster the salt is leached out. Reid (1932) found nevertheless that brief exposure of the sediments to tidal water will cause a return of interstitial salinity to near normal levels. He concluded that it is somewhat more difficult to decrease interstitial salinity than to increase it.

In a California study, Johnson (1967a) demonstrated that interstitial salinity on the upper beach was higher at a depth of 10 cm than at 20 cm below the sediment surface. This relationship did not hold throughout the beach profile, however. At an elevation of 1 m above sea level, the salinity at 10 cm equaled that at 20 cm. Below this elevation, the salinity of the interstitial water was less variable than that of the adjacent bay water.

Regarding the relationship between the abundance of benthic organisms and the salinity regime in which they are found, Cronin and Mansueti (1971) reported that the highest density of benthic species was often near the center of the salinity gradient. That location tended to be the area that received the widest diurnal salinity variation. The upper estuary would often remain nearly fresh, while the lower estuary would maintain relatively high salinity under normal conditions.

Large ranges in water chemistry do not necessarily relate to high standing crops of benthos, however. In the Pamlico River estuary of North Carolina, Tenore (1972) found both low diversity and low benthos density in an area characterized by a salinity range of 1 to 20 o/oo and a temperature range of 5 to 31 C. Those ranges may be somewhat greater, particularly for salinity, than the ones to which most midestuary benthic species are exposed, though such extremes may not be uncommon in temperate estuaries. Tenore (1972) observed vast seasonal changes in species composition, distribution, and density in the North Carolina benthic community.

Although samples obtained from the water column are often useful in predicting conditions to which the benthos are exposed, frequently close examination of the sediments and interstitial waters is also required. For example, in many estuaries aerobic sediments predominate, while in others discrete anaerobic layers lie immediately below the sediment surface. In a Washington state estuary studied by Pamatmat (1968), the sediments were found to contain no oxygen at a depth of 5 cm, though living algae were recovered from as deep as 10 cm. Though the sediments were representative of a reducing environment, alkalinity, pH, and salinity were the same as those of the overlying water column.

Holland et al. (1973) examined the benthos of Galveston Bay, Texas, and found good correlation between such factors as benthic diversity and water quality. Of five areas evaluated, three were judged to have normal water quality as indicated from the kind of benthic community living there. Poor water quality was found in two cases. In one of the latter cases environmental stress was attributed to natural salinity fluctuations; in the other, pollution was invoked as the probable stressor.

SEDIMENTARY RELATIONSHIPS

The quantity of benthic organisms per unit area may be influenced by sediment type. For example, Sanders et al. (1962) found that small benthos standing crops occurred in a Massachusetts estuary in areas where ripple marks (indicative of strong water movement) were present. In the absence of ripple marks, dense colonies of benthic algae (diatoms and dinoflagellates) clustered near large standing crops of macrobenthic species. In another study, Newell (1965) found that the density of the prosobranch, *Hydrobia ulvae*, and bivalve, *Macoma balthica*, in England varied with sediment type. Dense concentrations of both species appeared in fine sediments, with low population densities in coarse sediments.

Carriker (1967) concluded that muddy sand sediments tend to support larger populations of benthic organisms than do coarse, clean, unstable sands and gravels or soft muds. According to Yonge (1953), locomotion may be difficult in soft mud sediments; thus, those sediments could limit benthic organisms. In a study of benthic organisms in Long Island Sound, Sanders (1956) found the highest numbers in sediments containing between 13 and 25% silt and clay.

Sanders (1958) sampled nineteen stations in late 1955 and discovered that the number of benthic organisms present in Buzzards Bay, Massachusetts, ranged from 1,064 to 12,576/m². Muddy sediments were dominated by the lamellibranch, *Nucula proxima*, and polychaete, *Nephthys incisa*.

In finer sediments the characteristic fauna were primarily amphipods of the genus *Ampelisca*. In general, soft-bodied organisms dominate fine-grained sediments, while molluscs are more common in coarser ones.

Johnson (1967b) reported that most of the benthic infaunal organisms of mud and sand flats stay in the upper 15 cm of the substrate. Burrowing organisms, particularly large species, may go somewhat deeper—and their burrowing may be unique with respect to species.

Benthic species are not completely at the mercy of the sediments. Several studies have demonstrated that some species can actually alter the sediments and can, in fact, lead to changes in the distribution of species found in a given area. Intertidal flats, for example, may change as a result of animal activity. Animals that ingest sediments while feeding may increase the water content of the sediments and allow more resuspension and movement of the sediments than might otherwise occur (Rhodes and Young, 1970). This could lead to an alteration in mean grain size over time. In a study on Cape Cod, Massachusetts, Young and Rhodes (1971) demonstrated that polychaete tube mats bind and stabilize sediments and provide surfaces for the attachment of epizoans. The formation of oyster reefs is another way in which benthic organisms influence the sedimentary environment.

EXCLUSION STUDIES

The purpose of exclusion studies is to protect limited areas from potential predators in order to determine how those predators might affect the organisms of a particular environment. Exclosures have often been used in benthos studies to assess the impact of various predators on epibenthic and infaunal species. In general, exclosure studies have shown that large, motile predators usually control the density of benthic infaunal species on intertidal flats (Peterson and Peterson, 1979), though this may not always be the case.

Various exclusion studies, conducted both in the field and the laboratory, have demonstrated the significance of predation on the benthos. Bell and Coull (1978) established a group of microecosystems in laboratory tanks. They first allowed meiobenthic communities to become established for nine months, then introduced *Palaemonetes pugio* (grass shrimp) into some of the tanks, leaving others as controls. The total numbers of meiofauna, nematodes, oligochaetes, and polychaetes were significantly reduced in tanks containing the grass shrimp. No changes in diversity were noted in any of the tanks. That study was one of the first to demonstrate that benthic macrofaunal organisms can control the meiobenthos.

In a study of the benthos of the Indian River estuary in central Florida, Young et al. (1976) found that in two out of three cases over five months, species densities increased in cages designed to exclude predators. In the third case there was heavier predation in the cage than in control areas, probably because predatory decapod crustaceans had been allowed to remain in the cage over the study period. The authors concluded that the decapods did more damage to the benthos than would have been the case if fish had been allowed into the area. The fish would, presumably, have eaten some of the decapods and reduced overall predation, even if the fish had also preyed upon the infauna.

Virnstein (1977) conducted studies with benthic exclosures, into which various species of fish and blue crabs were introduced, to determine their relative rates of predation. Spot (*Leiostomus xanthurus*) and blue crabs (*Callinectes sapidus*) reduced infaunal densities in the exclosures, while hogchokers (*Trinectes maculatus*) did not. If the predators were removed from the exclosures, the density and diversity of benthic species increased greatly within two months. The density of all species increased once predators were eliminated, suggesting that benthos population control results not from competitive interactions among the infaunal species but largely from predation. Virnstein's (1977) experiment did not place food or space limitations on the benthos. If either of those factors became limiting, more competition among the benthic organisms would presumably develop.

In exclosure studies conducted in European waters by Reise (1976, 1977, 1978), predation was measured in intertidal flats. Three probable benthos predators were excluded by using 5 mm mesh exclosures. These exclosures, placed on a mud flat, developed a density of benthic organisms tenfold that of unprotected areas. No significant change occurred in exclosures placed in a seagrass bed as compared with natural seagrass areas. Reise (1976, 1978) concluded that the root system of the seagrass gave protection from predation, so little or no advantage was gained from the exclosures. Benthic animals on the mud flat, on the other hand, enjoyed no such protection, and their numbers greatly increased when protection was afforded. The predation of birds and flatfish affected large infaunal species more profoundly than small ones, and small epibenthic predators (shrimps, shore crabs, and gobies) were major determiners of species abundance on intertidal flats.

BENTHOS FEEDING STRATEGIES

Benthic organisms use various feeding strategies. Rhodes (1974) recognized five categories:

1. Herbivores—organisms that consume plant material
2. Carnivores and scavengers—animals that eat living or recently living material
3. Parasites—species that live on the fluids of other living organisms
4. Deposit feeders—animals that feed on detritus within the sediments
5. Suspension feeders—species that prey on organic particles or on organisms suspended in the water column

Five categories of benthic feeding strategies were also enumerated by Sanders et al. (1962): carnivores, omnivores, scavengers, deposit feeders, and suspension feeders. There is general agreement that many estuarine benthic species are either deposit or suspension feeders. Levinton (1972) reported that deposit feeders actually ingest the bottom sediments, while suspension feeders strain food particles from the water. The latter feed mainly on phytoplankton, though detritus is also often consumed. Levinton (1972) found that predictability of the amount of food energy available to deposit and suspension feeders using detritus as their primary food source was poor. Moul and Mason (1957) discovered levels of from 50,000 to 900,000 algal cells/cm^2 in the top 2.5 cm of sediments in Massachusetts. Such high concentrations of food are undoubtedly of great importance to deposit-feeding benthic species. In a study of the holothurian *Leptosynapta tenuis* in North Carolina, Powell (1977) noted that 51% of the material ingested by that deposit feeder came from the upper 0.5 cm of the sediments, 75% from the top 3 cm. Rate of feeding appeared to depend on temperature.

Various specializations have developed within the suspension-feeding strategy. For example, bivalve molluscs pump water through their gills and filter out food, which is primarily phytoplanktonic, though bacteria and protozoans also contribute. Other suspension feeders construct nets to entrap particulate matter that passes over them. Suspended sediments tend to clog the filter apparatus of suspension feeders, however, so in high levels of suspended solids, deposit feeders tend to displace suspension feeders. Woodin (1976) indicated that the species that first occupy an area may control later colonization. That notion goes back to the previously mentioned concept that benthic organisms not only colonize on the basis of existing conditions but, in addition, can influence the sedimentary environment.

Suspension feeders generally dominate in sandy sediments, while deposit feeders are most common in soft, muddy substrates (Sanders, 1958; McNulty et al., 1962; Newell, 1965; Rhodes and Young, 1970). The food and feeding habits of deposit feeders have been studied in several estuaries. For example, a study by Brenner et al. (1976) in a Massachusetts salt marsh revealed that the gammarid amphipod *Talorchestia longicornis* ingests blue-green algae available on algal mats. In another Massachusetts study, Whitlatch (1974) found that the large polychaetes, represented by *Pectinaria gouldii*, selected larger food particles than did smaller polychaetes. Hyllberg and Gallucci (1975) studied the mollusc *Macoma nasuta*, which feeds by ingesting the top millimeter of sediment. They found that about 97% of the dry weight of surface material in the sediments is passed through the worms as pseudofeces. The same authors reported that the fecal pellets were richer in organic matter than were the original sediments, indicating some selectivity in feeding or at least in assimilation.

Sanders et al. (1962) examined the gut contents of various benthic species in Massachusetts for two years and revealed that many species traditionally considered carnivorous were actually deposit feeders. Included were several species of polychaetes. In that study, deposit feeding predominated even though the sediments were sandy. A similar discovery was made by Jacobsen (1967), who reported that the lugworm *Arenicola marina* is a deposit feeder, even though earlier work by Kruger (1959, 1964) had labeled the species a suspension feeder. Jacobsen (1967) felt that data in the earlier work were misinterpreted.

Sharp boundaries have been found between benthic communities of deposit, as opposed to suspension, feeders. Woodin (1976) hypothesized that the boundaries result from interactions among established infaunal species and settling larvae. Deposit feeders do a significant amount of sediment reworking and feed in areas where larvae have settled in attempts to become established. Such larvae become prey for the deposit feeders, while burrowing polychaetes usually escape in significant numbers. Suspension feeders can also affect settling larvae by removing them from the water column. Burrowing polychaetes, which commonly live in tubes, alter the sediments by usurping available space and depositing fecal pellets on the sediment surface. The burrowing forms may have little direct impact on settling larvae. Woodin (1976) predicted that suspension feeders would exist largely alone, while burrowing polychaetes would be found with deposit feeders. Results of sediment reworking by deposit-feeding benthic organisms can lead to a fluid, fecal material–rich surface easily resuspended by tidal currents. Resuspension of the sediments may clog the filtering apparatus of suspension feeders, bury or discourage larval settling, and prevent the attachment of sessile epifaunal species (Rhodes and Young, 1970).

Fecal pellets are often richer in nutrients than the sediments upon which they are deposited. The pellets are also often readily available, and it is not surprising that some benthic species have become dependent upon them as a food source. The fecal pellets of the mud shrimp, *Callianassa major*, may be produced at the rate of 2,600/m²/day and contain carbon and nitrogen at 3 and 0.3% of dry weight, respectively. They are commonly consumed by hermit crabs and may be eaten by blue crabs and perhaps other beach inhabitants (Frankenberg et al., 1967).

Frankenberg and Smith (1967) examined coprophagy in the laboratory by offering fecal pellets to three species of polychaetes, four gastropods, three pelecypods, seven crustaceans, and three fishes (*Fundulus heteroclitus*, *F. majalis*, and *Mugil cephalus*). Fecal pellets were obtained from the polychaete *Onuphis microcephala*, gastropods, the oyster *Crassostrea virginica*, and the crustaceans *Callianassa major* and *Penaeus setiferus*. The animals tested consumed from 0 to 83% of their body weight in fecal pellets over forty-eight hours. Fecal ingestion rates were positively correlated with carbon and nitrogen contents of the pellets. Frankenberg and Smith (1967) concluded that coprophagy can aid the recycling of nutrients but that it may also lead to parasitism and possibly toxicity if pollutants have been concentrated in the fecal pellets.

Motile macrobenthic organisms commonly feed as scavengers or predators and are not usually classified as deposit or suspension feeders. Such species as the horseshoe crab (*Limulus polyphemus*), which lives along portions of the southeastern Atlantic coast and in the Gulf of Mexico, preys on clams, heart urchins, polychaetes, and other burrowing organisms, which it reaches by digging through the sediments (Gray, 1974).

The blue crab (*Callinectes sapidus*) is carnivorous and ranges widely over the bottom in search of food. That species will also feed upon dead and decaying animals. Laird and Haefner (1976) examined the oxygen consumption of *C. sapidus* and found that as the crabs increased in weight from 20 to 200 g, weight-specific oxygen consumption decreased. There was little effect on oxygen consumption over the salinity range from 10 to 30 o/oo, though consumption increased with temperature over the range 10 to 25 C, indicating increased activity—including, presumably, a higher feeding rate.

Other crabs, such as *Pagurus longicarpus* and *Petrochirus diogenes* (hermit crabs), appear to be omnivorous (Peterson and Peterson, 1979). Mud crabs (family Xanthidae) are common throughout the estuaries of the Southeast and the Gulf of Mexico. The life histories of five species from Chesapeake Bay were outlined by Ryan (1956). Xanthid crabs are abundant near Alabama oyster reefs. Their distribution is affected by salinity, substrate, and water quality. They appear to be commensals and scavengers instead of predators (May, 1974).

Various large gastropods are carnivorous and may even feed almost exclusively on other molluscs. The gastropods *Busycon contrarium* and *B. carica*, for example, eat primarily such clams as *Mercenaria mercenaria* and *Chione cancellata*, while *B. canaliculatum* consumes carrion (Peterson and Peterson, 1979). The abundance of various species of *Busycon* was studied in the vicinity of Beaufort, North Carolina, by Magalhaes (1948). The most common species was *B. carica*, followed by *B. canaliculatum* and *B. contrarium*, respectively. Periods of maximum activity varied among the species. All species were more active for short periods just before and just after low tide than at other times. Common foods of the gastropods included such other mollusc genera as *Tagelus*, *Chione*, *Venus (Mercenaria)*, *Dosinia*, and *Modiolus*. Paine (1963) conducted a study in Alligator Harbor, Florida, which demonstrated that *Busycon contrarium*, *B. spiratum*, *Murex*, *Polinices*, and *Sinum* were secondary consumers while such gastropods as *Pleuroploca*, *Fasciolaria tulipa*, and *F. hunteria* were tertiary consumers, with *Pleuroploca* at the top of the food web.

COMMUNITIES OF FOULING ORGANISMS

Anyone who has owned or had occasion to use a boat in an estuary will undoubtedly be familiar with the myriad organisms that become attached to the hull. Included are such species as barnacles, mussels, bryozoans, and tunicates. Other kinds of fouling communities (though made up largely of the same species as those found on boat hulls) can be found on pilings (figure 16), piers, intertidal rocks, and other hard substrates, either intertidally or subtidally.

Fig. 16. An intertidal fence post colonized by barnacles.

One group of animals often a problem for man is the boring organ-isms, including the isopod, *Limnoria* sp. (commonly called the gribble), and the shipworms, *Bankia* and *Toredo* spp. Most pilings are treated with creosote and resist the invasion of shipworms. Gribbles, however, will in-vade. Their maximum length is 5 mm, and a single piling may house bur-rows containing several hundred thousand (Lindgren, 1974). Untreated wood tends to be more severely affected by *Limnoria* sp. than treated wood (Beckman et al., 1957). An affected piling often has a normal diameter above the level of mean high tide and below the sediment surface but a reduced diameter between those locations. Eventually, the piling will either be eaten through, or, if unsupported, it will fall as it becomes weakened.

Whitten et al. (1950) examined the invertebrate fauna around jetties along the Texas coast. The organisms lived within temperature and salinity ranges of 9 to 30 C and 15 to 35 o/oo, respectively. The investigation, which concentrated on intertidal fauna, found the community to be composed principally of three species of barnacles, one limpet, the periwinkle *Littorina ziczac*, an anemone, a mussel, the gastropod *Thais floridna*, a hermit crab, and the isopod *Ligyda*.

In some areas attached algae are common. Sea lettuce, *Ulva* sp., is an example. Bryozoans, sea pansies (*Renilla* sp.), and whip coral (*Leptogorgia* sp.) are fouling organisms that resemble plants.

HERMIT AND FIDDLER CRABS

Such hermit crabs as *Clibanarius vittatus*, *Pagurus pollicaris*, and *P. longicarpus* have broadly overlapping shell use patterns along the Texas coast, and in some cases this overlap can lead to a shortage of shells. As hermit crabs grow, they must move to larger shells (figure 17). When suitable shells are not available, growth may slow as will clutch size (Fotheringham, 1976). In the winter, *C. vittatus* competes with *P. pollicaris* and *P. longicarpus* for gastropod shells in Galveston Bay, Texas (Wright, 1973). *C. vittatus* is aggressive and thus often is able to outcompete *Pagurus* spp. even if the latter are larger.

Kellogg (1976) studied occupancy of gastropod shells by hermit crabs in North Carolina. His study revealed that the crabs could be found in 58 to 99% of the available shells, with those not occupied by hermit crabs often containing sipunculids.

Fiddler crabs are a common sight in many estuaries as they scurry around during low tide. Their intertidal burrows provide shelter when inundated by water, but the crabs often forage when the burrows are exposed. They will quickly retreat to the safety of the burrows, which can be quite extensive, when danger threatens. Various species of fiddler crabs occur in the estuaries of the United States. Along the Atlantic coast, *Uca pugnax*, *U. pugilator*, and *U. minax* are common. *U. pugnax* is found throughout the *Spartina* salt marshes except at the edge, *U. pugilator* lives on the tidal

Fig. 17. Hermit crabs inhabit mollusc shells and leave distinctive tracks inter-tidally. Also visible are worm holes and the tube of the polychaete *Diopatra cuprea* (*upper right*).

creek banks and in the *Salicornia* and *Distichlis* marshes, and *U. minax* can be found in certain parts of the *Spartina* marsh (Teal, 1958).

Density of the marsh root mat within a particular area may be impor-tant in the distribution of *Uca pugnax*. Ringold (1979) found that distribution of that fiddler crab was reduced when thick root mats were present, since the roots limited the ability of the crab to burrow.

Near Mustang Island, Texas, three species of fiddler crabs were found by Bowers (1975). *Uca panacea* was the most common, inhabiting denuded areas from dry-damp sand flats to wet sand and muddy algal flats. *U. virens* lived within vegetated clumps of marsh and appeared to prefer wet, muddy substrates, while *U. longisignalis* was found in dry or damp sandy-mud zones of vegetation clumps.

MOLLUSC COMMUNITIES

Various communities of molluscs occur in estuaries, among them oyster reefs, clam beds, scallop beds, and mussel shoals. Other molluscs may be somewhat less conspicuous but may play an important role in energy cycling in estuaries. A variety of small pelycepods and gastropods inhabit the sediments in nearly all estuaries, though they may not be visible to the casual observer. Periwinkles climb up and down on the grasses around salt marshes, and nudibranchs commonly drift along in the water column as part of the zooplankton community.

The blue mussel, *Mytilus edulis*, is common along the Atlantic coast and the Gulf of Mexico. Mussels grow attached to some sort of hard substrate, much like oysters. Examination of the effects of temperature and salinity on the growth and survival of *M. edulis* larvae by Lough (1974) showed that the range of conditions required for maximum survival greatly differed from those required for growth. Temperature appeared to exert a strong influence on both growth and survival, while temperature-salinity interactions were not significant.

The razor clam (*Tagelus* sp.) is common in many estuaries. In South Carolina, the razor clam population was found to inhabit only stable sediments with more than 2% silt and clay and was characterized by a film of benthic algae (Holland and Dean, 1977). The clams, which filter suspended matter from the water column, constituted 93% of the biomass of the benthos community, though they accounted for only 3.2% of the total number.

Some of the most common clams in estuaries of the southeastern United States and the Gulf of Mexico are the common rangia, *Rangia cuneata*, and hard clams in the genus *Mercenaria*. Menzel (1963) found that the northern quahog (*M. mercenaria*) grew more slowly than did the southern species (*M. campechiensis*) in Alligator Harbor, Florida. The former species reached 67 mm after 3.5 years; the latter, 74 mm in 2 years. Laboratory setting experiments with larval northern quahogs demonstrated that pheromones and physical factors influenced setting. Clams prefered to set on sand as opposed to mud. In addition, sediments treated with clam extract were preferred to untreated sediments (Keck et al., 1974).

Among the often overlooked gastropods of estuaries, one of the more common is the mud snail, *Nassarius obsoletus*. That small mollusc is basically a deposit feeder that eats the microflora found on the sediments of intertidal flats. Dead organisms are also consumed when available but are not considered to be a primary food source for mud snails (Scheltema, 1964).

Many estuarine molluscs, such as oysters, mussels, and clams, are filter feeders. An investigation of the stomach contents of the scallop, *Aequipecten irradians*, by Davis and Marshall (1963) revealed that the primary food items were microflora, detritus, bacteria, and organic matter.

The filtering activity of molluscs can lead to concentration of toxicants, as has been clearly demonstrated by oysters. For example, oysters exposed to 1 ppb of the pesticide DDT for twenty-five days accumulated 25 ppm of the compound in their eggs. Although little obvious damage was observed, growth rate of the oysters was suppressed by 20% (Butler, 1966). The same study revealed that oysters with 151 parts per million DDT in their tissues were able to purge themselves of 95% of the pesticide within three months after being transferred to uncontaminated water. Trace metals can also be accumulated by oysters. Pringle et al. (1968) discovered that average tissue levels of copper, zinc, iron, and cadmium were all far greater than those found in natural waters.

Oyster reefs result from the attachment of young oysters (spat) to suitable substrates, such as other shells, rocks, man-made objects, or debris of some sort. In shallow waters and marshes, reef development may be in the form of a fringe of live oysters near the land; while in deeper waters, a shoal rising several meters above the bottom may emerge (Chestnut, 1974). Living reefs exist primarily within the photic zone, since oysters feed largely on living phytoplankton.

Loosanoff (1961) demonstrated that silt levels of 250 mg/l can significantly affect the development of oyster eggs. The egg does not develop at 1 to 2 g/l silt concentrations, but those levels are not common in most estuaries.

Oyster reefs can affect not only the standing crop of phytoplankton in the water column but, through feeding, they can also affect the surrounding sediments. A reef that develops in an area dominated by soft sediments will gradually convert the region to a solid mass of shell (Galtsoff, 1964). In contrast, solid bottom surrounding a developing oyster reef may actually become dominated by soft sediments as the reef reduces the current flow and allows suspended materials to be deposited (Grave, 1901).

Peterson and Peterson (1979) indicated that the oysters of North Carolina sand and mud flats are associated with a variety of other organisms. Among the more common are tunicates (e.g., *Styela* sp.), branching bryozoans (*Bugula* sp.), hydroids (*Pennaria* sp.), barnacles (*Balanus eburneus* and *B. amphitrite*), encrusting bryozoans (*Schizoporella* sp.), sponges (*Hymeniacidon* sp. and *Cliona* sp.), soft coral (*Leptogorgia* sp.), and small gastropods (*Bittium* sp.). The diversity on an oyster reef is often quite high, with a great deal of possible interaction among the species present—not the least important of which is predation upon the oysters by other species of molluscs.

Oyster predators are numerous on living reefs and can affect production considerably. The predators include other molluscs and such crabs as members of the Xanthidae and the blue crab, *Callinectes sapidus* (Carriker, 1959).

The predators of oysters and clams have been widely studied in the United States, but three studies, one each from Florida, Georgia, and Alabama, will illustrate the possible effects of other molluscs on oyster production. Menzel and Nichy (1958) examined the oyster predators of Alligator Harbor, Florida,. The whelk *Busycon contrarium* was widespread and destructive to oysters. That species was found to kill mainly by chipping edges from oyster shells and forcing the valves apart. Another mollusc, *Melongena corona*, fed by inserting its proboscis into relaxed and open oyster shells. By contrast, the oyster drill *Murex* sp. used its radula to bore a hole into living oysters, after which the tissues within were dissolved and ingested. Oyster drills occurred mainly below the intertidal reefs of Alligator Harbor, where they could attack only available individual oysters and did not severely damage the reef as a whole. The stone crab, *Menippe mercenaria*, and blue crab, *Callinectes sapidus*, also preyed on oysters. The former killed oysters by breaking the shells, while the latter attacked only small oysters.

A study of the hard clam, *Mercenaria mercenaria*, in Wassaw Sound, Georgia (Walker et al, 1980), revealed that whelks, drills, rays, and crabs, particularly *C. sapidus*, eat clams. Whelks migrated seasonally onto and off of intertidal flats containing clams. Whelk densities were highest in the fall and spring and lowest in summer and winter. The drill, *Urosalpinx cinnerea*, occurred at an average density of 35 drills/m^2, but blue crabs were the greatest threat to clams. In Alabama, another oyster drill, *Thais haemastoma*, was shown to be the most serious predator of young oysters. Mortalities as high as 95% have ravaged some areas, according to May (1968). Salinities above 15 o/oo are thought to favor oyster drills (Chapman, 1959), and their activity diminishes at salinities below 10 o/oo (Galtsoff, 1964). High survival of planted seed oysters in Alabama during 1968 and 1969 was thought to result from a lack of oyster drills (May and Bland, 1970).

Another aspect of oyster production is artificial culture. Although oysters represent only one among many species with potential or realized importance as mariculture species, oysters were among the first estuarine organisms to inspire interest in culture. Wallace (1966) reviewed the development of the oyster industry in the United States, noting that oyster farming began in New England in the early nineteenth century. Oyster (and clam) culture varies considerably from state to state. As an example, most oyster culture in the Middle Atlantic states is on lands leased to farmers by the states. Table 7 presents data from the Middle Atlantic states on oyster and clam production from 1960 through 1969. During an earlier period, Raritan Bay was the center for oyster production, but pollution has changed all that, according to Wallace (1971). Hard clams have been found to reproduce successfully in that bay, even though oyster production has dissipated.

Among the unusual niches within the estuarine environment is that filled by the periwinkle, *Littorina* spp. Periwinkles (small gastropods) can be found moving up and down the stems of marshgrasses in the intertidal zone, always maintaining their position above the water as the tides rise and fall. The growth rates of *L. irrorata* in three North Carolina *Spartina alterniflora* marshes were studied by Stiven and Hunter (1976), who determined that the growth rates of the gastropods differed among the three marshes. Although marsh production also varied from site to site, the relationships between marsh productivity and growth rates of the periwinkles were not clear. The authors of that study were careful not to draw too heavily on the apparent relationship between marshgrass standing crop and periwinkle size variability.

TABLE 7. Oyster and Hard-Clam Production in New York, New Jersey, and Delaware, 1960–69

Year	Oysters (Metric Tons)	Hard Clams (Metric Tons)
1960	524.5	3,147.3
1961	873.2	2,981.8
1962	1,073.6	2,979.1
1963	432.3	3,253.2
1964	616.4	3,506.4
1965	344.1	3,720.0
1966	426.8	4,327.3
1967	480.0	5,649.1
1968	683.6	4,431.8
1969	581.4	4,473.2

Source: Wallace, 1971.

Ricketts and Calvin (1952) suggested that the climbing up and down of periwinkles is a behavioral adaptation that allows the gastropod to avoid drowning; that explanation, however, has not been supported by bioassays. Bleil and Gunn (1978) showed that all periwinkles survived total water immersion for twenty-eight days. Another theory, which states that maintenance of their position above the waterline protects periwinkles from blue crab predation (Hamilton, 1976), may be the correct one.

INSECTS

Aquatic insects are routinely examined in relation to limnological research but are often ignored in estuarine benthic studies. In subtidal sampling programs insects are generally absent or may appear as contaminants either in the field or during subsequent sample washing and are not true representatives of the benthic community. Insects often live in intertidal sediments, however, particularly at the higher elevations within that zone, as well as in exposed marshlands. A few groups (for example, the family Staphylinidae) are common in estuarine intertidal sediments.

Insects perhaps affect estuaries most importantly through their association with exposed marshlands, though insects and their larvae have also been found to use submerged vegetation for both attachment and food (Martin and Uhler, 1939). Observations and collections in Georgia showed that the most important herbivores of living *Spartina* spp. are the grasshopper, *Orchelimum fidicinium* (common from May to September), and the leafhopper, *Prokelesia marginata* (present throughout the year). Smalley (1959) estimated that those insects consumed no more than 7% of annual marshgrass production.

Davis and Gray (1966) reported on the insects of North Carolina marshes obtained by sweep netting. Homoptera and Diptera dominated in all kinds of marshland (*Spartina, Juncus,* and *Distichlis*). Hemiptera, Orthoptera, Coleoptera, and Hymenoptera were present at all sampling locations but did not occur in large numbers. Most of the insects collected in that study were herbivorous. Spiders constituted the dominant predators, but such predaceous insects as beetles, asilids, mosquitos, and dolichopotid flies were also gathered.

SHRIMP

The estuaries along the southeastern Atlantic coast and the Gulf of Mexico are well known for the production of penaeid shrimp. Shrimp of the family Palaemonidae are also abundant, though not nearly as widely known to the general public. Palemonid shrimp in the genus *Macrobrachium*, commonly called freshwater shrimp, occur in many of the fresh waters of the region, but their larvae require some salinity for normal development. Thus, the females migrate to the estuaries, where their eggs hatch and the larvae develop. The developing shrimp move out of the estuaries and into fresh water as they grow. Several species of freshwater shrimp are found in the Rio Grande and other river systems in Texas. Reimer et al. (1974) found that *M. ohione* seemed to be limited by salinities above 15 o/oo. Other species common to Texas, such as *M. carcina* and *M. acanthurus*, are also sought after since they attain large size.

Various species of grass shrimp, *Palaemonetes* spp., live in the estuaries of the United States and can even be found in fresh water. Shrimp in the genus *Palaemonetes* are small, without any current commercial value. Grass shrimp, like the related freshwater shrimp, carry their eggs externally. Seasonal distribution of *P. pugio* in Galveston Bay, Texas, was studied by Wood (1967). The shrimp were found throughout the year but were present in greatest abundance from July through October and at salinities from 10 to 20 o/oo; in lowest abundance, in water of 1 o/oo. Growth to maturity (attained at 20 to 24 mm) requires only two or three months during the summer but is increased to four to six months during the remainder of the year. Longevity of the grass shrimp was found to be about one year.

Best survival was at 4 to 16 o/oo salinity and 16 to 25 C. Peak spawning occurred in early summer and early fall at 18 to 20 C.

Shrimp studies have concentrated on the commercially valuable species of estuaries along the southeastern Atlantic and the Gulf of Mexico. The dominant species are the white shrimp, *Penaeus setiferus*; brown shrimp, *P. aztecus*; and pink shrimp, *P. duorarum*. They occur with discontinuous distribution throughout the region. White shrimp seem to have a greater tolerance for low salinity than do brown shrimp. That is one reason why the Louisiana coast offers a more conducive environment for white shrimp than does the Texas coast, where brown shrimp are more plentiful (Gunter, 1961).

A fourth species, the seabob (*Xiphopeneus kroyeri*), occurs in the deep, cool waters of the Gulf of Mexico during the summer but may enter the bays in midwinter when salinity conditions are suitable (Gunter, 1961). Under some circumstances *X. kroyeri* also appear in inshore waters during the summer. Seabob shrimp were found in the Savannah River by Stickney and Miller (1974) when the salinity of the lower reaches of the river was high enough to support them.

The general life history of penaeid shrimp has been reviewed by Kutkuhn (1966) and that of shrimp in North Carolina by Williams (1955). The general life cycle includes offshore spawning, after which postlarvae move into the estuary (figure 18). Juvenile shrimp remain in the estuary throughout much of the year and may reach commercial size by autumn. In some cases this size is not attained until the following spring. Williams (1955) indicated that white shrimp generally reach commercial size by late summer, while only a portion of the pink shrimp of North Carolina are harvestable before growth is slowed by falling temperatures in autumn. In the Gulf of Mexico, most of the shrimp produced in the spring reach harvestable size by summer.

Williams (1955) determined that the growth of *P. setiferus*, *P. aztecus*, and *P. duorarum* in estuaries was 36, 46, and 52 mm/mo, respectively. Parker (1970) reported that brown shrimp immigrated into Galveston Bay at sizes between 70 and 100 mm and were abundant over a salinity range of 0.9 to 30.8 o/oo. According to Crowe (1975), 91.9% of the white shrimp in Caminada Bay, Louisiana, were found in 1 to 20 o/oo salinity, while 91.8% of brown shrimp juveniles occurred in water between 10 and 20 o/oo salinity.

Gunter et al. (1964) found the lower salinity limits of white, brown,

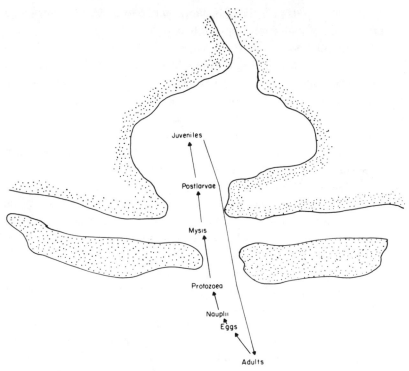

Fig. 18. Shrimp life cycle.

and pink shrimp to be 0.42, 0.80, and 2.5 o/oo, respectively. White shrimp were most plentiful in waters of less than 10 o/oo salinity, browns at 10 to 20 o/oo, and pinks at equal to or above 18 o/oo. Highest production of white shrimp was found in low salinity waters in Louisiana, while brown shrimp production peaked in high salinity areas in Texas. Pink shrimp production was greatest in the oceanic waters of south Florida. Gunter et al. (1964) reported that pink shrimp thrived in the Laguna Madre of Texas at salinities up to 65 o/oo, while white and brown shrimp did not occur above 45 o/oo.

The white shrimp fishery along the Texas coast began in the 1920s, but it was not until after the 1940s and the advent of widespread freezing that shrimp were generally introduced to U.S. consumers. Once the popularity of shrimp spread from coastal regions to inland areas, fishing pressure increased. Caillouet et al. (1980) examined catch records for white and brown shrimp in Texas and Louisiana from 1959 to 1976 and reported that the proportion of small shrimp of both species in the harvest increased significantly over the period of evaluation.

According to Wickham and Minkler (1975), white, brown, and pink shrimp in the Gulf of Mexico are nocturnal. *P. setiferus* were more active than the other two species and are the species most commonly caught during daytime trawling. *P. aztecus* did not burrow as actively as *P. duorarum*, while *P. setiferus* were not observed to burrow at all.

Sediment preference of shrimp has been evaluated in several studies. Springer and Bullis (1954) and Hildebrand (1954, 1955) reported that white and brown shrimp in the Gulf of Mexico occurred most commonly over bottoms dominated by terrigenous silt, while pink shrimp preferred calcareous mud and sand or sand and shell sediments. Williams (1958) also noted that white and brown shrimp preferred soft, muddy sediments while pink shrimp selected less muddy bottoms.

A correlation between shrimp harvest and annual rainfall patterns has been demonstrated. Gunter and Hildebrand (1954) found that shrimp yields were high during wet years while shrimp production was low during dry years. They concluded that salinity patterns were responsible for the differences in shrimp production.

Kutkuhn (1966) argued that appreciable reductions of freshwater inflow to estuaries would seriously hinder fertility by significantly limiting nutrient inflow, thus lowering shrimp production. He also concluded that turbid estuaries may yield higher shrimp production because of suspended detritus, which affords partial protection from predators by floating particles in the water.

LITERATURE CITED

Barbour, M. G., R. B. Craig, F. R. Drysdale, and M. T. Ghiselin. 1973. *Coastal ecology: Bodega Head*. Berkeley: University of California Press.

Beckman, C. R., J. Menzies, and C. M. Wakeman. 1957. The biological aspects of attack on creosoted wood by *Limnoria*. *Corrosion* 13: 162–64.

Bell, S. S. 1979. Short- and long-term variation in a high marsh meiofauna community. *Est. and Coast. Mar. Sci.* 9: 331–50.

Bell, S. S. and B. C. Coull. 1978. Field evidence that shrimp predation regulates meiofauna. *Oecologia* 35: 141–48.

Bleil, D. F., and M. E. Gunn. 1978., Submergence avoidance behavior in the periwinkle *Littorina irrorata* is not due to threat of drowning. *Estuaries* 1: 267.

Bowers, L. W. 1975. Fiddler crabs in a nontidal environment. *Cont. Mar. Sci.* 19: 67–78.

Brenner, D., I. Valiela, C. D. van Raalte, and E. J. Carpenter. 1976. Grazing by *Talorchestia longicornis* on an algal mat in a New England salt marsh. *J. Exp. Mar. Biol. Ecol.* 22: 161–69.

Butler, P. A. 1966. Fixation of DDT in estuaries. *Trans. N. Amer. Wildl. Conf.* 31: 184–89.

Caillouet, C. W., F. J. Patella, and W. B. Jackson. 1980. Trends toward decreasing size of brown shrimp, *Penaeus aztecus*, and white shrimp, *Penaeus setiferus*, in reported annual catches from Texas and Louisiana. *Fish. Bull.* 77: 985–89.

Carriker, M. R. 1959. The role of physical and biological factors in the culture of *Crassostrea* and *Mercenaria* in a salt-water pond. *Ecol. Monogr.* 29: 219–66.

———. 1967. Ecology of estuarine benthic invertebrates: A perspective, pp. 442–87. In: G. H. Lauff, ed. *Estuaries*. American Association for the Advancement of Science Publication no. 83. Washington, D.C.: AAAS.

Chapman, C. R. 1959. Oyster drill (*Thais haemastoma*) predation in Mississippi Sound. *Proc. Nat'l. Shellfish Assoc.* 49: 87–97.

Chestnut, A. F. 1974. Oyster reefs, pp. 171–203. In: H. T. Odum, B. J. Copeland, and E. A. McMahan, eds. *Coastal ecological systems of the United States*, Vol. II. Washington, D.C.: Conservation Foundation.

Coull, B. C., ed. 1977. *Ecology of marine benthos*. Columbia: University of South Carolina Press.

Coull, B. C., and J. W. Fleeger. 1977. Long-term temporal variation and community dynamics of meiobenthic copepods. *Ecology* 58: 1136–43.

Coull, B. C., S. S. Bell, A. M. Savory, and B. W. Dudley. 1979. Zonation of meiobenthic copepods in a southeastern United States salt marsh. *Est. and Coast. Mar. Sci.* 9: 181–88.

Cronin, L. E., and A. J. Mansueti. 1971. The biology of the estuary, pp. 14–39. In: P. A. Douglas and R. H. Stroud, eds. *A symposium on the biological significance of estuaries*. Washington, D.C.: Sport Fishing Institute.

Crowe, A. L. 1975. Population dynamics of two species of commercial shrimp in Caminada Bay, Louisiana. *Proc. La. Acad. Sci.* 38: 86–91.

Davis, L. V., and I. E. Gray. 1966. Zonal and seasonal distribution of insects in North Carolina salt marshes. *Ecol. Monogr.* 36: 275–95.

Davis, R. L., and N. Marshall. 1963. The feeding of the bay scallop, *Aequipecten irradians*. *Proc. Nat'l. Shellfish Assoc.* 52: 25–29.

Dexter, D. M. 1967. Distribution and niche diversity of haustoriid amphipods in North Carolina. *Ches. Sci.* 8: 187–92.

Elliott, P. B., and S. S. Bamforth. 1975. Interstitial protozoa and algae of Louisiana salt marshes. *J. Protozool.* 22: 514–19.

Fenchel, T. 1967. The ecology of marine microbenthos. I. The quantitative importance of ciliates as compared with metazoans in various types of sediments. *Ophelia* 4: 121–37.

———. 1968a. The ecology of marine microbenthos. II. The food of marine benthic ciliates. *Ophelia* 5: 73–121.

———. 1968b. The ecology of marine microbenthos. III. The reproductive potential of ciliates. *Ophelia* 5: 123–36.

———. 1969. The ecology of marine microbenthos. IV. Structure and function of the benthic ecosystem, its chemical and physical factors, and the microfauna communities with special reference to the ciliated protozoa. *Ophelia* 6: 1–182.

Fotheringham, N. 1976. Population consequences of shell utilization by hermit crabs. *Ecology* 57: 570–78.

Frankenberg, D., and K. L. Smith, Jr. 1967. Coprophagy in marine animals. *Limnol. Oceanogr.* 12: 443–50.

Frankenberg, D., S. L. Coles, and R. E. Johannes. 1967. The potential trophic significance of *Callianassa major* fecal pellets. *Limnol. oceanogr.* 12: 113–20.

Galtsoff, P. S. 1964. The American oyster *Crassostrea virginica* Gmelin. *Fish. Bull.* 64: 1–480.

Grave, C. 1901. The oyster reefs of North Carolina. Johns Hopkins Circular no. 151.

Gray, I. E. 1974. Worm and clam flats, pp. 204–43. In: H. T. Odum, B. J. Copeland, and E. A. McMahan, eds. *Coastal ecological systems of the United States*. Vol. II. Washington, D.C.: Conservation Foundation.

Gunter, G. 1961. Habitat of juvenile shrimp (family Penaeidae). *Ecology* 42: 598–600.

Gunter, G., and H. H. Hildebrand. 1954. The relation of total rainfall of the state and catch of the marine shrimp (*Penaeus setiferus*) in Texas waters. *Bull. Mar. Sci. Gulf Caribb.* 4: 95–103.

Gunter, G., J. Y. Christmas, and R. Killebrew. 1964. Some relations of salinity to population distributions of motile estuarine organisms, with special reference to penaeid shrimp. *Ecology* 45: 181–85.

Hamilton, P. V. 1976. Predation on *Littorina irrarata* (Mollusca: Gastropoda) by *Callinectes sapidus* (Crustacea: Portunidae). *Bull. Mar. Sci. Gulf Caribb.* 26: 403–409.

Hildebrand, H. H. 1954. A study of the fauna of the brown shrimp (*Penaeus aztecus* Ives) ground in the western Gulf of Mexico. *Publ. Inst. Mar. Sci., Univ. Tex.* 3: 233–316.

———. 1955. A study of the fauna of the pink shrimp (*Penaeus duorarum* Burkenroad) grounds in the Gulf of Campeche. *Publ. Inst. Mar. Sci., Univ. Tex.* 4: 171–232.

Holland, A. F., and J. M. Dean. 1977. The biology of the stout razor clam *Tagelus plebeius*. I. Animal-sediment relationships, feeding mechanism, and community biology. *Ches. Sci.* 18: 58–66.

Holland, J. S., N. J. Maciolek, and C. H. Oppenheimer. 1973. Galveston Bay benthic community structure as an indicator of water quality. *Cont. Mar. Sci.* 17: 169–88.

Hyllberg, J., and V. F. Gallucci. 1975. Selectivity in feeding by the deposit-feeding bivalve *Macoma nasuta*. *Mar. Biol.* 32: 167–78.

Jacobsen, V. H. 1967. The feeding of the lugworm, *Arenicola marina* (L.). Quantitative studies. *Ophelia* 4: 91–109.

Johnson, R. G. 1967a. Salinity of interstitial water in a sand beach. *Limnol. Oceanogr.* 12: 1–7.

———. 1967b. The vertical distribution of the infauna of a sand flat. *Ecology* 48: 571–78.

Keck, R., D. Maurer, and R. Malouf. 1974. Factors influencing the settling behavior of larval hard clams, *Mercenaria mercenaria*. *Proc. Nat'l. Shellfish Assoc.* 64: 59–67.

Kellogg, C. W. 1976. Gastropod shells: A potentially limiting resource for hermit crabs. *J. Exp. Mar. Biol. Ecol.* 22: 101–11.

Kerby, C. 1977. Life in the bottom–meiobenthos, pp. 656–60. In: J. R. Clark, ed. *Coastal ecosystem management*. New York: John Wiley and Sons.

Kruger, F. 1959. Zur Ernährungsphysiologie von *Arenicola marina* L. *Zool. Anz. Suppl.* 22: 115–20.

———. 1964. Messungen der Pumptätigkeit von *Arenicola marina* L. im Watt. *Helgolander wiss. Meeresunters.* 11: 70–91.

Kutkuhn, J. H. 1966. The role of estuaries in the development and perpetuation of commercial shrimp resources, pp. 16–36. In: A symposium on estuarine fisheries. American Fisheries Society Special Publication no. 3.

Laird, C. E., and P. A. Haefner, Jr. 1976. Effects of intrinsic and environmental factors on oxygen consumption in the blue crab, *Callinectes sapidus* Rathbun. *J. Exp. Mar. Biol. Ecol.* 22: 171–78.

Lee, J. J., H. D. Freudenthal, M. McEnery, W. A. Muller, and S. Pierce. 1965. Nutrition of certain littoral foraminifera: a bloom feeder hypothesis. (Abstract.) *Excerpta Medica Intern. Congr. Ser.* 91: 332.

Levinton, J. S. 1972. Stability and trophic structure of deposit-feeding and suspension-feeding communities. *Am. Nat.* 106: 472–86.

Lindgren, E. W. 1974. Treated piling system, pp. 301–17. In: H. T. Odum, B. J.Copeland, and E. A. McMahan, eds. *Coastal ecological system of the United States*. Vol. III. Washington, D.C.: Conservation Foundation.

Loosanoff, V. L. 1961. Effects of turbidity on some larval and adult bivalves. *Proc. Gulf and Carrib. Fish. Inst.* 14: 80–95.

Lough, R. G. 1974. A re-evaluation of the combined effects of temperature and salinity on survival and growth of *Mytilus edulis* larvae using response surface techniques. *Proc. Nat'l. Shellfish Assoc.* 64: 73–76.

McIntyre, A. D. 1969. Ecology of marine meiobenthos. *Biol. Rev.* 44: 245–90.

McNulty, J. K., R. C. Work, and H. B. Morore, 1962. Some relationships between the infauna of the level bottom and the sediment in south Florida. *Bull. Mar. Sci. Gulf Caribb.* 12: 322–32.

Magalhaes, H. 1948. An ecological study of snails of the genus *Busycon* at Beaufort, North Carolina. *Ecol. Monogr.* 18: 377–409.

Martin, A. C., and F. M. Uhler. 1939. *Food of game ducks in the United States and Canada.* Technical Bulletin no. 634. Washington, D.C.: U.S. Department of Agriculture.

May, E. B. 1968. Summer oyster mortalities in Alabama. *Prog. Fish-Cult.* 30: 99.

———. 1974. The distribution of mud crabs (Xanthidae) in Alabama estuaries. *Proc. Nat'l. Shellfish Assoc.* 64: 33–37.

May, E. B., and D. G. Bland. 1970. Survival of young oysters in areas of different salinity in Mobile Bay. *Proc. S.E. Assoc. Game and Fish Comm.* 23: 519–21.

Menzel, R. W. 1963. Seasonal growth of the northern quahog, *Mercenaria mercenaria*, and the southern quahog, *M. campechiensis*, in Alligator Harbor, Florida. *Proc. Nat'l. Shellfish Assoc.* 52: 37–46.

Menzel, R. W., and F. W. Nichy. 1958. Studies of the distribution and feeding habits of some oyster predators in Alligator Harbor, Florida. *Bull. Mar. Sci. Gulf Caribb.* 8: 125–45.

Moore, H. B., L. T. Davies, T. H. Fraser. R. H. Gore, and N. R. López. 1968. Some biomass figures for a tidal flat in Biscayne Bay, Florida. *Bull. Mar. Sci. Gulf Caribb.* 18: 261–79.

Moul, E. T., and D. Mason. 1957. Study of diatom populations on sand and mud flats in the Woods Hole area. *Biol. Bull.* 113: 351.

Newell, R. 1965. The role of detritus in the nutrition of two marine deposit feeders, the prosobranch *Hydrobia ulvae* and the bivalve *Macoma balthica*. *Zool. Soc. Lond.* 144: 25–45.

Nichols, M. M. 1974. Foraminifera in estuarine classification, pp. 85–103. In: H. T. Odum, B. J. Copeland, and E. A. McMahan, eds. *Coastal ecological systems of the United States.* Vol. I. Washington, D.C.: Conservation Foundation.

Paine, R. T. 1963. Trophic relationships of eight sympatric predatory gastropods. *Ecology* 44: 63–74.

Pamatmat, M. M. 1968. Ecology and metabolism of a benthic community on an intertidal sand flat. *Int. Rev. Gesampt. Hydro.* 53: 211–98.

Parker, J. C. 1970. Distribution of juvenile brown shrimp (*Penaeus aztecus* Ives) in

Galveston Bay, Texas, as related to certain hydrographic features and salinity. *Cont. Mar. Sci.* 15: 1–12.

Pearse, A. S., H. J. Humm, and G. W. Wharton. 1942. Ecology of sand beaches at Beaufort, North Carolina. *Ecol. Monogr.* 12: 135–90.

Peterson, C. H. and N. M. Peterson. 1979. The ecology of intertidal flats in North Carolina: A community profile. U.S. Fish and Wildlife Service Biological Services Program FWS/OBS 79-39.

Powell, E. N. 1977. Particle size selection and sediment reworking in a funnel feeder, *Leptosynapta tenuis* (Holothuroidea: Synaptidae). *Int. Rev. Gesampt. Hydro.* 62: 385–408.

Pringle, B. H., D. E. Hissong, E. L. Katz, and S. T. Malawka. 1968. Trace metal accumulation by estuarine molluscs. *J. San. Eng.* 94: 455–75.

Reid, D. M. 1930. Salinity interchange between seawater in sand and overflowing freshwater at low tide. *J. Mar. Biol. Assoc. U.K.* 16: 609–14.

———. 1932. Salinity interchange between seawater in sand and overflowing freshwater at low tide. II. *J. Mar. Biol. Assoc. U.K.* 18: 299–306.

Reimer, R. D., K. Strawn, and A. Dixon. 1974. Notes on the river shrimp, *Macrobrachium ohione* (Smith). *Trans. Am. Fish. Soc.* 103: 120–26.

Reise, K. 1976. Predation pressure and community structure of an intertidal soft bottom fauna, pp. 513–19. In: B. F. Keegan, P. O. Cerdigh, and R. J. S. Beaden, eds. *Biology of benthic organisms*. New York: Pergamon Press.

———. 1977. Predator exclusion experiments in an intertidal mud flat. *Helgolander wiss. Meeresunters.* 30: 263–71.

———. 1978. Experiments on epibenthic predation in the Wadden Sea. *Helgolander wiss. Meeresunters.* 31: 55–101.

Rhodes, D. C. 1974. Organism-sediment relations on the muddy sea floor. *Oceanogr. Mar. Biol. Ann. Rev.* 12: 263–300.

Rhodes, D. C. and D. K. Young. 1970. The influence of deposit-feeding organisms on sediment stability and community trophic structures. *J. Mar. Res.* 28: 150–78.

Ricketts, E. F., and J. Calvin. 1952. *Between Pacific tides*. Stanford, Calif.: Stanford University Press.

Ringold, P. 1979. Burrowing, root mat density, and the distribution of fiddler crabs in the eastern United States. *J. Exp. Mar. Biol. Ecol.* 36: 11–22.

Ryan, E. P. 1956. Observations on the life histories and the distribution of the Xanthidae (mud crabs) of Chesapeake Bay. *Am. Midl. Natur.* 56: 138–62.

Sanders, H. L. 1956. Oceanography of Long Island Sound, 1952–1954. X. The biology of marine bottom communities. *Bull. Bingham Oceanogr. Coll.* 15: 345–414.

———. 1958. Benthic studies in Buzzards Bay. I. Animal-sediment relationships. *Limnol. Oceanogr.* 3: 245–58.

————. 1960. Benthic studies in Buzzards Bay. III. The structure of the soft-bottom community. *Limnol. Oceanogr.* 5: 138–53.

Sanders, H. L., E. M. Goudsmit, E. L. Mills, and G. E. Hampson. 1962. A study of the intertidal fauna of Barnstable Harbor, Mass. *Limnol. Oceanogr.* 7: 63–79.

Scheltema, R. S. 1964. Feeding habits and growth in the mudsnail *Nassarius obsoletus*. *Ches. Sci.* 5: 161–66.

Smalley, A. E. 1959. The growth cycle of *Spartina* and its relation to the insect populations in the marsh, pp. 96–100. In: Proceedings of the salt marsh conference, Marine Institute, University of Georgia, Sapelo Island.

Springer, S., and H. R. Bullis. 1954. Exploratory shrimp fishing in the Gulf of Mexico. Summary report for 1952–54. *Comm. Rish. Rev.* 16: 1–16.

Stewart, H. B., Jr. 1958. Sedimentary reflections of depositional environment in San Miguel Lagoon, Baja California, Mexico. *Bull. Amer. Assoc. Petrol. Geol.* 42: 2567–2621.

Stickney, R. R., and D. Miller. 1974. Water chemistry and biology of the lower Savannah River. *J. Water Poll. Cont. Fed.* 46: 2316–26.

Stiven, A. E., and J. T. Hunter. 1976. Growth and mortality of *Littorina irrorata* Say in three North Carolina marshes. *Ches. Sci.* 17: 168–76.

Teal, J. M. 1958. Distribution of fiddler crabs in Georgia salt marshes. *Ecology* 39: 185–93.

Tenore, K. R. 1972. Macrobenthos of the Pamlico River estuary, North Carolina. *Ecol. Monogr.* 42: 51–69.

Virnstein, R. W. 1977. The importance of predation by crabs and fishes on benthic infauna in Chesapeake Bay. Ecology 58: 1199–1217.

Walker, R. L., M. A. Fleetwood, and K. R. Tenore. 1980. The distribution of the hard clam *Mercenaria mercenaria* (Linné) and clam predators in Wassaw Sound, Georgia. Georgia Marine Science Center Technical Report Series 80-8.

Wallace, D. H. 1966. Oysters in the estuarine environment, pp. 68–73. In: *A symposium on estuarine fisheries*. American Fisheries Society Special Publication no. 3. Washington, D.C.: American Fisheries Society.

————. 1971. The biological effects of estuaries on shellfish of the middle Atlantic, pp. 76–85. In: P. R. Douglas and R. H. Stroud, eds. *A symposium on the biological significance of estuaries*. Washington, D.C.: Sport Fishing Institute.

Whitlatch, R. B. 1974. Food-resource partitioning in the deposit feeding polychaete *Pectinaria gouldii*. *Biol. Bull.* 147: 227–35.

Whitten, H. L., H. F. Rosene, and J. W. Hedgpeth. 1950. The invertebrate fauna of Texas coast jetties: A preliminary survey. *Publ. Inst. Mar. Sci., Univ. Tex.* 1(2): 53–87.

Wickham, D. A., and F. C. Minkler III. 1975. Laboratory observations on daily patterns of burrowing and locomotor activity of pink shrimp, *Penaeus duo-*

rarum, brown shrimp, *Penaeus aztecus*, and white shrimp, *Penaeus setiferus*. *Cont. Mar. Sci.* 19: 21–35.

Wieser, W. 1960. Benthic studies in Buzzards Bay. II. The meiofauna. *Limnol. Oceanogr.* 5: 121–37.

Williams, A. B. 1955. A contribution to the life histories of commercial shrimps (Penaeidae) in North Carolina. *Bull. Mar. Sci. Gulf Caribb.* 5: 116–46.

————. 1958. Substrates as a factor in shrimp distribution. *Limnol. Oceanogr.* 3: 283–90.

Williams, R. B., and L. K. Thomas. 1967. The standing crop of benthic animals in a North Carolina estuarine area. *J. Elisha Mitchell Sci. Soc.* 83: 135–39.

Wood, C. E. 1967. Physioecology of the grass shrimp, *Palaemonetes pugio*, in the Galveston Bay estuarine system. *Cont. Mar. Sci.* 12: 54–79.

Woodin, S. A. 1976. Adult-larval interactions in dense infaunal assemblages: Patterns of abundance. *J. Mar. Res.* 34: 25–41.

Wright, H. O. 1973. Effect of commensal hydroids on hermit crab competition in the littoral zone of Texas. *Nature* 241: 139–40.

Yonge, C. M. 1953. Aspects of life on muddy shores, pp. 29–49. In: S. M. Marshall and A. P. Orr, eds. *Essays in marine biology*. London: Oliver and Boyd.

Young, D. K. and D. C. Rhodes. 1971. Animal-sediment relations in Cape Cod Bay, Massachusetts. I. A transect study. *Mar. Biol.* 11: 242–54.

Young, D. K., M. A. Buzas, and M. W. Young. 1976. Species densities of macrobenthos associated with seagrass: A field experimental study of predation. *J. Mar. Res.* 34: 577–92.

CHAPTER 9

Estuarine Fishes

Introduction

ESTUARIES support large commercial and sport fisheries in the Gulf of Mexico and along the coast of the southeastern United States. For many visitors, fishing is an important consideration in the selection of vacation spots. Heffernan and Green (1977) conducted a two-year creel survey in selected Texas bays and found the following:

1. About 185,000 anglers fished the eight areas surveyed
2. Anglers made 3,001,500 trips and spent 13,643,300 man-hours fishing
3. Boat users provided 47.7% of the man-hours; wade-bank fishermen, 38.3%; and lighted-pier fishermen, 14.0%
4. Mean catch was near 0.25 kg/man-hour expended in fishing
5. Spotted seatrout, *Cynoscion nebulosus*, was the most widely caught species
6. During the two-year study, over 5,000,000 kg of fish were taken from the survey areas
7. Sport fishermen accounted for 59.5% of total fish landings; commercial fisherman the remainder

Although such invertebrates as shrimp, oysters, crabs, and scallops are important staples in seafood restaurants and markets, flounder, red drum, black drum, seatrout, and mullet (all estuarine fishes) are favorites in many areas. All of these fishes are captured by sportsmen using hook and line or netting and are also important in the commercial catches. Other marketable species include menhaden (*Brevoortia* spp.), which are processed for fish oil and meal, and a host of other species used for pet food or for hydrolyzed protein products, which can be incorporated into a variety of foods for livestock or humans.

McHugh (1966) reported that nearly two-thirds of the commercial marine catch (expressed in monetary value) is composed of species that spend at least part of their lives in estuaries. The same paper also pointed out that there was no effective scientific management of any estuarine fishery. Little has changed since 1966, though some attempts have been made to manage estuarine fisheries. Of the ten species groups most important to commercial fisheries in the United States, seven are typically estuarine and make up 58% of the commercial catch (McHugh, 1968). Of those, three are fishes; two of them (menhaden and flounder) occur along the southeastern Atlantic coast and in the Gulf of Mexico.

The estuaries of the United States contain large numbers of fish species—many of which remain unknown to even the most avid fisherman, since they are not generally taken by rod and reel or castnet. The importance of such fishes as the killifish (genus *Fundulus*) and anchovy (genus *Anchoa*) lies primarily in their contribution to the estuarine food chain. Members of the family Sciaenidae, on the other hand, tend to dominate not only sport and commercial catches but also total biomass of estuarine fishes in the Southeast and the Gulf of Mexico. Some species within the Sciaenidae are important to commercial or sports fishermen, but others represent the by-catch of both kinds of fisheries. Commercially valuable sciaenids include red drum (*Sciaenops ocellatus*), black drum (*Pogonias cromis*), and spotted seatrout (*Cynoscion nebulosus*). The following smaller species, though less desirable as sports fish, often reach edible sizes: Atlantic croaker (*Micropogonias undulatus*), spot (*Leiostomus xanthurus*), weakfish (*Cynoscion regalis*), and star drum (*Stellifer lanceolatus*). Flounder (family Bothidae), particularly members of the genus *Paralichthys*, are also vital to both sport and commercial catches.

The coast along the Gulf of Mexico is, according to Gunter (1967a), the most productive fishery area in the world except for the coast of Peru. Information on the fishes of the region can be found in Hildebrand and Schroeder (1928) and Hoese and Moore (1977). Keys, depictions in photographs or drawings, and information on life history and distribution are provided in both books.

The kinds of studies that can be undertaken with estuarine fish differ widely depending upon intent, facilities, and funding level. Ranging from general surveys to highly specialized examinations of some biochemical feature within a species, the breadth of information that relates to fish ecology in estuaries is voluminous.

Great numbers of fishes, shrimps, and crabs enter estuaries as larvae or juveniles and remain in the estuarine environment for some time before migrating to the ocean. The belief that estuaries are nursery grounds for many important commercial species is widespread and appears to be supported by considerable scientific evidence. It is generally concluded that abundant food supplies are a primary reason for the influx of young marine organisms into estuaries. The upper reaches of estuaries and tidal creeks are heavily used by larval and juvenile fishes (Shenker and Dean, 1979). Table 8 presents a list of commercially important fishes and invertebrates that occur as juveniles in Tampa Bay, Florida.

Attempts have been made to indicate how many fisheries products are lost through such activities as filling. Stroud (1971) concluded that for every hectare of estuarine habitat lost, there would be an annual reduction of over 500 kg of fishery products.

According to Nixon (1980), total fish production would probably not be greatly affected if marsh productivity were reduced. He pointed out that other sources of estuarine and near-shore productivity might well be sufficient to support existing fisheries. For example, in regions without extensive marshes, freshwater inflow may be reponsible for bringing in the nutrients that support fishes.

Destruction of estuarine habitat by man is not, of course, the only factor that affects fish survival and distribution. Unusually cold winters, red tides, oxygen depletions caused by suspension and oxidation of organic-rich sediments during storms, and other natural phenomena can cause heavy fish mortalities in estuaries. Tabb and Jones (1962) reported that in September, 1960, Hurricane Donna caused heavy fish and invertebrate losses in Florida Bay. Many animals were stranded as retreating water left them above the waterline. Others suffocated in the mud or were killed when high turbidity clogged their gills. A subsequent oxygen depletion precipitated by the decay of large amounts of organic matter led to further fish and invertebrate deaths. Recovery of fish populations after severe mortality may be slow. Tabb (1966) reported that destruction of *Cynoscion nebulosus* populations in Virginia estuaries due to extremely cold weather decimated the fishery for several years. Recovery depended upon reproduction by individuals that had moved offshore during the cold period and were able to survive.

Pressing problems in the commercial seafood industry include high fuel costs, technological gaps, decreasing competition for fishery products at dockside, legislation considered an impediment to development, mar-

TABLE 8. Commercially Important Vertebrate and Invertebrate Species in the Gulf of Mexico, Recovered as Juveniles from Tampa Bay, Florida

Scientific Name	Common Name
Vertebrates	
Brevoortia patronus	Gulf menaden
Brevoortia smithi	Yellowfin menhaden
Mugil curema	White mullet
Mugil cephalus	Striped mullet
Mugil trichodon	Fantail mullet
Mycteroperca microlepis	Gag
Epinephelus morio	Red grouper
Scomberomorus maculatus	Spanish mackerel
Cynoscion nebulosus	Spotted seatrout
Cynoscion arenarius	Sand seatrout
Pomatomus saltatrix	Bluefish
Caranx hippos	Crevalle jack
Pogonias cromis	Black drum
Trachinotus carolinus	Florida pompano
Trachinotus falcatus	Permit
Archosargus probatocephalus	Sheepshead
Eucinostomus argenteus	Spotfin mojarra
Eucinostomus gula	Silver jenny
Diapterus plumieri	Striped mojarra
Leiostomus xanthurus	Spot
Invertebrates	
Penaeus duorarum	Pink shrimp
Callinectes sapidus	Blue crab

Source: Sykes, 1964. The fish names were verified in American Fisheries Society, 1980.

keting and management deficiencies, and extreme fluctuations in price. Some of those problems may be overcome through the imposition of the 200-mile fishery and economic zone limit that has been adopted by most nations (Fisher, 1975). Many of the problems found in offshore fisheries also exist in estuaries. Although the distance to the fishing grounds may be shorter, increased fuel costs still drive up the expense of fishing and consequently affect the price to the wholesaler, retailer, and consumer. Problems with marketing, management, and the bureaucracy plague estuarine fishermen as much as they do offshore fishermen.

Sports fishermen also exert an economic influence on estuarine regions. Money spent for bait, boats, motors, fishing equipment, licenses (which are required in some states such as Texas but are often not required in marine or estuarine waters), and ancillary needs like food, fuel, and lodging are responsible for a considerable fraction of the cash flow in many coastal areas.

Pelagic Fishes

Pelagic fishes are those that can be found in the water column, though they may feed in and around the sediments. Some are filter feeders that consume plankton, while others are carnivores that prey upon other fishes or on macroinvertebrates. Various fish species that inhabit oligohaline areas are pelagic, and many are also migratory. Included are the menhaden species *Brevoortia patronus* in the Gulf of Mexico and *B. tyrannus* along the Atlantic coast of the United States.

The striped bass, *Morone saxatilis*, is another example of a pelagic species found in the estuaries of the United States. Striped bass occur on both the East and West coasts of the United States as well as in the Gulf of Mexico (Copeland et al., 1974). In some cases the present geographic range of striped bass is a result of introductions from their native areas.

Pelagic species also inhabit the middle and lower reaches of estuaries and can even be found in hypersaline waters. Gunter (1967b) reported that such pelagics as the ladyfish (*Elops saurus*), striped anchovy (*Anchoa hepsetus*), and striped mullet (*Mugil cephalus*) occur in the Laguna Madre of Texas at salinities as high as 75 o/oo.

Since it is not possible to discuss in detail all of the pelagic species that exist in estuaries, anchovies, menhaden, striped bass, and mullet have been selected for brief consideration. The bay anchovy, *Anchoa mitchilli*, appears to be the most abundant fish along the Atlantic seaboard of the United States (McHugh, 1967), and perhaps in the Gulf of Mexico. The species ranges from Massachusetts through the Gulf of Mexico but is relatively unrecognized, since its small size eliminates it from sports and even most commercial catches. Reid (1955) collected fifty species of cartilaginous and bony fishes in Galveston Bay, Texas, and found the bay anchovy, along with its relative, *A. hepsetus*, to be among the most abundant species in the estuary. Although numerically dominant, bay anchovies constitute only a small fraction of total fish biomass. They may be an important food source for predatory fishes, but their actual importance to the food web has not been well documented.

Second in abundance to the bay anchovy in the estuaries of the southeastern United States and Gulf of Mexico are menhaden, *Brevoortia patronus* and *B. tyrannus* (McHugh, 1967). A research of the literature by Peters and Schaaf (1981) revealed that the menhaden population numbers about 8.5 billion in estuaries and that they annually consume between 183,000,000 and 276,000,000 kg of organic matter, or between 6 and 9% of phytoplankton production. Estimated daily consumption of food by menhaden in autumn ranged from 0.6 to 1.0 g/m^2, which is equal to the estimated average daily production of the primary producer community. Peters and Schaaf (1981) hypothesized that detritus may serve as an alternate food source for menhaden.

Juvenile menhaden use all or most of the estuaries from New England to the Mexican border and appear to be estuarine-dependent for most of the first year of life. According to Reintjes and Pacheco (1966), menhaden enter Atlantic coastal estuaries in New England from May to October, in the Middle Atlantic states from October to June, and in the South Atlantic states from December to May. Menhaden spawning occurs in the ocean. The gulf menhaden, *B. patronus*, spawns from October through March (Fore, 1970; Christmas and Waller, 1975). The related Gulf of Mexico species, *B. gunteri*, spawns during the winter in Texas (Gunter, 1945; Simmons, 1957), while *B. smithi* appears to spawn during the spring in Florida waters (Springer and Woodburn, 1960). Gulf of Mexico menhaden, which are spawned between December and March, probably enter estuaries a few weeks following hatching (Reintjes, 1969); thus, they could be expected to occur in estuarine waters between February and April or May.

Larval menhaden are within the range of 14 to 34 mm fork length when they arrive in the estuaries (Reintjes, 1961). Juvenile menhaden feed and grow for several months inshore and then leave the estuaries for offshore areas in the fall to overwinter (Reintjes, 1969). The adults can be found offshore in the Gulf of Mexico for a distance of about 40 km in the case of *B. patronus* (Christmas and Gunter, 1960).

The life cycle of *B. tyrannus* in the Atlantic seems to be similar to that of *B. patronus* in the Gulf of Mexico (June and Chamberlin, 1959). The former species may leave the estuaries in the northern part of their range as early as August, while they may remain inshore as late as January in the south. Tag returns from *B. tyrannus* revealed that a single population overwintered offshore along the southeastern Atlantic coast and that the population moved north during the spring (Nicholson, 1978). The population was found to stratify along the coast by size during spring and summer, after which it moved south again in the fall.

Between 85 and 90% of the gulf menhaden landed by commercial fishermen are members of age classes II and III. (A fish that has completed its second year of life is designated age class II; during its first year of life it is designated age class 0.) The gulf menhaden appears to be shorter lived than its Atlantic cousin (Reintjes, 1969). A two-year failure in recruitment could lead to a collapse of the commercial fishery.

Striped bass occur from the Saint Lawrence River in the north to the Saint Johns River in the south along the East Coast of the United States. Along the Gulf of Mexico, striped bass have been found from west Florida to Louisiana. The species has been introduced into the waters of Texas and along the West Coast (Raney, 1952).

Stripers reproduce in fresh water from April to July, and the young feed on fish and invertebrates in the estuarine environment (Raney, 1952). Because of interest by sport fishermen, artificial spawning and rearing of young striped bass have been developed in many coastal states to provide stock to augment natural supplies of the species. One concern of environmentalists is that this popular sport species is susceptible to estuarine pollution. For example, Talbot (1966) warned that dredging, bulkheading, and navigation projects are a threat to striped bass habitat.

Mullet may also be considered among the pelagic species, though they often feed on benthic algae and other organisms associated with substrates. Mullet are highly euryhaline. In Florida and other regions within their range, they can be found in freshwater habitats such as springs and rivers that connect with saline waters.

Striped mullet (*Mugil cephalus*) are commercially important in some parts of the United States, while in others they are not popular. In Florida and Hawaii, mullet bring attractive prices in the marketplace and are widely sold fresh or smoked. Along the Gulf of Mexico, however, particularly in Texas, mullet are difficult to market.

Demersal Fishes

Demersal fishes are those found in close association with the sediments. In the estuaries of the southeastern Atlantic and Gulf of Mexico, demersal species seem to dominate the nekton community. Reid (1955) found that such demersal species as spot (*Leiostomus xanthurus*) and Atlantic croaker (*Micropogonias undulatus*) were the most abundant demersal fish in Galveston Bay, Texas. The same two species are probably among the dominants in many other estuaries.

Several demersal species common in areas of relatively low salinity are also abundant in hypersaline lagoons. Many of the species of *Fundulus* can be found in nearly fresh water as well as in high salinity areas. Gunter (1967b) found *F. similis*, *Cyprinodon variegatus*, *Lagodon rhomboides*, *Cynoscion nebulosus*, *Pogonias cromis*, and *Micropogonias undulatus* in the Laguna Madre of Texas at salinities as high as 75 o/oo. The same species often thrive in intermediate to low salinities in positive estuaries.

As indicated in the case of the pelagic fishes, complete treatment of all demersal fish species is beyond the scope of this text, so only a few representative species are considered. Among them are some of the dominant species in the estuaries of the southeastern Atlantic and along the Gulf of Mexico.

Spot, *Leiostomus xanthurus*, live offshore as adults, eggs, and larvae. They migrate into estuaries as postlarvae. During fall, decreasing water temperatures and reduced daylight trigger migrations of juveniles from the estuaries into the near-shore ocean (Welsh and Breder, 1923; Hildebrand and Schroeder, 1928; Hildebrand and Cable, 1930; Subrahmanyam and Drake, 1975; Schauss, 1977; Pristas and Trent, 1978).

Maturation, followed by spawning, occurs in the ocean during winter (Hildebrand and Schroeder, 1928; Pearson, 1929; Hildebrand and Cable, 1930; Gunter, 1945; Dawson, 1958). Eggs and sperm are released into the water column where fertilization occurs. Larval development has not been completely described, but Hildebrand and Cable (1930) outlined the morphology of spot at various stages following hatching. Environmental conditions and predation appear to be the major controls on the survival of larval spot.

After yolk sac absorption, mouth parts appear to be sufficiently developed to allow postlarval spot to begin feeding. At that time, food may become the most important limiting factor. Postlarval spot begin entering the estuaries as temperatures begin to rise in the spring. Food supplies, water quality, predation, and currents all influence spot survival in estuaries. Juvenile spot make up a considerable portion of the catch of bay shrimpers in certain areas, and large individuals often enter sportsmen's creels.

Spot generally live no more than about three years (perhaps four years in some instances), and many may die following spawning (Welsh and Breder, 1923; Sundararaj, 1960; Pacheco, 1962; Joseph, 1972). Maximum size is between 300 and 400 mm (Hildebrand and Schroeder, 1928; Bigelow and Schroeder, 1953), with adults averaging 250 mm (Bigelow and Schroeder, 1953). Length-weight relationships for spot have been determined by Dawson (1958, 1965) and Parker (1973). A habitat suitability index model for spot was developed by Stickney and Cuenco (1982).

Directly competing with spot for food in the estuaries of Louisiana and Texas, if not elsewhere, is the Atlantic croaker, *Micropogonias undulatus* (Parker, 1971). Croakers have a life cycle similar to that of spot. Both are members of the family Sciaenidae. They spawn in the Gulf of Mexico off Louisiana and Texas from late October or November through April or June (Parker, 1971). Young croakers reside in the estuaries and migrate back into the Gulf of Mexico when they reach a length of 80–90 mm. Croakers reportedly begin entering the Delaware River on the northeast Atlantic coast of the United States by late October and are most abundant in early December (Thomas, 1971). Tagging studies aimed at following croaker migration in Chesapeake Bay showed that upstream migrations occurred in the spring, random movement during the summer, and oceanward migration in the fall (Haven, 1959).

Some croakers seem to remain in the estuaries of the Gulf of Mexico throughout the year (Parker, 1971), though most migrate offshore at the appropriate size as indicated above. Regarding their tolerance of environmental extremes in estuaries, Parker (1971) reported croakers from temperatures ranging between 0.4 and 35.5 C and in salinities from 0.2 to 35.1 o/oo. Croakers, like spot, are well adapted to life in temperate estuaries and are abundant at certain times of the year. They often make up a considerable proportion of the by-catch of commercial shrimpers. Moore et al. (1970) reported that *M. undulatus* and long-spine porgies, *Stenotomus caprinus*, accounted for nearly half of all fish captured by trawling in 7 to 10 m off Louisiana and Texas.

Croakers, like spot, are relatively short-lived. Successful recruitment can often dramatically affect the subsequent harvest in species with short life spans. Extremes in croaker populations were reflected in the catch of Virginia fishermen between 1945 and 1952, as documented by Massmann and Pacheco (1960). Those authors were able to relate declines in croaker abundance to below-normal winter water temperatures.

The spotted seatrout, *Cynoscion nebulosus*, is among the most popular fishes of the southeastern Atlantic and the Gulf of Mexico. Spotted seatrout range from Chesapeake Bay to Texas and are an important sport fish. The species has an extended spawning season compared with many other estuarine and marine species. In Chesapeake Bay, Florida, and Texas, *C. nebulosus* were found to spawn from March or early April through October (Pearson, 1929; Moody, 1950). Young spotted seatrout are most abundant on grass flats in the Cedar Key, Florida, area and are resident throughout the year (Moody, 1950). Their growth rate is relatively rapid: spotted seatrout can reach 130 mm by their first winter and may be as large as 250 mm by the onset of their second winter of life. Maturation occurs at between 240 and 250 mm (Moody, 1950).

The weakfish (*Cynoscion regalis*), which is fairly common along the southeastern Atlantic coast of the United States, and the sand seatrout (*C. arenarius*), found in the Gulf of Mexico, are less popular with sport fishermen than are the spotted seatrout. Weakfish and sand seatrout (which may actually be the same species) do not get as large as *C. nebulosus* (Hoese and Moore, 1977). The size differential is undoubtedly an important aspect of the popularity of the spotted seatrout over the other species in the genus.

Both *C. regalis* and *C. arenarius* can be found in the deep waters of estuaries and in the near-shore ocean waters (Thomas, 1971; Hoese and Moore, 1977). A related species in the Gulf of Mexico, the silver seatrout, *C. nothus*, is often confused with *C. arenarius*, but the former is usually collected further offshore than the latter (Hoese and Moore, 1977).

Thomas (1971) determined that the weakfish is an estuarine spawner in the lower Delaware River and that the young are present beginning in mid-June. *C. arenarius* have been found to spawn in deep channels within the bays along the Gulf of Mexico as well as in shallow offshore waters (Hoese and Moore, 1977).

Cyprinodont fishes are abundant in estuaries of the southeastern Atlantic and the Gulf of Mexico, though Gunter (1956) reported that one striking feature of Louisiana marshes was the virtual absence of cyprinodont fishes. In Texas, Simpson and Gunter (1956) listed the following common cyprinodonts (in decreasing order of abundance):

Cyprindon variegatus (sheepshead minnow)
Fundulus grandis (Gulf killifish)
Poecilia latipinna (sailfin molly)
Fundulus similis (long-nose killifish)
Adinia xenica (diamond killifish)
Gambusia affinis (mosquitofish)
Lucania parva (rainwater killifish)

Fundulus pulvereus (bayou killifish)
Fundulus jenkinsi (saltmarsh topminnow)

Abundant along open shorelines were *C. variegatus*, *F. grandis*, and *F. similis*, while the remainder of the species listed were most common in protected waters.

Simpson and Gunter (1956) found *C. variegatus* in salinities above 80 o/oo on several occasions and once discovered that fish in water having a salinity of 142.4 o/oo. The authors concluded that the fish did not select the high salinity water but appeared to be stranded in pools and sloughs where evaporation led to the increased salt level.

In the eelgrass beds of North Carolina, Adams (1976a) found that diversity was low and standing crop biomass high. The fish community was dominated by pinfish, *Lagodon rhomboides*. Pinfish were not only numerically dominant but also had the highest production level within the fish community (Adams, 1976b).

Pearcy and Richards (1962) reported that demersal fish eggs (those that fall to the bottom after being released and fertilized) were more common in fish species taken within estuaries than in those that were captured in neritic areas. They postulated that the production of demersal eggs may be an adaptive response of estuarine fishes to reduce dispersal of eggs offshore by currents. The authors (1962) observed that the larvae of fish with demersal eggs tended to remain low in the water column; such behavior, they postulated, may also be a means of preventing the newly hatched fish from being carried out of estuaries.

Food Habits

Feeding habits refer to the manner in which an organism obtains its food, while food habits relate to the kind of food ingested. The food habits of various estuarine fishes have been well documented, though for many species few data are available. Complete discussion of the food habits of even a fraction of the estuarine species along the coasts of the southeastern Atlantic and the Gulf of Mexico would require a prodigious amount of space. Therefore, information on the food habits of some of the more common and important species in the region are summarized in table 9. Each species listed in the table includes references that will provide the interested reader with additional information.

In most instances, the information on food habits presented for spe-

TABLE 9. Primary Foods of Some Estuarine Fishes of the Southeastern Atlantic and the Gulf of Mexico

Scientific Name	Common Name	Food Habits	References
Megalops atlanticus	Tarpon	Juveniles consume copepods, ostracods, grass shrimp, and fish	Harrington and Harrington (1960), Rickards (1968)
Brevoortia tyrannus	Atlantic menhaden	Algae, planktonic crustacea	Bigelow and Schroeder (1953), June and Carlson (1971), Kjelson et al. (1975)
Harengula jaguana	Scaled sardine	Harpacticoid copepods, amphipods, mysids, isopods, and chironomid larvae	Odum and Heald (1972)
Anchoa hepsetus	Striped anchovy	Copepods, mysids, isopods, molluscs, fish, zooplankton	Hildebrand and Schroeder (1928), Springer and Woodburn (1960), Carr and Adams (1973)
Anchoa mitchilli	Bay anchovy	Zooplankton, fish, decapods, amphipods, mysids, detritus	Hildebrand and Schroeder (1928), Reid (1954), McLane (1955), Darnell (1958), Springer and Woodburn (1960), Odum (1971), Odum and Heald (1972), Carr and Adams (1973)
Synodus foetens	Inshore lizardfish	Fish	Linton (1905), Hildebrand and Schroeder (1928), Reid (1954), Reid (1955), Springer and Woodburn (1960), Carr and Adams (1973)
Arius felis	Sea catfish	Amphipods, decapods, insects, molluscs, copepods, schizopods, isopods, hydroids	Darnell (1958), Harris and Rose (1968), Odum and Heald (1972)
Opsanus tau	Oyster toadfish	Crustaceans, molluscs, polychaetes	R. R. Stickney, unpublished data
Fundulus majalis	Striped killifish	Molluscs, crustaceans, insects, fish	Bigelow and Schroeder (1953)
Fundulus pulvereus	Bayou killifish	Insects, isopods	Simpson and Gunter (1956)
Fundulus similis	Longnose killifish	Harpacticoid copepods, ostracods, barnacle larvae, insects, isopods, amphipods	Stickney and McGeachin (1978)

Species	Common name	Diet	References
Cyprinodon variegatus	Sheepshead minnow	Plant detritus, small crustaceans, nematodes, diatoms, blue-green algae, filamentous algae, formas, insects	Simpson and Gunter (1956), Odum and Heald (1972), Stickney and McGeachin (1978)
Adinia xenica	Diamond killifish	Plant detritus, filamentous algae, amphipods, insects, small copepods, diatoms	Odum and Heald (1972)
Lucania parva	Rainwater killifish	Insects, crustacean larvae, annelids, mysids, amphipods, cumaceans, copepods, plant detritus, small molluscs	Simpson and Gunter (1956), Odum and Heald (1972)
Gambusia affinis	Mosquito fish	Amphipods, chironomids, insects, algae	Odum and Heald (1972)
Poecilia latipinna	Sailfin molly	Algae, diatoms, vascular plant detritus, inorganic matter	Odum and Heald (1972)
Menidia beryllina	Tidewater silverside	Isopods, amphipods, copepods, mysids, detritus, algae, insects, barnacle larvae	Hildebrand and Schroeder (1928), Reid (1954), McLane (1955), Darnell (1958), Springer and Woodburn (1960), Odum and Heald (1972), Carr and Adams (1973), Marsh (1973), Stickney and McGeachin (1978)
Membras martinica	Rough silverside	Copepods, barnacle larvae, amphipods, insects, shrimp, fish	Dixon (1974), Stickney and McGeachin (1978)
Morone saxatilis	Striped bass	Fish, crustaceans	Hollis (1952)
Lutjanus griseus	Gray snapper	Fish, crustaceans	Croker (1962), Odum and Heald (1972)
Diapterus plumieri	Striped mojarra	Mysids, amphipods, molluscs, ostracods, detritus, copepods	Odum and Heald (1972)
Eucinostomus gula	Silver jenny	Copepods, amphipods, molluscs, detritus, mysids	Odum and Heald (1972)
Eucinostomus argenteus	Spotfin mojarra	Amphipods, copepods, mysids, molluscs, detritus	Odum and Heald (1972)

TABLE 9. (*continued*)

Scientific Name	Common Name	Food Habits	References
Archosargus probatocephalus	Sheepshead	Shrimp, molluscs, small fish, crabs, other crustaceans, algae, plant detritus	Reid et al. (1956), Odum and Heald (1972), Stevenson and Confer (1978)
Lagodon rhomboides	Pinfish	Fish, crustaceans, vascular plants, algae, detritus, copepods, mysids, molluscs	Linton (1905), Smith (1907), Hildebrand and Schroeder (1928), McLane (1955), Hanson (1969), Odum and Heald (1972), Carr and Adams (1973), Kjelson et al. (1975), Adams (1976a)
Bairdiella chrysura	Silver perch	Decapods, schizopods, copepods, mysids, amphipods, polychaetes, ectoprocts, fish, detritus	Linton (1905), Hildebrand and Schroeder (1928), Hildebrand and Cable (1930), Reid et al. (1956), Darnell (1958), Thomas (1971), Odum and Heald (1972), Carr and Adams (1973), Stickney et al. (1975)
Cynoscion nebulosus	Spotted seatrout	Copepods, decapods, mysids, carideans, fish, molluscs	Moody (1950), Reid et al. (1956), Darnell (1958), Springer and Woodburn (1960), Odum and Heald (1972)
Cynoscion regalis	Weakfish	Polychaetes, copepods, amphipods, mysids, stomatopods, decapods, fishes	Thomas (1971), Stickney et al. (1975)
Leiostomus xanthurus	Spot	Polychaetes, copepods, isopods, amphipods, mysids, cumacea, fishes	Linton (1905), Welsh and Breder (1923), Hildebrand and Cable (1930), Reid (1954), Roelofs (1954), Darnell (1958), Diener et al. (1974), Stickney et al. (1975), Stickney and McGeachin (1978)

Species	Common name	Diet	References
Micropogonias undulatus	Atlantic croaker	Polychaetes, molluscs, amphipods, isopods, copepods, decapods, stomatopods, mysids, cumacea, ascidians, fish	Linton (1905), Welsh and Breder (1923), Gunter (1945), Roelofs (1954), Reid et al. (1956), Darnell (1958), Diener et al. (1974), Stickney et al. (1975), Roussel and Kilgen (1975), Stickney and McGeachin (1978)
Stellifer lanceolatus	Star drum	Amphipods, isopods, copepods, cumaceans, mysids, stomatopods, decapods, fish	Stickney et al. (1975)
Chaetodipterus faber	Atlantic spadefish	Small crustaceans, annelids, detritus, ctenophores	Smith (1907), Hildebrand and Schroeder (1928), Breder (1948)
Mugil cephalus	Striped mullet	Algae, detritus, vascular plants, crustaceans, bacteria, diatoms	Darnell (1958), Odum (1968), Odum and Heald (1972), Moriarity (1976)
Gobiosoma robustum	Code goby	Amphipods, mysids, insect larvae, cladocerans, algae, detritus, molluscs	Odum and Heald (1972)
Ancylopsetta quadrocellata	Ocellated flounder	Mysids, copepods, other crustaceans, polychaetes, fish	Stickney et al. (1974)
Citharichthys spilopterus	Bay whiff	Mysids, other crustaceans, fish	Stickney et al. (1974)
Etropus crossotus	Fringed flounder	Polychaetes, molluscs, copepods, isopods	Stickney et al. (1974)
Scophthalmus aquosus	Windowpane	Mysids, other crustaceans, fish	Stickney et al. (1974)
Trinectes maculatus	Hogchoker	Annelids, algae, amphipods, detritus, foraminifera, plant seeds, copepods, insect larvae, molluscs, cumaceans	Hildebrand and Schroeder (1928), Reid (1954), McLane (1955), Darnell (1958), Odum and Heald (1972), R. R. Stickney (unpublished data)
Symphurus plagiusa	Blackcheek tonguefish	Molluscs and crustaceans	Stickney (1976)

cies that reach large size is based on studies conducted on juveniles. This is because among estuarine fishes, the most numerous species rarely weigh over a few grams; thus, fishes that exceed one kilogram as adults can be considered large. With some exceptions, large fishes become increasingly piscivorous as they grow, though they may also eat significant numbers of shrimp, crabs, and other large invertebrates.

Many estuarine fishes are highly opportunistic in their food habits. Such species as the Atlantic croaker, which feeds by taking bites out of the bottom (Roelofs, 1954), show little selectivity in their foods, while spot (which feed in the same manner) appear to select copepods over other organisms within the sediments. Specialized as well as unspecialized species can be found in table 9.

In many cases food habits change rather dramatically as the fish grow. This is often because the array of foods available to large fish is greater than that available to small animals. It should be kept in mind, of course, that as fish increase in size and find new foods, they also eliminate other foods from their diets. Large fishes may be unable to ingest such small organisms as rotifers, protozoans, and copepods because these items will pass out through the opercles rather than becoming trapped on the gill rakers before being swallowed.

Most estuarine fishes are highly carnivorous. Although algae are sometimes recovered from estuarine fish stomachs, their presence can generally be considered incidental. Even fish larvae may begin feeding on animal rather than plant matter. Stickney and Shumway (1974) examined a number of marine and estuarine fishes for the presence of cellulase enzyme, which would indicate that the fish can digest cellulose and thereby derive some nutritional value from that complex carbohydrate. Although some of the fishes examined were species that consume algae, cellulase seemed to appear as often as or more often in strictly carnivorous species. It was concluded that the cellulase within the fish was of bacterial origin (no vertebrate is known to produce the enzyme independent of bacteria) and that the bacteria probably colonized stomachs after being introduced in food that was consumed by the fish.

Some general feeding patterns have been found in estuaries when the food habits of fish have been widely investigated. Diener et al. (1974) reported that the most frequently consumed foods of forty species of fish in the Clear Lake, Texas, area were polychaetes, copepods, mysids, penaeids, river shrimp, grass shrimp, detritus, mud, and sand. Since mud and sand are probably incidental in fish stomachs as a consequence of feeding on organisms that live in the sediments, those items have not been included in table 9, though mud and sand did appear in the stomachs of many of the species included in the table. In Lake Pontchartrain, Louisiana, two main food chains were found by Darnell (1958). The first proceeded from copepods (*Acartia*) through small fishes (*Anchoa*, *Brevoortia*, young sciaenids, and others) to large piscivores. The second began with small benthic invertebrates, went through larger invertebrates and small benthic fishes (sea catfishes, young sciaenids, and others), and ended in the large piscivores. According to Darnell (1958), detritus was prominent in the food of fishes and larger invertebrates, and detritus might play an important role in the food web of Lake Pontchartrain.

Odum and Heald (1972) investigated the food habits of many organisms in conjunction with their study of a Florida mangrove community. Many of the fish they evaluated are included in table 9. In addition to fishes, however, Odum and Heald (1972) also examined the food of various important invertebrates (table 10). From those studies and other data, they were able to determine the principal flow of energy in the mangrove swamp (Odum and Heald, 1975). The authors concluded that energy flowed from mangrove leaf detritus through bacteria and fungi into detritus consumers. From there, lower and higher carnivores completed the food chain.

Various other studies have evaluated the food of invertebrates commonly considered important in the diet of fishes. Barnes (1963) indicated that mysids are generally filter feeders, eating such foods as diatoms and finely divided detritus (Pennak, 1953; Cannon and Manton, 1927). They may also feed on copepods and dead amphipods (Green, 1968). Harpacticoid copepods feed on the bottom and browse on small algal cells and bits of detritus (Green, 1968). The fiddler crab, *Uca pugnax*, consumes detrital plant material on the sediment surface but appears to select detritus from plants that follow a specific photosynthetic pathway, probably because of palatability (Haines, 1976). Coprophagy is also thought to be of some importance in marine food webs (Johannes and Satomi, 1966).

Studies of food habits are often not the primary aim of estuarine research projects but, as indicated by DeSylva (1975), may be done as an afterthought once a large number of fishes have been collected for some other purpose. Because studying food habits may not be the main goal of a project, such studies are often not carefully planned. The greatest difficulty with many of these studies is the lack of sufficient environmental informa-

TABLE 10. Food Habits of Some Important Invertebrates in a Florida Mangrove Swamp Community

Species	Food Habits
Copepoda	
Acartia sp., *Cyclops* sp., and *Labidocera* sp.	Particles of vascular plant detritus, a few phytoplankters, and epiphytic diatoms
Isopoda	
Limnoria sp.	Microalgae and detritus obtained by scraping the surface of decaying leaves and submerged logs
Mysidacea	
Mysidopsis almyra	Vascular plant detritus, copepod parts, diatoms, inorganic particles, considerable amount of unidentified particulate matter
Taphromysis bowmani	Inorganic particles, diatoms, copepod parts, fine vascular plant detritus, unidentified particulate matter
Amphipoda	
Melita nitida	Detritus and microalgae
Decapods	
Palaemonetes intermedius	Microalgae, unidentified particulate matter, vascular plant detritus, animal remains
Penaeus duorarum	Unidentified animal remains, harpacticoid copepods, small molluscs, ostracods, benthic diatoms, filamentous green and blue-green algae, vascular plant detritus
Callinectes sapidus	Mussels, another crab (*Rhithropanopeus harrisii*), and amphipods
Rhithropanopeus harrisii	Inorganic particles, vascular plant detritus, diatoms, filamentous algae, amphipods, harpacticoid copepods, unidentified animal remains
Mollusca	
Brachidontes exustus	Unidentified particles, vascular plant detritus, phytoplankton, diatoms, inorganic matter
Congeria leucophaeata	Vascular plant detritus, inorganic particles, phytoplankton, diatoms

Source: Odum and Heald, 1972.

tion. Data often included in studies of food habits specify fish size and season of capture; thus, it is often possible to document changes in food habits as fish grow and become exposed to different temperatures. Information on depth, salinity, sediment type, and other environmental factors is often lacking, however. As an example of how the environment can affect not only food habits but also feeding behavior, the study by Peters and Kjelson (1975) is revealing. Those authors found that both feeding and growth of the southern flounder, *Paralichthys lethostigma*, were highest when temperatures were high and salinity low. The optimum feeding rate for maximum efficiency in food conversion was approximately 70 to 90% of the *ad libitum* rate and was relatively unaffected by temperature.

Estuarine Fish Management

Interest in management of marine and estuarine fisheries has increased in recent years as the impacts of both commercial and sport fishing on saltwater fishes have become apparent. Some states have imposed size limits on certain game species, and most coastal states have closed seasons for certain species of fish and shellfish. In many cases, the size limits and limited seasons have been recommended on the basis of scientific investigations, but some regulations have been promulgated through pressure from interested citizens who may not have scientific data to back up their demands. In the latter instance, the resulting legislation may not be appropriate with respect to serving the needs of all parties while still preserving the integrity of the fishery.

Gear restrictions are one way to regulate marine and estuarine fisheries. For example, the mesh size and length of a seine may be regulated by the appropriate state agency. The number of rods and reels per individual fisherman can also be controlled. Regulation includes commercial fishermen as well as sportsmen. Maximum sizes and numbers of nets to be pulled by a fishing boat are often set by state agencies. Seasons are also set by such agencies and may differ for sport and commercial fishermen interested in the same species. All of these regulations, and others, have been used to try to manage coastal fisheries.

Nonregulatory management of coastal and estuarine fisheries has been somewhat limited, but certain techniques have been effective. Early programs to stock estuaries with eggs and larvae of marine fish and shellfish were probably not very productive. Little evidence was ever collected to suggest that such stocking programs (which were common in the late 1800s and early 1900s) did anything but provide predators with a wider selection in their food supply. More recently, hatcheries have been maintaining such species as striped bass, red drum, flounder, and pompano until the fish reach at least a few centimeters in length, at which time they are somewhat less subject to predation upon release. Tagging studies have not revealed overwhelming changes in natural fish stocks resulting from artificial augmentation, but some encouraging signs have been observed.

Another nonregulatory program that has enhanced fishing in coastal regions involves establishing artificial reefs. Although these are often used in offshore areas, they have also been placed in estuaries. Tire reefs, composed of old auto or truck tires bound together with wire or filled with concrete, have been constructed in many areas. Such structures, which may comprise several thousand tires in a relatively small area, attract a diverse community of fishes and can provide excellent recreational fishing. Liberty ships have been sunk for use as artificial reefs. Car bodies, old streetcars, and other discards of society have also been used. In some cases, corrosion has limited the life of such reefs, but many can be expected to last indefinitely with little or no attention.

Care must be used in the placement of reefs so that they do not interfere with shipping lanes or encroach on commercial fishing grounds. In some instances, reefs have been known to move from the area in which they were dropped, destroying fishing gear as much as several kilometers from the intended reef site. This happened once when parts of some tire reefs, sunk off one southeastern state, were redistributed by currents into traditional shrimp fishing grounds. A certain amount of animosity was generated as a result.

Few states have generated marine fish management plans—Mississippi is an exception (Etzold and Christmas, 1979)—but various regions of the United States have organized fishery councils under federal statute to develop species management plans for the more important species in those regions. One such council is the Gulf Coast Regional Council. Each fishery council obtains advice from scientific experts on particular species. The available data are then evaluated, and a management plan is developed. These plans are dynamic in that they can be updated as the need arises or as new data are obtained. Plans for such species as menhaden, sharks, shrimp, and Florida lobsters are being developed or are already in place. The goal of most plans is to obtain optimum sustainable yield (OSY). Although many fisheries in the past have been regulated on the basis of maximum sustainable yield (MSY), the theory of OSY has been developed to ensure that no fishery will collapse as a result of fishing pressure. Although the total catch may be less under OSY, the population can be expected to be maintained even during years when recruitment is below normal. OSY has been accepted by many fishery managers across the country as the best way to maintain both a stable fishery and a normal balance among the species of the community.

LITERATURE CITED

Adams, S. M. 1976a. The ecology of eelgrass, *Zostera marina* (L.), fish communities. I. Structural analysis. *J. Exp. Mar. Biol. Ecol.* 22: 269–91.

———. 1976b. The ecology of eelgrass, *Zostera marina* (L.), fish communities. II. Functional analysis. *J. Exp. Mar. Biol. Ecol.* 22: 293–311.

American Fisheries Society. 1980. A list of common and scientific names of fishes from the United States and Canada. American Fisheries Society Special Publication no. 12.

Barnes, R. D. 1963. *Invertebrate zoology*. Philadelphia: W. B. Saunders Co.

Bigelow, H. B., and W. C. Schroeder. 1953. Fishes of the Gulf of Maine. *Fish. Bull.* 53: 1–577.

Breder, C. M., Jr. 1948. *Field book of marine fishes of the Atlantic coast from Labrador to Texas*. New York: G. P. Putnam.

Cannon, H. G., and S. M. Manton. 1927. On the feeding mechanism of a mysid crustacean, *Hemimyxsis lamornae*. *Trans. Roy. Soc. Edinb.* 55: 219–53.

Carr, W. E. S., and C. A. Adams. 1973. Food habits of juvenile marine fishes occupying seagrass beds in the estuarine zone near Crystal River, Florida. *Trans. Am. Fish. Soc.* 102: 511–40.

Christmas, J. Y., and G. Gunter. 1960. Distribution of menhaden, genus *Brevoortia*, in the Gulf of Mexico. *Trans. Am. Fish. Soc.* 89: 338–43.

Christmas, J. Y., and R. S. Waller. 1975. Location and time of menhaden spawning in the Gulf of Mexico. Gulf Coast Research Laboratory Publication. Mimeo.

Copeland, B. J., K. R. Tenore, and D. B. Horton. 1974. Oligohaline regime, pp. 315–57. In: H. T. Odum, B. J. Copeland, and E. A. McMahan, eds. *Coastal ecological systems of the United States*. Vol. II. Washington, D.C.: Conservation Foundation.

Croker, R. A. 1962. Growth and food of the gray snapper, *Lutjanus griseus*, in Everglades National Park. *Trans. Am. Fish. Soc.* 91: 379–83.

Darnell, R. M. 1958. Food habits of fishes and larger macroinvertebrates of Lake Pontchartrain, Louisiana, an estuarine community. *Publ. Inst. Mar. Sci., Univ. Tex.* 5: 353–416.

Dawson, C. E. 1958. A study of the biology and life history of the spot, *Leiostomus xanthurus* Lacepede, with special reference to South Carolina. *Cont. Bears Bluff Lab.* 28: 1–48.

———. 1965. Length-weight relationships of some Gulf of Mexico fishes. *Trans. Am. Fish. Soc.* 94: 279–80.

DeSylva, D. P. 1975. Nektonic food webs in estuaries, pp. 420–47. In: L. E. Cronin, ed. *Estuarine research.* Vol. I. New York: Academic Press.

Diener, R. A., A. Inglish, and G. B. Adams. 1974. Stomach contents of fishes from Clear Lake and tributary waters, a Texas estuarine area. *Cont. Mar. Sci.* 18: 7–17.

Dixon, C. A. 1974. A study of food habits of 2 species of silverside, *Menidia beryllina* (Cope) and *Membras martinica* (Valenciennes), in upper Galveston Bay, Texas. M.S. thesis, Texas A&M University, College Station.

Etzold, D. J., and J. Y. Christmas, eds. 1979. A Mississippi marine finfish management plan. Mississippi-Alabama Sea Grant Consortium Publication MASGP-78-046.

Fisher, N. P. 1975. *The future of Texas fisheries.* Austin: Texas Industrial Commission.

Fore, P. L. 1970. Oceanic distribution of eggs and larvae of the Gulf menhaden. *U.S. Fish and Wildl. Serv., Bur. Comm. Fish. Circ.* 341: 11–13.

Green, J. 1968. *The biology of estuarine animals.* Seattle: University of Washington Press.

Gunter, G. 1945. Studies on the marine fishes of Texas. *Publ. Inst. Mar. Sci., Univ. Tex.* 1: 1–190.

———. 1956. Some relations of faunal distributions to salinity in estuarine waters. *Ecology* 37: 616–19.

———. 1967a. Some relationships of estuaries to the fisheries of the Gulf of Mexico, pp. 621–38. In: G. H. Lauff, ed. *Estuaries.* American Association for the Advancement of Science Publication no. 83. Washington, D.C.: AAAS.

———. 1967b. Vertebrates in hypersaline waters. *Publ. Inst. Mar. Sci., Univ. Tex.* 12: 230–41.

Haines, E. B. 1976. Relation between the stable carbon isotope composition of fiddler crabs, plants, and soils in a salt marsh. *Limnol. Oceanogr.* 21: 880–83.

Hanson, D. F. 1969. Food, growth, migration, and abundance of pinfish, *Lagodon rhomboides*, and Atlantic croaker, *Micropogon undulatus*, near Pensacola, Florida, 1963–1965. *Fish. Bull.* 68: 135–46.

Harrington, R. W., Jr., and E. S. Harrington. 1960. Food of larval and young tarpon, *Megalops atlantica. Copeia* 1960: 311–19.

Harris, A. H., and C. D. Rose. 1968. Shrimp predation by the sea catfish, *Galeichtyes felis. Trans. Am. Fish. Soc.* 97: 503–504.

Haven, D. S. 1959. Migration of the croaker (*Micropogon undulatus*). *Copeia* 1959: 25–30.

Heffernan, T. L., and A. W. Green. 1977. *Survey of finfish harvest in selected Texas bays*. Austin: Texas Game Fish Commission.

Hildebrand, S. F., and L. E. Cable. 1930. Development and life history of fourteen teleostean fishes at Beaufort, North Carolina. *Fish. Bull.* 46: 383–499.

Hildebrand, S. F., and W. C. Schroeder. 1928. Fishes of Chesapeake Bay. *Fish. Bull.* 43: 1–388.

Hoese, H. D., and R. H. Moore. 1977. *Fishes of the Gulf of Mexico, Texas, Louisiana, and adjacent waters*. College Station: Texas A&M University Press.

Hollis, E. H. 1952. Variations in the feeding habits of the striped bass, *Roccus saxatilis* (Walbaum), in Chesapeake Bay. *Bull. Bingham Oceanogr. Coll.* 14: 111–31.

Johannes, R. E., and M. Satomi. 1966. Composition and nutritive value of fecal pellets of a marine crustacean. *Limnol. Oceanogr.* 11: 191–97.

Joseph, E. B. 1972. The status of the sciaenid stocks of the middle Atlantic coast. *Ches. Sci.* 13: 87–100.

June, F. C., and F. T. Carlson. 1971. Food of young Atlantic menhaden, *Brevoortia tyrannus*, in relation to metamorphosis. *Fish. Bull.* 68: 493–512.

June, F. C., and L. Chamberlin. 1959. The role of the estuary in the life history of the Atlantic menhaden. *Proc. Gulf and Caribb. Fish. Inst.* 11: 41–45.

Kjelson, M. A., D. S. Peters, G. W. Thayer, and G. N. Johnson. 1975. The general feeding ecology of postlarval fishes in the Newport River estuary. *Fish. Bull.* 73: 137–44.

Linton, E. 1905. Parasites of fishes of Beaufort, North Carolina. *Bull. Bur. Fish.* 24: 321–428.

McHugh, J. L. 1966. Management of estuarine fisheries, pp. 133–54. In: A symposium on estuarine fisheries. American Fisheries Society Special Publication no. 3.

———. 1967. Estuarine nekton, pp. 581–620. In: G. H. Lauff, ed. *Estuaries*. American Association for the Advancement of Science Publication no. 83. Washington, D.C.: AAAS.

———. 1968. Are estuaries necessary? *Comm. Fish. Rev.* 30: 37–45.

McLane, W. M. 1955. The fishes of the St. Johns River system. Ph.D. diss. University of Florida.

Marsh, G. A. 1973. The *Zostera* epifaunal community in the York River, Virginia. *Ches. Sci.* 14: 87–97.

Massmann, W. H., and A. L. Pacheco. 1960. Disappearance of young Atlantic croakers from the York River, Virginia. *Trans. Am. Fish. Soc.* 89: 154–59.

Moody, W. D. 1950. A study of the natural history of the spotted trout, *Cynoscion nebulosus*, in the Cedar Key, Florida, area. *Quart. J. Fla. Acad. Sci.* 12: 147–71.

Moore, D., H. A. Brusher, and L. Trent. 1970. Relative abundance, seasonal distribution, and species composition of demersal fishes off Louisiana and Texas, 1962–1964. *Cont. Mar. Sci.* 15: 45–70.

Moriarity, D. J. W. 1976. Quantitative studies on bacteria and algae in the food of mullet *Mugil cephalus* L. and the prawn *Metapenaeus bennettae* (Racek and Dall). *J. Exp. Mar. Biol. Ecol.* 22: 131–43.

Nicholson, W. R. 1978. Movements and population structure of Atlantic menhaden indicated by tag returns. *Estuaries* 1: 141–50.

Nixon, S. W. 1980. Between coastal marshes and coastal waters: A review of twenty years of speculation on the role of salt marshes in estuarine productivity and water chemistry, pp. 437–525. In: P. Hamilton and K. B. Macdonald, eds. *Estuarine and wetland processes—with emphasis on modeling.* New York: Plenum Press.

Odum, W. E. 1968. The ecological significance of fine particle selection by the striped mullet, *Mugil cephalus. Limnol. Oceanogr.* 13: 92–98.

———. 1971. Pathways of energy flow in a south Florida estuary. Ph.D. diss., University of Miami.

Odum, W. E., and E. J. Heald. 1972. Trophic analysis of an estuarine mangrove community. *Bull. Mar. Sci.* 22: 671–738.

———. 1975. The detritus-based food web of an estuarine mangrove community, pp. 265–86. In: L. E. Cronin, ed. *Estuarine research.* Vol. I. New York: Academic Press.

Pacheco, A. L. 1962. Age and growth of spot in lower Chesapeake Bay, with notes on distribution and abundance of juveniles in the York River system. *Ches. Sci.* 3: 18–28.

Parker, J. C. 1971. The biology of the spot, *Leiostomus xanthurus* Lacepede, and Atlantic croaker, *Micropogon undulatus* (Linnaeus). Ph.D. diss., Texas A&M University, College Station.

———. 1973. Length-weight relationship and condition of *Leiostomus xanthurus* and *Micropogon undulatus* in Galveston Bay, Texas. *Southwest. Nat.* 18: 211–27.

Pearcy, W. G., and S. W. Richards. 1962. Distribution and ecology of fishes of the Mystic River estuary, Connecticut. *Ecology* 43: 248–59.

Pearson, J. C. 1929. Natural history and conservation of the redfish and other commercial sciaenids on the Texas coast. *Bull. Bur. Fish.* 44: 129–214.

Pennak, R. W. 1953. *Fresh-water invertebrates of the United States.* New York: Ronald Press.

Peters, D. S., and M. A. Kjelson. 1975. Consumption and utilization of food by various postlarval and juvenile fishes of North Carolina estuaries, pp.

448–72. In: L. E. Cronin, ed. *Estuarine research*. Vol. I. New York: Academic Press.

Peters, D. W., and W. E. Schaaf. 1981. Food requirements and sources for juvenile Atlantic menhaden. *Trans. Am. Fish. Soc*. 110: 317–24.

Pristas, P. J., and L. Trent. 1978. Seasonal abundance, size, and sex ratio of fishes caught with gill nets in St. Andrew Bay, Florida. *Bull. Mar. Sci*. 28: 581–89.

Raney, E. C. 1952. The life history of the striped bass *Roccus saxatilis* (Walbaum). *Bull. Bingham Oceanogr. Coll*. 14: 5–97.

Reid, G. K., Jr. 1954. An ecological study of the Gulf of Mexico fishes in the vicinity of Cedar Key, Florida. *Bull. Mar. Sci. Gulf Caribb*. 4: 1–94.

———. 1955. A summer study of the biology and ecology of East Bay, Texas. II. The fish fauna of East Bay, the Gulf beach, and summary. *Tex. J. Sci*. 7: 430–53.

Reid, G. K., A. Inglis, and H. D. Hoese. 1956. Summer foods of some fish species in East Bay, Texas. *Southwest. Nat*. 1: 100–104.

Reintjes, J. W. 1961. Menhaden eggs and larvae from M/V *Theodore N. Gill* cruises, south Atlantic coast of the United States, 1953–54. U.S. Fish and Wildlife Service Special Scientific Report—Fisheries no. 393.

———. 1969. The Gulf menhaden and our changing estuaries. *Proc. Gulf and Caribb. Fish. Inst*. 22: 87–105.

Reintjes, J. W., and A. L. Pacheco. 1966. The relation of menhaden to estuaries, pp. 50–58. In: A symposium on estuarine fisheries. American Fisheries Society Special Publication no. 3.

Rickards, W. L. 1968. Ecology and growth of juvenile tarpon, *Megalops atlanticus*, in a Georgia salt marsh. *Bull. Mar. Sci*. 18: 220–39.

Roelofs, E. W. 1954. Food studies of young sciaenid fishes, *Micropogon* and *Leiostomus*, from North Carolina. *Copeia* 1954: 151–53.

Roussel, J. E., and R. H. Kilgen. 1975. Food habits of young Atlantic croakers (*Micropogon undulatus*) in brackish pipeline canals. *Proc. La. Acad. Sci*. 38: 70–74.

Schauss, R. P., Jr. 1977. Seasonal occurrence of some larval and juvenile fishes in Lynnhaven Bay, Virginia. *Am. Midl. Natur*. 98: 275–82.

Shenker, J. M., and J. M. Dean. 1979. The utilization of an intertidal salt marsh creek by larval and juvenile fishes: Abundance, diversity, and temporal variation. *Estuaries* 2: 154–63.

Simmons, E. G. 1957. An ecological survey of the upper Laguna Madre of Texas. *Publ. Inst. Mar. Sci., Univ. Tex*. 4: 156–200.

Simpson, D. G., and G. Gunter. 1956. Notes on habitats, systematic characters, and life histories of Texas saltwater Cyprinodontes. *Tulane Stud. Zool*. 4: 115–34.

Smith, H. M. 1907. The fishes of North Carolina. North Carolina Geological and Economic Survey II, pp. 1–453.

Springer, V. G., and K. D. Woodburn. 1960. An ecological study of the fishes of the Tampa Bay area. Florida State Board of Conservation Marine Laboratory Professional Paper, series 1.

Stevenson, J. C., and N. M. Confer. 1978. Summary of available information on Chesapeake Bay submerged vegetation. U.S. Fish and Wildlife Service Biological Services Program FWS/BA 78-66.

Stickney, R. R. 1976. Food habits of Georgia estuarine fishes II. *Symphurus plagiusa* (Pleuronectiformes: Cynoglossidae). *Trans. Am. Fish. Soc.* 105: 202–207.

Stickney, R. R., and M. L. Cuenco. 1982. Habitat suitability index models: Juvenile spot. U.S. Department of the Interior Fish and Wildlife Service FWS/OBS 82-10.20.

Stickney, R. R., and R. B. McGeachin. 1978. Food habits of fishes associated with marshland developed on dredged material. *Proc. Ann. Conf. S.E. Assoc. Fish and Wildl. Agencies* 32: 547–60.

Stickney, R. R., and S. E. Shumway. 1974. Occurrence of cellulase activity in the stomachs of fishes. *J. Fish Biol.* 6: 779–90.

Stickney, R. R., G. L. Taylor, and D. B. White. 1975. Food habits of five species of young southeastern United States Sciaenidae. *Ches. Sci.* 16: 104–14.

Stickney, R. R., G. L. Taylor, and R. W. Heard III. 1974. Food habits of Georgia estuarine fishes. I. Four species of flounders (Pleuronectiformes: Bothidae). *Fish. Bull.* 72: 515–25.

Stroud, R. H. 1971. Introduction to symposium, pp. 3–8. In: P. A. Douglas and R. H. Stroud, eds. *A symposium on the biological significance of estuaries.* Washington, D.C.: Sport Fishing Institute.

Subrahmanyam, C. B., and S. H. Drake. 1975. Studies on animal communities in two north Florida salt marsh fish communities. *Bull. Mar. Sci.* 25: 445–65.

Sundararaj, B. I. 1960. Age and growth of the spot, *Leiostomus xanthurus* Lacepede. *Tulane Stud. Zool.* 8: 41–62.

Sykes, J. E. 1964. Requirements of Gulf and south Atlantic estuarine research. *Proc. Gulf and Caribb. Fish. Inst.* 16: 113–20.

Tabb, D. C. 1966. The estuary as a habitat for spotted seatrout, *Cynoscion nebulosus*, pp. 59–67. In: A symposium on estuarine fisheries. American Fisheries Society Special Publication no. 3.

Tabb, D. C., and A. C. Jones. 1962. Effect of hurricane Donna on the aquatic fauna of north Florida Bay. *Trans. Am. Fish. Soc.* 91: 375–78.

Talbot, G. B. 1966. Estuarine environmental requirements and limiting factors for striped bass, pp. 37–49. In: A symposium on estuarine fisheries. American Fisheries Society Special Publication no. 3.

Thomas, D. L. 1971. An ecological study of the Delaware River in the vicinity of [an] artificial island. III. The early life history and ecology of six species of drum (Sciaenidae) in the lower Delaware River, a brackish tidal estuary. Ichthyological Associates, Bulletin no. 3. Ichthyological Associates, Ithaca, N.Y.

Welsh, W. W., and C. M. Breder. 1923. Contributions to the life histories of Sciaenidae of the eastern United States coast. *Fish. Bull.* 39: 141–201.

CHAPTER 10

Higher Vertebrates Associated with Estuaries

Introduction

IF asked to provide a list of vertebrates (other than fishes) that are commonly associated with estuaries, most people would probably give birds high priority, or even list them exclusively. Such birds as sea gulls, pelicans, blue herons, little green herons, and snowy egrets are familiar to those who reside on or near the seacoast or who have visited the seashore. Sandpipers might also be named but many other species also live in the estuarine environment. Most species of birds found at the coast also occur inland. Although they may be tied to water for food, the birds are generally not confined to only one kind of aquatic environment. All birds nest on land, so none is truly a marine organism, though many conduct most of their activities on or over water.

Birds are not the only nonfish vertebrates associated with estuaries. At the lower end of the taxonomic ladder are the amphibians and reptiles that, while not particularly numerous, do have estuarine representatives. Frogs and toads (families Ranidae and Bufonidae) are among the amphibians found in estuaries. Soft-shell turtles (family Trionychidae), sea turtles (family Chelonidae), and terrapins (family Emydidae) are also found in estuaries. The diamondback terrapin, *Malaclemys terrapin*, was once widely harvested from estuaries for human food. There is one native member of the family Crocodylidae in the United States (in Florida) and one native member of the family Alligatoridae. American alligators range from at least South Carolina southward throughout Florida and in all of the states bordering on the Gulf of Mexico. They have made an impressive comeback from the brink of extinction in recent years.

A marsh development site on Bolivar Peninsula, near Galveston, Texas, was surveyed for reptiles and amphibians (Webb et al., 1978). No examples of either group were found in the marshland habitats, but the ornate box turtle (*Terrapene ornata*), speckled king snake (*Lampropeltis getulus*), and Texas horned lizard (*Phrynosoma cornutum*) were present. Also found along the Texas coast are such species as the Gulf coast toad (*Bufo valliceps*), narrow-mouth frog (*Gastrophyrne carolinensis*), skink (*Eumences* sp.), six-lined race runner (*Cnemidophorus sexlineatus*), glass lizard (*Ophisaurus attenuatus*), southern garter snake (*Thamnophis sirtlalis*), salt-marsh snake (*Natrix faciata clarki*), and cottonmouth (*Ancistrodon piscivorous*). Of the species listed, the salt-marsh snake is the only one that feeds in the marshland, consuming crabs and crayfish as well as terrestrial organisms. The king snake and cottonmouth eat mammals and birds, while the remaining reptiles and amphibians feed primarily upon insects.

Mammals, including some truly marine species, can be found in U.S. estuaries along the coasts of the southeastern Atlantic and the Gulf of Mexico. Terrestrial mammals can be considered casual users of estuaries. They may traverse estuaries during migration and often feed in and along the water. Some mammals even reproduce within estuaries. None of the terrestrial mammals is, however, tied to estuarine conditions. Any species found in an estuary can also be found inland. At least fifteen families of mammals live near estuaries. Sources of information on the various groups of vertebrates, including those in coastal areas, can be found in the works of such authors as Bent (1962a, 1962b, 1963, 1964), Carr (1952), Wright and Wright (1957), and Walker (1975).

Relationships between vertebrates and marshland habitats include establishment of territories or parts of territories; usage of part or all of the home range; feeding; reproduction; and, in the case of birds, roosting. Plant cover in marshland provides refuge from predators and somewhat reduced temperature extremes as compared to the open beach (Shanholtzer, 1974). These may be important factors in the selection of marshland habitat by at least some terrestrial vertebrates.

Some species of birds feed upon marshgrass seeds (Shanholtzer, 1974), and deer, marsh rabbits, and rodents sometimes feed on the stems. Consumption of grass stems seems to be more common in the high marsh than in the low marsh. *Spartina patens*, for example, has been used as cattle forage for generations, while *S. alterniflora* is not generally used as livestock feed. Goats, rabbits, and other mammals will eat on *S. alterni-*

flora shoots, but once the grass has reached several centimeters in height, it does not seem to attract grazing animals.

In this chapter a few of the higher estuarine vertebrates are discussed. As in previous chapters, no attempt has been made to cover all of the species common to estuaries. Considerable attention has been focused on birds, and information on the distribution and food of various birds is provided. The occurrence of marine mammals in estuaries is also discussed. Special attention is given to the bottle-nosed dolphin, *Tursiops truncatus*, since it is the most common marine mammal in the region of interest. Amphibians and reptiles are not discussed in detail, though the reader should remember that they are present and may be important in certain instances. Certainly, in areas with high standing crops of alligators, these reptiles influence energy flow along with, in some cases, human behavior.

Estuarine Birds

Peterson and Peterson (1979) recognized six feeding guilds of birds on North Carolina tidal flats. Their list can probably be extended throughout the southeastern U.S. estuarine system and along the Gulf of Mexico. The guilds recognized were (1) waders, (2) shallow probing and surface searching, (3) deep probing, (4) aerial searching, (5) floating and diving, and (6) birds of prey. According to the same authors, birds often represent end points in food chains. Eggs and young, on the other hand, are often devoured by other birds or mammals.

Table 11 presents a list of some of the birds common to these estuaries. Even a cursory examination of the list of species in that table reveals great diversity among the birds. Some of the species are common, while others, like the brown pelican, bald eagle, and whooping crane, are rare or extremely rare. The whooping crane is among the rarest species on earth, and a great deal of effort has been expended to keep it from becoming extinct. Table 11 is not meant to provide a complete listing of species of birds found in estuaries. Lowery and Newman (1954) revealed that fully 90% of the birds of North America have been reported from the marshes of the Gulf of Mexico.

WATERFOWL

Many species of ducks and geese can be found in estuaries, either as permanent residents or as transients. Estuaries along the Gulf of Mexico

TABLE 11. Estuarine Birds of the Southeastern Atlantic and the Gulf of Mexico

Common Name	Scientific Name
Whistling swan	*Cygnus columbianus*
Snow goose (blue goose)	*Anser caerulescens*
White-fronted goose	*Anser albifrons*
Canada goose	*Branta canadensis*
Brant	*Branta bernicla*
Mallard	*Anas platyrhynchos*
Pintail	*Anas acuta*
Black duck	*Anas rubripes*
American widgeon	*Anas americana*
Gadwall	*Anas strepera*
Shoveler	*Anas* sp.
Green-winged teal	*Anas crecca*
Blue-winged teal	*Anas discors*
Wood duck	*Aix sponsa*
Ring-necked duck	*Aythya collaris*
Canvasback	*Aythya valisineria*
Redhead	*Aythya americana*
Scaup	*Aythya* sp.
Ruddy duck	*Oxyura jamaicensis*
Bufflehead	*Bucephala albeola*
Hooded merganser	*Mergus cucullatus*
Goldeneye	*Bucephala* sp.
Old-squaw	*Clangula hyemalis*
Coot	*Falica atra*
White pelican	*Pelecanus erythrorhynchoss*
Brown pelican	*Pelecanus occidentalis*
Cormorant	*Phalacrocorax* sp.
Great blue heron	*Ardea horodias*
Little blue heron	*Egretta caerulea*
Reddish egret	*Egretta rufescens*
Common or great egret	*Egretta alba*
Snowy egret	*Egretta thula*
Louisiana heron	*Egretta tricolor*
Cattle egret	*Bubulcus ibis*
Black-crowned night heron	*Nycticorax nyctocorax*
Yellow-crowned night heron	*Nycticorax violaceus*
Glossy ibis	*Plegadis falcinellus*
White ibis	*Eudocimus albus*
White-faced ibis	*Plegadis chihi*
Roseate spoonbill	*Platalea ajaja*
Bald eagle	*Haliaeetus leucocephalus*

TABLE 11. (*continued*)

Common Name	Scientific Name
Osprey	*Pandion haliaetus*
Whooping crane	*Grus americana*
Sandhill crane	*Grus canadensis*
Rail	*Rallus* sp.
Laughing gull	*Larus atricilla*
Herring gull	*Larus argentatus*
Ring-billed gull	*Larus delawarensis*
Tern	*Sterna* sp.

Source: Gruson, 1976.

often serve as overwintering grounds for waterfowl, though human encroachment into the coastal zone has led to some dispersion of the waterfowl out of their traditional areas of overwintering. Man's impact on waterfowl habitat has not been all bad, however. Rice fields on the Texas coastal plain support hundreds of thousands of geese during the winter. Grains left in the fields in more northerly states also support overwintering groups of waterfowl. The birds migrate south not to avoid cold weather but to find food, and if plentiful food is available inland, the birds will often take advantage of it and will not make their traditional migration to the Gulf coast and even farther south. About 350 thousand Canada geese, 550 thousand ducks, and thousands of whistling swans overwinter in the Chesapeake Bay region. Large concentrations of ducks and geese continue to migrate to the Gulf of Mexico, however. Palmisano (1967) reported that the marshes of Louisiana serve as wintering grounds for over six million ducks, geese, and coots—almost 25% of all U.S. waterfowl. Nearly two million waterfowl overwinter along the Texas coast (Lay and Culbertson, 1977).

Although the food habits of birds vary greatly, most waterfowl that prefer to live in estuaries feed on plants. Some species feed most heavily on freshwater or low salinity plants, while others seem to prefer plants in higher salinity water.

Glasgow and Junca (1962) found that mallard ducks ate mostly Louisiana grasses, among them not only freshwater grasses but also domestic rice. The ducks also consumed some animal matter, which made up less than 2% of the total food ingested. The same authors found a similar situation for pintail and teal ducks. Fall panicum (panicgrass) was the most common food for both pintails and teal, but millet and other terrestrial grasses were also commonly recovered. In a study of fifteen species of waterfowl in North Carolina, Quay and Critcher (1962) found that the fresh-water plants *Potamogeton*, *Ruppia*, and *Najas* were the most important foods. Examination of the food habits of seventeen species of ducks and geese by Chamberlain (1959) led to the recovery of forty-nine species of important food plants.

Similar results were obtained by Glazener (1946), who examined the gizzards of 117 geese and found that the food recovered was all of plant origin and represented thirty-one species of flowering plants and algae. More than 66% of the plant material recovered was in the form of grasses. Rice, corn, and sorghum were the most commonly consumed cultivated crops. Saltgrass, watercress, and panicgrass were commonly consumed aquatic species. Redhead ducks seem to prefer shoalgrass, while diving ducks in Florida do not seem to use turtlegrass and manateegrass (Stieglitz, 1966).

According to Chabreck (1968), blue and snow geese benefit by moderate cattle grazing on marsh plants. The waterfowl feed on the tender new growth that appears after the mammals have grazed on the coarser grass stems. Not all waterfowl feed exclusively on plants, however. Dabbling ducks in South Carolina were found to utilize the snail, *Najas quadalupensis*, as a major food, according to Kerwin and Webb (1971). The same ducks also ate the plant *Scirpus validus*. The greater scaup, a diving duck, was found to consume large quantities of animal foods in Apalachee Bay, Florida (Stieglitz, 1966).

Most species of waterfowl nest predominantly in the northern portions of their home ranges, but the mottled duck and Florida duck nest exclusively along the coasts of the southeastern United States and the Gulf of Mexico (Lynch, 1967). The southernmost portion of the nesting range of the black duck also lies in the southeastern Atlantic part of this country. Similarly, a few gadwalls and some colonies of blue-wing teal can be found nesting in Louisiana and Texas. Wood ducks nest both along the coast and inland while the fulvous tree duck, which is almost global, nests in Louisiana and Texas. The tropical black-bellied tree duck can be found along the Texas coast south of Corpus Christi (Lynch, 1967).

WADING BIRDS AND SHOREBIRDS

Many birds other than waterfowl inhabit the estuaries of the southeastern Atlantic and the Gulf of Mexico. A few species are presented in table 12 along with locations of the birds, notes on habitat preferences, and other information. Ogden (1978) compiled estimates of the number of

TABLE 12. Patterns of Use by Nonwaterfowl Bird Species in Estuaries of the Southeastern Atlantic and the Gulf of Mexico

Common Name	Location	Notes
Pelican	Southeastern Atlantic and Gulf of Mexico	Brown and white pelicans inhabit the whole region. White pelicans breed primarily in the interior, but many winter in Florida and Texas. Brown pelicans are present throughout the year. Both eat fish
Cormorant	Southeastern Atlantic and Gulf of Mexico	Double-crested cormorant is more abundant than the olivaceous cormorant. The latter is found only in marshes in Texas and Louisiana
Great white heron	South Florida	Small total population
Great blue heron	Southeastern Atlantic and Gulf of Mexico	Wide distribution in the United States. Less dependent on coastal zone than are other herons
Reddish egret	Texas	Rare over much of its range. Seems to prefer high salinities
Common egret	Southeastern Atlantic and Gulf of Mexico	Found from fresh to salt water but seems to prefer fresh to brackish water
Snowy egret	Southeastern Atlantic and Gulf of Mexico	Found from fresh water to salt water
Cattle egret	Southeastern Atlantic and Gulf of Mexico	Widely distributed in United States, this exotic is not dependent upon wetlands
Louisiana heron	Southeastern Atlantic and Gulf of Mexico	Major populations in Louisiana and Texas; favors salt to brackish water
Little blue heron	Southeastern Atlantic	Present in coastal colonies, this bird seems to prefer inland freshwater areas
Black-crowned night heron	Southeastern Atlantic and Gulf of Mexico	Found throughout the United States; not dependent upon coastal zone

Species	Region	Notes
Yellow-crowned night heron	Southeastern Atlantic	Breeds in freshwater locations but feeds in salt to brackish water
Wood ibis	South Carolina, Florida, Louisiana, Texas	Breeds only in Florida
Glossy ibis	Southeastern Atlantic and Gulf of Mexico	Breeds in freshwater areas of Florida with scattered colonies on the Atlantic coast. Occasionally breeds in Louisiana and Texas
White ibis	Southeastern Atlantic and Gulf of Mexico	Nests from freshwater to hypersaline areas
White-faced ibis	Mississippi Delta to Texas	Primarily a western U.S. bird; several large colonies live in the Gulf coast region
Roseate spoonbill	Southeastern Atlantic and Gulf of Mexico	Confined to the region of interest. Tolerant of wide salinity range for breeding and feeding
Bald eagle	Southeastern Atlantic and Gulf of Mexico	About 70% of the southern subspecies nest in this region
Osprey	Southeastern Atlantic and Gulf of Mexico	Heavily dependent upon fishes in the estuarine region
Crane	Gulf of Mexico	Nesting of whooping crane limited to a small area in Texas. Sandhill crane resident populations can be found in Florida, Alabama, and Mississippi
Rail	Southeastern Atlantic and Gulf of Mexico	Various species are present ranging from fresh water to seawater
Gull	Southeastern Atlantic and Gulf of Mexico	Species include the laughing gull, herring gull, and ring-billed gull, all of which heavily use estuaries
Tern	Southeastern Atlantic and Gulf of Mexico	Many species frequent the estuaries of the region to some extent

Source: Sprunt, 1967.

breeding individuals of several species of wading birds in the southeastern states from Virginia through Georgia (table 13). Those figures indicate that egrets, herons, and ibises constituted a community of nearly 200,000 birds in the surveyed states. Allen et al. (1958) reported that over 70% of all common egrets breed along the southeastern Atlantic and Gulf coasts, though the species travels north along the eastern seaboard as far as New Jersey and can also be found in California.

Herons, storks, and ibises depend on coastal environments of various types. According to Curry-Lindahl (1978), those birds can be found around marshes, coastal lagoons, mangrove swamps, rocky coastlines, shallow offshore waters, mud flats, coral reefs, and islands. The distribution of wading birds has been shown in some cases to relate to the distribution of their food; in others, to such environmental factors as wave action, substrate type, and cover (Wolff, 1969).

Pelicans are some of the most interesting birds living in estuaries. Ungainly on the ground, during takeoff, and on land, pelicans are graceful in flight and unique in their feeding method and in the possession of a pouch beneath the lower mandible.

Before 1920, native populations of the brown pelican, *Pelicanus occidentalis carolinesis*, ranged from 50,000 to 85,000 birds in Louisiana and Texas (King et al., 1977). By 1958, according to the same authors, brown pelicans had disappeared from two overwintering grounds and had suffered additional losses between 1959 and 1961. By 1963, no brown pelicans could be found in Louisiana, and only about 100 were observed in Texas. Among the causes attributed to the decline in brown pelicans were the use of such pesticides as DDT and Endrin, though all pressures against pelican survival cannot be related to those chemicals. Hunters and fishermen took their toll, as did hurricanes, disease, and prolonged cold weather (King et al., 1977). The brown pelican was placed on the endangered species list, and DDT was banned from use in the United States. Since then, the pelican population has increased somewhat.

Shorebirds form dense multispecies aggregations in the littoral zone of estuaries during migration (Recher, 1966). The availability of feeding space fluctuates with the tide. When the tide is out, particularly in areas with high tidal range and broad, flat intertidal zones, the feeding area may be extremely large. On the other hand, feeding grounds may be very limited at high tide. Many shorebirds feed extensively on intertidal benthos, sometimes selectively feeding to the point of almost destroying certain

TABLE 13. Estimated Populations of Various Breeding Birds in the Southeastern
United States, 1975

Bird	Virginia	North Carolina	South Carolina	Georgia
Great egret	800	1,600	2,500	8,000
Snowy egret	5,500	2,500	15,000	3,000
Cattle egret	1,500	4,500	10,000	15,000
Louisiana heron	4,000	6,800	7,000	4,000
Little blue heron	750	2,100	4,000	2,500
White ibis	—	5,000	50,000	15,000
Glossy ibis	4,100	1,000	1,000	200

Source: Ogden, 1978.

benthic species (Schneider, 1978). Broad overlap during peak bird abundance, inter- and intrahabitat distribution, and preferred prey can be
expected among intertidally feeding shorebirds. Competitive exclusion
among the bird species that participate in the aggregations, however, does
not seem to occur (Recher, 1966). Food is generally plentiful enough in the
littoral area to support large numbers of birds.

Food habits have been determined for various species of shorebirds.
One species of sandpiper, the dunlin (*Calidris alpina*), was found to feed
primarily on the polychaete, *Nereis diversicolor*, while a related species,
C. minuta, fed on insects on a sand flat in Sweden (Bengston and Svensson, 1968). The authors concluded that predation by wading birds was not
a major factor in the density of sand flat invertebrates. Other species of
sandpipers were studied by Baker and Baker (1973) during winter in southern Florida and during summer in the east Canadian Arctic. Included in
that study were the least sandpiper (*Caldris minutilla*), the semipalmated
sandpiper (*C. pusilla*), and the dunlin, as well as the short-billed dowitcher
(*Limnodromus griseus*), lesser yellowlegs (*Tringa flavipes*), and semipalmated plover (*Charadrius semipalmatus*). The authors reported that
winter populations were regulated by competition stimulated by such factors as prey density and behavior, amount of time available for foraging
and feeding, and locomotion rates.

Clapper rails (*Rallus longirostris*) in Georgia were found to feed on
sixty-one different kinds of food (Oney, 1951). Ten of the sixty-one food
types accounted for 97% of the total food consumed. During late fall, rails
consumed animal matter almost exclusively, except for trace amounts of

the seeds of *Spartina* sp. Crabs were the principal staple (75% of the food eaten), including the genera *Sesarma*, *Eurytium*, *Uca*, and *Panopeus*. The periwinkle, *Littorina irrorata*, was ingested whole. Insects, while plentiful in the area where the rails were feeding, were rare in the gizzards of the birds, with the exception of one insect in the family Phalaenidae. Spiders and small fish were also found but were considered to be of minor importance. The Georgia study was substantiated in Louisiana by Bateman (1965), who found that small crabs and snails dominated the food of rails in the fall. In another Louisiana study, Roth et al. (1972) determined that clapper rails ate fiddler crabs during the summer and consumed crayfish and snails during the winter.

Long-billed marsh wrens, *Telmatodytes palustris griseus*, feed on herbivorous and predatory animals as well as on detritivores in the marshes of Sapelo Island, Georgia (Kale, 1964); thus, that species appears to be much less selective than the clapper rail.

The song sparrow, *Melospiza melodia samuelis*, was studied by Johnston (1956) in a marsh near San Francisco Bay, California. The most important foods of the sparrow were invertebrates associated with saltmarsh plants in the genera *Spartina* and *Salicornia*.

Feeding behavior is also diverse among estuarine birds. Many of the wading birds move slowly through shallow water and capture fish and invertebrates swimming by. A large number of shorebirds peck in the sediments for food organisms, while others are primarily seedeaters. The black skimmer, *Rynchops nigra*, has a lower mandible that is longer than the upper. The skimmer feeds by flying low over the water with the lower mandible cutting the surface of the water. Upon striking food, the bird will snap its head down and close its bill upon the prey. The black skimmer also exhibits a variety of other behavioral patterns.

Many studies have examined the home range and nesting characteristics of shorebirds. The clapper rail provides an example of the kind of data that can be obtained. Radiotelemetry studies of clapper rails in Louisiana (Roth et al., 1972) demonstrated that the average minimum home range exceeded 50 m along canals and tidal ditches during the summer but expanded to over 150 m during winter. The difference may have stemmed from the need to search a wider area for food during winter.

In a study of clapper rails in North Carolina, Adams and Quay (1958) found that twenty-three of the thirty nests they inspected occurred in *Spartina alterniflora* of medium height (60 to 120 cm). Mean egg number per clutch was 10.5. Continuous parental care of the hatchlings required five to six weeks; the young birds began to fly at an age of nine to ten weeks.

The large rookeries found in estuaries have often been abandoned as man has encroached on their territory. Others continue to survive by being sufficiently remote to escape the disruptive activities of man. One alteration in estuaries that has actually expanded coastal rookeries, however, is related to dredging. Although maintenance dredging generally yields soft sedimentary material that does not build up to any extent when expelled over land, the initial material removed during a dredging operation (such as when the intracoastal waterway system was first established) often contains a large percentage of coarse-grained sediments. When spread over marshes, small spoil islands are formed, which have frequently been colonized by various species of shorebirds. Even when adjacent to the intracoastal waterway, spoil islands are often remote enough that passing vessels do not disrupt the normal activities of the birds.

Terrestrial Mammals

Many species of terrestrial mammals have been observed in estuaries. Although those mammals living near estuaries spend most of their time in upland areas, they may move into marshland, sand flat, or mudflat areas to forage for food. Many species even enter the water to feed or swim to another terrestrial portion of their range. No terrestrial mammals are obliged to remain in estuarine areas, though some are typically found near water.

On Bolivar Peninsula adjacent to Galveston Bay, Texas, the dominant small mammal groups are the cotton rat (*Sigmodon hispidus*) and the house mouse (*Mus musculus*), though a few others were also observed (Webb et al., 1978). Shrews and field mice of various kinds can be expected to live in the uplands around estuaries.

Among the large mammals that frequent estuaries are the white-tailed deer (*Odocoileus virginianus*), coyote (*Canis latrans*), raccoon (*Procyon lotor*), spotted skunk (*Spilogale putorius*), swamp rabbit (*Sylvilagus aquaticus*), opossum (*Didelphis marsupialis*), and muskrat (*Ondatra zibethica*). Common in Texas estuaries, but of diminishing importance eastward and rare to nonexistent in the southeastern United States, are the armadillo (*Dasypus novemcinctus*), nutria (*Myocastor copyus*), and collared peccary (*Pecari tajacu*).

Texas estuaries are also somewhat unusual in the United States in having various species of exotic big-game animals, including the nilgai antelope (*Boselaphus tragocamelus*), axis deer (*Axis axis*), sika deer (*Cervus nippon*), fallow deer (*Dama dama*), blackbuck antelope (*Antilope cervicapra*), and mouflon-barbados sheep (*Ovis* spp.). Those species are among the ones that have been released on coastal prairie ranches to augment native big-game species (Sheffield et al., 1971).

Domestic animals such as cattle, sheep, and goats can also be found around estuaries. *Spartina patens* has commonly been used as forage for domestic livestock. In most estuarine areas, however, livestock are not allowed direct access to marshgrasses or are amply provided with other foods, so that their encroachment into natural marshes is relatively uncommon. In the past, some marshlands were dewatered to provide forage for cattle. As a result, the affected areas were removed from use by waterfowl. Some benefit to such birds as snipes and rails has resulted when marshgrass is heavily grazed, however. In those cases, otherwise unavailable, thickly vegetated areas have been opened for use by non waterfowl bird species (Chabreck, 1968).

Muskrats probably use marshlands more extensively than does nearly any other terrestrial mammal. They can be found feeding, building their houses, and conducting other business in estuarine areas. Muskrats also use the water to a great extent. Three-cornered grass, *Scirpus olneyi*, was found to be the most important plant for the support of muskrat populations in Louisiana (O'Neil, 1949; Palmisano, 1972). Their preferred habitat was near that plant along with *Spartina patens*, and the muskrats constructed their homes out of *Scirpus*. The latter was also found to be a major source of food. Muskrat habitats can be significantly disturbed by any more than light to moderate grazing by cattle (Chabreck, 1968).

Raccoons are a common sight in estuaries. They have been known to gather food on exposed sand and mud flats, along beaches, and from stream bottoms at low tide (Ivey, 1948). They feed mostly on crustaceans and molluscs, especially intertidal oysters and mussels, which appear to be among their favorite foods. Raccoons will break open molluscs by beating them against a rock or other shells.

Marine Mammals

The presence of marine mammals along the coast of the southeastern United States and the Gulf of Mexico, including sightings, strandings, and captures, was documented by Schmidly (1981). That study outlined the distributions of thirty-three species of marine mammals within the study region, though only one, the bottle-nosed dolphin (*Tursiops truncatus*), normally occurs in estuaries. Some of the others may wash into estuaries when moribund or dead, or they may become stranded in estuaries after becoming disoriented for one reason or another. Their preferred habitat is, in all cases, the open waters of the ocean. Marine mammals are found in somewhat greater numbers in the waters of the southeastern United States and the Gulf of Mexico than along the Atlantic coast of Canada, where only nineteen species were reported by Sergeant et al. (1970), who surveyed records from 1949 to 1968. Other studies on the occurrence of marine mammals off U.S. coasts were conducted by Caldwell and Golley (1965), Caldwell et al. (1971), and Gunter and Christmas (1973).

Bottle-nosed dolphins are found throughout the tropical and temperate oceans of the world (Rice, 1977). In the western Atlantic they can be found in coastal waters from Massachusetts to Florida and throughout the Gulf of Mexico (Lowery, 1974). *T. truncatus* most commonly occur in inshore waters. They can be found in highest concentrations near passes connecting the larger bays with the ocean but are also found in back bays and the lower portions of rivers. Winn et al. (1979) cited evidence that two distinct stocks may occur: one that lives offshore and another that is restricted to inlets, lagoons, and confined salty areas of rivers.

According to Schmidly (1981), there is a consensus that bottle-nosed dolphins are organized into localized populations. Although no estimates exist on the number of bottle-nosed dolphins living along the southeastern Atlantic coast and the Gulf of Mexico, Prescott et al. (1979) estimated that the dolphins off the Florida coast and along the Gulf of Mexico number about 10,000. Orr (1977), who also estimated the number of offshore dolphins, came up with a population of 20,000 for the same area. Shane and Schmidly (1979) estimated that between 48 and 104 dolphins inhabited Aransas Bay near Corpus Christi, Texas, in October and that from 164 to 281 were present in January.

T. truncatus reach a length of 3.7 m and may weigh over 650 kg, though the average size of adult dolphins is somewhat smaller. Males mature at from 2.5 to 2.6 m (ten to thirteen years of age) and females at from 2.2 to 2.4 m (five to twelve years of age). Gestation requires approximately a year, with calving intervals of two to three years and lactation periods of up to 18 months (Schmidly, 1981).

242 ESTUARINE ECOLOGY OF THE SOUTHEASTERN UNITED STATES

Bottle-nosed dolphins consume a variety of fishes, molluscs, and arthropods. Leatherwood and Platter (1975) found that dolphins fed at least once every hour during daylight and that they ate a variety of organisms. Leatherwood (1975) discovered seven recurring feeding patterns for bottle-nosed dolphins:

1. Foraging behind working shrimpboats and consuming organisms disturbed by the nets
2. Feeding on trash fish dumped from the decks of shrimpboats
3. Feeding on fish attracted to nonworking shrimpboats
4. Herding schools of fish by encircling and charging the school or feeding on stragglers
5. Sweeping schools of bait fish into shallow water ahead of a line of dolphins and charging into the school or feeding on stragglers
6. Crowding small fish into shoals or mud banks, even driving the fish completely out of the water and then sliding up on mud banks to feed
7. Individual feeding

Bottle-nosed dolphins have been the subject of movies, television shows, and numerous printed stories. The brain of *T. truncatus* is convoluted in a manner similar to that of man and is in fact somewhat larger than the brain of man. Efforts at communication with dolphins have been unsuccessful, however, and most scientists feel that while the species is easily trained, it may not have the mental powers once attributed to it. Porpoises do seem to have some form of primitive communication among themselves, however. They also use a form of sonar or echo-location to identify objects and locate food. Dolphin sounds include whistles, barks, moans, and something that sounds like a squeaking door (Schmidly, 1981). Bottle-nosed dolphins are easily trained, appear to wear a permanent smile, seem to relate well to man when in captivity, and have amazing acrobatic ability. For these reasons, they are often popular attractions at marine parks.

Sea cows, or mantees (*Trichechus manatus latirostris*) are another marine mammal that inhabits part of the area of interest. Sea cows live in parts of Florida with low salinity to fresh waters and consume aquatic macrophytic vegetation. It was once thought that sea cows could help clear weed-choked canals in Florida, but their low metabolic rate appears to allow the weeds to keep ahead of consumption. Sea cow populations are not large, and the animal is being protected over its range. It is thought that the sea cow was the model upon which the legend of the mermaid was based, but close examination of a sea cow will cause one to pause and wonder how even the loneliest sailor could equate the two.

LITERATURE CITED

Adams, D. A., and T. L. Quay. 1958. Ecology of the clapper rail in southeastern North Carolina. *J. Wildl. Man.* 22: 149–56.

Allen, R. P., S. Sprunt, and A. Sprunt, Jr. 1958. A progress report on the wading bird survey. II. Report presented at the 54th annual convention, National Audubon Society.

Baker, M. C., and A. E. M. Baker. 1973. Niche relationships among six species of shorebirds on their wintering and breeding ranges. *Ecol. Monogr.* 43: 193–212.

Bateman, H. A., Jr. 1965. *Clapper rail* (Rallus longirostris) *studies on Grand Terre Island, Jefferson Parish, Louisiana.* Baton Rouge: Louisiana Wildlife and Fisheries Commission.

Bengston, S., and B. Svensson. 1968. Feeding habits of *Calidris alpina* L. and *C. minuta* Leisl. (Aves) in relation to the distribution of marine shore invertebrates. *Oikos* 19: 152–57.

Bent, A. C. 1962a. *Life histories of North American shorebirds.* Pt. 1. New York: Dover Publications.

———. 1962b. *Life histories of North American shorebirds.* Pt. 2. New York: Dover Publications.

———. 1963. *Life histories of North American diving birds.* New York: Dover Publications.

———. 1964. *Life histories of North American petrels and pelicans and their allies.* New York: Dover Publications.

Caldwell, D., and F. B. Golley. 1965. Marine mammals from the coast of Georgia to Cape Hatteras. *J. Elisha Mitchell Sci. Soc.* 81: 24–32.

Caldwell, D. K., H. Neuhauser, M. C. Caldwell, and H. W. Coolidge. 1971. Recent records of marine mammals from the coasts of Georgia and South Carolina. *Cetology* 5: 1–12.

Carr, A. 1952. *Handbook of turtles.* Ithaca, N.Y.: Comstock Publishing Associates.

Chabreck, R. H. 1968. The relation of cattle and cattle grazing to marsh wildlife and plants in Louisiana. *Proc. S.E. Assoc. Game and Fish Comm.* 22: 55–68.

Chamberlain, E. B. 1959. Gulf coast marsh vegetation as food of wintering waterfowl. *J. Wildl. Man.* 23: 95–102.

Curry-Lindahl, K. 1978. Conservation and management of wading birds and their habitats: A global overview, pp. 83–97. In: A. Sprunt IV, J. C. Ogden, and S. Winckler, eds. *Wading birds*. Research Report no. 7. New York: National Audubon Society.

Glasgow, L. L., and H. A. Junca. 1962. Mallard foods in southwest Louisiana. *Proc. La. Acad. Sci.* 25: 63–74.

Glazener, W. C. 1946. Food habits of wild geese on the Gulf coast of Texas. *J. Wildl. Man.* 10: 322–29.

Gruson, E. S. 1976. *Checklist of the world's birds*. New York: Quadrangle.

Gunter, G., and J. Y. Christmas. 1973. Stranding records of a finback whale, *Balaenoptera physalus*, from Mississippi and the goose-beaked whale, *Ziphius cavirostris*, from Louisiana. *Gulf Research Reports* 4: 169–72.

Ivey, R. D. 1948. Raccoon in the salt marshes of northeastern Florida. *J. Mammal.* 29: 290–91.

Johnston, R. F. 1956. Population structure in salt marsh song sparrows. Environment and annual cycle. *Condor* 58: 24–44.

Kale, H. W. 1964. Food of the long-billed marsh wren, *Telmatodytes palustris griseus*, in the salt marshes of Sapelo Island, Georgia. *Oriole* 29: 47–66.

Kerwin, J. A., and L. G. Webb. 1971. Foods of ducks wintering in coastal South Carolina, 1965–1967. *Proc. S.E. Assoc. Game and Fish Comm.* 25: 223–45.

King, K. A., E. L. Flickinger, and H. H. Hildebrand. 1977. The decline of brown pelicans on the Louisiana and Texas Gulf coast. *Southwest. Nat.* 2: 417–31.

Lay, D. W., and K. F. Culbertson. 1977. *Wildlife of the Texas coastal zone*. Austin: Texas Parks and Wildlife Department.

Leatherwood, J. S. 1975. Observations of feeding behavior of bottle-nosed dolphins *Tursiops truncatus* in the northern Gulf of Mexico and *Tursiops gilli* of southern California, Baja California, and Nayarit, Mexico. *Mar. Fish. Rev.* 37: 10–16.

Leatherwood, J. S., and M. R. Platter. 1975. Aerial assessment of bottle-nosed dolphins off Alabama, Mississippi, and Louisiana, pp. 49–86. In: D. K. Odell, D. B. Siniff, and G. H. Waring, eds. Tursiops truncatus *workshop*. Miami: Rosenstiel School of Marine and Atmospheric Sciences, University of Miami.

Lowery, G. H. 1974. *The mammals of Louisiana and its adjacent waters*. Baton Rouge: Louisiana State University Press.

Lowery, G. H., Jr., and R. J. Newman. 1954. The birds of the Gulf of Mexico. *Fish. Bull.* 89: 519–40.

Lynch, J. J. 1967. Values of the South Atlantic Gulf coast marshes and estuaries to waterfowl, pp. 51–63. In: J. D. Newsom, ed. *Proceedings of the marsh and estuary management symposium*. Baton Rouge: Louisiana State University Division of Continuing Education.

Ogden, J. C. 1978. Recent population trends of colonial wading birds on the Atlantic and Gulf coastal plains. In: A. Sprunt IV, J. C. Ogden, and S. Winckler, eds. *Wading birds*. Research Report no. 7, New York: National Audubon Society.

O'Neil, T. 1949. *The muskrat in the Louisiana coastal marshes*. New Orleans: Louisiana Department of Wildlife and Fisheries.

Oney, J. 1951. Food habits of the clapper rail in Georgia. *J. Wildl. Man.* 15: 106–107.

Orr, J. M. 1977. A survey of *Tursiops* populations in the coastal United States, Hawaii, and territorial waters. Report prepared for the Marine Mammal Commission, Washington, D.C.

Palmisano, A. W., Jr. 1967. Ecological factors affecting occurrence of *Scirpus olneyi* and *Scirpus robustus* in the Louisiana coastal marshes. *Proc. S.E. Assoc. Game and Fish Comm.* 21: 161–72.

———. 1972. Habitat preference of waterfowl and fur animals in the northern Gulf coast marshes, pp. 163–90. In: R. H. Chabreck, ed. *Proceedings of the coastal marsh and estuary management symposium*. Baton Rouge: Louisiana State University.

Peterson, C. H., and N. M. Peterson. 1979. The ecology of intertidal flats in North Carolina: A community profile. U.S. Fish and Wildlife Service Biological Services Program FWS/OBS 79-39.

Prescot, J. H., S. D. Kraus, and J. R. Gilbert. 1979. *Proceedings East Coast/Gulf coast cetacean and pinniped workshop*. Boston: New England Aquarium.

Quay, T. L., and T. S. Critcher. 1962. Food habits of waterfowl in Currituck Sound, North Carolina. *Proc. S.E. Assoc. Game and Fish Comm.* 156: 200–209.

Recher, H. F. 1966. Some aspects of the ecology of migrant shorebirds. *Ecology* 47: 393–407.

Rice, D. W. 1977. A list of the marine mammals of the world. 3d ed. National Oceanic and Atmospheric Administration, National Marine Fisheries Technical Report SSRF-711.

Roth, R. R., J. D. Newsom, T. Joanen, and L. L. McNease. 1972. The daily and seasonal behavior patterns of the clapper rail (*Rallus longirostris*) in the Louisiana coastal marshes. *Proc. S.E. Assoc. Game and Fish Comm.* 26: 136–47.

Schmidly, D. J. 1981. *Marine mammals of the southeastern United States coast and Gulf of Mexico*. Washington, D.C.: U.S. Fish and Wildlife Service Office of Biological Services, FWS/OBS 80-41.

Schneider, D. 1978. Equilisation of prey numbers by migrating shorebirds. *Nature* 271: 353–54.

Sergeant, D. E., A. W. Mansfield, and B. Beck. 1970. Inshore records of cetaceans for eastern Canada, 1949–1965. *J. Fish. Res. Bd. Can.* 21: 1903–15.

Shane, S., and D. J. Schmidly. 1979. *The population biology of the bottle-nosed dolphin*, Tursiops truncatus, *in the Aransas Pass area of Texas*. Springfield, Va.: National Technical Information Service.

Shanholtzer, G. F. 1974. Relationship of vertebrates to salt marsh plants, pp. 463–73. In: R. J. Reimold and W. H. Queen, eds. *Ecology of halophytes*. New York: Academic Press.

Sheffield, W. J., W. B. Ables, and B. A. Fall. 1971. Geographic and ecologic distribution of nilgai antelope in Texas. *J. Wildl. Man.* 28: 797–808.

Sprunt, A. IV. 1967. Values of the South Atlantic and Gulf coast marshes and estuaries to birds other than waterfowl, pp. 64–72. In: J. D. Newsom, ed. *Proceedings of the management symposium*. Baton Rouge: Louisiana State University Division of Continuing Education.

Stieglitz, W. O. 1966. Utilization of available foods by diving ducks on Apalachee Bay, Florida. *Proc. S.E. Assoc. Game and Fish Comm.* 20: 42–50.

Walker, E. P. 1975. *Mammals of the world*. Baltimore: Johns Hopkins Press.

Webb, J. W., J. D. Dodd, B. W. Cain, W. R. Leavens, L. R. Hossner, C. Lindau, R. R. Stickney, and H. Williamson. 1978. *Habitat development field investigations: Bolivar Peninsula marsh and upland habitat development site, Galveston Bay, Texas*. App. D. Propagation of vascular plants and postpropagation monitoring of botanical soil, aquatic biota, and wildlife resources. Vicksburg, Miss.: U.S. Army Corps of Engineers.

Winn, L. K., H. E. Winn, D. K. Caldwell, M. C. Caldwell, and J. L. Dunn. 1979. Report on marine mammals. Prepared by the Center for Natural Areas, Washington, D.C., for the Bureau of Land Management.

Wolff, W. J. 1969. Distribution of non-breeding waders in an estuarine area in relation to the distribution of their food organisms. *Ardea* 57: 1–28.

Wright, A. H., and A. A. Wright. 1957. *Handbook of snakes of the U.S. and Canada*. Ithaca, N.Y.: Comstock Publishing Associates.

CHAPTER 11

Man's Impact on Estuaries

Introduction

IN recent years, a broad range of opinions has been expressed concerning the importance of estuaries to coastal ecosystems and the sensitivity of estuaries to pollution and other human actions. Early in the controversy, and to some extent even now, there were those who relied on appeals to the emotions rather than upon scientific evidence to support their views. Although these emotional appeals did raise the consciousness of the general public with respect to environmental problems, they were often either erroneous or unduly pessimistic about the ability of the environment to recover from damage. As the scientific evidence about how estuaries respond to perturbations began to accumulate, it became clear that problems did indeed exist—but it was also clear that nature, given an opportunity, could recover from many of the disruptive changes imposed by man.

Although it is certainly possible for man to destroy estuaries, it is also apparent that the environment has a great capacity to absorb man-made changes. This does not mean that man's estuarine projects can continue unabated as they have for the last several decades. It does mean, however, that we have recognized the possible consequences of our actions before passing the point of no recovery. As a result, projects in estuaries are now being approved and implemented only after assessing the environmental impacts and weighing against them potential benefits to mankind. In addition, most developers seem to be honestly concerned that environmental damage be kept to a minimum when new projects are approved. A good deal of legislation was passed during the 1960s and 1970s that will serve as a guarantee that future generations will be able to enjoy and benefit from estuaries. The environment itself should continue to exist indefinitely in a manner similar to the present.

Regardless of what one may consider the appropriate uses of estuaries, man has had and will continue to have an impact on this environment. De la Cruz (1976) put together a list of man's uses, present and future, for coastal wetlands, as well as the species man gathers from the area for sport and food, including:

1. Habitat for birds and other species of wildlife
2. Nursery grounds for commercial fish and shellfish
3. Pasture for livestock
4. Recreation
5. Natural waste treatment
6. Transportation
7. Petroleum production
8. Aquaculture

Clark (1974) discussed in more detail man's uses of the coastal zone and elaborated upon what he felt to be the constraints necessary to protect the environment from the activities of man. Although all of those recommendations may not be adopted, they do serve as a sort of "want list" to ensure that perturbations are kept to a minimum. Clark (1977) provided guidelines for the control of development in the coastal zone (table 14). Although Clark's recommendations (1974, 1977) make good environmental sense, many of them may be difficult to follow precisely—but they do represent an ideal that seems worthy of pursuit.

Of concern in some circles but not addressed in the above listing is the use of off-road vehicles in coastal ecosystems. In studies by Brodhead and Godfrey (1977), Godfrey et al. (1978), and Godfrey (1979), it was determined that shorebirds become adjusted to passing vehicles if nests are not disturbed. Those authors also found that even light automobile traffic can severely affect certain kinds of dune vegetation.

The effects of man-made alterations on coastal environments may be easily and rapidly observable, or they may be subtle and require an extended period of time before distinct changes can be documented. Copeland and Nixon (1974) concluded that when biological communities that have been placed under stress are further disturbed, certain species may be eliminated more readily than if similar disturbances were confined to a less stressed environment. Examples of stress that can lead to the elimination of species from a community are impoundment (leading to increased rates of evaporation and sedimentation, thus to higher salinity and, perhaps, reduced oxygen), organic pollution, dredge spoiling, and the creation of navigation channels. Behrens (1966) reported that extremely hypersaline conditions in the Laguna Madre of Texas were reduced upon completion of the Gulf Intracoastal Waterway (GIWW), because natural sills at either end of the lagoon allowed an increased inflow of low salinity water. This was also discussed by Collier and Hedgpeth (1950).

Destruction of a vast expanse of marshland would seem to have a much more devastating local impact than would the filling of a few square meters. But as indicated by Gucinski (1978), since small marsh tracts have relatively more length of edge than do large tracts of the same total area, and since edges may be more useful in productivity and diversity than the interior marsh, good management plans should not overlook the value of preserving small tracts of marshland. This, of course, does not mean that large tracts should be sacrificed; it simply suggests that even a seemingly insignificant area of marshland may, when combined with numerous other areas of similar size, significantly contribute to total productivity.

The remainder of this chapter examines a few of the ways in which man has influenced estuaries. They include the environmental consequences of dredging, oil spills, and pesticide usage.

Dredging and Filling

Dredging and filling cause the loss of many estuarine habitats in the United States. The quantities of material dredged average 300 million cubic meters yearly for the maintenance of existing waterways and another 80 million cubic meters of new dredging. Annual costs in the early 1970s for dredging exceeded $150 million (Boyd et al., 1972). Many of the dredging projects are fairly small, though it has been found that major changes result from the cumulative effect of small projects that are individually insignificant (Thompson, 1961).

In Texas alone, the length of dredged channels approaches 1,600 km (McCoy, 1976). Over 40 million cubic meters of dredge material are removed by federal and nonfederal dredging programs annually in Texas (Espey et al., 1976). Channel depths in Texas and other areas range from about 2 m for shallow-draft boat passages to as much as 15 m in channels maintained for the passage of ocean-going ships. Estimates in 1973 indicated that if dredging in the Houston ship channel remained constant, the capacity of existing spoil disposal areas would be reached in 26.4 years. It was also noted that if Houston was to retain its ranking among U.S. ports,

TABLE 14. Guidelines for Protection of Wetland Areas in the Coastal Zone

Practice or Activity	Guidelines
Agricultural pollution	Farming should be controlled to protect coastal areas from fertilizers, biocides, sedimentation, and altered runoff
Farm layout	The planning of farm layouts should include insurance that water quality and vital areas are protected[a]
Feedlots	Feedlots and other operations in which livestock are concentrated should be placed on high ground, and waste discharge should be controlled
Airports	Airports should be designed and located in a manner that protects the coastal ecosystem from pollution and loss of vital areas
Beachfronts	Shore protection programs should be developed to preserve existing beach profiles. Regulations should be implemented to protect frontal dunes
Bulkheads	Bulkheads should be located shoreward of all wetlands and designed for ecological compatibility. Natural methods of erosion control (e.g., the planting of vegetation in sensitive areas) should be used when possible
Dams and water diversions	Nonstructural solutions for controlling freshwater flow should be used whenever possible
Estuarine flood protection	Estuarine floodplain management and ecosystem management programs should be combined and integrated. All structures on estuarine shores should be set back from the annual flood line; structures should be elevated above 100-year storm line; area-wide flood control structures should be avoided
Extractive industries	The location and operation of extractive industries (mining) should be controlled to avoid damage to the coastal ecosystem
Forest industries	Logging should be controlled in a manner that will maintain watershed runoff at preexisting quality, volume, and rate of flow
Groundwater extraction	Groundwater control should be included in a comprehensive water management program with the goal that withdrawal must not exceed recharge in order to prevent saltwater intrusion and land subsidence
Heavy industry	Heavy industry should be directed away from ecologically sensitive areas

TABLE 14. (*continued*)

Practice or Activity	Guidelines
Land drainage	The quality, volume, and rate of flow of coastal watershed drainage should be maintained
Marinas	Marina and small boat harbors should be planned in a manner that will minimize the threat of water pollution
Mosquito control	Appropriate water management techniques should be used as much as possible, and pesticide usage should be kept to a minimum
Navigational dredging and spoil disposal	Dredging projects should be designed to avoid erosion, circulation change, and disturbance of vital areas
Oil and gas industries	The development of oil and gas industries should be controlled to minimize environmental disturbance offshore, near shore, and onshore
Piers and docks	The encroachment of recreational boat landings into wetlands and coastal waters should be limited to the extent possible
Power plants	Power plants should be located in a manner that will avoid damage to vital habitat areas
Residential development	Residential development should be done only in compliance with ecosystem protection requirements
Roadways and bridges	Road systems should avoid impingement on vital areas or interference with surface or groundwater flows
Septic tanks	Septic tanks should be located and maintained to avoid water pollution
Sewage treatment systems	Sewage treatment plants, outfalls, pipelines, and storm sewers should be located where they will not disrupt vital areas
Solid waste disposal	Sanitary landfills should be located so as to prevent coastal water pollution
Tract and site preparation	Strict control of erosion during site preparation and construction should be exercised
Urban runoff	Impervious surfacing should be limited to the extent possible. Storm systems should be designed to simulate natural runoff patterns

Source: Clark, 1977.

[a]Clark (1977, p. 106) defined vital areas as "elements of such importance to the functioning of the coastal ecosystem that they must be preserved as intact units by disallowing uses that would alter them significantly."

the ship channel would have to be deepened and widened. This would put additional stress on the spoil disposal areas (Farmer, 1973).

Shoaling of the GIWW in Texas has been estimated at over 26 cm annually (Atturio et al., 1976). That study found that shoaling in the bays was about 7.5 cm/yr greater than in areas that were cut through high ground.

Various kinds of dredges have been used around the United States for both new and maintenance dredging. The following descriptions were adopted from Machemehl (1972):

> Dipper dredge: This dredge is basically a power shovel mounted on a barge. The barge has three spuds (two forward and one at the stern) for stability. Spuds are large-diameter pipes that can be raised and lowered to help hold the barge in position or allow it to pivot around a given point. Dipper dredges can handle up to nearly 10 m³ of hard material per cycle. They are commonly used to remove blasted rock or loose boulders. Dredged material is discharged within reach of the dipper boom. This kind of dredge is usually not used in water deeper than about 20 m.
>
> Ladder dredge: A ladder dredge is essentially an endless chain of buckets mounted on a barge. The barge is maintained in position by side cables. The buckets can each carry between one and two cubic meters of material. The excavated material is dumped into chutes or onto belts and is discharged over the side of the barge. Ladder dredges are generally not used in water over about 30 m.
>
> Bucket dredge: A bucket dredge is basically a crane mounted on a barge. The bucket (a clamshell, orange peel, or dragline type) can be changed to suit the job. The barge uses either spuds or anchor lines for stability. This kind of dredge can handle moderately stiff material in confined areas. It is generally used on small-scale dredging projects. The material is dumped within the length of the boom.
>
> Hydraulic pipeline dredge: This is the most versatile of the modern dredges and is also the most widely used. Using a cutter head, a hydraulic pipeline dredge can excavate material over the range from light silts to heavy rock. Dredged material is pumped through floating pipes and pipes laid onshore and can be discharged in areas remote from the dredge itself. Hydraulic pipeline dredges range in size and can work in depths of up to 20 m.
>
> Hopper dredge: A hopper dredge is a self-propelled vessel designed to dredge, load, and retain spoil in hoppers and haul it to aquatic disposal areas. Capacities for hopper dredges can exceed 10,000 m³. Such dredges can work in depths over 20 m.

According to Windom (1976), the hydraulic pipeline dredge accounts for some 69% of the total material handled. Hopper dredges make up about 24%, with the other types and combinations constituting the remainder.

Dredging can lead to three major kinds of environmental damage: (1) destruction of bottom habitats, (2) alteration of habitats from spoil deposition, and (3) impairment of water quality (Windom, 1972). More specific changes include loss of marshlands, alteration of shallow bay bottoms from channelization, segmentation of bays (which can lead to increased shoaling), increased rates of saltwater intrusion, longer flushing time, greater turbidity, altered rates of tidal exchange, changes in mixing and circulation rates, and loss of submerged aquatic vegetation (Chapman, 1967). Dredging and filling have had considerable impact on the salt marshes of the United States. Schmidt (1966) reported that over 18,000 ha of tidal marsh were destroyed between Maine and Delaware from 1954 to 1965 alone. In North Carolina a similar expanse of marshland was disturbed between 1952 and 1967 (Burdick, 1967).

James et al. (1977) examined some of the environmental effects of the GIWW of Texas. They found that the GIWW can sometimes facilitate the transfer of water, pollutants, aquatic plants, and animals from one river to another. That same study showed that normal operations of the GIWW did not appear to increase the levels of major pollutants, but elevated levels of nutrients and trace metals were associated with freshwater inflow to the waterway. Shoaling rates were significantly affected by current patterns adjacent to the GIWW channel in shallow, open bays. Finally, the presence of the GIWW and the nearby dredge spoil islands were found to be capable of modifying circulation patterns and salinity levels in surrounding bays and estuaries.

Not all the effects of dredging are harmful to the environment. The connection of isolated waters and marshes by dredging can make those areas more readily available as fish nursery grounds and can provide an escape route or refuge for fish during cold periods. Another positive result is improved water exchange and circulation, along with the release of trapped nutrients (Chapman, 1967).

Although sediments are removed and suspended through dredging, it is interesting to note that other activities may also cause substantial disturbance of the sediments. For example, Schubel et al. (1979) found that the volume of sediments disturbed by shrimping in Corpus Christi Bay, Texas, was ten to one hundred times greater than that disturbed by annual dredging in the same area. The maximum concentrations of suspended material in the trails left by shrimpboats were comparable to those in the plumes of dredge material discharged in the bay.

EFFECTS OF DREDGING ON WATER QUALITY

Various studies have examined the effects of dredging on water quality. Windom (1976) indicated that changes in water quality cannot be predicted from an examination of the material to be dredged. For example, sediments with high levels of trace metals often do not release those metals into the water column during dredging. The kind of spoil disposal is one important influence of water quality, though local conditions vary considerably and generalizations may be misleading.

Some conflicting reports exist with respect to the effects of dredging on water quality. The differences from study to study seem to stem from differences in sediment type and from the methodology employed in spoil disposal. Windom (1972) studied water quality before, during, and after dredging in areas dominated by both polluted and nonpolluted sediments in Georgia estuaries and found no detrimental changes in dissolved oxygen, chemical oxygen demand, biochemical oxygen demand (BOD), pH, or iron concentration. Mercury increased slightly in water samples during dredging, suggesting that the metal may have been released by dredging. Phosphate levels declined, perhaps due to absorption on suspended particulate matter during dredging.

Since there was little apparent change in water quality near the dredge, Windom (1972) began to evaluate water quality in disposal areas. He discovered that significant changes resulted from the use of the diked spoil disposal technique but that disposal over open marshland did not lead to gross changes in runoff water quality. When water in areas adjacent to a diked spoil disposal site was examined, it was determined that dissolved oxygen and pH were always lower in the unaffected area. Iron, copper, and zinc increased significantly in the diked disposal area. Changes in concentrations of trace metals appeared to be linked to salinity, while increases in dissolved oxygen and pH seemed to occur independent of salinity.

To further study the changes mentioned, water obtained from a diked disposal area was taken into the laboratory, and concentrations of trace metals were followed temporally. Initial concentrations in sediment-water suspensions were low, but they gradually increased. Windom (1972) postulated that the changes were associated with the oxidative state of iron. When buried in the sediments before dredging, iron is in the reduced (ferrous) form. As it becomes exposed to oxygen during dredging, iron is oxidized to the ferric state and will precipitate as ferric hydroxide. As the precipitate forms, other trace metals may be scrubbed from solution. Upon burial in a spoil disposal site, the ferric hydroxide will become dissociated as a reducing environment is established, and the iron will revert to the ferrous state. Metals bound in the precipitate will then be released. When water from dredging is impounded in diked spoil disposal areas, the released trace metals can migrate and become concentrated in the overlying water; they can, thus, be released in elevated amounts when the spoil area is drained. When the open spoil disposal technique is used, release of metals into the adjacent environment is much more gradual and no pulses of metal input are observed.

Stored sediment-water samples were also found to continually increase in both dissolved oxygen and pH when exposed to sunlight, as a result of primary production. The data collected by Windom (1972) indicated that bacteria present in the sediment-water suspensions were responsible for the formation of nitrate from other nitrogen compounds, thus supplying needed nutrients for algal production. Phosphate levels declined with increased algal growth as the plants incorporated phosphate into their tissues. The final result could be the development of highly eutrophic conditions in impoundments formed as a result of diked spoil disposal.

Oxygen-demanding materials released during dredging (e.g., organic compounds and certain inorganic chemicals) do not seem to be exposed to the water for enough time to allow the total exertion of their oxygen demand on the system (Windom, 1975). Decreases in dissolved oxygen during dredging can occur, however, and increased BOD may follow dredging as a result of increased levels of photosynthesis. Again, this situation applies primarily to diked spoil disposal areas. Windom (1976) concluded that the primary process responsible for changes in dissolved oxygen, pH, and BOD after sediment dispersion through dredging is related to the initial release of ammonia.

Although intuition might predict significant and detrimental changes in water quality through dredging, the evidence does not convincingly substantiate that notion. The conclusions of Windom (1972) were upheld by Engler (1976), who found that leaching of toxic metals from disposal areas into the water column was probably no greater than from normal sediments of similar character. The major impact found by Engler (1976) was physical mounding of spoil material.

Large amounts of organic-laden silts and clays are released into the water column of Texas bays as a result of various natural and human activities, including beach erosion, river inflow, storm resuspension, and dredging (Odum and Wilson, 1962; Masch and Espey, 1967). In most cases, however, such releases do not seem to cause significant or long-term changes in water quality. Information on the effects of suspended sediments on animal communities is considered below.

General patterns of change in water quality through dredging include the following, according to Windom (1975): (1) turbidity increases, which are most significant where natural turbidity is low; (2) relatively rapid return to normal turbidity levels after dredging; (3) the release of ammonia during dredging, which may increase nitrate levels, thus increasing algal production; and (4) initial decreases in concentrations of heavy metals near the dredge, but eventual increases in iron, copper, zinc, cadmium, and lead.

EFFECTS OF DREDGING ON ESTUARINE ANIMALS

In general, benthic communities are affected by dredging in all cases (Windom, 1976). If sediment type is not changed as a result of dredging, however, recolonization can be expected, with the same species that were there before dredging usually returning to the disturbed area. The rate of recolonization will depend upon locality and sediment type. Motile organisms, according to Windom (1976), are generally unaffected by dredging.

Various studies have been run on the effects of sedimentation on oysters, partly because those organisms would presumably be affected by increased levels of suspended sediment from dredging and would also quickly succumb to burial. Windom (1975) reported that oysters can be harmed if they are exposed to high enough levels of suspended sediments for extended periods. Short-term exposure of oysters to such stimuli can be overcome if the animals close their valves and cease pumping water until conditions improve. Oysters can protect themselves in that manner for periods of from several hours to several days, depending upon temperature and other physical conditions. Mackin (1961) compared oyster survival at a control level of 15 ppm turbidity with dredging levels of from 50 to 700 ppm and found that the experimental levels did not significantly increase mortalities. Only about 1% of the dredged material drifted away from the immediate vicinity. Thus, a few meters from the dredge, turbidity did not exceed normal levels. Lunz (1938) was among the first to find a lack of correlation between dredging and oyster mortality on beds adjacent to affected areas. Mortalities were found only in instances where the oysters were actually buried by spoil material.

Manning (1957) observed nearly complete oyster mortality in the path of a commercial soft-shell clam dredge and noted displacement and deposition of sediments up to 25 m downstream of the dredged area. Significant mortalities occurred as far as 8 or 9 m downstream of the dredge. Burg (1973) found that resedimentation of dredged material in San Antonio Bay, Texas, killed oysters nearly 500 m from the dredge site. Mortalities were attributed to the average of 30 mm of silt that was deposited on affected beds.

Dredging for clams, oysters, and even dead shells (mud-shell dredging) is practiced in many estuaries. Such activities must result in the disruption of not only molluscan communities but also communities of other benthic organisms. Mud-shell dredging has been practiced in Alabama since 1871 (Gunter, 1969), with an average of nearly four million cubic meters being produced annually. In Texas, mud-shell dredging began in Galveston Bay in 1880.

Sedimentation on oyster reefs as a result of mud-shell dredging was examined by Benefield (1976), who found that sedimentation rates were greater on low-profile reefs than on higher ones in Galveston Bay and San Antonio Bay, Texas. A reef rising from 0.91 to 1.22 m above the surrounding bottom did not receive sediments from a dredge located 90 m away, while a reef with a flat profile collected sedimentation from a dredge as far as 1,800 m distant. Sediment deposition of 10.2 to 15.2 cm caused oyster mortalities.

Harvesting on oyster, clam, and mussel beds by commercial fishermen can be considered a form of dredging. When enough fishermen are active, a considerable percentage of at least the surface sediments around mollusc beds can be disturbed, often several times, in a fishing season. Removal of oysters from their beds also removes cultch, the living and dead shell upon which larval oysters (spat) attach when they settle.

Burg (1973) found significant population decreases in the benthos due to siltation near a dredge. A 71% reduction in average numbers of individuals per unit area was found in conjunction with a spoil bank in upper Chesapeake Bay following dredging (Phitzenmeyer, 1970). A year and a half after dredging was completed, the number of individuals per unit area at the spoil site was about the same as before dredging.

Even burrowing organisms might succumb to spoil deposition if they are deeply buried. At the dredging site, complete removal of the benthic community is more often the case. The rate of recolonization will depend upon the organisms making up the benthic community and the kind of sediment involved. Rhodes et al. (1978) determined that the equilibrium benthos community is often not as productive as a pioneering community that becomes established after dredging; however, the former is the more predictable concerning production. Unless toxic materials are released or sediment type is greatly altered through dredging, the benthic community that becomes established either at the dredge site or on subtidal fill material is generally similar to that existing before dredging.

In Boca Ciega Bay, Florida, soft sediments in a dredged area were inhabited by fewer species of polychaetes, molluscs, blue crabs, and pink shrimp than were those in an undredged area characterized by sandy-shell sediments (Taylor and Saloman, 1968). Even after ten years, invertebrate colonization was negligible, and few benthic fishes were recovered. Such changes are not common in unpolluted areas or in estuaries not significantly altered by outside forces other than those imposed by dredging. In the Boca Ciega Bay, spoil placement along the northern end of South Bay after the dredging of a ship channel followed by maintenance dredging led to the filling in of a pass, which in turn eliminated circulation in South Bay. Average depth dropped from 1.2 to only 0.4 m (Breuer, 1962), and the oyster population perished due to lack of circulation. Low productivity in South Bay was observed by Odum and Wilson (1962) and was also attributed to a lack of circulation and the smothering of grass beds. Reduction in numbers of fishes and invertebrates was attributed to sedimentation. Thus, while dredging operations often have only transient impacts, at times dredging has caused enough environmental upheaval to greatly disrupt the biota.

Stickney and Perlmutter (1975) found that recolonization of soft-bottomed sediments by benthic infauna occurred within days after dredging. Probable reasons given for this rapid colonization included the virtual lack of change in the sedimentary structure following dredging and the fact that the forms present both before and after were short-lived species with relatively motile stages in their life cycles.

The effects of dredging on motile organisms are difficult to document. It is generally assumed that such animals merely leave the area being dredged and return when the environment becomes suitable once again. This return to satisfactory conditions may occur almost immediately after the dredging is completed in a given area. Although food may be scarce, at least with regard to benthic food organisms, fish and other motile animals do not seem to actively avoid freshly dredged areas. Ingle (1952) observed no mortality of finfish or motile crustaceans within 25 to 50 m of a shell dredge in Alabama. In fact, shrimp appeared to be attracted to the dredging area. Recolonization of benthic organisms following dredging is often rapid. Bybee (1969) determined that penaeid shrimp needed only three to four weeks to colonize an area that had been dredged. That same study revealed that the shrimp population needed about six months to reach commercial levels.

Bulkheading of shorelines is related to dredging and filling in that back-filling of bulkheaded areas is common, and the fill material is often dredge spoil. Bulkheads disrupt normal runoff patterns and may create upland areas from previously intertidal ones. Mock (1966) compared post-larval and juvenile brown shrimp (*Penaeus aztecus*) and white shrimp (*P. setiferus*) populations in an unaltered, vegetated shoreline area with those in a similar area that had been bulkheaded. He showed that 2.5 times more brown shrimp and 14 times more white shrimp postlarvae and juveniles occurred in the unaltered area. More food and shelter may have been available for shrimp in the nonbulkheaded study site.

Cuts through barrier islands and similar areas can cause significant changes in the biota after such alterations are complete. An example is the construction of Rollover Pass from the Gulf of Mexico into East Bay of the Galveston Bay system in Texas. As reported by Reid (1957), the Rollover Pass area was studied for three years: the year before, at the time of, and for a year following construction. During the third year, sedimentation partially closed the pass. Salinity distribution and fish and shrimp population densities were found to be similar before construction and following partial blockage of the pass. A different set of circumstances existed when the pass was open: some fish populations increased while others declined. The densities of brown and white shrimp were lower when the pass was open than before or after that time.

Stinson and Mathewson (1976) discussed the importance of regional geology as a subject for study when selecting a spoil disposal site. They suggested that topography, bathymetry, geomorphology, meteorology, and water circulation should all be considered. Since wind and waves tend to dominate physical changes in spoil deposition areas, they should be given particular attention. The authors also pointed out that dredge material should be placed on the down-drift side of the channel. Otherwise, the material will move back into the channel, and frequent dredging—which is both costly and much more harmful to the environment than infrequent dredging—will be required.

EFFECTS OF DREDGING ON PLANT COMMUNITIES

Plant communities are frequently disturbed by dredging, either in the actual dredge site or in spoil disposal areas. In maintenance dredging areas, submerged vegetation may exist, or the sediments may be vegetation-free. New dredging sites may also be vegetation-free, or they may have submerged or intertidal plants around them. In some cases, such as in parts of the intracoastal waterway system, terrestrial plants are affected when initial dredging cuts are made through supratidal areas. Spoil sites are often located in regions with vegetation. Upland spoil disposal is also practiced, so terrestrial vegetation may be buried. Marshlands and pools of open water are commonly selected as spoil deposition sites. Although some of these sites are protected by law, many are not or are exempt, as in the case of spoil deposition grounds used by the U.S. Army Corps of Engineers along the intrascoastal waterways. Although salt marshes can recover after suffering inundation with spoil material when the undiked technique is used, they will be destroyed when spoil is contained within dikes (Windom, 1972).

Few studies have attempted to determine the impacts of dredging on phytoplankton or benthic algal communities, though both could be greatly affected, at least locally. One study conducted by Corliss and Trent (1971), which was based in Galveston Bay, Texas, compared phytoplankton production in dredged and undredged areas. An undredged marsh was evaluated against an adjacent marsh that had undergone channelization, bulkheading, and filling. Average gross phytoplankton production (mg C/l/day) in the altered area was 8% higher than in the unaltered marsh and 48% higher than in the bay from January through August. Gross and net production were significantly higher in both marsh areas than in the bay, and differences between the two marshes were not statistically significant. Thus, in the situation examined by these authors, the modifications resulting from dredging did not adversely affect phytoplankton production.

Studies on the effects of dredging on submerged grass beds are not numerous, though some information is available. Godcharles (1971) examined grass-flat habitats in Florida that had been affected by clam dredges. A year following dredging, there had been no recolonization of the seagrasses *Thalassia testudinum* and *Syringodium filiforme* in any affected area. No faunal differences between dredged and undredged locations were noted from trawl and benthos samples except at one station.

Recent attempts have been made to stabilize dredge spoil material by planting native aquatic vegetation in subtidal, intertidal, or supratidal areas containing the material. One study, conducted by Eleuterius (1975), involved the planting of subtidal grasses on a spoil area. The submerged grasses *Thalassia testudinum*, *Cymodocea manatorum*, and *Diplanthera wrightii* were planted on dredged material in Mississippi Sound. *Diplanthera* was judged to be the best candidate for further study; no successful transplants on spoil deposits were achieved, however, because of erosion and sedimentation that exceeded the growth potential of these plants.

A considerable amount of work has been directed at the establishment of intertidal marshgrasses on spoil material. The goals behind much of that research have been to encourage the rapid growth of plants on dredged material in order to provide stability for the newly placed sediments and to hasten the reestablishment of the predredging environment. Replanting intertidal marshlands has generally involved the establishment of *Spartina alterniflora*, but other grasses such as *S. patens* have also been evaluated. Mechanized planting as well as hand planting have been used.

Both seeding and sprigging have also helped establish intertidal marshes. Sprigging involves the collection of cuttings from existing marshes or nurseries, while seeding entails collecting seeds from marshes or nurseries and storing them until they are planted. Broome et al. (1973) reported that *S. alterniflora* produces many viable seeds under the proper conditions. Seeds can be collected from vigorous stands and stored over winter submerged in water of estuarine or seawater salinity at 2 to 3 C. A brief period of dry storage before submergence has been shown to increase the percentage of germination. The authors concluded that seeding works well at high intertidal elevations but that sprigging is a better method in the lower intertidal zone.

Woodhouse et al. (1972) reported that the establishment of *S. alterniflora* marshes on spoil material is not only feasible but that complete coverage can be expected within two growing seasons. This has been confirmed by other studies, such as the one conducted by Webb et al. (1978). Sprigging of marshgrasses appears to be more widely adaptable than seeding (Woodhouse et al., 1972) but is more expensive. Broome et al. (1973, 1974) determined that the amount of protective cover provided by seedlings during the first growing season exceeded that produced from the transplantation of sprigs in the case of *S. alterniflora*. Seneca et al. (1975) found that seeding at the rate of 100 seeds/m² from April through May can result in complete coverage of *S. alterniflora* by the end of the first growing season.

According to Seneca et al. (1975), the length of tidal inundation and salinity should be considered when an elevational gradient is used to construct a marsh in which *S. alterniflora* is to be established. It only makes good sense to attempt to introduce a particular species of marshgrass into a region of appropriate elevation and salinity, provided that other environmental constraints do not interfere.

Spoil disposal along the intracoastal waterways, and certainly in other estuarine areas of the United States, can be expected to affect various kinds of vegetation, including upland species. This has been documented along the GIWW by Vaughan and Kimber (1977). Their study reported that erosion and splashing of water generated by passing vessels disturbed vegetation along the waterway; both dredging and spoiling, therefore, can be expected to affect terrestrial plants. Upland vegetation was considered in a study conducted in Galveston Bay, Texas, by Webb et al. (1978). Some species appeared to adapt well to dredge material while others died. Intolerance of atmospheric salt caused by proximity to the bay may have been as important or more important than an inability of the plants to survive in the dredge material. Soil fertility also affects the survival of plants on dredged material.

Successfully establishing a marshland on dredged material often depends upon proper protection of seedlings or sprigs during the early months of their growth. That is one reason why protective devices are sometimes provided when marshland planting is begun. Machemehl (1976) indicated that nylon bags can be used to construct relatively inexpensive groins, which can effectively stabilize a beach area. The economic life of such bags was determined to be two years on the beach. They may live considerably longer, however, in estuaries where the level of exposure to waves is significantly less than on an open beach.

Garbisch et al. (1975) reviewed the biotic techniques employed to stabilize shorelines and included in this review the technique of establishing marshlands on both unaltered shorelines and fill material. The authors concluded that (1) substrate characteristics do not seem to limit the establishment of vegetation; (2) periodic fertilization may be required in some instances; (3) mammal and waterfowl grazing may harm certain plant species in newly created marshes, leading to permanent removal of species that do not flower during the first growing season following planting; and (4) species of plants that can be most successfully established in brackish water areas are *S. alterniflora*, *S. patens*, *S. cynosuroides*, *Distichlis spicata*, *Phragmites australis*, *Panicum virgatum*, and *Ammophilia breviligulata*.

Thermal Effluents

Heated effluents that enter estuaries can result from various kinds of manufacturing processes or even from the release of geothermal well or spring water; thermal effluents, however, are most commonly associated with power plants. Whether conventional (coal, oil, or gas fired) or nuclear, steam electric power stations are responsible for the use of tremendous quantities of water for cooling. These stations operate by providing heat from burning fuel (or heat produced by fission, in the case of nuclear plants) to produce steam. The steam is used to turn turbine generators, after which it is condensed back into water and recycled to the boilers.

For each megawatt of electricity produced, 1.7 megawatts of heat are rejected by the typical steam electric station (Mihursky, 1975). Condenser cooling is accomplished by dissipating the waste heat into water. In conventional power plants, cooling water is allowed to flow through condenser pipes that touch the steam being condensed. In nuclear power plants, the steam is insulated from the outside world by a water jacket through which waste heat is dissipated. This water jacket provides integrity to the system, preventing the release of radioactivity into the environment.

The amount of water used for cooling purposes by power plants is staggering. In 1968, U.S. consumption of cooling water was over 180 x 10^{12} liters (Clark, 1969; Bienfang, 1971). Regulatory agencies generally require that the increase in temperature of water passing through a steam electric power station not exceed 10 F, so a large volume of water of ambient temperature must be continuously available.

Power plants are usually located adjacent to a lake, stream, or coast. In some cases, reservoirs have been constructed specifically to provide cooling water for power plants. In a typical power plant, incoming water is brought through an intake canal, passed over screens to keep out debris and living organisms, run through a system of condenser pipes, and ejected from the plant site through a discharge canal. In cases where environmental damage of unacceptable proportion might result if the discharged water were immediately returned to the natural environment, a cooling lake may be required near the discharge area.

The amount of published information on the environmental impacts of thermal wastes from power plants rose from seventeen papers in 1950 to over one hundred in 1960 (Kennedy and Mihursky, 1969) and would literally fill rooms today. Numerous studies on impingement (the trapping and destruction of organisms on the intake screens of power plants) and entrainment (the passage of organisms through power plants and the resulting effects) have been conducted. O'Connor and McErlean (1975) concluded that steam electric power plants can alter the productivity of fish populations, through both thermal and chemical discharges.

Fishes, and perhaps other animals, can be attracted to power plants, largely because of the thermal effluent. Gallaway and Strawn (1974) found that fish were attracted to a power plant on Galveston Bay, Texas, during all but summer months. The lowest elevated temperature that was avoided (by Gulf menhaden, *Brevoortia patronus*) was 30 C. Most fishes were abundant in temperatures as high as 33 to 35 C. Sea catfish and Atlantic croaker (*Arius felis* and *Micropogonias undulatus*, respectively) did not avoid the power plant effluent until the temperature reached 37 C. Sand seatrout (*Cynoscion arenarius*) and mullet (*Mugil* spp.) were collected from 40 C water, though that temperature would undoubtedly prove lethal upon long-term exposure.

Brungs and Jones (1977) reviewed the desired criteria for power plant operation that would avoid destroying freshwater fish through thermal impacts. Their criteria should also apply to estuarine organisms. First, the maximum weekly average temperature of effluent water should not exceed one-third of the range between the ultimate upper incipient lethal temperature and the optimum temperature for growth. Second, the temperature should not be so high that, if rapidly dropped to ambient, mortality would result. A third consideration is that the effluent temperature should not prevent successful reproduction and development of exposed fishes, nor should it prohibit normal species diversity.

Oil Production, Platforms, Pipelines, and Spills

The mention of oil-drilling platforms in the ocean commonly brings to mind the image of massive towers with multiple wells being drilled in depths of up to several hundred meters of water. Such platforms certainly do exist and are becoming increasingly common, yet most oil drilling along U.S. coasts is done in relatively shallow water or even on land adjacent to salt water.

Whether in the water or on land adjoining estuaries, oil wells disturb the environment to one degree or another. Besides the wells themselves, many related activities also have environmental effects. Oil refineries have most commonly been established in estuarine regions (figure 19). Refineries handle domestic oil along with imported petroleum. An extensive pipeline network has been constructed in the United States to carry petroleum products to and from the refineries. Pipeline construction requires a significant amount of dredging and filling through waterways and marshes, though such disruptions are temporary. Large port facilities for loading and unloading tankers are required, again necessitating a good deal of dredging and filling in most cases. Extensive tank farms for oil storage around refineries also demand space and may take wetland areas out of production. Of concern in all petroleum-related activities is the constant danger of oil spills.

The aesthetic impact of oil-drilling rigs, refineries, tank farms, and so forth has also been objected to by many environmentalists. Drilling itself is a transient activity. Once the well comes in or is abandoned, the drilling rig or platform is moved to another location; the original area will then either be returned to approximately its original appearance, or, if the well produces, a gas collection system or oil pump (figure 19) may be left to mark the site. One or more storage tanks may also be present. Wells drilled on land commonly have drilling mud pits (small ponds) near them that are filled after the well is completed. Producing wells also usually have roads leading to them, so some long-term changes can be expected in the area around a producing well.

Except for oil or natural gas that escapes into the atmosphere or water of an estuary, drilling platforms and land-based wells generally do a minimal amount of environmental damage, though that view is not always supported by public opinion. In 1979, attempts to obtain leases for offshore drilling in the Gulf of Maine by various oil companies met with stiff protests from environmental groups and fishermen. The antidrilling faction claimed that drilling in the Gulf of Maine posed an unacceptable threat to the fisheries of the region. A similar attitude has been expressed by environmental groups along the West Coast of the United States; in both

Fig. 19. An oil-drilling site on the edge of an estuary. Storage tanks and refinery towers are visible in the background.

areas, leasing of offshore areas has been curtailed or never initiated, though the issue is by no means dead.

A great deal of research emphasis has been placed on determining the effects of petroleum and petroleum fractions on organisms. Lee et al. (1980) outlined what happens to oil in the ocean. When oil is spilled into water, it forms a slick on the surface. Part of the oil will evaporate into the atmosphere where it will eventually become oxidized. Some of the rest will be directly ingested by marine organisms, and some will dissolve in the water. The remainder will form tar balls, become emulsified, or be degraded by microorganisms. Tar balls and emulsified oil can become sedimented, after which the materials will undergo chemical or biological degradation or will be ingested by marine organisms. Incorporation of part of the sedimented oil by these organisms may also result. Guard et al. (1975) suggested that, following volatilization of the light petroleum fractions, insoluble residues will form not only floating masses but also hard, pavementlike surfaces on sediments.

Sediments on the beaches of Chedabucto Bay, Nova Scotia, were found to act as a sink for stranded oil (Vandermeulen and Keizer, 1977). It was estimated that the oil could persist for up to 150 years. Significant contamination of eelgrass (*Zostera marina*) resulted.

An estimated 32,000 barrels of Bunker C fuel oil were spilled into Los Angeles Harbor in California during December, 1976, when the 70,000-ton tanker *Sansinena* exploded and burned. Studies conducted over the next several months at twenty-four stations (Soule and Oguri, 1978) revealed that intertidal areas were most heavily damaged. Benthos decreased through April, 1977, but returned to normal by November. Phytoplankton productivity dropped for two weeks but recovered by January, 1977. Zooplanktonic organisms were affected by oil and grease in the water in April and July, 1977.

Following a spill in Chesapeake Bay, oil was recovered from as deep as 10 cm in beach sediments (Roland et al., 1977; Hershner and Moore, 1977). Tides caused continuous uncovering of the oil and led to long-term contamination of the water. Oil was found to smother benthic organisms, including oysters. Edible oysters, clams, and crabs that were exposed but not killed had off-flavors; marshgrasses became oil-coated.

Some studies have focused on specific organisms as well as on communities or ecosystems. Among marshgrasses, DeLaune et al. (1979) indicated that *Spartina alterniflora* could tolerate large amounts of oil without demonstrating a decrease in aboveground biomass. A somewhat contradictory report was published by Lee et al. (1980). The latter authors determined that exposure of cordgrass to heavy fuel oil resulted in the yellowing and death of the leaves. After three years, green shoots were observed on plants that had been doused with oil in the fall. By the following spring, no differences were noticed in oiled and control areas of *Spartina*. The difference between the two studies may have been related to the kind of oil used, the manner of application, the time of year that oiling took place, or to some combination of factors.

A wide range of responses can be expected from plants exposed to crude oils. Baker (1979) found that some annuals, such as *Salicornia* spp., can be killed by oiling, while other species may tolerate successive monthly applications. Tolerant plant species may gain a competitive advantage after an oil spill. Burning, cutting, or treatment with chemical dispersants after a spill may not aid the recovery of an affected area but may, in fact, cause further harm. Acute toxicity of oil to plants may be attributable to the light aromatic fractions present in the oil. Some heavy and weathered oils actually appear to stimulate the growth of marsh plants (Baker, 1979).

Westree (1977) found that the practice of cutting oiled marshgrass was not always helpful in speeding the recovery process. He noted that the mixing of oil and sediments during cutting could lead to greater contamination than if the area were left alone. The theory advanced was that the oil becomes a long-term pollutant that contaminates rhizomes and burrowing organisms when mixed with the sediments.

Many studies have set out to determine the effects of oil on marine animals. For example, Lee et al. (1977) evaluated the toxicity of aqueous extracts of No. 2 fuel oil and southern Louisiana crude oil on the amphipods *Gammarus mucronatus* and *Amphithoe valida*. They found that the fuel oil was toxic at 0.8 ppm and the crude oil at 2.4 ppm. In a similar study by Cucci and Epifanio (1979), larvae of the mud crab, *Eurypanopeus depressus*, were exposed to Kuwait crude oil. The forty-eight-hour median tolerance limit was about 10 ppm for first-stage zoeae, while that for the second stage was 17 ppm. Chronic exposure to low levels of oil led to differential mortality and longer intermolt periods for all larval stages compared with controls. Concentrations of 4.3 and 8.7 ppm crude oil caused no increased mortality among juvenile crabs, regardless of exposure time. Exposure of crab larvae to crude oil led to the development of an extra and morphologically abnormal megalops stage.

Exposure of the American oyster, *Crassostrea virginica*, to various kinds of oil was the topic of a study by Anderson and Anderson (1976). They found that No. 2 fuel oil and Venezuela Bunker C oil were more toxic than either southern Louisiana or Kuwait crude oils.

Lee et al. (1980) discovered that benthic macrofauna respond to oil spills with either no change, an increase in population, or a decrease in population. Fiddler crabs, oysters, and mussels showed no changes when exposed to oil. Mud snail, *Nassarius obsoleta*, populations increased due to immigration of adults from uncontaminated areas. Adult periwinkles, *Littorina irrorata*, were killed in large numbers but recolonized within several months.

On June 3, 1979, an oil well located in the Bay of Campeche, Mexico, and designated as Ixtoc I blew out. Crude oil was released at the rate of 20,000 barrels per day into the Gulf of Mexico, with the resulting oil slick reaching Texas waters by late August of the same year (Amos, 1980).

Various studies set out to determine the effects of that oil spill on marine organisms. Among them was a study by Rabalais et al. (1981), which showed that larval red drum, *Sciaenops ocellatus*, died in large numbers when placed in mixtures of Ixtoc I oil and water. Eggs and larvae exposed to oil-contaminated water from the jetties at Port Aransas, Texas, also demonstrated high mortalities.

Grebes are among the birds that have suffered most from oil spills, though sea ducks (scooters and old-squaws), loons, murres, and cormorants have also been heavily damaged in many instances. Bunker C fuel oil consumed by many birds has been shown to be fatal to eggs produced by those birds (anonymous, 1971; Roland et al., 1977). The amount of damage suffered by birds is related to the kind of oil and the ambient temperatures at the time of exposure. The worst damage is caused by fresh, fluid oils that clog plumage and break down the insulating capacity of the feathers. Fuel oils, which are liquid until dispersed, cause more damage to birds than do crude oils, which quickly form tar balls. High temperature speeds the loss of volatile fractions, while low temperature does the opposite (Bourne, 1975).

Although oil spills have resulted in significant problems, not the least of which involves the aesthetic character of polluted areas, the overall effect of the oil production, distribution, and refining industry might be considered fairly small when the immense size of the industry is compared with the amount of environmental damage attributed to spills. A two-year synoptic study was conducted by Sharp and Appan (1978) to determine if twenty-five years of intensive oil drilling and production had disturbed Timbalier Bay and adjacent offshore waters in Louisiana. No biological, physical, chemical, or geological evidence of significant changes was found. The same general conclusion might obtain for other areas—but a single significant oil spill in a given estuary will have long-term effects that cannot be ignored.

An important aspect of oil spills relative to estuaries involves cleanup operations. Containment booms (floating devices that help confine spilled oil to small areas) are one means for gaining control. Emulsifiers (substances that help mix oil with water) are used to remove oil from beaches, rocks, sediments, boats, piers, and other objects. Hay has been spread over oiled beaches to help soak up spills, but the problems associated with disposal of the oil-soaked hay may be as perplexing as those of the oily beach.

After a spill of Bunker C fuel oil in Chesapeake Bay in 1976, some of the oil was used on roads, while some was put into barrels and burned (Wise and Brunk, 1977). The latter technique is usually not recommended because it produces polluting black smoke.

Various emulsifying agents have been developed to assist in oil-spill cleanup. Chadwick (1960) found that one commercial oil-spill eradicator of the emulsifying type was toxic to striped bass, *Morone saxatilis*, at low concentrations.

Oil spills are by no means insignificant problems in estuaries, though predicting their occurrence and effects is virtually impossible. Sometimes a great amount of damage, either short- or long-term, results while at other times the effects appear to be minimal. Laws on prohibition of intentional dumping are helpful but are not the whole answer. Everyone involved with petroleum products in any form should exercise extreme care to avoid spills. Current laws make even the spilling of a few drops of fuel during refueling an offense punishable by heavy fines.

Biocides

Scientific studies on the effects of biocides (pesticides and herbicides) on nontarget species have been conducted for many years, and massive amounts of data have been accumulated. The chlorinated hydrocarbons or organochlorines consist of such compounds as DDT, aldrin, BHC, chlordane, endrin, heptochlor, hexachlorobenzene, lindane, dieldrin, endosulfan, methoxychlor, perthane, and toxaphene. The chlorinated hydrocarbons are extremely long-lived: the original chemical or its breakdown products may survive for many years in the environment.

A second category of pesticides is the organophosphates. Those compounds usually break down into harmless compounds after a few days, though their overall toxicity while active is generally a great deal higher than that of the chlorinated hydrocarbon pesticides. Clark (1977) felt that such compounds as dursban, fenthion, naled, parathion, and ronnel were too dangerous to be used in coastal areas.

Because estuaries are often breeding sites for mosquitos and other pests, insecticides have been used with some frequency in certain regions. Areas adjacent to estuaries are often used as farmland, so pesticides and herbicides may enter the estuaries as runoff. Biocide runoff can also infiltrate estuaries from well upstream, particularly the long-lived compounds. The spraying of biocidal materials in estuaries, together with runoff, can lead to the accumulation of dangerously high levels of the compounds in estuarine organisms and may even cause mortality. Fatal chemicals may be directly toxic, or they may enter the affected animals through the food web. Early studies outlining the effects of pesticides on aquatic organisms were reviewed by Butler and Springer (1963). The Environmental Protection Agency (undated) also published a report detailing studies conducted on pesticide toxicity, which reviewed the literature through the early 1970s. A second Environmental Protection Agency publication (Courtenay et al., 1973) addressed the effects of toxaphene on various species of fishes and crustaceans.

The concept of bioaccumulation or biomagnification developed as a result of observations made on organisms exposed to pesticides—in particular, DDT. Biomagnification is the phenomenon by which each step in the food chain contains greater levels of a chemical than does the step below it. Biomagnification may not mean that the organism at the top of a food chain has lethal levels of the chemical, though sublethal effects are sometimes observed. For example, fish that consume insects killed by pesticides may not accumulate enough of the chemical to die, but their body burden may significantly exceed that of their food. Lesions of the brain, spinal cord, liver, kidneys, and stomach were reported in spot, *Leiostomus xanthurus*, exposed to sublethal levels of endrin (Lowe, 1964), to mention but one such study. Behavioral changes have also been reported in Atlantic salmon, *Salmo salar*, exposed to an organophosphate compound (Symons, 1973); and consistent changes in the levels of sodium, potassium, magnesium, iron, calcium, and zinc were observed in adult clams, *Mercenaria mercenaria*, exposed to the organophosphate methoxychlor (Eisler and Weinstein, 1967).

Direct mortality of fishes has been reported from the use of biocides in a number of instances. Dieldrin usage in an estuary led to the death of such fishes as tarpon, sea catfish, killifish, mosquito fish, mullet, and red drum, according to Harrington and Bidlingmayer (1958). Application of the chemical mirex, which was used to kill fire ants, reportedly brought about direct toxicity in fish as well as causing mortality through the food chain (Boudreaux et al., 1959).

More subtle but no less drastic impacts of pesticide usage have been reported. As a result of biomagnification, certain species of birds that feed heavily on aquatic organisms have collected high body burdens of pesticides. The story of how DDT led to decreased egg shell thickness of eagles, ospreys, and other species is widely known. Many eggs were broken during incubation, and the threat of extinction of certain species was very real, largely because of pesticide contamination. That incident helped lead to the ban that was ultimately imposed on the use of DDT. During 1981, waterfowl in Montana and adjacent states were found to have excessive levels of endrin, and a caution was issued to hunters to limit or forgo the hunting and consumption of ducks and geese in the affected flyway.

Many studies have examined the effects of biocides on estuarine organisms. Some of the earliest investigations focused on DDT since that compound was the first pesticide available; and, while touted as safe for nontarget organisms, it was found to bioaccumulate and persist in the environment for many years after use. Cottam and Higgins (1946) presented evidence not too long after the introduction of DDT suggesting that the application of the chemical to marshes for insect control resulted in toxicity to crustaceans, shellfish, fish, birds, and amphibians living in adjacent waters. Of perhaps equal or even more importance, Holland et al. (1966) found that some species exposed to sublethal concentrations of DDT showed increased sensitivity to reexposure and would later succumb to low levels of the chemical. A similar response was demonstrated for toxaphene by spot, *Leiostomus xanthurus*.

These responses are not common to all fish nor to all pesticides, however. Studies conducted by Vinson et al. (1963), Ferguson et al. (1964), and Lowe (1964) are among several showing that at least some fishes can become resistant to certain pesticides after exposure to subtoxic levels. Rosato and Ferguson (1968) found that mosquito fish, *Gambusia affinis*, when exposed to high concentrations of endrin were not killed because of resistance but were responsible for the deaths of such predatory animals as fish, reptiles, and birds. Other related studies were conducted by Ferguson et al. (1966) and Ferguson (1967).

The literature on the impacts of biocides on aquatic organisms includes work with microorganisms (Brown et al., 1975), copepods (Darrow and Harding, 1975), crab larvae (Epifanio, 1971), palaemoneid and penaeid shrimp (Chin and Allen, 1957; Nimmo et al., 1970; Conte and Parker, 1975; Provenzano et al., 1978), and oysters (Loosanoff, 1947), to name a few. Even with the massive amount of data accumulated on the subject, Butler (1966) reported that after the first twenty years of research, the effects of pesticides on estuaries were inadequately understood.

The presence of biocides in fish and shellfish may, in some cases, pose a threat to human health. Some reassuring information, however, has appeared on that subject. Butler (1974), after examining over eight thousand shellfish samples from estuaries, concluded that DDT levels were not an immediate threat to human health and that both the high and low extremes in concentration of that chemical and its metabolites were well defined geographically. Marked declines in DDT levels were found after 1968. The pesticide was banned in the United States in 1972.

A considerable amount of interest and research have been focused on the chlorinated hydrocarbon, toxaphene. That chemical has been widely used on croplands for pest control. In studies of rice fields around marshlands in Texas, Ginn and Fisher (1974) found that toxaphene led to one fish-kill incident, though long-term effects and bioaccumulation were not evident. That same report suggested that the use of aldrin on rice fields led to runoff into marshlands where the breakdown product, dieldrin, was recovered. Other chlorinated hydrocarbons, such as DDT and its metabolites DDE and DDD, were also found, though their origin could not be documented.

Reimold et al. (1973) documented the effects of toxaphene on a Georgia estuary over a period of three years. The study area contained a toxaphene manufacturing plant that underwent a program of pollution abatement during the study. As the effluent from the plant was cleaned up, the researchers were able to document a simultaneous drop in the body burden of toxaphene in plants, animals, and the sediments of the region.

Related research has concentrated on the polychlorinated biphenyls (PCB), which, although not used as biocides, are chemically similar. One of the main uses of PCB has been in electrical transformers, so those chemicals have been spread throughout the country by electrical utility companies. Release due to transformer rupture can result in severe environmental damage. One PCB was found to be toxic to juvenile pink shrimp, *Penaeus duorarum*, exposed to 1 ppb for fifteen days. Adult shrimp were less susceptible but were found to concentrate the chemical to levels as high as 510 ppm in the hepatopancreas (Nimmo et al., 1971). Levels of the same PCB as high as 184 ppm were recovered from fish livers (Duke et al., 1970). The latter study found that PCB was bioconcentrated in a variety of estuarine species. In pinfish, *Lagodon rhomboides*, the chemical persisted for about three months following removal of the fish from exposure to the chemical (Hansen et al., 1971). A study by Wildish

(1970) showed that the amphipod *Gammarus oceanicus* was killed by concentrations of PCB as low as 0.01 ppm and that molting or newly molted animals were highly susceptible to toxicity. Severe controls have been placed on the manufacture, use, and disposal of PCB.

Trace Metals

Many manufacturing processes lead to the emission of trace metals into the environment. Much of that release is into water, where concentrations may reach toxic levels. Though many trace metals are required for normal metabolism in plants and animals, excessive levels may prove to be toxic. For example, copper is required by many invertebrates as a component of the blood pigment cyanocobalamin. That substance is similar in action to the iron-based hemoglobin of vertebrates and some invertebrates. Although required by animals, both copper and iron can be toxic if present in high concentrations.

Other trace metals are also necessary for both plants and animals, though some have no biological function or may interfere with normal biochemical reactions. A great deal of attention has been given to such metals as mercury, cadmium, lead, and arsenic—none of which is required by either plants or animals, though each can and does accumulate in organisms exposed to the metals. Exposure to high levels of any of those metals can lead to pathology and, ultimately, death.

Mercury has received a great deal of attention by geochemists working on estuarine species. The metal occurs naturally in seawater at low concentrations, though many coastal regions have suffered contamination through mercury released from industrial plants, thereby increasing environmental levels. The recognition of relatively high levels of mercury in tuna and swordfish during the 1960s led to the imposition of controls on mercury levels in fish sold for human consumption. Interestingly, neither tuna nor swordfish are found in coastal waters, and it is difficult to document the mechanisms for offshore transport of mercury from coastal regions. Thus, the elevated mercury levels in tuna and swordfish as compared with many other offshore species appear to result from accumulation through the natural food web. Man can be affected by elevated mercury levels in tuna and swordfish only by consuming those fishes daily, or almost daily. Many coastal species have also been shown to have mercury levels that exceed Environmental Protection Agency standards. Levels exceeding 1 ppm were found in various species of estuarine fishes in Georgia (Stickney et al., 1975).

The dumping of mercury into estuarine waters has resulted in mercury toxicity. Perhaps the classic example is the pollution of Minamata Bay, Japan, during the 1950s. Mercury was discharged from a factory into the bay over a period of several years, causing shellfish in the bay to accumulate high concentrations in their tissues. When the shellfish were eaten, the metal was transferred to the nervous tissues of the people involved, leading to high incidences of brain damage and even death in a number of instances.

The phrase "mad as a hatter" comes from the earlier practice by persons involved in making hats of using mercury in the felting process. Years of exposure to the metal led to brain dysfunction.

Not all organisms concentrate mercury in the nervous tissues. For example, Stickney et al. (1972) found that the bottle-nosed dolphin, *Tursiops truncatus*, had highest mercury concentrations in organs other than the brain. The right lobe of the brain was found to contain 1.24 ppm mercury on a dry weight basis, while the kidneys contained up to 22 ppm and the liver up to 34.7 ppm. Muscle levels exceeded 3 ppm.

The contamination of estuaries by mercury has been a topic of considerable interest in recent years because of the belief that once contaminated, the environment will remain so for many years or even centuries after the source of pollution has been removed. Low levels of mercury contamination can be significant. For example, Green et al. (1976) found that 17 ppb mercury was acutely toxic to postlarval white shrimp, *Penaeus setiferus*. Once deposited, mercury was retained in animal tissues. Thus, removing the source of pollution will only slow or stop the buildup of the metal in the environment and its animals but will not result in depuration of the metal from animals harboring it.

Biomagnification does not seem to occur with all metals, however. For example, many invertebrates have, as indicated above, a requirement for and relatively high levels of copper in their tissues. Yet studies have demonstrated that fish feeding on such invertebrates do not accumulate high levels of the metal. In fact, fish generally have substantially less copper in their bodies than in their food (Stickney et al., 1975). Biochemical pathways for excreting excessive levels of some metals must exist, while other metals apparently cannot be metabolized.

Cadmium is a trace metal that can lead to toxicity in estuarine organisms and has been implicated in hypertension in man (Schroeder, 1965).

Cadmium is chemically similar to zinc, a metal rquired in small concentrations by animals for use as a cofactor in certain enzyme systems. When cadmium is present in tissues, it will compete for active sites on enzymes. If cadmium replaces zinc at such a site, the affected enzyme will be deactivated. Thus, the absolute concentration of cadmium may sometimes be less important than the ratio between cadmium and zinc. This is particularly true when both elements are present at sublethal levels.

Toxicity of cadmium to various estuarine organisms has been evaluated by many authors. Studies have ranged from those involved with diatoms (Jensen et al., 1976) to those that examined crabs (Hutcheson, 1974) and fish (Middaugh et al., 1975; Hawkins et al., 1980). Cadmium concentrations of as low as 10 ppb above ambient have caused increased tissue levels of the metal in the scallop, *Aequipecten irradians*, and the killifish, *Fundulus heteroclitus* (Eisler et al., 1972). Results of such studies appear to be affected by both temperature and salinity in addition to absolute cadmium concentration (Eisler, 1971; O'Hara, 1973a, 1973b).

Other Human Impacts on Estuaries

The topics discussed in preceding sections are only a few among the many that have been investigated. Among the remaining ones that deserve attention is sewage pollution. Studies by Lynn and Yang (1960), McNulty et al. (1960), and McNulty (1961) in Biscayne Bay, Florida, showed that seventy sewage outfalls entered the bay. The numbers of coliform bacteria per liter (one indicator of sewage contamination) rapidly declined seaward of the sewage outfalls, though no benthic organisms were found to recover within about 200 m of the outfalls.

Current federal regulations have severely limited the dumping of raw sewage into estuaries, though overflowing septic tanks from houses built in areas without centralized sewage systems may still pose problems. Another source of estuarine sewage has been boats, which until recently almost always dumped sewage overboard. Current federal law requires that all toilets on boats be of the type that retain wastes until the boats can return to port, where tanks can be pumped out into a sanitary sewer system (figure 20).

Industrial pollution of estuaries has continued for decades in the United States, though the recent implementation of strict pollution regulations has led to abatement programs, many of which have been highly suc-

Fig. 20. Modern marinas feature pump-out stations for all boats with toilets.

cessful. As a result, the effluents from manufacturing plants have been largely cleaned up (figure 21), though toxic chemicals have not been completely eliminated. Improvement of the air has been accompanied by increased water purity as effluents from factories are treated before being released into receiving streams. Stressed environments in many cases have rapidly recovered, though the battle is far from won.

Estuaries have received virtually all kinds of effluents from manufacturing, agricultural, and social activities. In the Pacific Northwest, nearly all estuaries are highly developed ports and industrial sites. Salo and Stober (1971) reported that sulfite wastes from paper mills have become an important problem in the region because of the probable effects of the waste on fish, benthos, larval forms, and phytoplankton.

Seafood processing has also been found to pollute estuaries when wastes dumped from the industry lead to nutrient enrichment (eutrophication). The effects of dumped wastes from seafood processing plants were evaluated by Heald and Odum (1974), who concluded that (1) blooms of

Fig. 21. Coastal industrial plants, once major sources of pollution in estuarine areas, have been more closely regulated in recent years with respect to effluents. The result has been fewer pollutants emitted into both air and water from such plants.

phytoplankton, particularly nannoplanktonic species of green flagellates, blue-greens, and small diatoms, may be encouraged; (2) a slight excess of respiration over photosynthesis may occur because the input nutrients are high in organic matter; (3) diurnal changes in dissolved oxygen concentration become magnified; (4) incidences of patchiness may appear as localized areas of nutrient-rich water are formed; (5) phosphorus levels increase; (6) species diversity decreases; (7) the water column may become stratified; and (8) some organisms become adapted to feeding on the refuse.

Indiscriminate dumping of human wastes into estuaries is no longer allowed in this country. Various state and local regulations have been developed to ensure that the air and water of the country are protected as much as possible. The Fish and Wildlife Coordination Act of 1958 gave the U.S. Fish and Wildlife Service the responsibility of investigating proposed projects (federal and nonfederal) for potential damage to fish and wildlife resources. Such activities as dredging and construction in estuarine areas come under that act. The Rivers and Harbors Act of the late nineteenth century has served as the basis for the permit system used by the U.S. Army Corps of Engineers. Permits must be obtained from the corps for dredging, bulkheading, jetty construction, and other related activities in navigable waters. Input from the Fish and Wildlife Service and other agencies is solicited as a part of the permit process.

Many other agencies may also require permits for various kinds of activities in estuaries. In Texas, the Antiquities Board is one of the state agencies that is approached during the permit process. Construction is normally not allowed until it is clear that no historical artifacts are on the site. Construction may be disallowed or held up until the antiquities can be documented and, in many cases, removed.

Mariculture

Mariculture, or marine aquaculture, is the rearing of marine organisms under controlled or semicontrolled conditions. In other words, mariculture is underwater agriculture as practiced in salt water. Because of the severe problems of engineering offshore mariculture facilities that will withstand the rigors of wind and waves, marine aquaculture is largely restricted to coastal waters and is most often practiced in estuaries.

Although intensive culture systems (tanks, raceways, raft culture, and cages) have been used in estuaries with some success, most culture is undertaken in coastal ponds. The science (or art, as practiced in many areas) is particularly well developed in Southeast Asia, Japan, Israel, and parts of Europe. U.S. mariculture is not well developed, though a great deal of interest currently exists. A major problem confronting prospective U.S. mariculturists is competition for desirable estuarine areas. Current costs for many otherwise suitable coastal sites are too high to permit a reasonable return on investment.

Mariculture ponds, located immediately adjacent to the water or on the upper beach, may be filled by water percolating through the sediments, by tides, or by pumping. Pond drainage may be by gravity, in conjunction with the ebbing tide, or by pumping. An adequate supply of fresh water is required to replace evaporative losses from ponds, since the addition of more salt water would lead to increased salinity.

Although production varies considerably depending upon the species under culture, climate, management intensity, and the skill of the culturist, annual harvests of two to three metric tons per hectare can generally be anticipated. For an individual mariculturist in a developing nation, one or two ha of land may be sufficient to support the food needs of a family with some fish left over for sale. In developed nations and throughout the world in commercial operations, larger facilities will be required in order to accrue profits. Commercial mariculture may be conducted on one or a few hectares if intensive culture is employed, but as many as several hundred hectares of ponds may be required for less intensive operations.

Mariculture may or may not represent a source of pollutants to estuaries. Although pond fertilization and the use of prepared feeds add nutrients to the water that would not otherwise be there, the primary goal of the culturist is to provide the best possible environment for the species under culture. Release of culture water into the environment may add some nutrients, but—at least in the warm waters of the southeastern Atlantic and Gulf of Mexico—the increases in nutrient levels would nearly always be insignificant.

There are few commercial mariculture enterprises in the United States at present, though interest is increasing, and active research programs exist. Properly integrated, mariculture might be one way in which estuarine areas can be exploited without damaging the environment. Mariculture will, however, require regions that are relatively unpolluted, with large amounts of water of suitable quality and some proximity to markets.

LITERATURE CITED

Amos, A. F. 1980. *Longhorn* reports: The Ixtoc oil spill. I. Field observations: July–November 1979. Report of NOAA Environmental Research Laboratory and Department of Transportation, U.S. Coast Guard Scientific Institute, Port Aransas Marine Laboratory.

Anderson, R. D., and J. W. Anderson. 1976. Oil bioassays with the American oyster, *Crassostrea virginica* (Gmelin). *Proc. Nat'l. Shellfish Assoc.* 65: 38–42.

Anonymous. 1971. Treatment of oiled birds in California. *Mar. Poll. Bull.* 2: 132.

Atturio, J. M., D. R. Basco, and W. P. James. 1976. *Shoaling characteristics of the Gulf Intracoastal Waterway in Texas*. College Station: Ocean Engineering Program, Texas A&M University, TAMU-SG-76-207.

Baker, J. M. 1979. Responses of salt marsh vegetation to oil spills and refinery effluents, pp. 529–42. In: R. L. Jefferies and A. J. Davy, eds. *Ecological processes in coastal environments*. London: Blackwell Scientific Publ.

Behrens, E. W. 1966. Surface salinities for Baffin Bay and Laguna Madre, Texas, April 1964–March 1966. *Publ. Inst. Mar. Sci., Univ. Tex.* 11: 168–73.

Benefield, R. L. 1976. *Shell dredging sedimentation in Galveston and San Antonio bays 1964–69*. Austin: Texas Parks and Wildlife Department.

Bienfang, P. T. 1971. Taking the pollution out of waste heat. *New Scientist and Sci. J.* 51: 456–57.

Boudreaux, J., K. Strawn, and G. Callas. 1959. Fire ants, heptachlor, and fish kill. *Southwest. Nat.* 3: 7–12.

Bourne, W. R. P. 1975. Temperature and the seasonal and geographical occurrence of oiled birds on west European beaches. *Mar. Poll. Bull.* 8: 173.

Boyd, M. B., R. T. Saucier, J. W. Keely, R. L. Montgomery, R. D. Brown, D. B. Mathis, and E. J. Gruice. 1972. *Disposal of dredge spoil*. Vicksburg, Miss.: U.S. Army Corps of Engineers Waterways Experiment Station, Technical Report H-72-8.

Breuer, J. P. 1962. An ecological survey of the lower Laguna Madre of Texas, 1953–1959. *Publ. Inst. Mar. Sci., Univ. Tex.* 8: 153–83.

Brodhead, J. M. B., and P. J. Godfrey. 1977. Off-road vehicle impact in Cape Cod National Seashore. *Internat. J. Biometeor.* 21: 299–306.

Broome, S. W., W. W. Woodhouse, Jr., and E. D. Seneca. 1973. An investigation of propagation and the mineral nutrition of *Spartina alterniflora*. North Carolina University Sea Grant Publication UNC-SG-73-14.

———. 1974. Propagation of smooth cordgrass, *Spartina alterniflora*, from seed in North Carolina. *Ches. Sci.* 15–214–21.

Brown, L. R., E. G. Alley, and D. W. Cook. 1975. *The effect of Mirex and Carbofuran on estuarine microorganisms*. Corvallis, Ore.: National Environmental Research Center, Office of Research and Development, Environmental Protection Agency.

Brungs, W. A., and B. R. Jones. 1977. *Temperature criteria for freshwater fish: Protocol and procedures*. Ecological Research Series no. EPA-600/3-77-061. Washington, D.C.: U.S. Environmental Protection Agency.

Burdick, G. 1967. An investigation of the alteration of coastal marshes in North Carolina. Proceedings of the North Carolina interagency council on natural resources, Department of Conservation Development, Division of Commercial and Sports Fish.

Burg, T. M. 1973. The effects of mudshell dredging on the biological and physical parameters of a special permit area of San Antonio Bay, Texas. Special Report for the Coastal Fisheries Branch, Texas Parks and Wildlife Department, Austin.

Butler, P. A. 1966. The problem of pesticides in estuaries, pp. 110–15. In: A symposium on estuarine fisheries. American Fisheries Society Special Publication no. 3.

———. 1974. Trends in pesticide residues in shellfish. *Proc. Nat'l. Shellfish Assoc.* 64: 77–81.

Butler, P. A., and P. F. Springer. 1963. Pesticides: A new factor in coastal environments. *Trans. N. Amer. Wildl. Conf.* 28: 378–90.

Bybee, J. R. 1969. Effects of hydraulic pumping operations on the fauna of Tijuana Slough. *Cal. Fish and Game* 55: 213–20.

Chadwick, H. K. 1960. Toxicity of Tricon Oil Spill Eradicator to striped bass (*Roccus saxatilis*). *Cal. Fish and Game* 46: 371–72.

Chapman, C. 1967. Channelization and spoiling in Gulf coast and south Atlantic estuaries, pp. 93–106. In: J. D. Newsom, ed. *Proceedings of marsh and estuary management symposium.* Baton Rouge: Louisiana State University Division of Continuing Education.

Chin, E., and D. W. Allen. 1957. Toxicity of an insecticide to two species of shrimp, *Penaeus aztecus* and *Penaeus setiferus. Tex. J. Sci.* 9: 270–78.

Clark, J. R. 1969. Thermal pollution and aquatic life. *Sci. Amer.* 220(3): 18–27.

———. 1974. *Coastal ecosystems.* Washington, D.C.: Conservation Foundation.

———. 1977. *Coastal ecosystem management.* New York: John Wiley and Sons.

Collier, A., and J. W. Hedgpeth. 1950. An introduction to the hydrography of tidal waters of Texas. *Publ. Inst. Mar. Sci., Univ. Tex.* 1: 120–94.

Conte, F. S., and J. C. Parker. 1975. Effect of aerially-applied malathion on juvenile brown and white shrimp *Penaeus aztecus* and *P. setiferus. Trans. Am. Fish. Soc.* 104: 793–99.

Copeland, B. J., and S. W. Nixon. 1974. Hypersaline lagoons, pp. 312–30. In: H. T. Odum, B. J. Copeland, and E. A. McMahan, eds. *Coastal ecological systems of the United States.* Vol. I. Washington, D.C.: Conservation Foundation.

Corliss, J., and L. Trent. 1971. Comparison of phytoplankton production between natural and altered areas in West Bay, Texas. *Fish. Bull.* 69: 829–32.

Cottam, C., and E. Higgins. 1946. DDT: Its effect on fish and wildlife. U.S. Fish and Wildlife Service Circular 11.

Courtenay, W. R., Jr., M. H. Roberts, Jr., and R. J. Irwin. 1973. *Environmental effects on toxaphene toxicity to selected fish and crustaceans.* Washington, D.C.: U.S. Environmental Protection Agency, EPA-R3-73-035.

Cucci, T. L., and C. E. Epifanio. 1979. Long-term effects of water-soluble fractions of Kuwait crude oil on the larval and juvenile development of the mud crab *Eurypanopeus depressus. Mar. Biol.* 55: 215–20.

Darrow, D. C., and G. C. H. Harding. 1975. Accumulation and apparent absence of DDT metabolism by marine copepods, *Calanus* spp., in culture. *J. Fish. Res. Bd. Can.* 32: 1845–49.

de la Cruz, A. A. 1976. The functions of coastal wetlands. *Assoc. Southeast. Biol. Bull.* 23: 179–85.

DeLaune, R. D., W. H. Patrick, Jr., and R. J. Buresh. 1979. Effect of crude oil on a Louisiana *Spartina alterniflora* salt marsh. *Envir. Poll.* 20: 21–31.

Duke, T. W., J. I. Lowe, and A. J. Wilson, Jr. 1970. A polychlorinated biphenyl (Aroclor 1254R) in the water, sediment, and biota of Escambia Bay, Florida. *Bull. Envir. Contam. Toxic.* 5: 171–80.

Eisler, R. 1971. Cadmium poisoning in *Fundulus heteroclitus* (Pisces: Cyprinodontidae) and other marine organisms. *J. Fish. Res. Bd. Can.* 28: 1225–34.

Eisler, R., and M. P. Weinstein. 1967. Changes in metal composition of the quahaug clam, *Mercenaria mercenaria*, after exposure to insecticides. *Ches. Sci.* 8: 253–58.

Eisler, R., G. E. Zaroogian, and R. J. Hennekey. 1972. Cadmium uptake by marine organisms. *J. Fish. Res. Bd. Can.* 29: 1367–69.

Eleuterius, L. N. 1975. Submergent vegetation for bottom stabilization, pp. 439–56. In: L. E. Cronin, ed. *Estuarine research.* Vol. II. New York: Academic Press.

Engler, R. M. 1976. Environmental impacts of the aquatic disposal of dredge material: Fact and fancy, pp. 220–35. In: *Proceedings of the eighth dredging seminar.* College Station: Texas A&M University Sea Grant Publication, TAMU-SG-77-102.

Environmental Protection Agency. Undated. *Effects of pesticides in water: A report to the states.* Washington, D.C.: U.S. Environmental Protection Agency.

Epifanio, C. E. 1971. Effects of dieldrin in seawater on the development of two species of crab larvae, *Leptodius floridanus* and *Panopeus herbstii*. *Mar. Biol.* 11: 236–62.

Espey, Huston & Associates. 1976. *A study of the placement of materials dredged from Texas ports and waterways: Executive summary.* Austin: Espey, Huston & Associates.

Farmer, J. 1973. Present status of spoil disposal areas along the Houston ship channel, pp. 88–89. In: *Proceedings of the fifth dredging seminar.* College Station: Texas A&M University Sea Grant Publication, TAMU-SG-73-102.

Ferguson, D. E. 1967. The ecological consequences of pesticide resistance in fishes. *Trans. N. Amer. Wildl. Conf.* 32. 103–107.

Ferguson, D. E., D. D. Culley, W. D. Cotton, and R. P. Dodds. 1964. Resistance to chlorinated hydrocarbon insecticides in three species of freshwater fish. *BioScience* 14: 43–44.

Ferguson, D. E., J. L. Ludke, and G. G. Murphy. 1966. Dynamics of endrin uptake and release by resistant and susceptible strains of mosquito fish. *Trans. Am. Fish. Soc.* 95: 335–44.

Gallaway, B. J., and K. Strawn. 1974. Seasonal abundance and distribution of marine fishes at a hot-water discharge in Galveston Bay, Texas. *Cont. Mar. Sci.* 18: 71–137.

Garbisch, E. W., Jr., P. B. Woller, W. J. Bostian, and R. J. McCallum. 1975. Biotic techniques for shore stabilization, pp. 405–26. In: L. E. Cronin, ed. *Estuarine research*. Vol. II. New York: Academic Press.

Ginn, T. M., and F. M. Fisher, Jr. 1974. Studies on the distribution and flux of pesticides in waterways associated with a ricefield-marshland ecosystem. *Pestic. Monit. J.* 8: 23–32.

Godcharles, M. F. 1971. A study of the effects of a commercial hydraulic clam dredge on benthic communities in estuarine areas. Florida Department of Natural Resources Marine Research Laboratory Technical Series no. 64.

Godfrey, P. J. 1979. Response of coastal ecosystems to the mechanical stress of off-road vehicles, pp. 641–42. In: R. L. Jeffries and A. J. Davy, eds. *Ecological processes in coastal environments*. London: Blackwell Scientific Publ.

Godfrey, P. J., S. A. Leatherman, and P. A. Buckley. 1978. Impact of off-road vehicles on coastal ecosystems, pp. 581–600. In: *Coastal zone '78 proceedings*. New York: American Society of Civil Engineering.

Green, F. A., Jr., J. W. Anderson, S. R. Petrocelli, B. J. Presley, and R. Sims. 1976. Effect of mercury on the survival, respiration, and growth of postlarval white shrimp, *Penaeus setiferus*. *Mar. Biol.* 37: 75–81.

Guard, H. E., L. Hunter and L. H. DiSalvo. 1975. Identification and potential biological effects of the major components in the seawater extract of a bunker fuel. *Bull. Envir. Contam. Toxic.* 14: 395–400.

Gucinski, H. 1978. A note on the relation of size to ecological value of some wetlands. *Estuaries* 1: 151–56.

Gunter, G. 1969. Reef shell or mudshell dredging in coastal bays and its effect upon the environment. *Trans. N. Amer. Wildl. Conf.* 34: 51–74.

Hansen, D. J., P. R. Parrish, J. I. Lowe, A. J. Wolson, Jr., and P. D. Wilson. 1971. Chronic toxicity, uptake, and retention of Aroclor® 1254 in two estuarine fishes. *Bull. Envir. Contam. Toxic.* 6: 113–19.

Harrington, R. W., Jr. and W. L. Bidlingmayer. 1958. Effects of dieldrin on fishes and invertebrates of a salt marsh. *J. Wildl. Man.* 22: 76–82.

Hawkins, W. E., L. G. Tate, and T. G. Sarphie. 1980. Acute effects of cadmium on the spot, *Leiostomus xanthurus*, teleostei: Tissue distribution and renal ultrastructure. *J. Toxic. Envir. Health* 6: 283–96.

Heald, E. J., and H. T. Odum. 1974. Seafood waste ecosystems pp. 112–22. In: H. T. Odum, B. J. Copeland, and E. A. McMahan, eds. *Coastal ecologi-*

cal systems of the United States. Vol. III. Washington, D.C.: Conservation Foundation.

Hershner, C., and K. Moore. 1977. Effects of the Chesapeake Bay oil spill on salt marshes of the lower bay, pp. 529–33. In: Proceedings of the 1977 oil spill conference. American Petroleum Institute Publication 4284.

Holland, H. T., D. L. Coppage, and P. A. Butler. 1966. Increased sensitivity to pesticides in sheepshead minnows. *Trans. Am. Fish. Soc.* 95: 110–12.

Hutcheson, M. S. 1974. The effect of temperature and salinity on cadmium uptake by the blue crab, *Callinectes sapidus*. *Ches. Sci.* 15: 237–42.

Ingle, R. M. 1952. Studies on the effect of dredging operations upon fish and shellfish. Florida State Board of Conservation, Technical Series 5.

James, W. P., S. Giesler, R. DeOtte, and M. Inoue. 1977. *Environmental considerations relating to operation and maintenance of the Texas Gulf Intracoastal Waterway*. College Station: Texas A&M University Sea Grant Publication, TAMU-SG-78-204.

Jensen, A., B. Rystad, and S. Melsom. 1976. Heavy metal tolerance of marine phytoplankton. II. Copper tolerance of three species in dialysis and batch culture. *J. Exp. Mar. Biol. Ecol.* 22: 249–56.

Kennedy, V. S., and J. A. Mihursky. 1969. Addendum to: Bibliography on the effects of temperature in the aquatic environment. Natural Resource Institute, University of Maryland, Reference no. 69-8.

Lee, R. F., B. Dornself, F. Gonsoulin, K. Tenore, R. Hanson, and J. Blanton. 1980. *Fate and effects of oil on Georgia coastal waters and marshes*. Skidaway Island: Georgia Marine Science Center, Technical Series 80-7.

Lee, W. Y., M. F. Welch, and J. A. C. Nicol. 1977. Survival of two species of amphipods in aqueous extracts of petroleum oils. *Mar. Poll. Bull.* 8: 92–94.

Loosanoff, V. L. 1947. Effects of DDT on setting, growth, and survival of oysters. *Fish. Gaz.* 64(4): 94, 96.

Lowe, J. I. 1964. Chronic exposure of spot, *Leiostomus xanthurus*, to sublethal concentrations of toxaphene in seawater. *Trans. Am. Fish. Soc.* 93: 396–99.

Lunz, R. G. 1938. Oyster culture with reference to dredging operations in South Carolina I. The effects of flooding of the Santee River in April 1936 on oysters in the Cape Romain area of South Carolina. II. Report to U.S. Engineer Office, Charleston, S.C.

Lynn, W. R., and W. T. Yang. 1960. The ecological effects of sewage in Biscayne Bay: Oxygen demand and organic carbon determinations. *Bull. Mar. Sci. Gulf Caribb.* 10: 491–509.

McCoy, D. S. 1976. Dredging operations in the Galveston District, pp. 54–81. In: *Proceedings of the eighth dredging seminar*. College Station: Texas A&M University Sea Grant Publication, TAMU-SG-77-102.

Machemehl, J. L. 1972. Mechanics of dredging and filling, pp. 49–51. In: *Proceedings of the seminar on planning and engineering in the coastal zone*. Washington, D.C.: Coastal Plains Center for Marine Development Service.

————. 1976. Dredge material containment in nylon bags in the construction of mini-projects for beach stabilization, pp. 82–122. In: *Proceedings of the eighth dredging seminar*. College Station: Texas A&M University Sea Grant Publication, TAMU-SG-77-102.

Mackin, J. G. 1961. Canal dredging and silting in Louisiana Bays. *Publ. Inst. Mar. Sci., Univ. Tex.* 7: 262–314.

McNulty, J. K. 1961. Ecological effects of sewage pollution in Biscayne Bay, Florida: Sediments and distribution of benthic and fouling organisms. *Bull. Mar. Sci. Gulf Caribb.* 11: 394–447.

McNulty, J. K., E. S. Reynolds, and S. M. Miller. 1960. Ecological effects of sewage pollution in Biscayne Bay, Florida: Distribution of coliform bacteria, chemical nutrients, and volumes of zooplankton, pp. 189–202. In: Biological problems in water pollution. Robert A. Taft Sanitary Engineering Center, Technical Report no. W60-3.

Manning, J. H. 1957. The Maryland soft shell clam industry and its effect on tidewater resources. Maryland Department of Research and Education, Biological Laboratory Report no. 11.

Masch, F. D., and W. H. Espey. 1967. Shell-dredging: A factor in sedimentation in Galveston Bay. Center for Research in Water Resources, University of Texas. Technical Report no. 7.

Middaugh, D. P., W. R. Davis, and R. L. Yoakum. 1975. The response of larval fish, *Leiostomus xanthurus*, to environmental stress following sublethal cadmium exposure. *Cont. Mar. Sci.* 19: 13–19.

Mihursky, J. A. 1975. Thermal discharges and estuarine systems. Paper prepared for the U.S. Environmental Protection Agency.

Mock, C. E. 1966. Natural and altered estuarine habitats of penaeid shrimp. *Proc. Gulf and Caribb. Fish. Inst.* 19: 86—98.

Nimmo, D. R., A. J. Wilson, Jr., and R. R. Blackman. 1970. Localization of DDT in the body organs of pink and white shrimp. *Bull. Envir. Contam. Toxic.* 5: 333–41.

Nimmo, D. R., R. R. Blackman, A. J. Wilson, Jr., and F. Forester. 1971. Toxicity and distribution of Aroclor® 1254 in the pink shrimp *Penaeus duorarum*. *Mar. Biol.* 11: 191–97.

O'Connor, S. G., and A. J. McErlean. 1975. The effects of power plants on productivity of the nekton, pp. 494–517. In: L. E. Cronin, ed. *Estuarine research*. Vol. I. New York: Academic Press.

Odum, H. T., and R. F. Wilson. 1962. Further studies on reaeration and metabolism of Texas bays, 1958–1960. *Publ. Inst. Mar. Sci., Univ. Tex.* 8: 23–55.

O'Hara, J. 1973a. Cadmium uptake by fiddler crabs exposed to temperature and salinity stress. *J. Fish. Res. Bd. Can.* 30: 846–48.

———. 1973b. The influence of temperature and salinity on the toxicity of cadmium to the fiddler crab, *Uca pugilator*. *Fish. Bull.* 71: 149–53.

Phitzenmeyer, H. T. 1970. Benthos, project C, pp. 26–38. In: Gross physical and biological effects of overboard spoil disposal in upper Chesapeake Bay. NRI Special Report no. 3.

Provenzano, A. J., Jr., K. B. Schmitz, and M. A. Boston. 1978. Survival, duration of larval stages, and size of postlarvae of grass shrimp, *Palaemonetes pugio*, reared from Kepone® contaminated and uncontaminated populations in Chesapeake Bay. *Estuaries* 1: 239–44.

Rabalais, S. C., C. R. Arnold, and N. S. Wohlschlag. 1981. The effects of Ixtoc I oil on the eggs and larvae of red drum (*Sciaenops ocellata*). *Tex. J. Sci.* 33: 33–38.

Reid, G. K. 1957. Biologic and hydrographic adjustment in a disturbed Gulf coast estuary. *Limnol. Oceanogr.* 2: 198–212.

Reimold, R. J., P. C. Adams, and C. J. Durant. 1973. Effects of toxaphene contamination on estuarine ecology. Georgia Marine Science Center Technical Report, Series no. 73-8.

Rhodes, D. C., P. L. McCall, and J. Y. Yingst. 1978. Disturbance and production on the estuarine seafloor. *Am. Sci.* 66: 577–86.

Roland, J. V., G. E. Moore, and M. A. Bellance. 1977. The Chesapeake Bay oil spill—February 2, 1976: A case history, pp. 523–27. In: Proceedings of the 1977 Oil Spill Conference, American Petroleum Institute Publication no. 4284.

Rosato, P., and D. E. Ferguson. 1968. The toxicity of endrin-resistant mosquito fish to eleven species of vertebrates. *BioScience* 18: 783–84.

Salo, E. O., and O. J. Stober. 1971. The effects of pollution on estuaries of the northwest Pacific coast, pp. 85–95. In. P. R. Douglas and R. H. Stroud, eds. *A symposium on the biological significance of estuaries*. Washington, D.C.: Sport Fishing Institute.

Schmidt, R. A. 1966. Needed—a coastline comprehensive program for development of estuaries, pp. 102–109. In: *Symposium on estuarine fisheries*. Washington, D.C.: American Fisheries Society, Special Publication no. 3.

Schroeder, H. A. 1965. Cadmium as a factor in hypertension. *J. Chron. Dis.* 18: 647–56.

Schubel, J. R., H. H. Carter, and M. W. Wise. 1979. Shrimping as a source of suspended sediments in Corpus Christi Bay (Texas). *Estuaries* 2: 201–203.

Seneca, E. D., W. W. Woodhouse, Jr., and S. W. Broome. 1975. Salt-water marsh creation, pp. 427–37. In: L. E. Cronin, ed. *Estuarine resarch*. Vol. II. New York: Academic Press.

Sharp, J. M., and S. G. Appan. 1978. Cumulative effects of oil drilling and production on estuarine and near-shore ecosystems, pp. 57–73. In: M. L. Wiley,
ed. *Estuarine interactions*. New York: Academic Press.

Soule, D. F., and M. Oguri, eds. 1978. *The impact of the* Sansinena *explosion and
Bunker C spill on the marine environment of outer Los Angeles Harbor*. Ma-
rine Studies in San Pedro Bay, California, pt. 15. Los Angeles: University of
Southern California.

Stickney, R. R., and D. Perlmutter. 1975. Impact of intracoastal waterway dredging on a mud bottom benthos community. *Biol. Conserv.* 7: 211–26.

Stickney, R. R., H. L. Windom, D. B. White, and F. Taylor. 1972. Mercury concentration in various tissues of the bottle-nosed dolphin (*Tursiops truncatus*).
Proc. S.E. Assoc. Game and Fish Comm. 26: 634–36.

————. 1975. Heavy-metal concentrations in selected Georgia estuarine orga-
nisms with comparative food-habit data, pp. 257–67. In: F. G. Howell, J. B.
Gentry, and M. H. Smith, eds. *Mineral cycling in southeastern ecosystems*.
Springfield, Va.: U.S. Energy Research and Development Administration,
CONF-740513.

Stinson, J. E., II, and C. C. Mathewson. 1976. Physical factors affecting dredged
material islands in a shallow water environment, pp. 1–7. In: *Proceedings of
the eighth dredging seminar*. College Station: Texas A&M University Sea
Grant Publication, TAMU-SG-77-102.

Symons, P. E. K. 1973. Behavior of young Atlantic salmon (*Salmo salar*) exposed
to or force-fed fenitrothion, an organophosphate insecticide. *J. Fish. Res. Bd.
Can.* 30: 651–55.

Taylor, J. L., and C. H. Saloman. 1968. Some effects of hydraulic dredging and
coastal development in Boca Ciega Bay, Florida. *Fish. Bull.* 67: 213–41.

Thompson, S. H. 1961. What is happening to our estuaries? *Trans. N. Amer. Wildl.
Conf.* 26: 318–22.

Vandermeulen, J. H., and P. D. Keizer. 1977. Persistence of non-alkaline compo-
nents of Bunker C oil in beach sediments of Chedabucto Bay, pp. 469–73. In:
Proceedings of the 1977 Oil Spill Conference, American Petroleum Institute
Publication no. 4284.

Vaughan, R., and C. Kimber. 1977. *Maintenance dredging effects on vegetation
adjacent to the Gulf Intracoastal Waterway—Cedar Lakes Section*. College
Station: Texas A&M University Sea Grant Publication, TAMU-SG-77-207.

Vinson, S. B., C. E. Boyd, and D. E. Ferguson. 1963. Resistance to DDT in the
mosquito fish, *Gambusia affinis*. *Science* 139: 217–18.

Webb, J. W., J. D. Dodd, B. W. Cain, W. R. Leavens, L. R. Hossner, C. Lindau,
R. R. Stickney, and H. Williamson. 1978. *Habitat development field inves-
tigations: Bolivar Peninsula marsh and upland development site, Galveston
Bay, Texas*. App. D. Propagation of vascular plants and postpropagation

monitoring of botanical soil, aquatic biota, and wildlife resources. Vicksburg, Miss.: U.S. Army Corps of Engineers.

Westree, B. 1977. Biological criteria for the selection of cleanup techniques in salt marshes, pp. 231–35. In: Proceedings of the 1977 Oil Spill Conference, American Petroleum Institute Publication no. 4284.

Wildish, D.J., 1970. The toxicity of polychlorinated biphenyls (PCB) in sea water to *Gammarus oceanicus*. *Bull. Envir. Contam. Toxic.* 5: 202–204.

Windom, H. L. 1972. Environmental aspects of dredging in estuaries. *J. Waterways, Harbors and Coastal Engineering Division, ASCE* 98(WW4): 475–87.

————. 1975. Water-quality aspects of dredging and dredge-spoil disposal in estuarine environments, pp. 559–71. In: L. E. Cronin, ed. *Estuarine research*. Vol. II. New York: Academic Press.

————. 1976. Environmental aspects of dredging in the coastal zone. *Critical Reviews in Environmental Control* 6: 91–109.

Wise, N., and P. A. Brunk. 1977. Black oil disposal techniques, pp. 277–79. In: Proceedings of the 1977 Oil Spill Conference, American Petroleum Institute Publication no. 4284.

Woodhouse, W. W., Jr., E. D. Seneca, and S. W. Broome. 1972. Marsh building with dredge spoil in North Carolina. Bulletin 445, Agricultural Experiment Station, University of North Carolina.

Index